Personalism

Personalism

a critical introduction

Rufus Burrow, Jr.

Chalice Press
St. Louis, Missouri

Biblical quotations, unless otherwise noted, are from the *New Revised Standard Version Bible*, copyright 1989, Division of Christian Education of the National Council of Churches of Christ in the United States of America. Used by permission. All rights reserved.

Cover Art: Harvey L. Sibley
Cover Design: Ross Sherman
Art Director: Elizabeth Wright
Interior Design: Wynn Younker

This book is printed on acid-free, recycled paper.

Visit Chalice Press on the World Wide Web at
www.chalicepress.com

10 9 8 7 6 5 4 3 2 1   99 00 01 02 03

Library of Congress Cataloging–in–Publication Data

Burrow, Rufus, 1951-
    Personalism : a critical introduction / by Rufus Burrow, Jr.
        p.   cm.
    Includes bibliographical references and index.
    ISBN 0-8272-2955-0
    1. Personalism   I. Title.
    B828.5.B87   1999
    141′ .5—dc21   99–43444 CIP

Printed in the United States of America

*For my teachers, Peter Anthony Bertocci (1910–1989)
and Walter George Muelder, who, through their teaching,
example, and mentoring taught me the philosophical
value of personalism. Although my parents taught me
the practical value of what I came to know as personalism,
these men also modeled the true meaning of this way of
thinking and living. It was these two elderly white men
who introduced me to what I consider the most reasonable
philosophical basis of two crucial beliefs in Afrikan
American religio-cultural tradition: that God is personal
and cares about us, and that all persons have etched into
their being the image of God and thus are heirs to a legacy
of absolute dignity and worth.*

Contents

Foreword

A half-century ago an introductory, systematic work of this kind would not have been necessary, for personalism as a well-known option in philosophy and theology was widely read. Thinkers like Albert C. Knudson were appreciated among philosophical theologians and by seminarians and liberal pastors. Scores of college departments in philosophy and religion were chaired by graduates of Boston University, the principal center of personal idealism. In addition, a thriving journal under the editorship of Ralph Tyler Flewelling, *The Personalist*, was published at the University of Southern California. Flewelling was a follower of the thought of Borden Parker Bowne, founder of American Personalism. Then there was Edgar Sheffield Brightman, who was president of the American Philosophical Association in 1936. His widely used textbook *An Introduction to Philosophy* appeared in 1925 and his equally respected *A Philosophy of Religion* was published in 1940. Flewelling, Knudson, and Brightman are but three of a large host of writers in epistemology, metaphysics, ethics, philosophy of religion, and theology who belong to the tradition inaugurated by Bowne in 1876 when he began his teaching career at Boston University. That tradition, to which Professor Rufus Burrow, Jr., claims adherence, is now in its fifth generation and is the longest continuous line of any school of philosophical thought associated with a single university. Indeed, the tradition is often referred to, not entirely accurately, as Boston Personalism.

Like idealism generally, personalism is today not center stage, and the writings of its chief proponents of yesteryear are often not in print. Nevertheless, there is a lively interest in this type of philosophy. The claim that personality is the basic explanatory principle, as John H. Lavely says, evokes a lively dialogue with claimants to metaphysical truth. A personalist discussion group comprises a current section of the American Philosophical Association. International conferences on personalism attract not only self-avowed adherents, but also critical scholars whose roots are in alternative metaphysical heritages. Personalism is thus one of the living options in a global arena of inquiry in its fields of concern.

The time is ripe for a systematic introduction designed to present both a tradition and a creative option to college, seminary, and graduate students. Rufus Burrow, Jr.'s, text should meet this need in a helpful way and supplement a significant volume, *The Boston Personalist Tradition in Philosophy, Ethics and Theology*, published in 1986 and edited by Paul Deats, Jr., and Carol Robb. This book is a symposium by writers in the third, fourth, and fifth generation of personalists from Boston University: F. Thomas Trotter, John H. Lavely, Walter G. Muelder, Peter A. Bertocci, S. Paul Schilling, Dianne Carpenter, L. Harold DeWolf, and the editors. That volume acknowledged certain historical debts of personalism to thinkers like Kant and Hegel, but also saluted individuals like Bowne, Francis J. McConnell, Knudson, Brightman, and Georgia Harkness, and then presented personal essays by living contemporaries.

Person, personality, personalism, personal idealism, personal realism—why all the fuss? Everybody knows what a person is—or do they? If person is the basic explanatory principle for ultimate reality, it is inevitable that hundreds of social groups and individuals should seize on the term person and exploit it for their own purposes. It is, moreover, not a recent invention. "Person" has an ancient and continuous usage. The derivation is uncertain in philosophy and theology. In his *Philosophy of Personalism* Knudson pointed out that in ancient times the term person had a double source, one coming from the Greek word *hypostasis* that denoted concrete individuality and the other from the Latin word *persona*. This latter term was a translation of *hypostasis*, but it originally designated an actor's mask. Later it referred to the actor himself and, even later, to a party in a legal dispute. It was in the trinitarian and christological dispute of the early church associated with certain great councils that the term person acquired theological and philosophical importance. The reader is referred to Knudson's long historical review in the above work. Boethius (ca. 475–524) defined it as follows: *persona est naturae rationabilis individus substantia.* Accordingly, a "person is the individual substance or subsistence of a rational nature." Knudson holds that "individual substance" corresponds to hypostasis and the "rational nature" to the social or universal element in persona. In any case, Boethius' definition was standard usage in the medieval period. After tracing various transmutations of the terms person and personality, Knudson offered a definition of personalism as "that form of idealism which gives equal recognition to both the pluralistic and monistic aspects of experience and which finds in the conscious unity, identity, and free activity of personality the key to the nature of reality and the solution of the ultimate problems of philosophy." This definition follows quite closely the thought of Borden P. Bowne, under whom Knudson studied.

Of course, such a definition is variously nuanced in dealing with the great range of human experience and the diverse fields of philosophy. The richness, depth, and uniqueness of individual and community life invites this. If personal experience, both private and communitarian, is the key to interpreting the ultimate reality of which it is a part, then many emphases in defining its aspects are to be expected. Nevertheless, in all cases personalism is a serious philosophical endeavor to be clearly distinguished from the usage of terms like person, personality, personalistic, personal, and so on, that abound in advertising, popular culture, and even in some scientific literature. Personalism takes the real person seriously, not superficially.

As a century-old school of thought personalism embraces a system that includes ancient and traditional ideas and ways of thinking. Its uniqueness lies not in a quest for novelty, but for grasping experience holistically and interpreting it coherently; its method of reasoning places analysis within a synoptic vision; its criterion of truth is empirical and rational coherence; and its understanding of reason is the whole relational activity of the mind. Reason does not stand as an intellectual opponent or alternative to the nonrational or irrational givens in human experience, but reason's work is to relate experiences of all kinds to one another coherently and synoptically with modes of analysis, hypothesis, and verification appropriate to each and to the whole. This introductory book shows how this is done. Philosophy's work begins and ends in conscious personal experience.

Personalism embraces all the disciplines of philosophy in its system of metaphysics. This means that it deals with the traditional disciplines. Bowne wrote on psychological theory, epistemology, ethics, metaphysics, philosophy of religion, and theology. Nothing human is alien to personalists. Yet each of these disciplines has undergone significant developments since Bowne's era. Each discipline has entered into serious dialogue with contemporary schools of thought. Each thinker in succeeding generations has developed distinctive interpretations both of problems and solutions. But the distinctiveness of personality as the explanatory principle unifies the tradition. In 1940 a group of personalists formulated a personalistic platform to bring out the common agreements and differences. Fifty years later many of these propositions as recorded in W. H. Werkmeister's *A History of Philosophical Ideas in America* are still subscribed to by the members of the personalist discussion group in the American Philosophical Association, but some of this group would propose other propositions in agreement and in disagreement. Philosophy changes through the logic and dialectic of its own internal development and by interaction and dialogue with new facets of experience and conflicting points of view. Hegel said that philosophy is its history, but it is also its future. Personalism is devoted to empirical coherence and therefore is open-ended; its coherence is emergent. Consequently, the philosophical, theological, and ethical hypotheses and conclusions of personalists sometimes differ widely. The different generations of the tradition illustrate this fact.

In the first generation, Bowne struggled against the impersonalism of nineteenth-century naturalism and absolute idealism, regarding them as metaphysical failures; he embraced the doctrine of evolution while reinterpreting the relation of science and religion; he defended historical biblical criticism; and he accommodated his ethics to the productivity of capitalism. In the second generation, Francis J. McConnell became famous as a theologically liberal bishop of the Methodist Episcopal church, as a social reformer in the industrial sphere, as a biographer of Bowne, and as an ecumenist. Meanwhile, Knudson clung to theistic absolutism when dealing with the problem of good-and-evil, favored reform capitalism, and defended a "just war" policy in World War II. On the other hand, Brightman put forward a controversial theory of God as finite, greatly developed moral law and axiology, took the pacifist position in World War II, and supported the socialism of Norman Thomas. In the third generation, Georgia Harkness, a student of Brightman's, became the first full-time woman theologian in an American theological seminary; she adopted a distinctive metaphysical synthesis called personal realism, supported pacifism, and made contributions in poetry and hymnody. Her work showed the influences of Whitehead, Hocking, Reinhold Niebuhr, and Tillich. With different accents,

L. Harold DeWolf followed the theistic absolutism of Bowne and Knudson, supported the "just war" theory in social ethics, became a leader for a sane nuclear policy, rejected capital punishment, and strongly supported the civil rights struggle led by Martin Luther King, Jr. Walter Mueder and S. Paul Schilling followed Brightman with respect to limitations on God's power. They also adopted pacifism and socialism. Muelder and DeWolf developed Brightman's "moral law" theory in an explicitly communitarian direction. Schilling made contributions in dialogue with contemporary continental theologians and secular atheists. John Lavely was prominent as a critic and teacher in philosophy of religion. Peter Bertocci probed the psychological and ethical dimensions of personality and wrote extensively on sexuality and related issues.

Continuity with respect to basic methods and metaphysical principles continued into the fourth generation. Diversity persisted as well. Most prominent was Martin Luther King, Jr., whose method of nonviolent social action grounded in personalistic metaphysics and the black church experience became the hallmark of the civil rights revolution. Scores of books have been written describing and evaluating his life and work. Less known was the social research work of Glen Trimble. He dialogued with Marxism. In empirical studies he developed analyses of cooperative Christianity in urban settings. Paul Deats, Jr., laid out the principles of strategy for social change. He explored the relation of religion to sociology and cultural anthropology. He was also active in the Fellowship of Reconciliation and participated in the churches' dialogue on peace issues with Christians in eastern Europe and what was once the Soviet Union. Dianne Carpenter and the author of this volume are numbered among the fifth generation of Boston-based personalists. Others of the fourth and fifth generation are widely scattered in their work and influence in America and abroad.

All of the above-mentioned thinkers and writers maintained a positive view of religious values, were broadly committed to ecumenism, and were staunch advocates of civil liberties, civil rights, and academic freedom, thus exhibiting in social action the meaning of freedom that Bowne made a central doctrine in his definition and defense of personality as a principle. All displayed the principle that inquiry begins in personal conscious experience, proceeds to analysis of its contents and objective reference, explores the interplay of fact and value, and moves finally to synoptic interpretation of experience in relation to reality.

Rufus Burrow, Jr., has written a lucid introduction to this century-long tradition as related to Boston University. He makes a contribution to the future as well as to the history of philosophical ideas.

Walter George Muelder

Preface

It was my good fortune to be able to spend two weeks each with my former teachers and mentors, Peter A. Bertocci and Walter G. Muelder, during the summer of 1989. Long before this I had been told that both men were gravely ill, and that Muelder was in worse shape than Bertocci. However, to my surprise and pleasure, Dr. Muelder's condition was in remission when I arrived at his home. At that time I discovered that he was very spirited and full of energy. But for previous knowledge of his degenerating health I would not have known during our two weeks together that he had been suffering from a serious illness. As I often commented to my former student, James L. Kirby, who at the time was a doctoral candidate taking courses under Dr. Muelder:

> He is still the same energetic, quick of mind, caring teacher I remember from my student days at Boston University. Ask him a question and you never have to worry about an incomplete answer. You get instead a very full response. He still tends to respond to questions by first placing the issue in its total historical setting. He then indicates the contemporary significance of the issue, gives his own critique, and then ponders the implications for today and tomorrow. His mind is still as sharp as ever!

Dr. Bertocci's condition that summer was such that he struggled, albeit gallantly and with much character, to get through each of the seven nearly two-hour sessions in his home. Like Dr. Muelder, his mind was very sharp and alert, although he spoke in a raspy, low whisper and experienced much discomfort from his condition. How he made it through that period with me I shall never know. My suspicion, however, is that he was able to carry on because it was, in part, a way for him to continue to "button up" some things, since he knew that his condition was not significantly improving. But in addition, I think he was able to make it through the sessions because I, a former student, called for help. In fact, in a letter he dictated to one of his sons a few weeks before I was to arrive in Boston, he said that his condition had degenerated to the point that he did not think he would be able to be of much help to me. But because I had a deep inner feeling of urgency—that I needed to get his guidance on Borden Parker Bowne's metaphysics and epistemology that summer—he decided that he would give it a try.

I found Dr. Bertocci to be very methodical and informative in our sessions. In this regard he had not changed. But it was also very evident that there was a good deal of urgency in all that he said during those two weeks, and consequently there was not as much opportunity for question and answer, although I had many questions to ask. But I sensed that he needed to do the talking. One of his sons told me later that Dr. Bertocci often had to go to bed to rest after our sessions. Indeed, he often appeared weak during these sessions and would take periodic breaks.

During our last week together he informed me that he had some things he wanted to give me and that I was to use the items in any way I saw fit as support for my work in personalism. The items included more than a half dozen copies of seven course syllabi he had used over the years. There were also copies of a couple of articles he had written. In addition, during the June 24 session he gave me a copy of *Waiting for the Lord*, a book of meditations that his good friend, the late Gordon W. Allport, offered in Appleton Chapel at Harvard University from 1938 to 1966. The book was edited by Dr. Bertocci. The inscription to me read: "For Rufus Burrow, with meaningful memories." I was deeply moved by this particular gift, and have on a number of occasions wondered whether my teacher was also "waiting for the Lord," and in fact believed the Lord to be near. On October 17, Jimmy Kirby phoned me to ask if I had heard that Dr. Bertocci died in his sleep, in his own bed, four days earlier.

I had known that he was not getting better. When I returned to Indianapolis we corresponded a couple of times, and he sent comments on an article on which I was working. I was not able to decipher his handwriting and had to get the faculty secretary to help me. I knew from his handwriting that his health was failing—that he was losing the battle for life in this world, while making preparations to enter the next.

To have spent two weeks helping a former student, despite his own illness and discomfort, says more about Peter Anthony Bertocci than words can convey. I was his last teaching assignment, as John Lavely remarked at the memorial service held in Boston University's Marsh Chapel. The best thing I can say about Dr. Bertocci is what I often heard him say about those he perceived to be great personalities: *What a person he was*! He was to the end a personalist and a great teacher, which is to say that he *lived* the personalistic faith that had become to him the most reasonable way of life.

Having studied both Bowne's theory of reality and theory of knowledge with Dr. Bertocci in Arlington, I then went off to Newton Centre to study Bowne's ethics with Dr. Muelder. This, too, was a very full and rich experience, as we worked our way through Bowne's classic work *The Principles of Ethics* and made the connections with his metaphysics. It was amazing to me that this man, then in his early eighties, was able to recall specific passages and the page numbers on which they appeared in that text. As with Dr. Bertocci, Dr. Muelder made Bowne's personalism live. The method used to teach during those two weeks was different, however. I was required to begin each session with questions and observations on assigned readings. This was followed by Dr. Muelder's commentary. There was a constant interchange of ideas and interpretations of Bowne's ethics. Based on the time spent with Muelder and Bertocci that summer, I wrote articles on Bowne's metaphysics and doctrine of God, and on his ethics.[1]

My teachers and I agreed that there is still much work to be done to clarify the key issues of personalism, and that there is need for a text to introduce the personalist conceptuality to the present generation and to propel this tradition into the twenty-first century. When Dr. Bertocci and I talked about this he said: "You write it!" Dr. Muelder's response was that he would be pleased to see such a text written in language that is intelligible for today.

I have pondered long and hard to determine how best to begin such a project. There are many ways one may approach the writing of an introductory text on the type of personalism that was developed by Bowne. Since my hope is that this book will be comprehensible to a broad audience, including college, seminary, and graduate students, as well as professors, pastors, and lay people, I intend to give a broad overview of the personalism developed by Bowne and some of his disciples. To this end I begin with a discussion of the meaning, origin, and development of personalism, and then proceed to an exposition of issues such as the doctrine of God and personalistic ethics. The book ends with a consideration of why personalism has been unpopular and what may be some new directions for it if it is to remain a viable framework for thinking about and doing philosophy, theology, and ethics.

Although my interpretation is influenced by Peter Bertocci and the careful eye and diplomatic critique of Walter Muelder, it is, finally, my interpretation. Therefore, I alone am responsible for any errors. However, if after being introduced to this work persons feel that they have a better sense not only of what personalism is, but why the personalist option is so important in the world today, I will have been at least partially vindicated.

I want to offer special thanks for the research assistance of Linda Sue Hewitt. In addition to this, she prepared the select bibliography and the index. Anyone who has done either or both of these knows how tedious and time consuming such tasks can be. Linda performed these with great care, alacrity, and attention to detail.

Introduction

> *...the main reason personalism is unpopular is because it fights against the dehumanization and depersonalization of all people. In understanding the subversiveness of this statement, it means that gays and lesbians are not to be oppressed, nor are women.*
>
> Rachel Metheny[1]

Personalism as a philosophy is fundamentally a metaphysics. That is, it is a way of thinking about the whole of reality and experience; of trying to see how all things hang together. It is a worldview. As such, personalism has profound implications for the way we think about humanity, God, nature, animal life, evil and suffering, freedom, ethics, and a host of other things relevant to human and other life forms. Since personalism makes *person* its central interpretive principle, it promotes the idea of the profundity of the worth and sacredness of all persons. For example, from the standpoint of ethics, personalism holds that all ethical principles must be conditioned by the highest conceivable estimate of the worth of persons as such. Not only does personalism require the highest possible conception of the worth of humanity, it conceives of reality itself as personal. The idea that reality is personal may be personalism's most controversial trait.

Strands of personalism appear early in the history of thought. Although Albert C. Knudson (1873–1953) traced important contributions to the development of personalism back to the time of the pre-Socratic thinkers in Greece, Edgar S. Brightman (1884–1953) at least acknowledged an awareness of contributions in the Orient. However, neither of these personalists linked strands of personalism to the Afrikan continent, despite the fact that Afrika is considered the cradle of civilization. In addition, it is known that some of the key ideas of some ancient Greek philosophers were actually learned and developed when they studied on that continent. Nevertheless, as far as we know, both the term *personalism* and its systematic formulation are of relatively modern origin.

As a philosophy, personalism received its first systematic and methodological formulation in the work of American Borden Parker Bowne (1847–1910).[2] Bowne was considered "the most outstanding champion of personalism..."[3] Personalism arose in part as a reaction against absolute idealism, and argued against the idea that the person is a mere attribute of some absolute whole (whether God or some other entity). Instead, it asserts that the person is ultimately real and valuable.

Bowne, unlike the great majority of his contemporaries, with the possible exception of George Holmes Howison (1836–1916), endeavored to push the personalistic argument to its logical conclusion in metaphysics, epistemology, philosophy of religion, theology, and ethics. Arguably, not all of Bowne's conclusions were as empirically adequate as they could have been.

1

Yet he was the first to make the effort to develop personalism systematically and methodologically.

The type of personalism discussed in this book is more than a philosophy or doctrine to be taught in the classroom. Likewise, it is not merely a theory to be written about. At its very best, personalism is an attitude, or better still, *a way of life—a way of living in the world*.[4] Although a number of the chief proponents of personalism were excellent scholars, they were generally not ivory tower dwellers who separated themselves from the blood and guts issues of life. They were, to be sure, a peculiar group of metaphysicians who did not seek to live in an abstract realm that is divorced from human experience. Instead, they were (and are) metaphysicians in the best sense, insisting that metaphysics (the study of reality) begins and ends in experience—human experience—and that the work of the metaphysician is first and foremost for the uplifting and enhancement of persons. The personalistic metaphysician, then, always tries to keep one foot "in the gutters of life" where so many persons have been relegated. The great aim of personalistic metaphysics is, finally, to establish a way of living and thinking about life that will motivate us to eradicate all behavior and practices that demean and crush the dignity of persons as if they were but things or objects to be manipulated and dehumanized.

If personalism has what approximates liberation theology's "preferential option," it is an option for a fully human life and all that that implies morally, spiritually, and substantively for every person. The option is not merely for physical life, but for life with dignity. The type of personalism that is the subject of this work is not selective in who it considers to be a person. That is, the worth and value it attaches to any person necessarily applies to all persons, regardless of race, gender, class, age, health, or sexual preference, although not all of the early progenitors of personalism were as clear about this as others.

Possibly the greatest compliment to be paid personalists is that their lives generally reflect the philosophy they teach and write. It has been said of the first three generations of personalists that they lived the personalistic faith in much of what they did. Robert Neville implies this in his review of a text on the Boston Personalist tradition. "Few people are Personalists because of books or ideas rather than because of direct contact with the living members of the tradition, usually at Boston University."[5] Although Neville's view that personalists have not produced a comparable text to that of Alfred N. Whitehead's *Process and Reality* (1929) is debatable, there is much to commend in his contention that large numbers of persons are personalists not because they have read much of the literature, but because of their personal contact or association with the heavyweights in the personalist tradition.

It may also be said that many persons are unknowing adherents of personalism long before they read or hear about it, or meet chief proponents. Prior to formal contact with personalism they simply have not had the language to articulate what they already believed and lived. Long before such persons even hear the term *personalism*, they have talked the language of personalism and lived as personalists ought to live. John Lavely, a third-generation personalist, has reflected on his experience with students and colleagues who have had similar experiences.

> I have frequently had students or associates concede that they were personalists when they came to the School of Theology [at Boston University] though they did not know it. I vividly recall the theological student who spoke to me at the start of a course in philosophy of religion. He said, "I'm a personalist, and I'm taking this course to find out what a personalist is."[6]

Paul Deats, Jr., a confessed fourth-generation personalist, makes the claim that he discovered he was a personalist only after he was thirty years old.[7] He made the discovery after he entered Boston University as a graduate student. Many of these persons who have unknowingly lived as personalists are adherents of the Christian faith as well, although some are members of other faith traditions.

A popular American philosophy from the late nineteenth century through the 1960s, personalism has seldom received sustained attention in universities and seminaries outside Boston University, which was once the great bastion of personalistic studies in this country. At this writing it is questionable as to whether it even receives much attention at the latter institution. With the retirement of key third-generation personalists from Boston University, little attention is given personalistic studies. There are, no doubt, many reasons for this lack of attention to what was once a vibrant philosophy.

In 1921 Brightman wrote about "the unpopularity of personalism." He was optimistic that there would be a resurgence of interest in personalistic philosophy,[8] although by 1925 he was still disturbed by the hostility against personalism and other forms of idealism.[9] Much of this hostility had to do with the fact that personalism is unabashedly and unashamedly theistic and acknowledges the truth and value of religion. Nevertheless, Brightman believed that at least three things needed to happen to prepare the way for a renaissance in the philosophy of personalism. First, personalists should not concede their position to other systems of thought merely because of the existing social and intellectual climate. This means that they should not become what Deats referred to as "closet personalists." In addition, it is important that personalists consciously and intentionally write, teach, and lecture about personalism in order to broaden the circle of awareness and understanding.

Second, personalists should encourage a stronger emphasis on philosophical study in educational institutions, including graduate theological seminaries. This will sharpen their analytical skills, critical thinking, and ability to more reasonably ground their theological and faith claims. This too will contribute to the coming renaissance of personalistic philosophy.

The third thing Brightman proposed was that ministers make a conscious effort to include philosophical literature in their daily reading regimen. In this way they will become familiar and comfortable with the methods of philosophy and the need for critical thinking.[10] It might further be added that it would be of great value if ministers and professors included in their sermons and lectures (on a regular basis) explicit references to the inherent and absolute sanctity of persons as such. Those ministers and professors who believe God to be personal should help their audience to understand that this God is the Source of the dignity and sanctity of persons. Thus, a violation of persons in this world is also a violation of the Source of their existence.

Despite Brightman's suggestions, however, the renaissance has not yet come. There was a great deal of writing and lecturing on personalism from the 1930s through the 1960s. Yet by all accounts personalism has not been a popular philosophy. J. Deotis Roberts points to this as well, claiming that "personalism does not receive the attention it deserves in the treatment of American religious thought."[11] Although I will address the question of the unpopularity of personalism in more detail in the final chapter, I want now to give some preliminary observations regarding this phenomenon.

The quotation at the beginning of this introduction makes the excellent point that personalism is not popular today because "it fights against the dehumanization and depersonalization of all people." Personalism requires that all persons treat themselves and other persons with dignity and respect. The cold truth is that we are presently living in an age in which little value is placed on the worth of persons as such. When we see the opposite practice displayed, it is very often done selectively. That is, particular individuals or groups are singled out to be treated like beings who possess inestimable worth. In this country general disrespect for persons is exhibited in social, economic, political, and legal practices. There is simply no other way to account for the existence of massive numbers of unemployed and underemployed people in the richest nation in the world. How else does one account for the continued practice of state-sanctioned murder (i.e., capital punishment) and the fact that since 1932 nearly 55 percent of the men murdered in this way have been Afrikan Americans? This general disrespect for persons is also seen in the suicidal-genocidal tendencies of the nation's youth. Another sign of this is seen in the ease with which drug trafficking occurs, and with which young men can obtain automatic and semiautomatic weapons that are then used indiscriminately in drive-by shootings that lead to the serious injuries and deaths of innocent bystanders on a near-daily basis throughout large- and small-town America.

On a more ideological level, it is commonly held that with the emergence of existentialism after the two world wars the importance of philosophical idealism in the United States began to wane. The failed attempts to resurrect the absolute idealism of Josiah Royce (1855–1916) in the 1950s was considered a key symptom of this.[12] This notwithstanding, from around the mid-1940s through much of the sixties, the chief writers and teachers on personal idealism were two generations removed from Bowne. Like their philosophical predecessors, these third-generation personalists, for example, Peter A. Bertocci, Walter G. Muelder, Ralph T. Flewelling, Nels F. S. Ferré,

Georgia Harkness, and L. Harold DeWolf were prolific writers who intentionally did their work as exponents of personalism. In addition, they were popular teachers who sought to combine theory and practice and exhibited special concern for the welfare of those with their backs against the wall. For these personalists neither the term personalism nor the personalistic tradition was something about which they felt shame and sought to conceal in the closet. They were proud to be members of this school of thought and did not hesitate to introduce their students to its major tenets, assumptions, and implications for life.

However, as members of the third generation approached retirement, many who had been their students devoted less and less attention to the problems and arguments of personalism and its continued viability as a philosophical and theological option. To be sure, dissertations continued to appear on aspects of the thought of Bowne, Brightman, Muelder, and some others. But as a viable philosophy, theology, and system of ethics, personalism was no longer in vogue.

A third preliminary comment as to why personalism lost its popularity in and beyond the classroom is that fourth- and fifth-generation personalists have not been as productive in a literary sense as their teachers in the tradition. In addition, they have not identified themselves as writers and teachers in the personalist tradition. In this regard they have done nothing to keep the tradition not only alive, but alive as a vibrant option in philosophy, theology, ethics, and other disciplines. Some fourth-generation personalists, for example, J. Philip Wogaman, have been prolific writers in their fields but have not openly identified themselves as personalists in the tradition of Bowne. Wogaman, more than many in this generation of personalists, at least credits various third-generation personalists, such as Muelder and DeWolf, as having influenced the way he thinks about the field of Christian social ethics.[13] Yet he at no point characterizes himself as a personalist, although the influence of personalism is evident in much of his writing. But as I say this about Wogaman, I know that Brightman, for example, was not very concerned about labels. These were not, according to him, important in the least. The truth is what is important, and we arrive at it through rational, coherent thought. Yet there is much to be said for naming one's self and one's experience. This is a prominent principle in present-day liberation theologies and is, in my view, appropriate to the present discussion.

It should be pointed out that Martin Luther King, Jr., also a fourth-generation personalist, intentionally did the work of Christian social ethics as a personalist. He claimed the tradition and its influence on his metaphysical and ethical thinking. But King was a different type of scholar than most theistic personalists, with the possible exception of Francis J. McConnell and John Wesley Edward Bowen, Sr. (a lesser-known personalist who will be discussed in chapter 3). McConnell was a scholar outside the academy who was called to church administration and Christian social activism. He therefore devoted his life to applying the principles of personalism to critical social issues of his day. Bowen actually set the precedence for social personalism. King would later apply the principles of personalism to critical socioeconomic issues of his day. There is no question that King was, in this sense, personalism's greatest disciple.

But by and large, personalism has been out of sight and out of mind for many persons over the past thirty years, primarily because fourth- and fifth-generation personalists have not carried the tradition forward. Suffice it to say that personalism will be revived only as present-day adherents intentionally teach it, allow its basic principles to inform all of their work, and write about it, not hesitating to include "personalism" in the title of their articles, monographs, books, and so on. "The prospects for personalism," writes Lavely, "depend on the projects personalists are willing to undertake."[14] In addition, many need to do what Paul Deats has done: come out of the closet and unhesitatingly affirm their identification with the personalist tradition.

These things notwithstanding, one does see evidence here and there of an emerging interest in personalism. Part of this has to do with the activity of the Personalistic Discussion Group that meets annually. Part of it has to do with the conversations that have occurred between American and British personalists over the past few years. But it is also due to the concern that many sensitive persons express as a result of the impersonal and dehumanizing way that vast numbers of persons are treated in this and other sociopolitical and economic systems throughout the world that place so little emphasis on the dignity and worth of persons. People, especially those among the most socially distressed, seem to be crying out for a return to respect for persons, a fundamental principle of personalism. This is most assuredly the case in the Afrikan American and Hispanic communities as a response to the massive violence and too-frequent murders among the young men of these communities.

But where does one turn for recent literature on personalism that discusses it in language that is both intelligible and takes seriously the experiences of traditionally excluded groups such as Afrikan Americans and Hispanics who have been systematically forced to the socioeconomic margins of American society? Without question the first three generations of American Personalists were very productive, and through their prolific writings and teaching in the personalist tradition they were successful in spreading its basic doctrines.

I have taught a course on personalism for several years. I am frequently asked by scholars, students, pastors, and others whether there is a current text available on the meaning, history, and development of personalism. It is quite evident that there is need for a book that will introduce personalism to the present generation of college, seminary and graduate students, professors, clergy, and lay persons. Knudson wrote the only book on the history of the development of personalism nearly seventy years ago.[15] He sought to uncover the philosophical strands of personalism in the West. His study culminates in the systematic, methodological personalism of Bowne. In this sense DeWolf was accurate when he said that it is to Knudson that we owe thanks for historically situating Bowne's personalism. That is, for giving it place among the great traditions in philosophy, for elaborating "systematically its relations with the more important rival systems," and for classifying it "among the various types of personalistic philosophy."[16]

Knudson's book was written primarily for a more philosophical, scholarly audience and is therefore replete with technical philosophical language that proves an impediment for numerous persons interested in knowing what personalism is and how it developed. Having used Knudson's book several times in my course on personalism, I believe it is not an exaggeration to say that it requires the reader to have a good background in the history of philosophy generally and idealistic philosophy more particularly. Even the brightest nonphilosophically trained students tend to have difficulty with the language in the book. I did not fare much better when I used Bowne's books. To further exacerbate the problem, most of the texts written by the first three generations of personalists are long out of print and inaccessible. The few that can be purchased must be secured through reprint companies at exorbitant cost. At any rate, it quickly became apparent that there is a need for a book on personalism that does not presuppose prior systematic study in philosophy, and one that provides an accurate exposition of its history and development, albeit primarily from the stance of the so-called Boston Personalists.

In addition to Knudson's book, William H. Werkmeister (1901–1993) wrote *A History of Philosophical Ideas in America* (1949) in which he includes three excellent chapters on personalism: "The Personalism of Bowne," "The Pluralistic Personalism of Howison," and "Recent Personalism."[17] However, like the Knudson text, Werkmeister's massive study is also long out of print and nearly impossible to locate in many libraries.

Werkmeister originally taught at the University of Nebraska and was called to teach philosophy at the University of Southern California in 1953. This was significant because one of Bowne's students, Ralph T. Flewelling, was teaching philosophy there. Flewelling was the founder and editor of *The Personalist*. Werkmeister shared with him the editorial and related responsibilities for the popular journal. He also edited Flewelling's autobiography[18] and was more influenced by Flewelling's interpretation of Bowne's personalism than that of Bowne's students (e.g., Brightman and Knudson) teaching at Boston University. Werkmeister himself was offered a permanent position at Boston University when he was a visiting professor there in 1940.[19] In light of his relationship with Flewelling, it is not surprising that he considered Flewelling (not Brightman!) to be the "dean of contemporary personalists."[20]

Although there are ways in which the more recent *A History of Philosophy in America* (1977) transcends Werkmeister's massive volume, it does not, like his, give extended attention to the Bowne-Brightman type of personalism. Instead, the authors focus on the personal idealism of George Holmes Howison. The work of Bowne is treated at best as an afterthought or an appendage to that of Howison. After devoting several pages to Howison's thought, the authors write: "Undoubtedly the closest to Howison among the younger idealists was Bowne, whose lineal descendants are of influence today."[21] The authors say nothing of Bowne's or of these lineal descendants' work, however.

When I have had to resort to technical jargon in this book, I have taken great pains to explain what is meant. In addition, I include (but do not exhaust) sources or strands of personalism that Knudson did not, for example, Afrikan and Afrikan American contributions. Also, my focus is not primarily that of interpreting Bowne's philosophy and giving it historical place. Unlike Knudson's, my book pays more attention to personalistic ethics, social ethics, and moral laws or principles.[22] It will become evident early in the book that I am more Brightmanian than Bownean. But even more noteworthy, there is an ongoing dialogue between this Bowne-Brightman personalism and my Afrikan American heritage. Much of this will be subtle, although some will be quite pronounced. The personalism emerging from my own research and reflection is really more Afrikan and Afrikan American than anything else. Bowne, and more specifically Brightman, would not be troubled by this development were they alive, for it is consistent with their synoptic-analytic approach, which requires the inclusion of all of the facts of experience,[23] and especially that which has traditionally been left out (such as the experiences of blacks, Native Americans, Hispanics, *all* women, etc.). As we will see in chapter 5, both men stressed this latter point and were adamant that the truth is the thing, and that it is never static and complete, for experience itself is dynamic and always changing. This means that the truth seeker must always be open to new facts and evidence, for these are always forthcoming and will need to be critically considered in light of other things believed to be true.

In the final chapter I consider several challenges or new directions for personalism. My hope is that this discussion will contribute to personalism's continued viability and intelligibility as we speed toward the twenty-first century. Although the rudiments of some of these new directions appear in germinal form in the personalism of Bowne and some of his students, it will become clear that they need to be pursued much more explicitly and vigorously.

Knudson sought to be a thoroughgoing personalist. It will be seen that neither he nor Bowne was as thoroughgoing at some points as their own personalistic method demanded. This leads me to raise the question of whether theirs was, as Knudson so forcefully argued, the most typical, "normative," or truest form of personalism, especially since they (as white middle-class males) left out the experiences, interests, questions, and opinions of over half the American population. Today it is generally not acceptable that any group assume that its stance is normative for everybody else. The difference in social location causes different groups to raise different issues and questions. In part this helps to explain why there were Afrikan Americans who studied with major personalists at Boston University, but did not become academic teachers of personalism. Instead, almost every one of them was a scholar-activist, with emphasis on social activism.

My book is also different from Knudson's and those of the majority of the chief proponents of personalism in that most of them wrote as white middle-class males who enjoyed the benefits of the racist-sexist-capitalist society of which some—not all!—of them were among the most consistent and scathing critics. Unfortunately, the experiences of Afrikan Americans, Native Americans, Hispanics, and women of all races and classes were not included in a serious way. For example, Bowne, a staunch advocate for women's rights and those of children,[24] did not explicitly address either the rights of black women in particular, or those of blacks in general in his book on ethics. In addition, he did not include elements of their experiences that contribute in positive ways to culture in this country.

Since most of the major books by the first three generations of personalists are out of print and difficult to locate in many libraries, I have quoted liberally from many of them, as well as from articles and other literature that are difficult to access. It is not my intention to undertake an exhaustive study of personalism. Instead, I want to consider and discuss its meaning, some of its history, sources, essential principles, methodological aspects, metaphysical and ethical considerations. There will be little comparison with other than personalistic systems of thought.

The work of Bowne and Brightman will receive much attention, although I consider key ideas of their students as well as personalists outside the Boston tradition. My reason for focusing on Bowne and Brightman is that the literature on personalism reveals that as for the most important issues for personalists, most adherents find themselves aligned with the Bowne or Brightman camp, with some nuancing of their respective positions. Brightman was Bowne's student and became the chief interpreter of his personalism. He always adhered to the main outlines of Bowne's personalism, but he clearly diverged from and went beyond his teacher in several key respects. One of the major differences we find between the two is the way each developed and responded to the doctrine of God and evil.

In chapter 3, I include a discussion of the personalism (or personal idealism) developed by Bowne's contemporary George Holmes Howison, who taught at the University of California. I mention Howison here because the relationship between him and Bowne has been something of a mystery. For several years both men lived in close proximity to each other in the Boston-Cambridge area. Howison was not, like Bowne, a voluminous writer but was an excellent teacher. I include him in this volume because it is important we remember that although Boston University was long considered the great center for personalistic studies, there was also a strong, vibrant personalist contingent on the West Coast under the leadership of such men as Howison, Flewelling, and John Wright Buckham. Although it is not known whether Bowne and Howison corresponded with each other about their work, we do know that they were at least acquainted with each other. Both men were present, for example, at the 1904 meeting of the Congress of the Arts and Sciences in St. Louis. Bowne was the chairperson of the philosophy division and read the Chairman's Address. Howison followed him with the reading of a major paper on philosophy.

In addition, I include a discussion on Afrikan American personalism.[25] I show that Martin Luther King, Jr., was not the only, or the first Afrikan American who studied personalism at Boston University, and that an Afrikan American actually studied personalism under Bowne. Also, and unlike Knudson, I include more extensive treatments of two women personalists, Mary Calkins and Georgia Harkness. Knudson provides a brief treatment of Calkins only.

Early personalists in the Bowne tradition did not distinguish between personality and person, but tended to use the two terms interchangeably. This text makes the distinction. Where early personalists used the term *personality* when referring to a metaphysical category, I substitute the term *person*.

I hope that my book will help give new life to a once vibrant philosophical tradition. Perhaps greater literary productivity on the part of present-day proponents of personalism will follow the publication of this book. In addition, the writing of this book is the best way I can say "thank you" to the two teachers outside the Afrikan American community—Walter G. Muelder and the late Peter A. Bertocci—who made such an indelible impression on my thinking.

1

What Is Personalism?

The Meaning of Personalism

Ernest N. Merrington wrote that Borden P. Bowne (1847–1910) built his metaphysical system upon "personality as an ethical concept."[1] It is more accurate to say that Bowne built his philosophy upon person as a metaphysical concept. Personalism does, of course, have an ethical theory. But as a philosophy, the Bowne type of personalism is essentially a metaphysics. It maintains that reality is a society of selves and persons with a Supreme Person (God) at its center. Person was, for Bowne, the fundamental principle of explanation, capable of explaining all other principles but itself.[2] Indeed, one has to assume mind, intelligence, or person in order to do any explaining, any discoursing at all. This is why we can speak of person as the assumption of assumptions, or as "the master principle." It is that principle without which no other principle matters or can be known. As an "ultimate fact" there is an element of mystery regarding person, and this will always be the case for us since we are finite and limited and, thus, not omniscient. Because person is ultimate, we can neither build it out of something else, nor tell how it is, or can be, a fact. Yet we always have a choice of mysteries. For example, we can choose the mystery of person, which leaves less to be explained in experience, or we can choose the mystery of some form of impersonal mechanism, which raises more questions than it answers. The mechanistic view does not have an adequate explanation for the existence of mechanistic forms of explanation. But person can at least give an explanation of itself, as well as of impersonal explanatory principles.

Just think about this: Can an impersonal, unthinking substance explain anything at all? Mind, intelligence, or person may not be able to fully explain itself and precisely how it came to be, but it goes a long way toward explaining all other things. How we are persons, how we can and will act, or how we can even be conscious we do not—and may never—know. But *that* we are, and of these things (and more) we are "absolutely sure."[3] In addition, we are sure that as potentially rational beings we, not some unconscious, impersonal we-know-not-what, are the most likely to unravel some of the mysteries of our being.

Personalism is a form of idealism. Idealism holds that mind is the ultimate reality, or reality is of the nature of mind, spirit, or intelligence. It is the opposite of materialism, which maintains that material things are the basis of reality. Materialism holds that mind or spirit emerges from the material or impersonal and is also reducible to it. Idealism of all kinds rejects this, maintaining instead that mind is not reducible to some material substance, nor does it emerge from such.

Personalism or personal idealism maintains that person is "the supreme philosophical principle." This means that one who is interested in ultimate causes and reasons for things must seek for their explanation in mind or person. Edgar S. Brightman (1884–1953) characterized personalism as that system of philosophy that holds that the universe is a society of interacting and intercommunicating selves and persons, united by the will of God, who is creator and sustainer of all things.[4] This description of personalism emphasizes the unity and interrelatedness of reality. In addition, it stresses what Brightman called a qualitative monism, which means that reality is of the nature of a single quality or type. In the case of personalism it means that only conscious processes (selves and persons) are real. We will see later that as a result of conversations with persons like his former student Georgia Harkness, and his critical reading of Alfred N. Whitehead, Brightman ultimately conceded that there are other realities as well. This is consistent with dualistic types of personalism such as that represented in the thought of Harkness. Yet we should be quite clear that for the Bowne-Brightman type of personalism, ultimate reality is personal. More will be said about this subject when we examine some of the key types of personalisms.

Another emphasis we see in Brightman's characterization of personalism is what he referred to as a relative quantitative pluralism. This means that the Supreme Person is neither the sole reality, nor is identical with created persons and selves, although these are dependent upon the Supreme Person (Creator). That they are not identical with or mere modes of the Creator is significant because one of the basic tenets of personalism is that being is characterized by freedom. In order for created persons to retain their sense of freedom and individuality, they cannot be completely identified with the Creator (such as we find in some forms of absolute idealism). Their freedom is preserved only as they retain a degree of separateness from the Creator and other persons.

There are nearly a dozen—and possibly more—types of personalisms.[5] My primary focus will be on that most typical form of personalism that grew up on the east coast of the United States under the direction of Bowne in the late nineteenth century and the first decade of the twentieth. The preceding discussion is about that type of personalism. It is not uncommon to refer to this type of personalism as typical personalism, "normative" personalism, typical theistic personalism, personal idealism, Bownean or Brightmanian, or Boston Personalism. Unless specified otherwise, any reference to personalism will be to the Bowne-Brightman type.

It was Albert C. Knudson (1873–1953) who designated Bowne's personalism as the "normative" type, a designation that I challenge for reasons to be clarified later. However, what Knudson sought to convey was the idea that personalism in its most thoroughgoing sense is reached only when it "becomes a philosophical method as well as a body of conclusions."[6] That is, in addition to being the basic principle of explanation, personalism must be pushed to its most logical conclusions. Only then may it be viewed as typical or thoroughgoing personalism. That is, person must be seen as a self-sufficient principle and the fundamental explanatory principle; that principle around which all the problems of philosophy and life are organized and solved. Bowne, more than any of his contemporaries, sought to present personalism in this way. This led Knudson to describe Bowne's philosophy as "systematic methodological personalism."[7]

Two early works by Bowne's students sought to situate his philosophy in the history of Western thought. Ralph T. Flewelling (1871–1960) was one of the last of the well-known, second-generation personalists to study under Bowne. He did his doctoral work under Bowne in 1909. Bowne died the next year. Flewelling taught for many years at the University of Southern California. It was there that he founded and edited the journal *The Personalist* in the early 1920s. Like most of the early personalists, he was a prolific writer and expositor of the Bowne type of personalism.

In 1915, five years after Bowne's death, Flewelling, inspired by Rudolf Euken,[8] undertook the task of writing a compact book on Bowne's personalism in relation to other major philosophical systems in the West. He compared Bowne's views on reality, space, and time, that is, "the main questions" of philosophy, with those of major thinkers down to "modern times." Flewelling gave his book the title: *Personalism and the Problems of Philosophy: An Appreciation of the Work of Borden Parker Bowne.* He did not seek an exhaustive treatment of Bowne's philosophy in relation to other systems, but was the first to begin the work of situating Bowne's personalism in Western philosophy. He himself pointed to the need for "a more detailed and technical work" than his own.[9] Albert C. Knudson answered the challenge.

In 1927 Knudson published *The Philosophy of Personalism: A Study in the Metaphysics of Religion.* The prepublication working title of this text was *Bowne and Personalism.*[10] This text far exceeds the Flewelling text in comprehensiveness. The audience for this book is advanced philosophy students and professional philosophers. And yet the style is so clear that most serious readers can successfully work through it and understand the basic principles of Bowne's personalism. After discussing five less typical or less thoroughgoing types of personalism, Knudson introduces Bowne's as the most typical, or as he liked to say, "normative,"[11] type. He then devotes separate chapters to the epistemology, metaphysics, and theology of personalism. He concludes with a discussion of "militant personalism" and "the personalistic hall of fame." He cites and responds to chief criticisms made against personalism and then clarifies why he believes it to be the most reasonable of the philosophical systems.

It was Knudson who provided the classic definition of the Bowne type of personalism. Characterizing it as "the most distinctive form of personalism," Knudson said that personalism is "that form of idealism which gives equal recognition to both the pluralistic and monistic aspects of experience and which finds in the conscious unity, identity, and free activity of personality the key to the nature of reality and the solution of the ultimate problems of philosophy."[12] Knudson saw as his task unpacking this definition in his book and providing a systematic account of Bowne's personalism.

There is no question that Bowne was a personalist long before he gave his philosophy the name personalism. We will see momentarily that his was a systematic and intentional movement toward a philosophy for which person would be the central category. Thus it made sense to give it a name that had "person" in it.

And yet Bowne was rather late in appropriating the term personalism—sometime between 1905 and 1907—as the way to designate his philosophy. He named his philosophy personalism not long before he died. In addition, he was not the first to coin the term. Friedrich Schleiermacher did that in 1799, although neither he nor others who later used the term developed it philosophically.

There is some confusion as to precisely when Bowne first became aware of the term personalism and when he actually began to appropriate it. There is also some fuzziness as to when the West Coast personalist George Holmes Howison first used the term. I consider the latter first.

James McLachlan agrees with Ralph Barton Perry's contention that it was Howison who was the "author" of the term personalism. Writes McLachlan: "Howison had used it in the Conception of God debate in 1896 and Perry noted 'his prior title to it is clearly valid.'"[13] In fact, Perry claimed that Howison used the term *personal idealism* "repeatedly" in his contribution to the text that resulted from that debate.[14] It is important to observe, however, that Perry specifically attributes the term personal idealism to Howison, not personalism. Furthermore—and this is where the confusion arose—it appears that Perry was actually quoting Howison's claim that he had referred to the term personal idealism a number of times in the Conception of God debate in 1896. In the 1904 revised edition of *The Limits of Evolution*, Howison wrote:

> Throughout the many years that I have held the metaphysical theory here presented, I have called it by the name of Personal Idealism; and when, three years ago, I published these essays, I placed this name in their title-page and explained it at length in the Preface; I had also several times used the name, with the same explained meaning, in the volume called *The Conception of God*, published four years earlier in cooperation with Professors Royce, Le Conte, and Mezes.[15]

Perry may or may not have been in attendance at the Conception of God debate in 1896. It is therefore not known whether he actually heard with his own ears Howison's alleged use of the term personal idealism "several times" during the debate. What Perry did do, however, was to cite the preface to the revised edition of Howison's book as the place where Howison *wrote* that he used the term several years prior to the original publication of the book.[16]

But there is yet another disturbing point to be noted. Howison was the editor who wrote the introduction to *The Conception of God* in 1897, months after the debate. Howison wrote that his opposing view to Royce may be called "Pluralistic Idealism," or "Ethical Idealism," but that he "would prefer, simply Personal Idealism."[17] Howison cites the term but one time in that introduction, written only *after* the actual debate. In addition, he three times used the term *pluralistic idealism*[18] as synonymous with personal idealism. He also used the term *idealistic pluralism*[19] as a synonym of personal idealism. Therefore, Howison's statement in the preface of the revised edition of *The Limits of Evolution* (1904) that he used the term personal idealism "several times" in *The Conception of God* debate is at best misleading. For in the first place he did not mention the term that frequently in the written text of his presentation. In the second place he only cited the term twice—not several times—in his introduction to that book. Howison's response to Royce in *The Conception of God* was in the form of a paper entitled "The City of God, and the True God as its Head." There he reveals that his aim was to set forth a pluralistic form of idealism against that of Royce's monistic idealism.[20] In addition, a half dozen or more times Howison observes that the idealism of Royce and Le Conte diverged early from the type that he advocated.[21] Howison clearly defined his type of idealism in his presentation. However, there is not a single use of the term personal idealism. It is, of course, possible that Howison used the term in his oral presentation, and it did not find its way into the written text that was published. And whether he did or did not use the term verbally, it is quite possible that Howison was the author of the term personal idealism.

However, McLachlan's claim that Howison was the "author" of the term personalism does not square with other things known about the authorship of the term, that is, that it was first introduced by Schleiermacher in 1799.[22] Nor does his claim square with the use of the term personalism by other American thinkers both during and prior to Howison's day.[23] Now, what about Bowne's use of the terms personalism and personal idealism?

In "Flewelling and American Personalism," Wilbur Long maintains that Bowne first employed the term personalism two years before he died.[24] Long dates Bowne's use of the term to the publication of his book *Personalism*, in 1908. This was not an uncommon practice, for most who knew of Bowne's work were aware that he came to use the term late in his career. Indeed, Frank W. Collier even argued that Bowne was, from the beginning to the end of his philosophical career, a staunch personalist. According to Collier, one sees in every book by Bowne "the ardent personalist."[25] There is no question that there were elements of personalism in Bowne's work from the beginning, and that the personalistic tone became more pronounced with almost every publication. And yet one wonders about the wisdom of actually naming Bowne a personalist before he himself came to the term. We know that Bowne actually called himself a personalist one year before he died, and quite possibly before that time. So when did Bowne first use the term personalism, and when did he first appropriate it as the best way to characterize his own philosophy? The following discussion is intended to provide some clarification on these questions.

In his book *Boston University School of Theology 1839–1968*, Richard Morgan Cameron wrote that Bowne actually got the term personalism "from a footnote of William James about the French philosopher [Charles B.] Renouvier."[26] Cameron did not name the specific book by James. It is known, however, that in *Some Problems of Philosophy* (1911), James, in the process of acknowledging Renouvier's influence on his own thought, cites his teacher's book *Le Personnalisme* (1903).[27] Since there is a considerable amount of evidence that James and Bowne were close friends and frequently read and critiqued each other's work, it is quite possible that Bowne saw a reference to Renouvier's book on personalism in one of James's books.

Cameron makes the further claim that Bowne "began to use the term [personalism] only about 1905."[28] Influenced by George C. Cell's article, "Bowne and Humanism,"[29] on this matter, Cameron unfortunately misrepresents key aspects of Cell's argument, thereby causing confusion. For example, the James footnote does not mention Renouvier's name either explicitly or implicitly.[30] Furthermore, Cameron's claim that Bowne only began using the term personalism in 1905 is not accurate, as we will see momentarily.

Cell actually said the following:

> While James was in Europe in 1900 he picked up in an article by the great French personalist, Renouvier, a new term…James was just then working away on his epoch-making treatise on The Varieties of Religious Experience…In a foot-note (p. 501) he used quite casually the term personalism for the first time, I believe, in American philosophy as the natural name for "this more personal style of thought…" In the same foot-note there occurs also a striking reference to Bowne's writings combining a high compliment with a keen criticism.[31]

An examination of the footnote to which Cell refers reveals no reference to Bowne's writings. However, in note number 2 on the next page James praises Bowne's "wonderfully able rationalistic booklets (which every one should read)": The Christian Revelation (1898), The Christian Life (1899), and The Atonement (1900).[32]

Cell then continues by saying that having always been a personalist, Bowne, upon seeing the term personalism in that footnote, was indelibly impressed and spellbound. "Thus a foot-note is the gateway through which the term personalism passed over into American philosophy," Cell continued. To Bowne this was the perfect term for what he had long taught, believed, and lived. Cell then maintains that in 1904 "Bowne announced in the course of a masterful lecture which the writer had the good fortune to hear that 'this style of philosophy might in short well be called personalism,' since it made personality the key to philosophy."[33] He then points to Bowne's use of the term in *The Immanence of God* (1905).[34] Cell believed his to be the most accurate account of how Bowne came to call his philosophy personalism. But Cell's line of argument needs to be examined, for even if Bowne saw James's casual footnote reference to personalism in *The Varieties of Religious Experience,* the question still remains as to whether that precise citing led to his adoption of the term.

It is quite possible that Bowne was aware of Renouvier's text on personalism since it was published in 1903. But it is also possible that Bowne was aware of the term personalism through his familiarity with the likes of William T. Harris (1835–1909),[35] Walt Whitman (1819–1892), and Amos Bronson Alcott (1799–1888). Each of these used the term personalism in his work, but did not develop it philosophically. Indeed, Ralph T. Flewelling, a former student of Bowne's, argued this point as well. Flewelling observed that, having studied under Rudolph Hermann Lotze in Germany in the early 1870s, Bowne would have likely been "familiar with the German use of the term."[36] In addition, Flewelling argued that Alcott may have been the first American to use the term personalism in more than a casual way to designate his philosophical system in 1857. Whitman used the term a number of times in *Democratic Vistas* and also published an essay in 1868 entitled "Personalism." In addition, John Grote, an English scholar, used the term in 1865.[37] The term was used by William Stern (1871–1938) in his pantheistic personalism in a 1906 publication. Brightman contends that after the term personalism was popularized, it had "widespread" use in Europe, Latin America, and the United States.[38]

Howison most assuredly used the term personal idealism in the introduction he wrote to *The Conception of God* in 1897. However, I have not found evidence that he used the term personal idealism during the actual debate with Royce in 1895. In addition, as far as I can tell, Bowne's first published use of that term, as well as the first public use of the term personalism, was in the Chairman's Address he gave at the Congress of Arts and Sciences in St. Louis in 1904.

In his essay "Bowne and Personalism," Francis J. McConnell wrote that it was five years before Bowne's death that he first heard him refer to his philosophical system as personalism.[39] This would have been around 1905. McConnell's claim was in fact given credence by Bowne himself, for in 1904 Bowne gave the aforementioned Chairman's Address before the Department of Philosophy at the Congress of the Arts and Sciences, which met in St. Louis that year. I know of no other place in Bowne's published writings prior to 1904 and before his lectures in 1907 (published in 1908 as *Personalism*) where he even used the terms personalism and personal idealism. Although Bowne did not actually characterize his own philosophical system as personalism in that 1904 address, he made it quite clear that in his judgment the best tendencies in metaphysics were moving in the direction of personalism. Here we also find for the first time an attempt on Bowne's part to define personalism. Said Bowne:

> In the field of metaphysics proper I notice a strong tendency toward personal idealism, or as it might be called, Personalism; that is, the doctrine that substantial reality can be conceived only under the personal form and that all else is phenomenal. This is quite distinct from the traditional idealisms of mere conceptionism. It holds the essential fact to be a community of persons with a Supreme Person at their head while the phenomenal world is only expression and means of communication.[40]

Notice that Bowne used personal idealism and personalism synony-
mously. Of course, it is important to note that George Holmes Howison was
present at that Congress. I will return to the Bowne-Howison relationship in
the discussion on Howison's teleological personalism in chapter 3. But what
is most important for our purpose is that it was Bowne who first systematized personalism and developed it into a philosophical method.

It was in 1909, a year before his death, that Bowne made a public decla-
ration of what he called himself. During Bowne's absence from the city of
Boston a number of persons inquired of Mrs. Bowne how he characterized
his philosophy. She wrote to her husband and put the question to him. Bowne
responded in the now famous letter he wrote to his wife on May 31 of that
year.

> It is hard to classify me with accuracy. I am a theistic idealist, a person-
> alist, a transcendental empiricist, an idealistic realist, and realistic ide-
> alist; but all these phrases need to be interpreted. They cannot well be
> made out from the dictionary. Neither can I well be called a disciple of
> any one. I largely agree with Lotze, but I transcend him. I hold half of
> Kant's system, but sharply dissent from the rest. There is a strong smack
> of Berkeley's philosophy, with a complete rejection of his theory of
> knowledge. I am a Personalist, the first of the clan in any thorough-
> going sense.[41]

It will be instructive to discuss several of the descriptions Bowne cites
in his letter, for a number of these are various ways that he characterized his
philosophy before finally naming it personalism. For our purpose I include:
objective idealism, the influence of Berkeley, Kant, and Lotze, and transcendental empiricism. These influences will be noted elsewhere as well.

Objective Idealism

We may refer to the objective idealism stage as the first phase of Bowne's
movement toward personalism. In *Metaphysics* (1882), Bowne said that historically his position might be called objective idealism.[42] Since this type of
idealism maintains that the object of perception is independent of the subject perceiving it, it holds that something in reality exists that created persons find, but do not make or create. It is given. We humans are not all there
is in existence. There is something in existence (not ourselves) that conditions us[43] and creates other things as well. This implies an objective ground
of our sensations, which in turn implies an Author or Creator; for the question immediately comes: If we did not create this "given" that we find in
our own experience, who did? Where did it come from? In the early stage of
his development Bowne began insisting that "we cannot help admitting that
we are conditioned by something not ourselves."[44] We may not know precisely what it is or its precise nature, but we know that something is there.

Objective idealism is essentially the view that the object of perception is
"a phenomenon of an objective fact of some kind." It is, in a word, caused
by something else. In holding this view of the object (which he also refers to

as phenomenalism[45]), Bowne was arguing against both common sense realism and subjective idealism. The former maintains that the object of our perceptions is real. It must be real, or have some type of reality about it in order to produce sensations about it. Subjective idealism, on the other hand, holds that the object is little more than a presentation in the mind. According to Bowne, physical objects are an order of the energizing of divine thought and will "which, when viewed under the forms of space and time, of causality and substance, appear as a world of things."[46] The world of things or physical objects is an objective fact, rather than the subjective idealist's view that it is a mere series of presentations in the mind. Objective idealism contends that the world of things has no existence apart from mind, but that they do have a level of reality about them. But that reality is not as essential as the reality of mind. Francis J. McConnell wrote an insightful summary of Bowne's objective idealism:

> For him the active self reads off the messages, sees the pictures, feels the forces of an outside world—an outside world which is the expression of the divine mind but of nothing outside of all mind. The universe consists, then, of the world-ground, which is the supreme self, and of other finite selves in a common objective system where they can come into touch with one another.[47]

In the revised edition of *Metaphysics* (1898), Bowne observed that his position might be described as Kantianized Berkeleianism, and transcendental empiricism.[48] There were several points at which Bowne agreed and disagreed with Kant and Berkeley.

Influence of George Berkeley

Francis J. McConnell, one of the best early commentators on Bowne's work, maintained that near the end of his life Bowne was preoccupied with the work of Berkeley. Just prior to Bowne's death, plans were being made for him to deliver a series of lectures on Berkeley in a European university. Although Bowne died before he could even write the lectures, McConnell was convinced that the trend of his later thinking was toward Berkeleianism.[49] Indeed, he believed this the case when Bowne changed the name of his philosophy from objective idealism to personalism. What did Bowne find influential in the work of Berkeley?

Bishop George Berkeley (1685–1753), more than any thinker before or during his time, denied the metaphysical existence of matter, but not its phenomenal existence. Rather, metaphysical reality was conceived by him in terms of mind or spirit. Only mind or spirit has metaphysical reality. One who does not read Berkeley far enough or closely enough may erroneously conclude that he completely identified physical objects with ideas or presentations in the mind. This would leave him open to the charge of subjective idealism, a criticism that has often been made of him both historically and in more modern times. Berkeley held that matter or material objects have no metaphysical existence. They are not the cause of that higher reality, mind. It is the mind of God, not some unknown, inert, impersonal, inactive substance, that both causes our perceptions and provides the assurance of the continued existence of objects, (e.g., a chair, pen, desk, or the paper on which I am writing) when we do not perceive it. Physical objects, according to Berkeley, are produced by the energizing of God's will. Accordingly, the entire visible world is nothing but the visual language of God. It is one of the chief ways that God communicates to us humans.[50] Brightman interpreted Berkeley to mean: "Nature is literally the living garment of the Deity. The world of nature...is a divine, visual language."[51] Bowne himself liked to describe nature as the energizing of God's will.[52] He maintained that, according to metaphysics, all "impersonal existence" is reduced to "a flowing form of the activity of the fundamental reality."[53] God is very prominent in Berkeley's philosophy. John Wright Buckham (1864–1945) was not wrong when he described Berkeley as "the most ardent of theists." Berkeley was adamant that created persons and God are able to communicate "primarily by direct, spiritual intercourse,"[54] such communication being initiated by God.

Berkeley's immaterialism has influenced all forms of idealism, including the personal idealism of the Bowneans. Bowne maintained that Berkeley denied the reality of material objects apart from mind, and held that such objects are but ideas or presentations produced in human minds by God. What we know of physical objects are their qualities and our perceptions of them, and we can only know these in the mind. And yet it was this latter concept, and not the idea that physical objects are presentations in the mind, that was Berkeley's major contribution. He wanted to get the emphasis off the external or outside world of physical objects and focus on mind.

Essentially Berkeley would say that the paper I am writing on is white, thin, and rectangular in shape. But these, according to Berkeley, are qualities that emerge as ideas in my mind. The paper as such has no metaphysical reality. What Berkeley rejected, and this was a crucial point, was the idea that there is some inert, inactive matter or physical substance that is the cause of these qualities or ideas. Quite the contrary. In Berkeley's view God and God only is the cause. The only metaphysical realities, he maintained, are souls or spirits and God. Yet Berkeley believed sensations and presentations in the mind to have an objective and spiritual ground that is an absolute necessity of thought. What Berkeley questioned was "the external existence of the object in perception, and reduced it to an effect in us."[55] Yet it should be remembered that although Berkeley considered himself to be an immaterialist, he denied nothing that the senses can apprehend, for example, a chair or tree. Continuing with the example of the paper on which I write, I can both see and feel it, and thus the paper has a reality. That is, it really exists. What Berkeley rejected was the tendency of philosophers to hold that there is a material substance that is the cause of the paper (although to David Hume it was questionable as to whether Berkeley was right in suggesting against John Locke that the cause is a spiritual substance). Said Berkeley:

Whatever we see, feel, hear, or any wise conceive or understand, remains as secure as ever, and is as real as ever...I do not argue against the existence of any one thing that we can apprehend, either by sense or reflection. That the things I see with mine eyes and touch with my hands do exist, really exist, I make not the least question. The only thing whose existence we deny, is that which philosophers call matter or corporeal substance.[56]

According to Berkeley the paper on which I write is but sensations or ideas (which are inactive and powerless), and these exist only in my mind, or in some mind, that perceives them. Only in this sense does the paper exist. But it was claims such as this that left him open to the charge of subjective idealism, whether he was in fact that or not. Berkeley rejected matter, or what he characterized as "an inert, senseless substance," that is the cause of the paper I write on. However, if the senses can bear witness to an object, it exists. What does not exist is some unknown object to the senses, which is presumably the cause of the object.

What was really novel about Berkeley's view was that he went much further than the common sense view that the object to which my senses bears witness exists. Berkeley went on to insist that the being of any object whatsoever depends on its being perceived by some mind. To be is to be perceived. Therefore, if my paper is not being perceived either by my mind or by some other mind—human or divine—it does not exist. Berkeley took as one of the most obvious truths the view that:

> [A]ll the choir of heaven and furniture of the earth, in a word all those bodies which compose the mighty frame of the world, have not any subsistence without a mind, that their being (*esse*) is to be perceived or known; that consequently so long as they are not actually perceived by me, or do not exist in my mind or that of any other created spirit, they must either have no existence at all, or else subsist in the mind of some eternal spirit...[57]

It is also important to point out that while Berkeley said that to be is to be perceived, this statement also implied that the deeper metaphysical reality is that which perceives, namely, the mind or self. Mind is implied in his formula, and thus it can be said that mind, not the object perceived, is the most significant reality. This is an important point, since idealists emphasize the centrality of mind.

Bowne understood that when Berkeley said that nothing could be external to mind he did not mean that nothing could be external to his individual mind. Berkeley essentially made God's mind "all-embracing," which included the constant working of divine will and thus has a constancy about it that makes it possible for persons to experience it. The object one perceives is therefore not a delusion, even if the perceiver leaves the room momentarily. As Bowne often said, the "blizzard is not merely a tumult in a man's consciousness."

Even the Berkeleian idealist regards the order of phenomena as constant, and views given phenomena as the permanent sign of the possibility of other phenomena. Berkeley himself insisted upon this point so strongly and so frequently that it is inconceivable that any presumably rational beings could have thought it relevant to urge him to knock his head against a post, or to thrust his hand into a fire.[58]

According to Bowne, physical objects exist not only in finite minds, but in the mind and will of God. "This constitutes its reality and universality." It also distinguishes Bowne's objective idealism from the idealism of Berkeley.[59]

Personalism has benefited much from Berkeley's demolishing of materialism, although it questions the reasonableness of any thoroughgoing immaterialism. The logical conclusion to be drawn from this is that material objects are but delusions, mere presentations in the mind. This was not what Berkeley intended, although some of his principles left him vulnerable to this criticism. Personalism, on the other hand, "affirms the complete phenomenality of matter."[60] This was Bowne's way of correcting Berkeley, who was vulnerable to the criticism that according to his theory physical objects do not exist. According to Bowne, physical objects have phenomenal, not ontological, reality. But they *are* real. This is why Bowne said that his idealism could well be classified as phenomenalism, for the visible phenomenal object does have a reality of its own. Otherwise, how does one explain the sensations produced in the mind by an object? So the object must have a reality of its own, although not metaphysical.

In addition to rejecting what he considered a too thoroughgoing immaterialism, Bowne rejected Berkeley's psychology and theory of knowledge.[61] However, he appropriated Berkeley's idea that "matter could not exist except as the creation of mind and that since it was the expression of mind it could not continue to exist if mind were withdrawn." Both Bowne and Berkeley were anxious to remove the emphasis from the outside world. Things either come into thought or they must go out of existence.[62] This has the effect of giving prominence to the activity of mind.

Both Bowne and Berkeley emphasized freedom.[63] However, only Bowne made freedom one of the two touchstones of his philosophy, arguing for both its "speculative" and ethical significance. Unlike Berkeley and many idealists after him, Bowne lifted freedom up as a chief regulative principle in his philosophy. Along with George Holmes Howison, this is one of the places at which Bowne's idealism is distinguished from other types. Indeed, for Bowne, reason itself requires freedom, and would become "shipwrecked" without it. I will return to this point later.

Berkeley and Bowne each wrote a book during their youth that contained most of the chief ideas that they later developed more systematically.[64] Unfortunately, Bowne did not seek the publication of his book. Instead, he destroyed it, causing it to be lost to the history of thought forever. It is also important to observe that both men were also "thoroughgoing evangelicals,"[65] although Berkeley was not an evangelical in the strict sense, inasmuch as he was no longer on the scene when the evangelical movement flourished.

Both Berkeley and Bowne held that idealism is the best argument for the existence of God. They differed in that Berkeley believed it could also tell us about the moral nature of God. Bowne rejected this, claiming instead that the most idealism could do is establish the existence of a mind back of the universe, but by itself it could not tell us enough about that mind's moral nature. Berkeley, on the other hand, maintained that we infer a worthy God by argument from what God does. The reason for their disagreement may be that Berkeley lived during the Age of Enlightenment, a period when there was a "glorification of reason," with little emphasis on faith. Although a very acute thinker much like Berkeley, Bowne had a better sense of where reason ends and faith begins. Berkeley seemed to think he could prove through reason more about God than was warranted. Bowne and personalists who follow his line of thought push reason as far as they can when addressing ultimate things, but do not hesitate to acknowledge that some mystery remains.

According to Bowne, the strength of Berkeley's argument lay in his analysis of the object. Berkeley rejected John Locke's notion of the mind as a *tabula rasa* (a blank sheet on which ideas are imprinted), and his view of matter as "only a complex of simple sensations," and thus "capable of existing only in sensibility." In addition, Berkeley had little use for Locke's view of matter as "pure passivity and inertness," for "matter, as thus conceived, would account for nothing, and could only be an idea."[66] Although Berkeley recognized the self as active, he did not acknowledge this as consistently and cogently as did Kant. The self as agent was not given primacy in Berkeley's philosophy, although he periodically pointed to the activity of mind. Perhaps, had Berkeley lived during or after Kant's time rather than fifty years before him, he, like Bowne (who lived a century after Kant), might have given the idea of the self as active a central place in his thought. Berkeley's failure to stress the activity of the mind left him open to the charge of skepticism. McConnell said that the chief difference between Berkeley and Bowne was the time that each lived in relation to Kant, who placed a great deal of emphasis on the activity of the self.[67] Bowne was very much influenced by this aspect of Kant's philosophy. Yet we will see in Bowne's transcendental empiricism that he criticized Kant for not making the self more central than the categories of thought, and for failing to see that the self, not the categories of thought, does the interpreting.

Influence of Immanuel Kant

From the German philosopher Immanuel Kant (1724–1804), Bowne appropriated several ideas that influenced his personalism. These include a rejection of John Locke's view that the mind is a passive tabula rasa (blank sheet) that is basically a receptacle for external stimuli such as sensations. Kant convincingly showed in *The Critique of Pure Reason* (1781) that if this were the case, the mind would be little more than a mess of disconnected impressions, or what he described as "an elusive phantasmagoria without intelligible contents." If the mind were merely passive it could neither connect nor make sense of impressions received, for it would not have the capacity to do anything at all with them other than to receive them into itself. It could perform no functions upon them. Knowledge, according to Kant, is not possible without an active thinking mind or intelligence that is capable of creativity. Therefore, he adopted the view that mind is both receptive and active. Kant went well beyond Berkeley's occasional reference to the mind as active. Mere sensations or impressions in the mind have no meaning, unity, or identity whatever. These are possible only through active thought or mind. Personalistic theory of knowledge, then, is activistic.

Bowne's idealism is essentially Kantian, although he was quick to point out that he rejected Kant's refusal to admit noumenal knowledge or knowledge of the ultimately real.[68] He believed Kant to have erred greatly when he failed to apply the categories of thought to noumena, or things in themselves. His failure in this regard "left the noumena without any ground of existence." Without rules or principles of thought for noumena, not only do these so-called "things in themselves" not exist for the mind, they do not exist at all. Bowne argued that any such doctrine that "denies the applicability of the categories to reality" ends in self-destruction. "When no law of thought is allowed to be valid for things, the things themselves become not only unaffirmable but also meaningless and empty of all contents." They become little more than verbal phrases "to which neither reality nor conception corresponds."[69]

Bowne maintained that Kant's doctrines of phenomena and noumena were "obscure" and confusing. He could not see the meaning in Kant's notion that phenomena are objects that we actually experience in the visual world, while noumena cause these. However, noumena are presumably unknowable to the human mind. In fact, according to Kant the phenomena masks or even distorts the noumena or power that causes them. Therefore, Bowne rejected outright "the conceptions of a world of reality altogether apart from mind and antithetical to it…"[70] Bowne described this as "Kant's strange doctrine."[71]

For Bowne, Kant's proof that there are categories or rules of thought "which are regulative in the mental life…was his great service to philosophy."[72] But according to Bowne, he then destroyed his system when he concluded that the categories of thought do not apply to noumena or things in themselves. Bowne reasoned that if the categories of thought do not apply to noumena, then the noumenal world does not exist. If they do apply, the question is what is the relation of the noumenal to the phenomenal world.

Bowne's response to Kant is that the rules of thought apply to all reality or to none, and that there are two types of reality—phenomenal and ontological or causal. Although both are real they are not real in the same way. "The phenomena are not causal or substantial," said Bowne, "but they are real in the sense that they are no illusions of the individual. If one is unsure of this he need only bang his head against a wall. Phenomena are abiding elements in our common-sense experience. They are not, then, phantasms or errors or hallucinations."[73] Phenomena are nothing but "forms of experience," and when we endeavor to go behind them the aim must not be to determine their reality, for they are real. Rather the aim should be to determine their cause. This is possible only through thought. Thought can penetrate to the reality or cause behind phenomena because all reality is of the nature of thought. So an important point to remember in personalism is that both the phenomenal and ontological worlds are real in their own way—even when it is said that the ontological is most "truly real." This is a Berkeleian influence and is what personalism means when it maintains that only mind is real. For it also acknowledges that the phenomenal world is "real in and for experience," but is not ontologically real. Bowne also rejected Kant's view that the phenomenal world masks and distorts the ontological. Instead, in Bowne's philosophy the phenomenal world is seen as a revelation of the ontological world.

In correcting and going beyond Kant, Bowne revealed a thoroughgoing theistic idealism. If all reality is of the nature of mind or thought, then in some way both the phenomenal and ontological worlds are caused by mind. But only mind or thought can penetrate both these realities and explain them as far as possible. Whatever the human mind can know of reality, it can know because both the phenomenal and ontological worlds are of the nature of mind. Bowne put it this way.

> But if all things lie within the thought sphere, if things are the product and expression of some creative thought, they might well, then, be commensurate with our intelligence…If things originate in thought and express thought, there is no difficulty in principle in their reappearing in thought. In that case the objects of experience, being products of thought, are commensurate with our thought, and it is altogether conceivable that our thought should be able to know them as they are. The world itself, though more than a thought, is essentially the expression of thought and hence lies open to our intelligence.[74]

If all reality is of the nature of thought and is actually produced by a Supreme Intelligence, the door is open for finite mind to get in touch with reality—even ultimate reality—and in some sense to know it as it really is. Perfect knowledge of reality may not be possible to humans, but since both they and reality are of the nature of mind, it is possible to know something about reality. This idea of Bowne's effectively destroyed Kant's idea of an unknowable thing-in-itself behind phenomenal objects. Personalism maintains that the phenomenal world is really a thought world and expresses thought. This is how Bowne managed to harmonize thought and thing, for he claims that the latter is itself rooted in thought. Therefore, there are not two separate orders—matter and spirit—but one. And that order is of the nature of mind or spirit.

Speaking of two types, or levels, of reality—phenomenal and ontological—can be confusing. Upon hearing my discussion on the influence of

Berkeley and Kant on Bowne's way of thinking about reality and his efforts to make clear that both phenomenal and ontological objects are real, a student of mine from Nigeria said that it might be an improvement to say simply that persons are created in a way that they can be in touch with reality, although not the whole of reality. When I look at another human being, for example, I see a real person. Yet I know that I do not see all that she is. There is more to her than the reality of her body.

It seems to me that to drop the language of phenomenal and ontological reality is reasonable, particularly if we remember that personalism is a thoroughgoing theistic idealism *and* realistic idealism; that ultimately the world is a thought-world, that is, that objects on any level have a reality about them. The key, according to the personalist framework, is that all objects are of the nature of thought or mind and are both caused and sustained by mind or thought. The paper on which I write is real. Period. That which causes the paper is real. Period. Reality is of one order, and that is a thought or spirit order. By saying it this way we also vastly reduce the tendency to distinguish between a sacred and secular order. There is, according to personalism, one order caused and sustained by a Supreme Mind. Persons are created in such a way that they can get in touch with and know something about reality, even when they cannot know the whole of reality in a perfect sense.

Although Kant's doctrine of the creative activity of thought is important for personalistic epistemology (theory of knowledge), it is more important for personalism because of its metaphysical implications. In the first place, thought as a creative process implies both unity and identity of the self. "If the mind were wholly passive and perception a mere act of receptivity, we might conceivably get along without a self."[75] It is inconceivable that we humans could be considered rational selves without the unity of self. Without self-identity the mind would be in a constant state of flux and utter confusion.

A second metaphysical implication of the doctrine of the creative activity of thought is that it opens the door to an idealistic worldview. This follows from Kant's view that the world of experience or the phenomenal order is made possible by the categories of mind, and not the other way around. Thought or mind prescribes its laws to nature or the world of experience as we know it. Experience or nature depends on the forms of mind or intelligence. With Kant, then, Bowne rejected the earlier empiricist view that mind or thought is dependent on experience or nature. Instead, these are dependent upon mind. This is the so-called "Copernican revolution" that Kant introduced into philosophy. It is thought, mind, or understanding that makes nature and experience, and not the other way around. Bowne took this to mean that intelligence cannot be understood through its own categories. That is, it is not the laws of thought (e.g., time, space, being, number, freedom, necessity, purpose) that understands intelligence. Rather, the laws of thought must be understood through our experience of intelligence.[76] This gives centrality or prominence to the self, which is precisely what Bowne was seeking to do. We will see later that this was the gist of his transcendental empiricism. At any rate, knowledge does not come, in this view, ready-made, but is "built up" in the mind.[77] More about this in a moment.

Bowne also appropriated Kant's idea of the primacy and centrality of the good will or holiness for ethics. In addition, he accepted Kant's emphasis on the practical reason. Since we are not able to arrive at the deepest truths about reality through intellectual processes alone, we must depend upon the ethical and practical aspects of our nature. In this respect Kant made value central in philosophy, and Bowne appropriated this idea as a key aspect of his theory of knowledge. Religion is based on morality or the goodness and righteousness of God. Knowledge about reality may be derived not only through intellectual processes, but through our ethical nature. Indeed, since reality always retains an element of mystery, there is a point beyond which rational human thought cannot go. For example, through rational demonstration we can prove neither the existence of God nor that immortality is a fact. This is why personalism tends to be more voluntaristic (laying stress on the will) than rationalistic (emphasizing the intellect).

Thought about reality is not reality. Reason alone cannot erase the gap between thought and reality. Something more is needed. For Bowne, this translated into faith. That is why he enjoyed saying with William James and his teacher, Rudolph Hermann Lotze that life is deeper and richer than mere logic alone.[78] In the final analysis all knowledge begins and ends in faith. For example, knowledge begins with the assumption or the faith that the universe is intelligible and that we are capable of understanding or getting in touch with it. Yet we do not know this with absolute, demonstrable certainty. We accept it on faith, and faith is essentially an act of will. Faith "springs out of the vital needs and interests of the mind. These needs and interests are subjective; they are practical and ideal in nature, a kind of *modus vivendi* with the universe; and they are also fundamental."[79] Furthermore, in order to even proceed on the path to knowledge it is necessary that we have faith even in the trustworthiness of reason itself. Indeed, if there is to be any discoursing at all, said Bowne, there must be a basic trust in reason. What Bowne would have us remember is that many of our statements about ultimate things, for example, God, freedom, and immortality, are practical postulates, not knowledge gained through reason alone. They are more dependent on faith than on knowledge.

Transcendental Empiricism

In addition to characterizing his system as objective idealism and Kantianized Berkeleianism, Bowne also at one time called it transcendental empiricism, which was alluded to previously in the reference to the Copernican revolution that Kant introduced into philosophy, that is, the view that experience or nature depends on the categories or forms of mind rather than the other way around. Mind makes and interprets experience and nature. These latter do not make and interpret mind or thought. Kant's contribution in this regard went a long way toward establishing the centrality of mind or thought in the knowing process, although the self still did not come to utmost prominence in his philosophy. This would be a chief contribution of Bowne. Kant stressed the role of the categories of mind. Bowne emphasized the role of the self in interpreting the categories.

Transcendental empiricism has primarily to do with Bowne's theory of knowledge or how persons come to know. Different from the traditional sense empiricism of Bowne's day, transcendental empiricism is the view that the categories of thought (e.g., being, space, time, notion, purpose, etc.) find their explanation in active, intelligent mind. That is, thought or mind is the explanation of the categories. The categories do not explain thought or intelligence, but are, rather, explained by it. Bowne said that "instead of testing our fundamental experience by the categories, we must rather find the meaning of the categories in experience. This experience, however, is not the passive experience of sense, but the active self-experience of intelligence."[80] Mind is active, subject to no laws beyond itself, or to any abstract principles within itself. "Living, active intelligence is the source of all truth and reality, and is its own and only standard."[81] This is Bowne's transcendental empiricism, the point of which is that all thought about reality must be rooted in experience, that is, the active self-experience of mind or intelligence.

Bowne's transcendental empiricism was crucial to his movement toward personalism. It was, writes Charles B. Pyle, "the kernel of his whole system."[82] The categories of thought do not determine or create our experience, but are instead revealed and understood in our experience. Intelligence can explain or at least give a better explanation of everything but itself. "It knows itself in living and only in living, but it is never to be explained by anything, being itself the only principle of explanation."[83] Transcendental empiricism made the self more central in Bowne's philosophy, and as he matured the self took on even more significance, a point of no small importance in the development of systematic methodological personalism.

Rudolph Hermann Lotze

Because Rudolph Hermann Lotze (1817–1881) was Bowne's teacher, and Bowne himself acknowledged his influence no less than three times, it will be instructive to say more about the nature of the Lotzean influence. There was deep respect between Bowne and Lotze. McConnell reported an interesting exchange between the two men during Bowne's student days:

> Lotze himself always paid high tribute to the work of Bowne. One afternoon in his student days Bowne called on Lotze. As Bowne left he called attention to a heavy thunderstorm coming up a valley. "That is nothing," said Lotze, "to the storm of questionings you have raised in my mind concerning my own philosophic system."[84]

From this it is difficult to know which man influenced the other most. It is important to remember that by the time Bowne went to Germany to continue his studies in 1873 he had already laid considerable foundation for his own philosophy through the writing of numerous articles. Therefore, without qualifying his statement, George Santayana misleadingly wrote in his dissertation that Lotze influenced Bowne even more than he influenced George T. Ladd, a Lotze scholar who taught at Bowdoin College and later at Yale.[85] The trouble with Santayana's statement is that he implied that Bowne was more influenced by Lotze than might have been the case. In addition, Bowne published his first book, *The Philosophy of Herbert Spencer*, the year after his study under Lotze, which means that even during his student days he was working on his first book to be published. So by the time Bowne studied under Lotze, he was by no means a novice in philosophy. Bowne declined to take the doctorate under Lotze because of his disdain for degrees.[86]

Bowne tells us only that he was much influenced by Lotze. In his second book, *Studies in Theism* (1879), he acknowledged his "general obligation to [his] friends and former instructors, Professor Ulrici, of Halle, and Professor Lotze, of Göttingen."[87] But Lotze is the only teacher whose ideas Bowne actually cites in his work.[88] On the dedication page of *Metaphysics* (1882) Bowne wrote: "In grateful recollection to the memory of my friend and former teacher Hermann Lotze." Lotze died the year before this book was published. In the preface Bowne cites the Lotzean influence, telling the reader that the conclusions reached in that book "are essentially those of Lotze," although for the most part they were reached "by strictly independent reflection; but, so far as their character is concerned, there would be no great misrepresentation in calling them Lotzean."[89] It will be recalled that Bowne also mentioned Lotze in the famous letter to Mrs. Bowne in 1909. Although Bowne did not say explicitly where he transcended Lotze, several things may be said.

Bowne Transcends Lotze

Bowne primarily went beyond Lotze by making both person and freedom touchstones of his philosophy. He built his entire philosophy around these, thus solidifying the centrality and role of the self. Although Lotze recognized the significance of both person and freedom, it was Bowne who argued their centrality both systematically and methodologically. For example, Lotze stopped just short of applying the category of person to God, thereby leaving "the fundamental reality only less vague than Hegel's absolute." Bowne, on the other hand, "presses on to the assertion of personality in the World-Ground with all that such an assertion implies." This, said Flewelling, "is the chief point of difference between Lotze and Bowne."[90]

We see Bowne's movement beyond Lotze most vividly in the revised edition of *Metaphysics* (1898). Both men were much influenced by Kant. However, Lotze failed to correct what Bowne understood to be a major Kantian error. More than any thinker before or during his day Kant stressed the activity of the mind. However, Bowne believed he undermined the importance of the mind's active role in the knowing process. In Bowne's judgment Kant seemed to give the categories of mind more prominence in the knowledge process than the role of the self. Bowne, as we have seen, wanted the emphasis not on the categories or rules of thought, but on the self. The centrality of the self is what Bowne sought to establish. This was fundamental to his movement toward personalism.

By the publication of the revised edition of *Metaphysics* Bowne had solidified his belief that the categories of thought are not more fundamental than the self. To claim otherwise would be an abstraction. It is precisely here that Bowne differed with Lotze. He was adamant about giving the self primacy over the categories. The categories of thought do not determine or create our experience, but are revealed and understood in our experience, that is, the experience of the self. In this respect the self is the basic metaphysical fact, and explains everything—as far as it can—but itself. This was Bowne's transcendental empiricism.

Bowne's Popularization of Personalism

As noted previously, Bowne did not begin, but ended his career, as a thoroughgoing personalist. As an objective idealist he held that there is an objective order outside persons that we do not create but find. This order exists independently of us. Bowne maintained that one must begin one's philosophizing with the actual world (which is independent of us) and never lose sight of this fact.

If one reads the entire Bowne corpus, it is possible to see a consistent progression in his thought from objective idealism in the early phase (1874–1895), to transcendental empiricism in the middle stage (1896–1904), and finally to the personalism stage near the end of his life (1905–1910). One can see in each phase an emphasis on the significance of the self, an emphasis that became more pronounced as Bowne moved into each new stage. By the personalism stage it was clear that person now had unequivocal prominence in his philosophy. According to McConnell, this is why in 1905 Bowne decided on the name personalism for his mature philosophy rather than the earlier objective idealism. McConnell was concerned that such a change would minimize the idealistic element in his philosophy, and "asked why he did not call it personal idealism. He replied that he wanted the emphasis kept unmistakably on the personal element."[91]

Bowne wrote *Personalism* (1908) one year before he wrote the famous letter to his wife. Although he understood his philosophy to be eclectic in the sense that he appropriated the relevant ideas of several thinkers, Bowne was now putting the scholarly world on notice that his philosophy was different from anything that had gone before or that existed during his day. Though others had introduced the term personalism into common parlance and emphasized certain aspects of personal idealism, Bowne's was the most thoroughgoing type. He considered all philosophical problems and their solutions in light of person, and he made person the central interpretive principle or category of his philosophy.

Bowne had little patience with those who insisted on trying to go behind mind or intelligence in attempts to explain it. "Uncritical minds always attempt to explain the explanation," he wrote, "thus unwittingly committing themselves to the infinite regress. Accordingly, when they come to living intelligence as the explanation of the world, they fancy that they must go behind even this."[92] For Bowne, of course, once one reaches this living, active intelligence there is nowhere else to go. Only in active intelligence or person do we find the fundamental explanation of the world and what happens in it. We have no way of knowing the *why* of mind or person, that is, precisely why or how person came to be. Nor do we know the nature of any explanation behind it. This is part of the mystery of person. Thoroughgoing personalism contends that only the Supreme Person can know the true nature of mind and the explanation of how and why it came to be.

Personalism's Point of Departure

Personalism is a philosophy that takes experience seriously. However, it is never quite accurate to say that personalism's point of departure is experience. Experience by itself is an abstraction. Experience, personalism maintains, presupposes a self or subject of experience that is having the experience or is aware of the experience. Without a self or subject, experience would have neither grounding nor meaning. It need only be remembered that personalism elevates active intelligence or the self to a place of prominence. Whatever meaning we can make of experience we do so through the self. Self, then, is the basic assumption of all experience.

It is therefore more accurate to say that personalism begins with the experience of the self or with self-experience. In other words, one begins with personal conscious experience and always returns here to check for consistency in argument. As part of the method of personalism, experience of the self is fundamental. Personalists are more sure of the experience of the self than of anything else. This was a basic premise of Saint Augustine (353–430), of whom Knudson writes:

> Augustine might in a sense be called the first personalist. To him we owe (1) a more highly developed conception of the unity of the mental life, (2) a new insight into the significance of the will in the life both of God and man, (3) the earliest clear formulation of the great truth that self-certainty is more immediate than our knowledge of the external world and hence should be used as the starting-point of philosophy, and (4) the first clear grasp of the fact that a valid metaphysics must be based on the self-knowledge of the finite personality.[93]

The idea of the primacy of self-certainty as the point of departure in philosophy and the belief that any adequate metaphysics must be based on the self-knowledge of created persons were revolutionary principles.

However, these principles were not firmly established until the French philosopher René Descartes (1559–1650) began writing philosophy in the seventeenth century. Descartes made the primacy of self-certainty fundamental to his philosophical method. Bowne believed that there is much about the self we cannot answer adequately. However, "the self itself as the subject of the mental life and knowing and experiencing itself as living, and as one and the same throughout its changing experiences, is the surest item of knowledge we possess."[94] Because the experience of the self is so important in personalism, it is crucial that any exposition of it include a discussion of the self and its nature. This will be taken up in chapter 4.

Personalists find in the self the clue to the nature of the world and reality. But it is important to remember that the self is not a mirror of the world. That is, we do not find in the self a perfect one-to-one correspondence between our thoughts and ruminations about reality. Our thoughts about God, for example, are neither identical with God, nor are they God. Yet the clue to the only knowledge we can have about God, nature, other selves and persons is found in the self and its experiences. The key to the solution to the basic problems of philosophy and life, then, is found in the self. We know nothing about change, for example, without looking to the source of affirming change, namely, the self. This means that the self must, in some sense, be unchanging or identical in order to be able to affirm change. We know change, then, only on the personal plane, and only as a result of an unchanging, abiding self that knows both itself and the changes occurring. In this regard every person is what Peter A. Bertocci called a "changing-same-self." More about this in the discussion on the meaning of person.

In addition to the emphasis on the primacy of self-certainty, personalism advocates a particular way of thinking about *being*. Accordingly, all being is characterized by activity. "Those things exist which act...," writes Bowne.[95] Reality is through and through causal or active. "Being and action are inseparable; the inactive is the non-existent." To be is to act or be acted upon. Persons never experience being without activity.

> The postulate of action is an agent, but this agent is not temporally antecedent to the action. Action is a dynamic consequence of being, and is coexistent with it. Neither can be thought without the other, and neither was before the other. Being did not first exist, and then act; neither did it act before it existed; but both being and action are given in indissoluble unity. Being has its existence only in its action and the action is possible only through the being...Metaphysically considered, being is self-centered activity, without distinction of parts or dates.[96]

Persons experience neither being without activity nor activity without being. Neither existed before or after the other. Being and activity have always existed in an integral, "indissoluble unity."

In discussions on being, personalism argues against the materialist claim to be able to picture ultimate things. Thinking, or mind, for example, cannot be pictured. Activity of thought cannot be pictured. Values cannot be pictured. The human inclination is to want to picture all things, but we simply cannot. Indeed, early personalism maintains that all we can picture of ourselves is our bodily manifestation. Bowne writes, for example, of "the impossibility of construing our own minds,"[97] and we certainly cannot construe the mind of any other person—human or divine.

The point about not being able to picture reality is probably among the most difficult of the personalistic teachings. We humans are so accustomed to seeing material objects that we easily conclude that the real is that which we can see or picture. We assume that if we cannot see an object, it must not be real. Following Plato, Bowne described all who insist that the real can be known only through the senses as "the children of the dragon's teeth." Such persons are completely lost to, and "embrangled"[98] in, sense experience. They are, said Bowne, "disciples of the senses."[99] Such persons believe that if a thing cannot be seen, touched, or smelled, for example, it must not be real. But the Berkeleian influence on personalism caused proponents to reject this emphasis on the senses. Berkeley, it will be recalled, maintained that all objects in the visible world are the result of God's thought and will.[100] Personalism therefore insists on the immateriality of matter. That is, all material objects in the world are the activity of God. They are the energizing of the divine will and mind. Visible objects in nature are caused only by God's thought and will.

Personalism, then, proposes a theistic solution to the problem of knowledge and reality. When I see the mountain in the distance, I *do* see the mountain. That is, the mountain does have phenomenal reality, and thus is not an illusion. At least to this extent one can say that there is an element of phenomenalism in Berkeleian idealism. At any rate, the mountain as the activity of God is not the mountain as I perceive it. That is, I do not see the mountain in all of its splendor and detail because of the distance and the limitations of my eyesight. But it also means that the mountain as phenomenal object is not all there is. For example, I do not *see* what causes the mountain to be. And as Berkeley pointed out, using the illustration of a castle in the distance, the castle that I see in a far-off distance is not the castle as it actually is close up.[101] And yet there is an obvious connection between the castle that I see in the distance and the castle that I see close up. There is always a connection between the object of my perception and my perception; a connection between what I perceive in mind and the object perceived. That I do not know the precise connection between the two is not an argument against some sort of relationship between them. However, God is still the ultimate reality causing the castle (or any object) that is being perceived. The point to be made here is that the ontologically real is not something we can picture, while the phenomenal reality, for example, the mountain, is the revelation of the ontological reality. From its inception personalism fought notions of lumpy being, insisting instead on a movement from a world of lumps to a world of energy.[102] The deepest problems for reality are problems not for sense, but for thought or mind. There is a kinship between ontic reality and thought that makes it possible for the latter to know what it can about the former.

The doctrine that ontological reality is not picturable is a tough one, and is likely to be a major challenge for many persons when they first encounter it. However, one cannot hope to understand personalism if one fails to grasp the importance of the doctrine of the unpicturableness of reality. It is a hard concept to grasp simply because most of us are inclined to the commonsense view that the real is that which we can bear witness to via our senses.

However, it cannot be reiterated enough times that in its metaphysics (thinking about reality) personalism is against all picture-thinking. Ultimate reality is not mirrored. It is an active process, not a picture book sort of thing.[103]

Many humans want desperately to actually *see* God putting things or physical objects out in space. But personalism maintains that space is interpreted as the activity of those things.

> We must not attempt to construe the infinite [God] spatially, whether in itself or in its relation to the world…space is only phenomenal and has no application to ontological reality. With this result it follows that the world is neither in, nor out of, God in a spatial sense; and that God is neither in, nor apart from, the world in a spatial sense. The world depends unpicturably upon God, as our thoughts depend unpicturably upon the mind, and God is in the world as the mind is in its thoughts, not as a pervading aura or spatial presence, but as that active subject by which all things exist.[104]

God, like mind and thought, has no spatial form and therefore does not occupy space as does a physical object. It is this fact that makes it possible to speak intelligibly of God's omnipresence. God can be everywhere at once precisely because God does not occupy space. Our thoughts (which we cannot see) depend upon our mind (which we cannot see or construe). In an analogous sense we can say with Bowne that God is in the world as the mind is in its thoughts. Thought has no spatial presence in mind. In like manner God has no spatial presence in the world. Rather, God's presence in the world may be likened unto "that active subject by which all things exist." The infinite (God) "comprises all reality in the unity of its immediate activity, and hence is everywhere. For by omnipresence we can mean nothing more than this immediate action upon all reality."[105]

Conclusion

Having considered the meaning of personalism and its point of departure, I want now to turn to a matter that has only been implied up to this point. The chief concern of this book is a critical exposition of personalism in its most typical or thoroughgoing form. This implies that there are other, less typical types of personalisms. Knudson did an admirable job of delineating and discussing six of these, concluding that the Bowne type of personalism is the truest form. Rather than give detailed accounts of all of the less typical types of personalism, I list and discuss eight of these, having suggested that there are at least twelve types of personalisms. I include a chief representative of each of the types discussed. In addition I include some of the major ideas of each type and provide a brief critique of each one.

My method of presenting the types of personalisms to be discussed will be essentially Hegelian. In this it is similar to the approach of Knudson and L. Harold DeWolf,[106] both of whom have written on varieties of personalisms, although their discussions are not as extensive as mine. In other words, I will begin with the most abstract or least typical form and proceed to the most concrete or most thoroughgoing form of personalism. I list and discuss ten tenets of personalism elsewhere in this work.[107] For now suffice it to say that personalism in its most typical or thoroughgoing sense must, minimally, exhibit each of these traits: (1) centrality of person, both metaphysically and ethically; (2) fundamentally and thoroughly idealistic; (3) theistic; (4) creationist; (5) freedomistic; (6) radically empirical; (7) coherence as criterion of truth; (8) synoptic-analytic method; (9) activistic and dualistic epistemology; and (10) reality is through and through social or relational. These are the minimal traits of theistic personalism. The less typical types may be characterized by one or more of these traits, but not by all. Nor are these types thought to be a systematic method for addressing the deepest problems of philosophy, ethics, philosophy of religion, and humanity in the world.

Unless otherwise stated, the term personalism is used throughout to refer to the most typical or thoroughgoing type. It is this type of personalism and this type only that I have in mind when I say that personalism is not, chiefly, a philosophy or doctrine to be taught or written about, but rather is a way of life—a way of living together in God's world. So the chief aim is to teach persons how to *live* the personalistic faith.

I discuss the least and most typical types of personalisms in chapters 2 and 3, respectively. I challenge Knudson's claim that Bowne's is the "normative" type of personalism. It is reasonable to conclude that Bowne's is more thoroughgoing than other types of personalisms, but this should not be taken to mean that it is the normative type. It may well be the truest, most systematic type, but it does not necessarily follow that it is normative. Later I will show that although Bownean personalism is more thoroughgoing than other types, it has shortcomings that we do not find in some of the others.

The hope is that we will get a sense of the progression from the most abstract to the most concrete type of personalism, and that increasingly we will sense the significance of this philosophical framework. This approach also points to the eclectic nature of personalism, that is, the willingness of proponents to consider all viewpoints and not hesitate to appropriate the element(s) of truth in competing views. In this respect personalism is "a philosophy of conciliation." Personalism is "of the mediating type"[108] of philosophy. Andrew J. Reck seems to have this in mind as well when he writes that as a philosophy, personalism "has been better able to assimilate the newer modes of thinking which stress change, temporality, existence, novelty, and creativity."[109] However, personalism's eclecticism is not to be construed as being its most distinctive feature. That honor goes to personalism's keen insight into the metaphysical, epistemological, and ethical significance of person.

2

Some Less Typical Types of Personalism

Atheistic Personalism (John M. E. McTaggart)

The chief representative of atheistic personalism was John McTaggart Ellis McTaggart (1866–1925). McTaggart, an Englishman, was considered to be a hardheaded, thorough, "acutely logical…metaphysician."[1] He was one of the most incisive and striking of commentators on the philosophy of Hegel. Since he did not believe in a personal God, McTaggart was not a theist. That he was not a theist places his ideas in the category of the least typical form of personalism. And yet McTaggart reflected long and hard on just what the nature of God would be *if* God existed. McTaggart argued that *if* God existed, and *if* any conception of God were to be adopted, it should be that of a God whose power is finite or limited. He based this on his view that experience clearly reveals that some evil exists in the world. Accordingly, the cause or allowance of evil is only justifiable in a God whose power is limited. McTaggart argued that evil would neither be justifiable nor possible were God omnipotent. Said McTaggart:

> It seems to me that when believers in God save his goodness by saying that he is not really omnipotent, they are taking the best course open to them, since both the personality and the goodness of God present much fewer difficulties if he is not conceived as omnipotent. But then they must accept the consequences of their choice, and realize that the efforts of a non-omnipotent God in favor of good may, for anything they have yet shown, be doomed to almost total defeat.[2]

Therefore, even *if* God exists, the trait of omnipotence would be inconsistent with personality and goodness in God. However, McTaggart does hold that if God exists God would be "a being who is personal, supreme, and good," although the term "supreme" is not intended to imply that *only* an omnipotent God could exist.[3] This means, according to McTaggart, that a supreme being would have to be "much more powerful than any other self, and so powerful that his volition can affect profoundly all else that exists."[4] So if God did, in fact, exist, God would have the traits of personality and would be infinitely supreme and good. In addition, McTaggart held that even if God did exist, God would not be "more fundamental in the universe" than other selves. Neither would God be the creator, since time is essential for creation, and McTaggart argues against the idea of the reality of time. He reasons that if there is no time (and for him there clearly is not!) there can be no creation. So for McTaggart, even if God exists, God would not be the creator. But we have already seen that creationism, like theism, is

6

a chief trait of typical theistic personalism. McTaggart's personalism falls short on both counts.

McTaggart, then, was not a theist. He was, however, a metaphysical personalist, inasmuch as he believed that "nothing but eternal persons exists." His "central doctrine is that of the ultimateness of finite selves, and the consequent need for conceiving reality as a unity of system, and not of self-consciousness."[5] L. Harold DeWolf contends that McTaggart was "unequivocal in maintaining the personalistic ontological position that 'the only substances are selves, parts of selves, and groups of selves.'"[6] This stance places McTaggart in the personalist camp, although in the most minimal sense.

McTaggart was an atheist inasmuch as he saw no reason why a unifying cosmic person was needed in addition to the society of eternal persons. He characterized the Absolute (not to be identified with the God of theism) as "a system of selves," and as "a spiritual unity." But McTaggart's Absolute or spiritual unity is not personal. Ultimate reality is, for McTaggart, no more than a "harmonious spiritual system" made up of finite selves. McTaggart is a personalist because for him reality is a system of selves. Ultimate reality consists of a system of infinite, uncreated, eternal selves. The Absolute is a unity made up of persons, but is not itself a person. William Sahakian illustrates the relationship between McTaggart's idea of the Absolute and its infinite selves:

> The Absolute is related to its parts in the same way that a college is related to its members. Both the college and its members are spiritual entities but only the individual members may properly be considered persons, for the organization as a whole merely brings them together as a single unit. Accordingly, for McTaggart, reality is essentially spiritual in nature, consisting of spiritual selves or persons.[7]

I know of no place in McTaggart's writings where he calls himself a personalist. But what makes him a personalist is the emphasis he placed on the centrality and ultimacy of the self. The most miminal personalist gives primacy to the self. McTaggart surely was not a thoroughgoing personalist. Indeed, Knudson's comment is quite to the point when he says that McTaggart's brand of personalism "stands apart from the main current of personalistic thought, and impresses one as a more or less artificial variation from the accepted type,"[8] that is, the Bownean type.

A fundamental limitation in McTaggart's personalism is his characterization of ultimate reality as a system of selves. The problem here is that this way of describing ultimate reality leaves us wondering about the cause of the system of selves if not because of a creator. We are left wondering where the finite selves came from. Characterizing ultimate reality as a system of selves does not provide an explanation for how the system came to be. We must ask whether the human mind can accept McTaggart's view as ultimate. Does the mind drive us to ask, What is the cause of the system of selves? Is the system of selves, as McTaggart claims, uncreated and eternal?

Is there a need for both a creator and a unifying principle? If the human mind drives us to raise these questions, it would then be necessary to ask whether the unifying principle necessarily has to be other than the system of selves. Indeed, can the system of selves find its unity in anything other than a superior intelligence or mind? A personal God? It would seem that for the completion of what McTaggart calls a "harmonious spiritual system" there is a need for the existence of such a being.

Another crucial question is whether, according to McTaggart's system, persons have real freedom. McTaggart himself claimed that persons are self-determined. But he also seemed to think that self-determination is compatible with determination from outside. But if this is the case, freedom is essentially destroyed at the outset. For we cannot have it both ways, that is, self-determination (freedom within limits) and determination from the outside. Since theistic personalism is freedomistic, McTaggart's denial of freedom and the existence of a personal God makes his a very untypical type of personalism. Personalism in its most typical form considers freedom and person to be touchstones of reality. When Martin Luther King, Jr., studied personalism under L. Harold DeWolf at Boston University he wrote a paper on McTaggart. King's study of Bowne convinced him of the metaphysical and ethical significance of freedom. He believed that had McTaggart studied Bowne he would not have rejected freedom. "In rejecting freedom," King wrote, "McTaggart was rejecting the most important characteristic of personality."[9] To be a person is to be free. To be free is to be a person. McTaggart's personalism, then, is neither theistic, creationist, nor freedom-centered.

Pantheistic Personalism (William Stern)

William Stern (1871–1938) had been a professor at the University of Berlin before being exiled by associates of Adolph Hitler in the early 1930s. A philosophical psychologist by profession, Stern joined the faculty of Duke University where he taught with William McDougall. Stern developed the Intelligence Quotient (I.Q.) as an instrument to assess intelligence.[10] Stern is remembered best as a result of his personalistic approach to the study of persons, "which on its philosophical side he called 'personalism' and on its psychological side 'personalistics.'"[11] Stern's view of the person is summed up in his statement: "The 'person' is a living whole, individual, unique, striving toward goals, self-contained and yet open to the world around him; he is capable of having experience."[12]

The personalism developed by Stern is completely pantheistic. Pantheism literally means "all God." It holds that reality is composed of a single being (in this case a personal God), and all things are either modes, expressions, moments, or appearances of God. There is one Supreme God, and all else in existence are parts of that God. There is no degree of independence or separateness between Creator and created. The world emanates from God, much like the rays of the sun emanate from it. As the rays of the sun have no real individuality of their own, created persons have no individuality of their own. In this case there is no need to even mention the subject of freedom, for it makes no sense to talk about human freedom if one has no individuality in relation to the Creator.

Stern actually named his theory "critical personalism." By this he meant to convey the idea that all reality is unified in the supreme personal being or God. Since all other beings are included in God, we may refer to God as Absolute. Pantheism stresses the nearness of God to creation, which is important, especially if God is to be deemed worthy of worship. In addition, and also on the positive side, George F. Thomas maintained: "The philosophical impulse behind pantheism has been the drive of reason for unity in its view of the world."[13] Since personalism at its best seeks to give a view of reality as a whole, this aspect of pantheism is a significant contribution.

The pantheistic stance of Stern is problematic because of its too close identification of the world and persons with God. Since pantheism claims that the Absolute is one with the world, and all finite persons are parts of the Absolute, we are confronted with the troublesome question of whether God is responsible in an ethical sense for human behavior and actions in the world. If the price of unity is the denial of human freedom, can humans ever be held morally accountable for wrongful deeds? In addition, pantheism does not account rationally for sin and evil in the world. If the pantheistic view is taken as true, sin and evil are not caused by created persons at all. Rather, they are caused by God, in whom created persons lose their sense of individuality and relative independence. Both of these—individuality and relative independence—are necessary for real freedom. If Creator and created are one, sin and evil must be included in the divine nature. But how could such a God be worthy of worship? A God who is morally responsible for all the crimes and other evil deeds committed by humans cannot be trusted to keep promises to created persons. Peter A. Bertocci rightly observes that if God and created persons are one, God, not created persons, is responsible for evil.

In pantheistic personalism the idea of divine immanence is too absolute. And yet if we were to relax this somewhat, as happens in pan*en*theism, it would still be possible to say that God is *in* all things. However, God would not be so closely identified with created persons, for example, that the sense of individuality and relative independence would be lost. In addition, it would be possible to proclaim that God, while immanent in the world, is also transcendent, and therefore is *more* than the world. That God is transcendent is a significant point. For although creation is dependent for its existence and continuation upon God, God is not dependent upon it in the same way. It therefore becomes possible to maintain that God is the highest unity, but a unity in multiplicity.

Like the atheistic personalism of McTaggart, Stern's pantheistic personalism conceives of God in less personal terms than traditional theism and normative personalism. Neither McTaggart's nor Stern's God is a worthy object of worship. In addition, their systems are essentially deterministic, not freedomistic. Furthermore, although Stern describes his philosophy as "critical personalism," he sometimes wrote about persons in a way that suggested that he had something impersonal in mind. He tells us, for example, that "person" is a "psycho-physically neutral term." Such a description of person may or may not imply consciousness.

Absolutistic Personalism (Mary Whiton Calkins)

This type of personalism has been espoused by several outstanding thinkers in modern philosophy. These include, but are not limited to: Francis H. Bradley (1846–1924), Josiah Royce (1855–1916), Bernard Bosanquet (1848–1923), and Mary W. Calkins (1863–1930). Only Calkins actually described herself as a personalist. Each of these thinkers was influenced in various ways by the father of absolute idealism in the West, Georg W. F. Hegel (1770–1831). Bowne characterized absolute idealism as "the most pretentious form of idealism."[14]

Absolute idealism essentially maintains that reality is one absolute mind, spirit, or person. Similar to pantheism, it holds that all created beings are literally included within the absolute mind. The emphasis in absolutism is on the wholeness of reality, organic unity, and refusal to admit anything separate from the Absolute. The Absolute is "spirit," a rational unity, and alone is capable of solving all the problems of antinomies or opposites, such as the problem of freedom and determinism, the finite and the infinite, and the problem of change and identity. Absolutism is the view that "the universe is essentially one person or mind or mindlike whole." The "idea of a spiritual whole, a unitary and all-comprehensive experience…is the key to Hegelian absolutism."[15]

For our purpose we shall look briefly at Mary W. Calkins as a chief representative of absolutistic personalism. I do this intentionally for several reasons. First, the contributions of women to the development of personalism have not been given much attention. In addition, I do it with the full knowledge that Calkins was not a student of Bowne or any of his disciples, and therefore was not a Boston Personalist. That is, Calkins, unlike those who studied personalism under Bowne or his disciples, was never a student at Boston University. Under Bowne's leadership this university was one of two major centers for personalistic studies in the United States. The other was the University of California under the leadership of George Holmes Howison, whose personalism or personal idealism will be discussed later.

Calkins earned her bachelor's and master's degrees from Smith College in Massachusetts. From there she gravitated toward Harvard College in the 1890s, a time of much excitement and intellectual fervor. There she studied psychology under William James and Hugo Munsterberg, and philosophy under Josiah Royce. Having specialized in psychology, Calkins arrived at her psychology of the self both through her experimentations in the psychological laboratory she developed at Wellesley College and through the influence of the thinking of James and Royce.[16]

There is a second reason I have chosen to discuss the personalism of Mary Calkins. Although an absolutistic personalist, Calkins' stance is closer to typical theistic personalism than that of the personal absolutists who influenced her most: Hegel, Francis H. Bradley, and her "great teacher" Josiah Royce.[17] Calkins went beyond these in at least two respects: (1) She placed more emphasis on the centrality and significance of the self or person; and (2) along with Royce she affirmed the personal nature of the Absolute. Said Calkins: "For a universe conceived as mental but impersonal would consist in an aggregate of mental phenomena instead of constituting an individual whole. A consistent idealistic absolutist must accordingly conceive of the Absolute as person."[18] But in addition, and unlike other personal absolutists mentioned, it was Calkins who actually designated her system as absolutistic personalism. To her this seemed the logical outcome of combining the notions of the universe as mental, personal, and absolute.[19] I know of no instance in which Hegel, Royce, or Bradley actually referred to themselves as personalists. However, it is interesting to note that in a letter written to Edgar S. Brightman in 1913, Royce said that although he did not know the precise relation between his and Bowne's philosophy, he believed that the agreements between them were increasing near the end of Bowne's life.[20] Calkins was so prominent a representative of personalism that Knudson described her as "the most conspicuous representative of personalism in the form of absolute idealism."[21]

In her major publication on philosophy, *The Persistent Problems of Philosophy* (1907), Calkins did not mention any of the personalists in the Bowne tradition, either in the body of her discussions on personal idealism,[22] nor in the index. However, her discussion on personal idealism primarily focused on the work of George H. Howison. Calkins, it seems, actually used the term personalism to describe her philosophical stance just prior to or right around the time that Bowne did (sometime between 1905 and 1907). Indeed, Calkins recalled that long before actually naming her system personalism, she had adopted the personalistic point of view. Unable to date with precision when she adopted the personalistic stance, she said it was during the 1890s while she was studying and teaching psychology. In addition, she recalled being especially influenced during this period by "the famous ninth chapter of James's *Principles of Psychology*, in which he declares that 'the universal conscious fact is not "feelings and thoughts exist" but "I think" and "I feel".'"[23] Calkins took this to be indicative of the personalistic point of view, inasmuch as James seemed to make the self or person, the "I," central. Ralph T. Flewelling concurs with this view, claiming that James's discussion on self-consciousness in the text and chapter to which Calkins referred is "outstanding and conclusive evidence of his essential personalism."[24] Calkins further recalled that her "earliest published avowal of the personalistic standpoint in psychology" was in "Psychology as Science of Selves," an article she published in *Philosophical Review* in 1900, though she did not actually use the term personalism at this time.

What is interesting, however, is that in earlier editions of *The Persistent Problems of Philosophy* Calkins refers often to the personal idealism of Howison, a contemporary of hers and Bowne's. It is strange indeed that she does not include a discussion on the personalism of Bowne. Perhaps the reason for this may be attributed, in part, to the fact that both Howison and Calkins made the rounds of philosophy clubs and professional philosophical society meetings. Bowne was hampered from doing this on a regular basis because as dean of the graduate school at Boston University he had the added burden of heavy administrative responsibilities. However, there is no question that both Calkins and Howison were aware of Bowne, if not of his work. Howison taught at the Massachusetts Institute of Technology (M.I.T.) from 1872–1878 and remained in the Boston area until 1884. At this time he joined the philosophy department of the University of California. Bowne was called to the philosophy department at Boston University in 1876 and remained there until his death in 1910. By the time Howison left for the University of California, Bowne had published three books and was well on the way to developing what he eventually called personalism. I return to the Bowne-Howison connection in chapter 3. Although Calkins did not mention Bowne in earlier editions of *The Persistent Problems of Philosophy*, she at least lists Bowne's as a recent type of philosophy.[25] She did not, however, comment on or actually discuss his personalism as she did the personal idealism of Howison. A search into the *why* of Calkins' omission regarding Bowne should make a fascinating study and, at the same time, be an important contribution to personalistic studies.

Mary Calkins lived at a time when it was not popular for women to study philosophy, let alone to desire to earn the Ph.D. degree from one of the top academic institutions in the nation. Calkins audited enough courses in the Harvard philosophy department to have been awarded a doctorate. By all accounts she was a very astute, promising philosopher. Calkins petitioned Harvard officials to be awared the doctorate. Her teacher and mentor, Hugo Munsterberg, wrote a letter of support for his "best pupil." However, her petition for the degree was denied. The reply from Harvard, written in the early 1890s, must have been most discouraging to Calkins. "The Corporations are not prepared to give any Harvard degree to any woman no matter how exceptional the circumstances may be."[26]

But in addition to being a first-rate philosopher, Mary Calkins was made of tough moral fiber. When the occasion arose that would have led to receipt of a doctorate, but from Radcliffe (a women's college) "to insure its academic reputation," she declined, although Munsterberg urged her to accept it. Calkins was adamant that she had earned and therefore deserved a Harvard doctorate, and she would receive it from there or she would settle for being addressed as "Miss Calkins." And so it was! She did not receive the degree. Calkins was one of the earliest women "tokens" among American philosophers who made contributions to feminism, though she did not consider herself a feminist in the sense that we understand the term today.

The self was clearly central in Calkins' psychology, ethics, and metaphysics. Her self-psychology "is a theory of the self as a guide to the ways of consciousness, the ways of conduct, and the way of thought, generally."[27] Her belief that it is in the self that we find the clue to reality and the solution to fundamental philosophical and ethical questions places her squarely in the personalistic camp. "The self must be regarded not only as related to any reality in any sense beyond it but also as the relater, or unifier, of the different parts or aspects of itself."[28] Her views on religion, morality, and ethics are also based on her self-psychology.[29]

Calkins later qualified her views on ethics "as she came to see that it was the Absolute, rather than God, that served the purposes and objectives of religion and morality."[30] She came to believe that some may view God as Absolute and others not. She therefore concluded that it is wise not to identify the Absolute with God.

There is no question that Calkins considered herself a personalist. We see this in several places in her writing. In a 1919 essay, "The Personalistic Conception of Nature," she writes that "a completely personalistic doctrine must maintain, not that selves exist along with other real though non-mental beings, but that the world consists wholly of persons, or selves…"[31] By definition this admission places Calkins in the personalist camp. The fully personalistic doctrine of reality consists in "innumerable selves, or persons, of different levels and degrees, more or less closely related to each other."[32] The thoroughgoing personalistic view reveals that all existents are mental (including so-called material objects); that mental beings are at bottom personal; and that the Absolute self is not the only self in existence.

In the "Personalistic Platform" Calkins and Brightman collaborated on, adopted on May 25, 1929, we find the following: "The total universe is a system of selves and persons [Calkins and Brightman], who may be regarded either as members of one all-inclusive person who individuates them by the diversity of his purposing [Calkins] or as a society of many selves related by common purposes [Brightman]."[33] Brightman thought highly of Calkins both as a person and philosophical colleague. He acknowledged her for having read and offered helpful suggestions for the first edition of his book *An Introduction to Philosophy*.[34]

In yet another publication, "The Philosophical Credo of an Absolutistic Personalist" (1930), Calkins highlighted the four metaphysical principles in her philosophy:

1. The universe contains distinctive mental realities. There may or may not be nonmental entities, but if there are they would, at bottom, be mental in nature. Calkins drew this conclusion on the empirical grounds that she had direct experience of mental phenomena.

2. All mental realities are fundamentally personal in nature. Calkins writes "that the mental phenomena which I directly observe are not precepts, thoughts, emotions, and volitions, in unending succession, but rather perceiving, thinking, feeling, and willing self or selves." These and other activity potentials are not found just floating about loosely and disconnected in the world of persons. Experience reveals that mental realities exist, and these are either selves, aspects of, or experiences of selves.

3. Personalism is a philosophy that is unqualifiedly idealistic or mentalistic. Calkins was led in the direction of idealism by her first

teacher in philosophy, Professor Charles E. Garman. The universe, whatever else it may be and contain, is through and through mental. The real is mental, and therefore personal, or an aspect or process of some personal being.

4. The universe is an Absolute self or being, all-embracing, independent, and holds within itself and relates the many mental entities or selves that are its genuine parts. "As I have tried to show, to account consistently for my own experience," wrote Calkins, "I must regard myself as included in a greater self. And this Greater Self, unless all-including, must...itself be included in a still-greater self."[35] Everything conceivable is included within the Absolute. As the all-including self "no shred of reality however trivial, however futile, however base, can be outside it."[36] In light of this aspect of Calkins' *Credo* we see that she was not only a personalist, but by her own admission she was an absolutistic personalist. For reasons to be noted momentarily this aspect of absolute idealism raises more questions than it answers.

Clearly from points 3 and 4 it is evident that Calkins was both a personalist and an absolutist. But it is important to reiterate that unlike many absolutists she affirmed that God is personal. "A consistent idealistic absolutist must...conceive the Absolute as person." Calkins further contends that both Bradley and Hegel were personal absolutists.[37] Here she agreed with Royce that "Bradley's Absolute...escapes from selfhood...only by remaining to the end a Self."[38] Calkins seems to place as much emphasis on the Absolute as person, as she does on the all-embracingness or all-inclusiveness of the Absolute. In light of the former (i.e., emphasis on the Absolute as person) her personalism was closer to the thoroughgoing personalism of the Bownean school.

Generally, however, the more typical personalist is critical of absolutistic personalism. In addition, although there has been a "sympathetic relation" between the latter and historical theism and Christianity, there has not been complete accord between them. As noted previously, it is only in exceptional cases that absolutistic personalists have been more concerned with the Absolute as person than with "its all-embracing unity." Those who have stressed such all-embracing unity contribute to the denial of both the privacy and the relative independence of created persons. But as seen in the discussion of pantheistic personalism, this leads to a denial or cancelling of human freedom.

Although some personalists, for example, Knudson, make a distinction between absolutistic personalism and personalistic absolutism,[39] it is important to point out that Calkins made no such distinction. Instead, she maintained that they are "equivalent terms."[40] According to Knudson, personalistic absolutism places emphasis on the all-embracingness of the Absolute. The absolutistic personalism of Mary Calkins, on the other hand, focuses more on the Absolute as person. Personalistic absolutism's emphasis on the all-embracingness of the Absolute is problematic for typical personalism, for it implies a metaphysical union or a swallowing up of the individual in the Absolute.

Bowne maintained not only that absolute idealism is "the most pretentious form of idealism," but that it "could only result in a static pantheism."[41] Troubled by the idea of an Absolute that seems to swallow up all created existents, Howison offers a sharp but helpful critique of absolute idealism:

> But if the Infinite Self *includes* us all, and all our experiences—sensations and sins, as well as the rest—in the unity of one life, and includes us and them *directly*; if there is but one and the same final Self for us each and all; then, with a literalness indeed appalling, He is we, and we are He; nay, He is *I*, and *I* am He…Now, if we read the conception in the first way, what becomes of our ethical independence?—what, of our *personal* reality, our righteous and reasonable responsibility—responsibility to which we *ought* to be held? Is not He the sole *agent*? Are we anything but the steadfast and changeless modes of His eternal thinking and perceiving? Or, if we read the conception in the second way, what becomes of *Him*? Then, surely, He is but another name for *me*…[42]

Bowne provided an equally cogent criticism of the all-embracingness of the Absolute that we find in personalistic absolutism:

> It is no doubt fine, and in some sense it is correct, to say that God is in all things; but when it comes to saying that God is all things and that all forms of thought and feeling and conduct are his, then reason simply commits suicide. God thinks and feels in what we call our thinking and feeling; and hence he blunders in our blundering and is stupid in our stupidity. He contradicts himself also with the utmost freedom; for a deal of his thinking does not hang together from one person to another, or from one day to another in the same person. Error, folly, and sin are all made divine; and reason and conscience as having authority vanish. The only thing that is not divine in this scheme is God; and he vanishes into a congeries of contradictions and basenesses.[43]

Absolutism, declared Ralph T. Flewelling, ultimately makes God little more than "a moral monster" responsible for all of the worst moral traits in created persons.[44]

However, it should be reiterated that Calkins considered herself to be an absolutistic personalist rather than a personalistic absolutist. In part by designating herself as she did, Calkins hoped to avoid the type of criticism raised by Howison, Bowne, and their disciples. Furthermore, we should remember that absolutists like Royce and Calkins fought hard to preserve and protect the status of the individual self. Howison's critique of absolutism and its tendency to destroy or consume the finite self actually influenced Royce's thought, causing him to alter his thinking.[45] With this in mind, the advice of R. F. Alfred Hoernle is important for all who find fault with absolute idealism. "To any young American student of philosophy who rejects Absolute Idealism I would say that he has no right to dissent or condemn, unless he has first earned that right by a thorough study and understanding of Royce."[46] But just here it is important to observe that some scholars on personalism maintain that the type of critique that Howison, Bowne, and other personalists made against Hegel's absolute idealism is of the Kierkegaard variety, which, they contend, is not completely accurate. John J. Ansbro is one such scholar.

> It would seem...that Kierkegaard was not accurate in some of his criticisms of Hegel. Kierkegaard's criticism that Hegel's system was pantheistic ignored Hegel's emphasis on the eternal Trinity, distinct from and prior to creation, which is its manifestation...His further criticism that Hegel emphasized the importance only of the movements of the World-Spirit or Absolute in the development of "objective truth" and deprived the individual of his self-identity, self-determination, and dignity neglected Hegel's emphasis on the value of the individual's achievement of "subjective freedom" by consciously interiorizing and contributing to the rational elements in the objective political, artistic, religious, and philosophical orders.[47]

Ansbro argues further that the two Kierkegaardian, and hence personalist, critiques of Hegel that his notion of the Absolute swallows up the person, thereby destroying human individuality and freedom, and that Hegel's absolutism is actually pantheistic are fallacious.

However, according to early personalists like Howison and Bowne, absolute idealism destroys human persons, the moral order, and any sense of moral responsibility among created persons. It negates that freedom that is so fundamental to *person* and moral endeavor. If the Absolute includes within itself all persons and other created existents, it would necessarily have to include all their contradictions, errors, sins, crimes, and, as Brightman maintained, "it must include them as they actually occur. Consequently, the Absolute must believe everything that any person believes, and must commit every sin that every person commits."[48] What Brightman was really saying is that if it is true that the Absolute includes everything within itself as Calkins argued, then it includes everything exactly as it occurs in human experience. Therefore God, not human persons, is responsible for the near genocide of Native Americans; for American slavery, racism, and its several hundred years of negative consequences including intracommunity violence and murder among young Afrikan American males on an unprecedented scale; the Jewish Holocaust; starving, homeless babies in Ethiopia, Sri Lanka, and the United States; the systematic rape of women and girls in Bosnia; the Rwanda tragedy, and so on. Surely such a God cannot be deemed a worthy object of worship.

That religion seeks a certain kind of union with God cannot be denied. But, writes Knudson, "it is a union of will, of fellowship, a union that presupposes rather than excludes metaphysical otherness."[49] Personalism points not to a metaphysical or mystical union between God and created persons, for such union implies being swallowed up or absorbed by God. Such absorption implies a destruction of human individuality, thus raising ethical concerns about God. Therefore, personalism of the thoroughgoing type points to another type of union between God and persons. Knudson characterizes it as "a union that grows out of reciprocal intercourse, a union of heart and will and intellect; and such a union is possible only between personal beings. Only the personality of God makes possible the union of communion with him."[50] This is the best way that personalism knows how to account rationally for this basic religious value, namely, fellowship with God. Any philosophy of religion worthy of the name will therefore protect the individuality, freedom, and relative separateness of created persons.

There is no question that Mary Calkins fought hard to preserve and protect the individuality of the person. And yet it will be recalled that in "The Philosophical Credo of an Absolutistic Personalist" she said that the Absolute includes everything within itself, and that "no shred of reality however trivial, however futile, however base, can be outside it." Thoroughgoing personalism clearly views this as problematic, since it opens the door to the idea of a God who is potentially immoral.

There is another point at which absolutism falls short of typical theistic personalism. It has no doctrine of creation. Creation, rightly understood, implies a sense of otherness and relative independence, as well as privacy. The existence of created persons, for example, is dependent upon the Creator, but they are not parts or modes of the Creator. Persons cannot be literal parts or expressions of the Absolute without contradiction, "and the word 'create' celebrates this fact."[51] The absolutistic strand in Hegelianism therefore undermines the individuality that is so important for personalism.

But there are other problems with absolutism as well. The idealistic element in it is contrary to that in typical personalism. In absolutistic personalism there is not a real distinction between knowing and being. The reality of the individual is suspect, and one wonders whether, for example, there is a real distinction between the individual and a divine thought. Are these one and the same? If the absolutistic view is true, the answer must be affirmative. One's notion of an object and the object itself are one and the same, which means that one can know the thing or object itself and then compare it with one's notion of it. This makes the absolute idealist an epistemic monist (one who believes that the object does not need mind to exist). Thoroughgoing personalism, on the other hand, contends that there is a dualism between idea and object, even though there is an unquestionable relation between idea and object. This must be the case. Otherwise how does one even claim to have a notion or idea of an object? But this does not mean that one's idea of the object and the object itself are one and the same, or more accurately, that "the object is immediately present as idea."[52] Furthermore, personalism maintains that one does not know the object as such. Rather, the most one can know is his conceptions of the thing or object. And since we are never able to transcend our conceptions, we cannot really know the thing itself.[53]

Thoroughgoing personalism contends that the individuality of created persons is fundamentally other, and more than an idea in the mind of the Absolute. The individual has an existence for herself, and therefore she is not completely identified with God. Possibly the greatest error of absolutism of the Hegelian type is its total identification of human and divine self-consciousness.

Relativistic Personalism (Charles B. Renouvier)

This type of personalism is found in the work of Charles B. Renouvier (1815–1903). His system has often been referred to as neocritical personalism. This personalism is characterized by empiricism, relativism, finitism, and pluralism. Renouvier stressed the ultimacy of personal experience, the finitism of God's power, human freedom, and immortality. Radoslav A. Tsanoff contends that Renouvier was a leader in modern personalism.[54]

An American philosopher who was greatly influenced by Renouvier was William James. Having studied under Renouvier, James later wrote a book (published posthumously) in which he acknowledged his teacher's influence.

> [Renouvier] was one of the greatest of philosophic characters, and but for the decisive impression made on me in the seventies [1870s] by his masterly advocacy of pluralism I might never have got free from the monistic superstition under which I had grown up. The present volume, in short, might never have been written. This is why, feeling endlessly thankful as I do, I dedicate this text-book to the great Renouvier's memory.[55]

We can distinguish three stages in the development of Renouvier's philosophy. The first (1842–1854) is the eclectic period. He advocated no definite system of his own during this period of development. Rather, he was much like a sponge, eager to soak up all that he could about the various philosophical systems in existence. He took Hegel quite seriously during this stage and had deep appreciation for Hegel's rejection of "either-or" approaches in favor of the "both-and" approach. Such a stance enabled Renouvier to affirm antinomies such as the infinite *and* finite, unity *and* plurality, freedom *and* determinism.

His neocriticism or phenomenalism marked the second stage of his development. During this period a philosophy distinctly his own began to take shape. He now rejected Hegel's idea of the Absolute, Kant's doctrine of *das Ding-an-sich* (the idea that there are unknowable, unreachable "things-in-themselves" behind phenomenal objects that humans experience from day to day). Renouvier now believed physical things to be phenomena, which is similar to Bowne's stance. Bowne, it will be recalled, rejected the thoroughgoing immaterialism of Berkeley, insisting instead that physical objects are not just ideas in God's mind, but are phenomena, and thus have a reality of their own. According to Renouvier we can have knowledge of nothing but physical and mental phenomena. Physical phenomena are those objects we can perceive with the senses, for example, the paper on which I write. Mental phenomena are those perceived through introspection, such as, sensations or ideas. Unlike Kant, Herbert Spencer, and others,

Renouvier concluded that there is no unknowable reality behind or beyond the world of appearance, a stance similar to that of typical personalists.

The three most important concepts during the middle period of Renouvier's development (1854–1885), were: human freedom (as a necessary presupposition of the moral life), the law of relativity, and the principle of contradiction. Because the latter two principles meant something quite different for Renouvier than others who appealed to them it is appropriate to discuss them briefly.

The law of contradiction maintains that two contradictory propositions, for example, A equals B, and A does not equal B, cannot both be true at the same time. Renouvier used this law not to show that knowledge (epistemology) is relative, but that reality (metaphysics) or being is relative and finite. Through the principle of contradiction Renouvier argued against the Hegelian view that there are fundamental antinomies, for example freedom and necessity, finite and infinite, that may be reconciled in the Absolute. Instead, he argued that experience reveals that there must be one *or* the other—freedom *or* necessity, not both at once. The principle of contradiction requires the either-or approach, which he rejected in the first stage of his philosophical development. Renouvier held that the principle of contradiction also requires that reality be conceived as finite and many. Reality, after all, is constituted or built up by the categories that mask (hide or conceal) and limit our apprehension of it. "All reality is 'relative' to the categories, and so must be finite."[56] The principle of contradiction has to do with both thought (epistemology) and reality (metaphysics). But Renouvier was more concerned with its relation to reality. He wanted to know the metaphysical implications of the principle of contradiction. For truly if reality is "relative" to the categories of thought or mind, as Renouvier claimed, it would seem that reality, including Supreme reality, must also be finite.

Likewise, by relativity, Renouvier did not mean what Kant meant in his theory of knowledge, namely, that all true knowledge of reality is hidden or veiled, since the categories of thought build up its world of experience, thereby masking true knowledge of reality. According to Kant true knowledge of reality is forever and completely hidden from us, since the conditions of thought itself (i.e., the categories) block such knowledge. Therefore, all knowledge is relative, a conclusion that landed Kant in epistemological agnosticism.

But Renouvier rejected relativism in the agnostic sense. That is, he rejected epistemological relativism while adopting metaphysical relativism. He believed phenomenal objects constitute all reality, and each implies "a perceptual process," which means that each is "relative to consciousness." Phenomenal objects do not exist in isolation, but in relation, and in this sense too, they are relative. Renouvier believed, like typical personalists, that the fact that we cannot know absolute truth about reality does not mean that we cannot know something about it. We can know degrees of probable truth if nothing else. If phenomenal objects are the result of God's thought and will in action, we may say that they too are phenomenal realities, and therefore are kin to reality. Because of this kinship it must be possible for created persons, for example, to know something about the Creator, despite our inability to ascertain perfect knowledge of God. The discussion on personalistic method and criteria of truth later on in this work will give us a clearer sense of how personalists arrive at knowledge and truth.

In the sense that everything is in relation, all is relative. Relationality is more than a universal category. It is a law of both reality and thought. Interpreting Renouvier, Knudson writes: "Reality is constituted by phenomena, and so is as relative in its structure as the phenomena themselves. There is no such thing as an absolute or unrelated being."[57] Therefore, Renouvier's was a metaphysical, not an epistemic relativism.

The metaphysical period marked the third stage of Renouvier's philosophical development. During this period he began to deal with ultimate questions of reality such as the existence and nature of God, the problem of evil, the origin, nature, and destiny of the world. It was also during this period that he dropped the designation neocriticism and adopted personalism as the best way of characterizing his philosophy. He considered this change a logical progression and end of his system. However, Renouvier did not give up the emphasis on relativism, or his belief that all consciousness is a series of relations.

At several points Renouvier's personalism is superior, and therefore closer to typical personalism than is absolutistic personalism. One instance of this is Renouvier's relativism, which gives freedom a central place in the moral life. Since he believed that the universe is not a closed system or "block universe," the individual retains a measure of separateness or independence that is so important for freedom. In addition, Renouvier defended the doctrine of immortality, which opens the way for hope in the mortal life—hope that if created persons do not achieve all the good they can in this life, they will be able to continue to strive for the achievement of ideal value even beyond death. A good and loving God would have it no other way. We do not get this sense of hope in absolutism, since absolutistic personalists believe individuals are literally swallowed up in the Absolute.

Renouvier's is also a more acceptable form of personalism because he affirmed the doctrine of creation in his mature years (having rejected it at an earlier stage). Creation, he held, also points to God's finitism. That is, he viewed God as quantitatively finite, that is, finite in power and knowledge. However, Renouvier believed God to be qualitatively infinite in terms of moral perfection. God is therefore ethically perfect, although finite in power and knowledge. This view is very similar to Brightman's doctrine of the finite-infinite God. Renouvier arrived at the conclusion that God must be finite not through consideration of the problem of evil as many thinkers do, but through theoretical speculation. As can be seen, Renouvier's was a type of dipolar theism, since for him God has both a finite and an infinite aspect. God is finite in power and infinite in moral perfection. At any rate, the emphasis that Renouvier placed on individuality, freedom, immortality, and creation makes his a more acceptable type of personalism.

One of Knudson's chief criticisms of Renouvier centered on his finitistic conception of God.

> By rejecting the idea of the absolute and by insisting on a relativistic and finitistic view of reality, [Renouvier] gave to personalism a one-sided and defective expression. Personalism is as much interested in unity as it is in plurality, and, if it is developed in a thoroughgoing and consistent way, cannot dispense with the conception of an absolute Person.[58]

It is clear where Knudson himself stood regarding the doctrine of God. For him God has none but self-imposed limitations, for example, as results from human freedom. But in this view, since God grants human freedom, this is little more than an argument for God's omnipotence. However, at some point those interested in the problem of evil and suffering in the world must ask whether Knudson's doctrine of an Absolute who is omnipotent is the most empirically adequate view, or whether it is consistent with personalism in its most thoroughgoing sense. This subject will be taken up in chapter 6.

Other criticisms of Renouvier's personalism include the claim that only phenomena are real. This does not answer the question of the cause of the phenomena. Renouvier was right to reject Kant's claim that we cannot (through speculative reason) know the reality (noumena) behind the phenomena. But he went too far in the other direction in his attempt to correct Kant. Kant at least postulated the existence of a reality behind the phenomenal object, denying only that we can—through speculative thought—know that reality. Renouvier, on the other hand, denied the very existence of a noumenal reality behind the phenomenal. Unlike Bowne he did not distinguish between phenomenal and ontological reality. Nor did he say explicitly, like Bowne, that phenomenal reality is caused by ontological reality. The active, inquisitive nature of the mind forces us to want to know the cause behind the phenomenal objects we experience.

Unlike relativistic personalism, thoroughgoing personalism proposes the existence of at least two levels of reality: phenomenal and ontological, the latter being the cause of the former. But both types of objects are real in their own spheres. Knudson, following Bowne, was concerned that if only the phenomenal is real this would make the categories of time and space as valid for the ultimately real (God) as are the other categories. This, in his view, contributes to a less typical form of personalism.

Another criticism of relativistic personalism has to do with its emphasis on relatedness as a metaphysical principle. Relatedness as a principle is an abstraction when thought of independently of the self or person. One must inquire what it means, for example, to speak of relationality or any category apart from the person. No category has independent existence apart from active intelligence or the self. And if they do have independent existence, there would then be the question of *who* would know about it, other than God. According to Bowne's transcendental empiricism all categories are interpreted through thought or mind. It is not the categories that somehow interpret mind.

In addition, and also by way of criticism, we must wonder whether the individual person gets lost in Renouvier's thoroughgoing relational view of reality if we do not—as he certainly did not—speak explicitly of persons-in-relation. On a less thoroughgoing view of relationality there is less fear of the possibility of the loss or consumption of the individual self. In addition, there would be fewer openings to write or speak of the categories as if they can explain either themselves, mind, or intelligence. The individual does not have to get lost or consumed in such a view, but one must not speak of the categories as if they can either explain themselves or can explain mind.

By now we are getting a sense of the progression from more abstract, less theistic types of personalism to more concrete, theistic types. We are also getting a sense of the most important traits of the more typical types of personalism. In the next chapter I focus on even more typical theistic forms of personalism.

3

Some More Typical Types of Personalism

Beginning with George H. Howison's noncreationist but ethical personalism, this chapter discusses its chief tenets and limitations. In addition, there is a brief discussion of Howison and Bowne's relationship and some similarities and differences in their thought. There is then a consideration of the realistic or dualistic personalism of Georgia Harkness. Although, by her own admission, Harkness remained in the Boston Personalist camp, she made a turn that led to the development of her own unique personalistic synthesis.

I next discuss what was for Knudson and his followers the most typical, or what he liked to refer to as "normative," type of personalism. This, according to Knudson, is the truest type. I challenge Knudson's designation, normative, and give my reasons that, in part, have to do with the fact that this normative, truest form of personalism that Knudson so forcefully defended excluded the voices and experiences of Afrikan Americans and other racial-ethnic groups. Since the Bowne type of personalism essentially grew up in this country, one must wonder whether normative adequately takes into consideration the contributions of groups other than white men. If not, in what sense can this personalism be deemed normative?

It should be noted, however, that these omissions were not as pronounced among Brightman's disciples. This was due both to Brightman's deeper radical empiricism and his commitment to truth, which forced him to insist on the Hegelian principle that the true is the whole. Brightman interpreted this to mean that that which has been traditionally excluded both in the quest for truth and in the ethical field must now be included. Unfortunately, the term he adopted to designate what had historically been excluded is "the negative." Nevertheless, the emphasis on including what had been left out, he believed, was consistent with personalistic method. The traditionally excluded must be included. This includes the voices and experiences of Afrikan Americans, the poor, and even more recognition of all racial-ethnic womens' voices and experiences. Brightman was interested in truth, not in defending labels. Many of his students pushed much further his view about the need to include the traditionally excluded. Many of these became, for example, forceful advocates for the rights and freedom of Afrikan Americans. This chapter also includes a discussion on Afrikan American contributions to personalism. Any study on the origin and development of personalism in this country would be incomplete without it.[1]

Teleological or Ethical Personalism (George Holmes Howison)

Bowne's teacher, Hermann Lotze,[2] may also be characterized as an ethical personalist. However, for my purpose I focus on George H. Howison

(1836–1916), who called his metaphysical system *personal idealism*.[3] He sought to present "an idealistic system that shall be thoroughly personal."[4] John W. Buckham and George M. Stratton tell us that as Howison's philosophical stance was developing he easily and readily made friendships with idealists and personal idealists, "believers in the power and the glory of the personal spirit."[5] Interestingly, they do not indicate whether he became a friend or acquaintance of Bowne's, or whether he was even familiar with Bowne's work.

Both because Howison (born in the South) and Bowne (born in the East) lived and worked in close proximity to each other for approximately eight years (1876–1884) in the Boston area, and because of the similarities and differences between their philosophies, it is appropriate to discuss any relationship that might have existed between the two men and their work. In the progression of personalistic philosophy on the way to the most typical form, Knudson considered Howison's personalism to be more typical than all but Bowne's, and this because there are several key similarities between their personalism and their commitment to it as not merely a philosophical system, but as a way of living and relating in the world. I also think it important to discuss these two men together—albeit briefly—because presently I know of no published comparative study on them. In addition, other than William Werkmeister,[6] who devotes an entire chapter to each man's thought, the general tendency of scholars has been to treat one or the other (and most often, Howison). My discussion is not intended to be exhaustive, but to whet the appetite for a more thorough investigation of the similarities and differences between the personalism of Howison and Bowne.

Howison and Bowne

In an important footnote, John W. Buckham, a prolific writer on personalism and a younger contemporary of Bowne and Howison, wrote that these two men were "two productive and independent thinkers [who] did not realize how much their philosophies had in common. This could only appear in the light of the subsequent development of Personalism."[7] This implies that Howison and Bowne were at least aware of each other's existence and had a general sense of each other's work. No one has documented this relationship at this writing, although by virtue of their close proximity for several years in the Boston-Cambridge area, they surely were at least acquainted and knew of each other's work. However, there need no longer be any uncertainty as to whether the two men at least knew about each other. For in fact, each man heard the other make at least one public presentation. It is known, for example, that both Howison and Bowne were present at the International Congress of Arts and Sciences held in St. Louis in 1904. Bowne was the chairman of the philosophical section and gave the chairman's address. This was followed immediately by Howison's lecture, "Philosophy: Its Fundamental Conceptions and Its Methods."[8] Not much more than this is known at present about the extent of the Howison-Bowne connection. Although Buckham implied that Howison wrote extensively, he did not. He did, however, make his rounds of the various philosophical societies. Since Bowne did little of this, it is unlikely that their paths crossed much in such gatherings. Howison wrote only one primary text, with which Bowne may or may not have been familiar. Bowne, on the other hand, wrote many major books, one or more of which Howison may have been familiar with. However, until further research is done we can only speculate about a Bowne-Howison connection.

Depending on where one is located in the United States, the tendency has been to point to either Bowne or Howison as the chief architect of American Personalism. Buckham, who was more influenced by Howison than any other thinker, and who taught at Pacific Theological Seminary in California, considered Howison to be the leader of American Personalism. Having described both men as "two productive and independent thinkers," he then implied—misleadingly—that personalism actually got its start in this country during the first decade of the twentieth century with the publication of Howison's only book on the subject, *The Limits of Evolution,* in 1901. He then immediately cites Bowne's book *Personalism,* published in 1908, as if to imply that it was actually Howison who led in the systematizing of personalism. But we need to take a closer look at this.

In the first place, there is no question that both men were independent thinkers. Although each was well read in the history of Western philosophy, the ideas that appear in their writings are essentially their own. But in the second place, how are we to understand Buckham's claim that *both* men were productive? The implication is that both were prolific writers. But we know that to not be the case. For Howison wrote only one book, which provides at best the basic outlines of his personal idealism. It is true that he wrote a number of articles, but he did not develop his personalism in a systematic way beyond his book.

On the other hand, the publication of *Personalism* essentially capped Bowne's long movement toward his description of himself as "a Personalist, the first of the clan in any thoroughgoing sense." His movement to this mature stage of his thought is easily seen in the fourteen books he published between 1874 and 1908. In other words, Bowne's, unlike Howison's, was a systematic movement from objective idealism, to transcendental empiricism, then to Kantianized-Berkeleianism, and finally to personalism. This movement or progression is clearly reflected in his writings. At every stage after the objective idealism phase he made the self more central or prominent in his philosophy. We will recall the East Coast personalist, Knudson, who described Bowne's philosophy as systematic methodological personalism. This was Knudson's way of distinguishing Bowne's personalism from all that preceded his. On the other hand, Howison simply did not write enough for us to get a clear sense of his movement toward a systematic personal idealism.

With this in mind, it is understandable why those affiliated with Boston University on the East Coast have generally looked to Bowne and his disciples as having developed personalism in a systematic, methodological sense. Although it has already been established that Bowne is considered the father of American Personalism by virtue of his prolific writing on the subject and his efforts to push the personalistic argument to its logical conclusions in metaphysics, epistemology, philosophical psychology, ethics, philosophy of religion, and theology, what many have not been aware of is that precisely during the period that Bowne was developing his personalism on the East Coast, Howison was doing the same thing at the University of California (beginning in 1884). As noted, a major difference between them is that Howison was not as prolific a writer as Bowne. This may help to explain in part why Bowne did not mention him in his work. Neither did Howison cite Bowne, but it would seem that he should have both known of Bowne's work and cited it because of the latter's more extensive writing. But as noted elsewhere, Bowne did not, for various reasons, join and participate in professional philosophical societies, which may be one of the reasons he did not get the exposure that other philosophers did.

Although both Howison and Bowne were considered excellent and caring teachers, Howison was thought to be a teacher *par excellence*. He disseminated his ideas more through lectures in and out of formal academic circles. As a teacher and conveyor of ideas to his students he was second to none. Howison stressed the importance of his students' doing their own thinking rather than uncritically buying into his or anyone else's system of thought. One would be mistaken, then, to gauge Howison's influence only by his limited writing.[9] The fact that he did not publish as much as Bowne may be attributed in part to his coming to the teaching of philosophy rather late in his life (at age fifty) because he was unable to find a steady position in philosophy when he began his teaching career. He therefore wrote one book on his personal idealism, *The Limits of Evolution* (1901, revised 1904). Here we find the major outlines of his philosophy and some of the fundamental questions he encountered, raised, and endeavored to respond to.

Both Howison and Bowne were sharp critics of Herbert Spencer's agnosticism and his philosophy of "the Unknowable"; of all materialistic systems of thought; and of the absolutism of Hegel and the neo-Hegelians of their day, particularly where it seemed to them that the individuality and freedom of the person is undermined or collapsed in the Absolute. Howison and Bowne gave person and freedom a place of prominence in their philosophy that was uncommon in their day. Both sought to make clear the limits and strengths of science and metaphysics or speculative thought. Each man insisted that the current evolutionary theorists claimed too much for their views, for example, that theirs were superior theories of the origin of life and even mind.[10] Howison and Bowne each emphasized the communal, interactive nature of person.[11] Both rejected pantheistic interpretations of divine immanence because these "confound God in unethical identity."[12] Both held that freedom is a central factor in person.[13] But there were other similarities between their systems of thought as well.

Both men adhered to the nontemporality of God, claiming that God is not affected by time.[14] Here they were both influenced by Kant. Although Bowne was clearly ambivalent on this issue, sometimes implying that God is indeed affected by the temporal order,[15] he most often opted for the non-temporality of God.[16]

In addition, Howison and Bowne were influenced by Berkeley's immaterialism and his contention that only minds and ideas exist. For Howison the similarity with Berkeley ceases here.[17] We have already seen in chapter 1 that Bowne rejected completely Berkeley's theory of knowledge. Both men rejected thoroughgoing immaterialism and opted instead for the phenomenalism of all objects. That is, they believed that all natural objects have a reality of their own. Natural objects are not just ideas in God's or someone else's mind, which smacks of subjective idealism. Indeed, the rejection of the latter is possibly the chief difference between personal idealism and most other idealistic systems.[18] In this sense, Howison and Bowne each distinguished between phenomenal and metaphysical reality and were able to maintain that because the phenomenal or natural object has a reality of its own, it does not mask reality, as Kant proposed, but is a derivative of the metaphysical reality.[19] Both phenomenal and noumenal objects are real, but they do not have the same kind of reality, said Bowne. The noumenal object *causes* the phenomenal object, and although the latter is not causal, it is real in the sense that it is not a mere idea or an illusion in some mind, but is an actual object of our sense experience. The phenomenal object is the result of the energizing of God's thought and will.[20] This is actually a rejection of Kant's epistemological agnosticism. However, the idea that all of nature or the visible world is but the sensible expression of God's reason and will is fundamentally Berkeleian.[21]

Both men were also influenced much by Kant.[22] They found Kant's emphasis on the active nature of the mind[23] to be useful, while rejecting his idea that nothing can be known about the ultimately real, and that phenomenal objects are but masks of the real.[24] In their ethical writings Bowne and Howison were each influenced by Kant's doctrine of the person as an end in itself.

Howison and Bowne were unquestionably more Kantian than Berkeleian,[25] although each made it clear that his system was not to be identified solely with Kantianism.[26] Bowne said he accepted half of Kant's philosophy and rejected the rest.

In addition, the two men believed evil to be primarily the product of human contrivance or misuse of human freedom.[27] God, according to Howison, "has no part whatever in the causation of evil." Similarly, Bowne held that "the difficulty lies solely in human nature." Both rejected classical pantheism and Hegel's idealism precisely because these systems seemed to make God responsible for evil, inasmuch as the individual appeared to be collapsed in the Absolute, which effectively destroyed human freedom. Neither Bowne nor Howison took seriously the theories of theistic finitism that held that God is limited in either power or goodness (but most often power).[28] Theistic finitism offered an alternative to absolutistic theories of God and evil. As we shall see later, Brightman was a chief proponent of theistic finitism.

I find another interesting similarity between Bowne and Howison. Nowhere in their writings do we find explicit statements against racial discrimination in the United States. We find no reflections on the Reconstruction era (1867–1877) and its aftermath, particularly regarding the plight of blacks. Nowhere do we find express acknowledgment of the humanity, dignity, and freedom of blacks. And yet, in principle, both men had to be against American slavery, lynchings of black men, and discrimination, for each maintained that to be human is to be free and of inestimable worth. The treatment of blacks during Bowne's and Howison's day was, therefore, a clear contradiction of their personalistic principles. And yet neither man made this connection explicitly in his published work. On principle, the treatment of blacks was a major assault on the personalistic outlook and on Christianity, particularly if Knudson was right in characterizing personalism as the Christian philosophy par excellence.[29] Buckham held similarly when he said that "it can hardly be gainsaid that Christianity has closer and more complete affiliations with Personalism than with any other philosophy."[30] One wonders whether Howison and Bowne, like very many whites of their day, thought only of the Anglo-Saxon race as fully human and therefore had only them in mind when they wrote so eloquently about the absolute dignity and sacredness of all persons.

Howison and Bowne each held that only mind is real,[31] a view that would be challenged by realists such as Alfred N. Whitehead, and even realistic personalists like Georgia Harkness, a point to be further explored later in this chapter. Neither Howison nor Bowne had children, which may help to explain their deep affection, care, and concern for their students. In addition, neither possessed an earned doctorate.

Unlike Bowne, Howison completely rejected Berkeley's creationism,[32] holding instead that creation is at best a metaphor.[33] Although a theist, Howison believed God to be *final* cause rather than *efficient* cause.[34] In this sense God did not create persons. Instead, persons are the eternally existent ultimate realities. God is but one person among a plurality of persons who, like them, has obligations and regrets. Persons are "attracted to God as their perfect final cause." The lives of persons are purposive only as they intentionally strive toward God, who is our guiding perfection. Indeed, the key to Howison's personal idealism is found in the primacy he gave to final cause,[35] or the idea of God as "attracting Ideal"[36] rather than Creator. Final cause, according to Howison, is the chief explanatory principle.[37] Human persons, then, are the only efficient causes.[38]

Although this is not an exhaustive treatment of the similarities and differences between Howison and Bowne, enough has been said for us to see just how similar and different were their thoughts. Some of the similarities are striking, considering that Howison and Bowne were not close colleagues (even when they lived and worked within a few minutes of each other!) and did not correspond or cite each other's work in their own publications. I have noted very few of the differences between the two men but will treat this more fully in the critical assessment of Howison.

Howison's Popularity

Because Howison traveled more extensively in Europe, having made three trips and staying for at least a year,[39] it is likely that he was better known there than Bowne and was cited more frequently by European philosophers. Yet there were also European thinkers who knew and respected Bowne's work. One of these, James Iverach, wrote a letter to James Hastings in 1920 praising the strengths of Bowne's work and the acuteness of his mind.[40] Another was Rudolph Eucken, who only knew Bowne vicariously through correspondence "which was, indeed, most hearty and intimate." Eucken believed theirs was a "close and most friendly" relation.[41] Bowne, according to Eucken, "was a philosopher of America, and as such all America may be proud of him and of his memory."[42] He meant by this that as a philosopher Bowne was not only American grown, but he was a profound thinker and a chief American philosopher of his day. But in any case, it is conceivable that Howison's work was better known than Bowne's in England and Europe. Buckham wrote of the popularity that Howison's book, *The Limits of Evolution*, had in England. He said that it "was received with an attention even more marked in Great Britain than in America."[43]

In books on American philosophy and philosophers Howison is frequently mentioned and examined, while Bowne is too often omitted.[44] Brightman may have said it best in 1926 when he pointed out that most histories of philosophy only treated Bowne casually, if at all, and that he was "seldom quoted in philosophical discussions or monographs."[45] Indeed, we even find this to be the case in the fairly recent two volume work, *A History of Philosophy in America*. Here the authors discuss only the personal idealism of Howison.[46] Bowne and Brightman are mentioned only in passing.[47] In addition, the authors erroneously write that Bowne taught at Cornell,[48] which of course he did not. His entire teaching career was spent at Boston University. At any rate, some of the reasons for the tendency to ignore Bowne include his failure to join professional philosophical societies; his propensity to not quote the work of his philosophical peers, but to do his own thinking; his tendency to be almost vicious and insensitive in his criticisms of other thinkers; and the fact that he did not travel much, but was basically confined to the East Coast where he was best known. Although it appears that Howison received more attention in basic history of philosophy texts than did Bowne, William James, a mutual friend of both men, more often cited Bowne's than Howison's works. James believed that Bowne would leave a tremendous legacy.[49]

James frequently appealed to Bowne's work. In *Varieties of Religious Experience* James mentioned Bowne near the end of the book.[50] In the classic work *The Principles of Psychology*, James includes a two-page, single-spaced quotation from Bowne's *Metaphysics*.[51] In *Pragmatism* he critiqued Bowne's personalism, placing it in the category of the "tender-minded philosophies" that have "the air of fighting a slow retreat." In addition, James said that Bowne's philosophy and those like it were not radical, but "eclectic, a thing of compromises."[52] Although James intended this as a criticism, personalists of the Bowne type insist that it is no devastating blow to the real genius of personalism, which is its emphasis on respect for persons and its insistence that persons live in a way that reflects their recognition of and respect for humanity in self and others. Personalism *is* eclectic, but this is not its most distinguishing feature. And yet it is considered by personalists to be a strength, and not a weakness, that personalism is eclectic and has been able to assimilate the strong points of other systems of thought.

Although James was critical of much of Bowne's work, he had high regard for both Bowne and his ability as a thinker, and thus was much influenced by him. In fact, James believed that he and Bowne were very close at some points in their philosophies. Having read Bowne's book *Personalism* shortly after it was published in 1908, James wrote to him about it.

> It seems to me a very weighty pronouncement, and form and matter taken together a splendid addition to American philosophy…It seems to me that you and I are now aiming at exactly the same end, though, owing to our different past, from which each retains special verbal habits, we often express ourselves so differently. It seemed to me over and over again that you were planting your feet identically in footprints which my feet were accustomed to—quite independently, of course, of my example, which was what made the coincidences so gratifying.[53]

Howison's Personal Idealism

There is no question that person has centrality in Howison's philosophy. Indeed, he called his idealism *personal* idealism precisely because it makes persons the highest and central realities. As a matter of course Howison believed in and respected persons. He was both tender and careful in the way he showed respect for persons. This was not limited to members of his own or a higher socioeconomic class. George Stratton recounts an instance of this.

> He saw the fine texture of plain men and women, and knew how to express some of the value he set upon them. Thus each year as the holidays approached he regularly provided some additional cheer for the janitor of the building which housed the Department of Philosophy…Howison's unusual and characteristically careful way was to go himself to market and buy the materials for a good dinner for the man and his wife—turkey and all. I remember the glow with which the old janitor told me of this regular expression of the professor's good will.[54]

Howison lived his personal idealism, and in this sense was similar to Bowne. For example, Bowne's biographer cited an instance in which he exhibited his disgust and outrage while in India when he witnessed his host mistreat and disrespect an Indian servant by saying he could not sleep in his house, but could sleep under the porch.[55]

Unlike Bowne, Howison founded no school of thought and had no disciples as such. Indeed, when once congratulated on his own success as teacher and scholar and the fact that so many of his own students held distinguished chairs of philosophy in American universities, Howison is reported to have "replied grimly: 'Yes, but not one of them teaches the truth.'"[56] Howison meant by this that unlike himself they were not personal idealists. Although he wanted his students to do their own thinking rather than to uncritically accept his or some other philosopher's system, he was confident that personal idealism was the most reasonable path, and consequently the one to follow. Apparently many of his students decided otherwise.

As noted in the discussion of absolutistic personalism, Howison was critical of absolute idealism because he believed it denied individuality and human freedom, which in turn undermined the uniqueness and moral nature of persons. He described the "foundation-theme" of idealism as:

> that explanation of the world which maintains that the only thing absolutely real is mind; that all material and all temporal existences take their being from mind, from consciousness that thinks and experiences; that out of consciousness they all issue, to consciousness are presented, and that presence to consciousness constitutes their entire reality and entire existence.[57]

Howison's basic metaphysical stance may be summed up in the statement that all reality (existence) is mental or mind, or the experiences of some mind.[58] There is not just one Absolute mind as in absolute idealism, but many minds that are in "mutual recognition of their moral reality" and "the determining ground of all events and all mere 'things,'" and therefore "form the eternal (i.e. unconditionally real) world." Howison believed that in this sense persons "constitute the 'City of God.'"[59]

As can be seen, Howison's personalism is both a qualitative monism (i.e., reality is of the same quality—mind), and a quantitative pluralism (i.e., there is not one, but a plurality of minds). This stance is also identical with the Bowne type of personalism.

Like Renouvier, Howison was a pluralist. Freedom is a touchstone of his philosophy. But unlike Renouvier, he was not a relativist, nor did he consider himself a theistic finitist.[60] However, according to Knudson, there is one way Howison limits God even more than Renouvier. We saw earlier that according to Howison, God is not the first, but the final cause of the world! Howison was quite certain that God reigns in the "Eternal Republic" (City of God) "not by the exercise of power, but solely by light; not by authority, but by reason; not by efficient, but by final causation..."[61] To deny that God is Creator places an even graver limitation on God's power, according to Knudson.

Howison argued that the key to his personal idealism:

> is found in its doctrine concerning the system of causation. It reduces Efficient Cause (*causa efficiens*) from that supreme place in

philosophy…and gives the highest, the organizing place to final cause (*causa finalis*) instead. Final cause becomes now not merely the guiding and regulative, but actually the grounding and constitutive principle of real existence…[62]

There is therefore no doctrine of creation in Howison's personalism. Human persons are not created by God. Rather, they and God are coeternal.[63] According to Howison, the members of the City of God or the Eternal Republic have no origin: "no source in time whatever. There is nothing at all, prior to them, out of which their being arises…They simply are…"[64] Human persons are, in a word, *causa sui* (self-caused). Although not the Creator, God is the goal or end (*telos*) toward which humans aim or strive. (This is why it is reasonable to refer to Howison's as teleological or ethical personalism.) God's influence over other beings may be reduced to a kind of spiritual attraction, so that God's influence is ethical in nature.[65] Created persons are free to move toward the kind of life God is.

For Howison the traditional idea of creation implies an occurrence or event dated in the life of God. He, therefore, preferred to think of creation metaphorically. As noted earlier he opposed the idea of the temporality of God. God, accordingly, is not subject to time. Creation, therefore, is at best a metaphor that symbolizes "such an eternal dependence of other souls upon God that the non-existence of God would involve the non-existence of all souls, while his existence is the essential supplementing Reality that raises them to reality; without him they would be but void names and bare possibilities."[66]

Whether he had adequate grounds for it or not, what Howison feared most was that creationism implies the loss of relative otherness or independence of persons. This he simply could not abide, for it would mean the destruction of human freedom. He argued for "the full *otherhood*" of all creation, "so that there shall be no confusion of the creature with the Creator, nor any interfusion of the Creator with the creature."[67]

Freedom, according to Howison, is essential to both person and the pursuit of the moral ideal, but he believed the idea of the sole causality of God (which we find in pantheism) implies the destruction of both freedom and immortality.[68] This was his chief criticism of pantheism and absolutism. At any rate, Howison considered as reprehensible any doctrine that was incompatible with human freedom. Werkmeister rightly contends that "the pivot of [Howison's] philosophy, was his concern for the moral responsibility of the human person."[69] This was the criterion by which he judged the value of all philosophical systems. Howison rejected any system that was incompatible with the freedom and responsibility of persons. He advocated a thoroughly personal idealism, "an eternal or metaphysical world of *many* minds, all alike possessing personal initiative, real self-direction, instead of an all-predestinating single Mind that alone has real free-agency."[70] That *every* person is free means that each is morally responsible for her actions toward self, others, God,[71] and the world. There is no moral evil in the world for which God is responsible. For the cause of moral evil one need only look to created persons. But this also means that in these are found the key to the solution to evil and suffering in the world. In this, too, Howison was in line with the Bowne type of personalism.

Howison was so keen on the idea of metaphysical pluralism that he rejected both pantheism *and* creation. Rejection of classical pantheism is not what causes his system to fall short of the more typical form of personalism, however. In fact, such rejection moved him closer to Bowne's personalism. It is, rather, Howison's denial that God is first cause, and thus his rejection of creation, that makes his a less typical type of personalism.

Howison did not show satisfactorily how creationism destroys human freedom and the moral life. He believed that if God created persons, all freedom and moral endeavor would be cut off, since "the Creator cannot…create except by exactly and precisely conceiving…The created nature must therefore inevitably register the will and the plan of the Creator…"[72] On this view persons can do only what the Creator designed them to do. This, according to Howison, opens the door to determinism. Clearly this line of thought has bearing on the problem of moral evil, for Howison argued that if God is first cause, then God must be responsible for moral evil and sin. "The predestinating Sovereign, the universal Maker, cannot escape the contagion of the evil and the wickedness that pervades the world which he creates and from moment to moment sustains."[73] Howison's answer is that final cause must be the chief explanatory principle. The "new view" (as he labeled it) "holds to an Eternal Pluralism of causal minds, each self-active, though all recognizant of all others, and thus all in their central essence possessed of moral autonomy, the very soul of all really moral being."[74]

Precisely at this point of difficulty in Howison's personalism Bowne could have been a helpful conversation partner. Both men argued cogently against pantheism. And yet when Howison wrote on creationism his language had the sound of one who believed that *if* God were considered the Creator, it would mean that somehow persons and the rest of creation are created out of God. But this implies that God is a physical thing, stuff, or substance. Bowne got around this implication in a nice way by declaring that metaphysics shows that reality is not this, but rather is an agent. Ultimate reality, or God, is agent, not a stuff of some kind out of which all things are created. Although both men rejected substantiality in favor of causality, Bowne seemed more willing to reason out the implications for God as Creator. Said Bowne:

> Metaphysics…shows that every agent is a unit, uncompounded and indivisible. God, then, is not the infinite stuff or substance, but the infinite cause or agent, one and indivisible. From this point all the precious views of the relation of God to the world disappear of themselves. He has no parts and is not a sum. Hence the world is no part of God, nor an emanation from him, nor a sharer in the divine substance; for all these views imply the divisibility of God and also his stuff-like nature. His necessary unity forbids all attempts to identify him with the world, either totally or partially. If the finite be anything real, it must be viewed,

not as produced from God, but as produced by God; that is, as created…For the finite, if real, is an agent, and as such it cannot be made out of anything, but is posited by the infinite.[75]

According to Bowne persons are created or posited, "not made, for making implies a pre-existent stuff."[76] And although Howison did not intend to imply that creation would mean that persons are made from some preexistent stuff, his argument against creationism does in fact imply this. "Creation means to posit something in existence which before was not," writes Bowne. That was all he meant by it. As the "all-powerful" deity, God "caused the world" and persons to exist. God "caused a new existence to begin…"[77] God caused to exist that which had not before existed. And yet Bowne was not hesitant to say that we humans do not know how God does this. "[W]e have no recipe for this process. Creation is a mystery; but any other view is a contradiction of thought itself."[78] If persons are not made by God, as Howison's language seems to imply, but rather are caused by the energizing of God's thought and will, the problem of otherness between Creator and created that was so important to Howison is no longer a problem.

Francis H. Bradley (1846–1924) said that "not to know how a thing can be is no disproof that the thing must be and is."[79] This statement applies to Howison's argument that all views of God as efficient or first cause (creationism) destroy freedom and immortality. Since Howison could not understand how God could create persons without also violating the principle of self-determination, he concluded that God cannot be Creator, but must be final cause, the goal toward which all persons aim.

At this point Howison would have done well had he simply concluded (as did Bowne) that ultimate truth is not demonstrable, even when we humans have gone as far as we can go through rigorous use of intellect and practical reason. In such a quest we will always be confronted at some point with mystery—a point beyond which human mind or thought processes cannot go, a point at which we should have the good sense to appeal to faith or belief based on the best that reason allows us to know at the time. At such moments we should admit this and be willing to say that having done all we can we are left, not with final, demonstrable truth, but with the most reasonable, coherent hypothesis based on the best evidence available. Every effort should be made to avoid basing our conclusions solely on our belief in a particular God-concept. For example, one should not allow her belief in an absolutely perfect God to cause her to draw conclusions about God, persons, and the rest of creation that are inconsistent with the facts and with other things known to be true. In other words, we should avoid forcing a theory or belief on the evidence. On the issue of creationism, for example, Howison strayed from the path of his otherwise rigorous empirical method when he tried to force his theory of God on the evidence, rather than revising his theory in light of the evidence. The latter approach would have been more consistent with personalistic method.

We do not find in Howison's personalism an adequate accounting of the existence of the plurality of selves and persons. Indeed, for him these are uncreated beings who, because of their freedom, may choose to aspire toward God (the final cause). But it is not clear why these uncreated persons would want to aspire toward a God who is not their creator—a God who is not the Father-Mother of all creation. Inquiring and curious minds will find it difficult to be at peace with Howison's noncreationist view. Furthermore, why would a noncreator God really, truly care for creation, and what would be the grounds for believing this to be the case? In agreement with so much of Howison's philosophy, John Wright Buckham sharply rejected his anticreationism. Buckham contended that persons are not only aware of their selfhood and freedom, but following Schleiermacher, he said that "we are equally conscious of *dependence*" on something greater than ourselves:

> This consciousness of dependence will not consent to any theory of original and underived human self-hood, but wistfully and insistently asserts its receptive relation to a Higher Self.[80]

He went on to say that this consciousness of dependence is more than the need for a final cause or goal toward which to strive. It is also the need, the necessity for an originating or efficient cause. There is no question of the need for a final cause toward which to aspire, but according to Buckham "unless this Final Cause is my Originating Cause as well, I am left without any adequate understandings of that inherent superiority to myself of the Supreme Self which makes Him my Final Cause."[81] Without an originating cause, from whence would come the innate sense we humans have of our own sacredness and worth? From whence would come our inherent sense that we stand in relation to that which nothing greater can be thought? Buckham believed that Augustine's adage "Thou has formed us for Thyself, and our hearts are restless till they find rest in Thee" is apropos.[82] We have the sense of dependence on something or some being not ourselves precisely because we are summoned into existence by a being greater than we; summoned by choice and in love. God made us for God's self. If this is so, it stands to reason that we would have etched into the uttermost depths of our being a consciousness of dependence. Buckham finally quoted Benjamin Whichcote approvingly: "We cannot be ultimate and final to ourselves, who are not Original to ourselves."[83]

If God does not create or call persons into existence, the theist is left wondering what evidence there is that we can believe in and depend on divine friendship. If God is not the Creator, why would God feel obligated to be our Savior? Bowne held that God is obligated in this regard precisely because God called us into existence.[84] If God is not responsible for willing and loving us into existence, but instead is only final cause, how can Howison reasonably characterize God as our "heavenly Judge, the unfailing Beholder and Sympathizer?"[85] If God is not the Creator, on what grounds can Howison argue (as he does) for our eternal dependence upon God?

In addition, Howison argued that God is a nontemporal being, and thus is not affected by time. In this he is close to Bowne. But in both cases it may be argued that these personalists were not as thoroughgoing in their empiricism as they might have been. If, as both argued, God is truly personal, then God, like all persons, must be affected by time in some way. Indeed, how can God be affected by time, or affect the world and human persons, if God is not in some way in time? How can it be claimed that we can ever hope (even through prayer!) to get in touch with a God beyond or above time? Consistent, thoroughgoing personalism does not permit changing the rules to accommodate God or one's theological faith claims about God. The requirement, instead, is that we reason from the facts and draw the most reasonable conclusion from the evidence.

Because of their close proximity for several years in the Boston area, the fact that there are strong similarities in their personal idealism, and the fact that no one has yet been able to document whether Howison and Bowne corresponded in any way, one might be tempted to wonder whether the two men in fact knew each other. Although it is not known how well they knew each other, it was noted earlier in this discussion that both men were present and made presentations at the International Congress of Arts and Sciences held in St. Louis in 1904.

Realistic or Dualistic Personalism (Georgia Harkness)

Both the idealistic and the realistic personalist believes that person is the fundamental, irreducible reality. The basic difference is that the former postulates the existence of one world, while the latter postulates two (a world of mind and a world of matter), and is therefore dualistic in the way she conceives of reality. In addition, the conception of matter espoused by these two types of personalists is different. This point will be taken up momentarily.

The chief proponent of metaphysical dualism is "the father of modern philosophy" in the West, René Descartes (1596–1650). Considered "the most famous exponent of this view," Descartes had to turn to miraculous properties in the pineal gland in the brain to unify the radically separate realities of mind and matter. We find this dualism in Plato and Aristotle as well. Plato, for example, made a sharp distinction between the material and immaterial worlds, while Aristotle made a sharp distinction between form and matter.

For our purpose Descartes is the chief exponent of metaphysical dualism, or what Alfred North Whitehead referred to as the "bifurcation of reality." This is the view that there is not one, but two realities or worlds—matter and mind. Descartes ultimately had to resort to the belief that only in the unifying substance (God) is there explanation for this and other dualisms. But this solution may be questioned, since the dualism between matter and mind is so radical, and Descartes' view of God was so abstract and remote from human experience.[86]

There are unquestionably dualisms and conflicts in the world. We know this from day-to-day experience. But this is quite different from postulating metaphysical dualism, as did Descartes. For this implies that there are essentially two worlds that will never be unified. If this is the case, we must wonder whether it will ever be possible to bring some sense of unity and harmony of things at all. If there is no essential harmony or unity in the nature of things (reality itself), how can we ever expect to develop a faith or means to achieve unity in the affairs of an already devastatingly divided world? If there is a basic disunity or dualism at the very seat of reality, why should we expect that we can have anything but disunity in lived experience in the world? Is there a unifying principle in a fundamentally divided world? Since we get our idea of unity from personal, conscious experience, that is, the self or person, is it possible that herein lies the clue that unity, not disunity or dualism, is a fundamental trait of ultimate reality?

Dualistic personalism contends that the worlds of matter and spirit are each irreducible, and neither is the ultimate explanation of the other. Person, according to dualistic personalism, is fundamental being. Matter, the visible world or nature, however, is not intrinsically personal, as in idealistic personalism. Nor is it of the nature of mind, or the energizing of God's will and thought. Matter, the dualist believes, is created by God. It has a separate existence in the sense that it is real, just as persons are real. The world of matter, accordingly, has an existence quite apart from that of persons.

One of the first Ph.D. candidates under Brightman at Boston University,[87] and an avowed personalist, Georgia E. Harkness (1891–1974) began her career as a thoroughgoing personalist. Brightman became her mentor and was the first to introduce her to the Bowne type of personalism during the second year of her master's degree program.[88] At the time of the publication of her book *Conflicts in Religious Thought* (1929), Harkness was essentially an idealistic personalist. However, by the time of the publication of *The Recovery of Ideals* (1937) and other writings, she had revised her view in the direction of another type of personalism. Still adhering to much of the Boston Personalist tradition in which she was nurtured, Harkness pointed to differences that led to her move in the direction of "theistic realism" or realistic personalism. Although during a leave of absence from Elmira College in the fall of 1926 Harkness worked with William Earnest Hocking and Alfred North Whitehead at Harvard,[89] it would be nearly a decade before her writings began to reveal a shift away from the idealistic personalism she was so deeply immersed in while studying under Brightman. In a moment we will see how the influence of Whitehead affected her new personalistic synthesis.

Before going further it is important to point out that Harkness was a very special kind of scholar. So popular was she as a lecturer in the 1930s that a major publication referred to her as the "famed woman theologian."[90] Harkness was the first woman theologian in this country to be appointed full-time at a major seminary. In 1940 she was called to Garrett Biblical Institute as professor of applied theology.[91]

Harkness wrote several early books whose primary audience was university and graduate students and scholars. However, having established impeccable credentials as a teacher and scholar, Harkness felt the need to devote the remainder of her writing career to teaching and instructing the laity, which in no way meant that her writing would be less scholarly and careful. It meant only that she would primarily address a different audience;

one that hungered for knowledge about the Christian faith, but in language that they could understand and appropriate. However, this was not deemed a popular move in academic circles. Indeed, many of Harkness' colleagues tended to view her work as a scholar differently when she began to write intentionally for the more popular audience of laity and pastors.[92] But this notwithstanding, Harkness soon became known as the theologian for the laity.[93]

From her early twenties Harkness "embarked upon her lifetime vocational journey of 'making theology understandable to people.'"[94] She was the quintessential "folk theologian" or theologian of the folk.[95] She was not only a prolific writer of books that became commonplace in church study groups, but all that she wrote was informed by excellent scholarship and was written with a wonderful clarity in nontechnical language that the average person in the pew could understand. Some of her more popular titles for the laity include: *Toward Understanding the Bible*, *Understanding the Christian Faith*, *Beliefs that Count*, *Prayer and the Common Life*, *Be Still and Know*, *The Dark Night of the Soul*, *The Gospel and Our World*. And indeed, there are many more.

Harkness' biographer, Rosemary Skinner Keller, maintains that she was likely the most widely read theologian in the mid-twentieth century.[96] Harkness was also considered to be a master teacher who loved and cared for her students. This is a view that is confirmed by many now-retired United Methodist pastors and elderly laypersons who either studied under Harkness or read her books. I have personally heard such sentiments expressed by United Methodists of all races.

Like Mary Calkins, Harkness, too, was the victim of sexism. In her case she was denied a number of teaching positions because she was a woman.[97] She did not hesitate to use her position and fame to address the problem of discrimination against women in the church and the academy. Her book *Women in Church and Society* (1972), published two years before she died, is not a radical manifesto in feminist theology; it is consistent with her choice to work from within structures to influence them toward change. Nevertheless, that book is evidence of her passion regarding the treatment of women. Hers was a very strong voice in favor of women's ordination. This is an important point, and when we understand that early in her career this affected Harkness in a personal way, we will understand why she would later use all of her prestige and energy to challenge the practice against women's ordination. Robert A. Mulligan, a student of Harkness' and a retired United Methodist pastor, maintains that Harkness was not only a theologian of the laity "without distracting from her reputation as a true scholar," but "she spoke out for women's ordination before it was popular." Mulligan contends further: "I remember President Horace Greeley Smith telling me that Dr. Harkness was ordained with the tacit understanding that she would not ask for assignment as pastor of a church but would confine her ministry to teaching!"[98] Smith was the president of Garrett Biblical Institute who extended the invitation to Harkness to teach applied theology in 1939.

Smith was actually pressured by a number of forces within the faculty as well as outside the school to hire Harkness. It would therefore not be accurate to say that he was one of her major supporters when she finally arrived at Garrett. Rosemary Skinner Keller reports that an interview with some of her longtime confidants during her tenure at Garrett revealed that Harkness was periodically pushed to tears as a result of her relationship with Smith.

> Dorothy Leiffer recalled that Georgia at times would come into her office and cry, simply saying that "sometimes it is hard to be here." Murray [Leiffer] tied these expressions directly to her interaction with Horace Greeley Smith. Though Smith hired Harkness, he backed off in supporting her after she had been on the faculty a short time. She was never confident of her relationship to President Smith, Murray Leiffer explained.[99]

According to those interviewed by Keller, the difficulty was President Smith's inability or unwillingness to fully accept Harkness as an equal peer because she was a woman. Despite the fact that he was married to a woman, he apparently had difficulty relating well to strong, intelligent, assertive women who were his intellectual equals or superiors. Keller writes of the "heavy-handed sexism in the way Horace Greeley Smith exerted his presidential power over" Harkness. "And the wider reflections of persons who knew Smith and Harkness confirm the injustice involved and her feelings of hurt."[100] The fact that Harkness' popularity, both on the Garrett campus and through her writings, continued to increase was perhaps, in Smith's mind, "such a threat to the long-established order of male dominance that he drew back his original support of her."[101] Harkness finally decided in 1950 to leave Garrett "on cordial terms" to join the faculty at Pacific School of Religion in Berkeley, California. There she became the second woman faculty member.

Because Harkness understood how power works, she had to find ways to influence change that would not quickly lead to her own demise. In her day she often found herself alone on committees in the academy and the church. In addition, it may be that she was a "centrist" in thought and action,[102] and by temperament as well. But in any case, regarding issues such as the ordination of women, she primarily fought the battle from within church structures.

Theistic Realism

Theistic realism "admits the existence of one or more kinds of non-mental being considered as independently co-eternal with God, eternally dependent upon Deity, or as a divine creation."[103] Harkness writes of this change in perspective, which seems to turn on the fact of her disagreement with the Bowne-Brightman idea that there is but one fundamental reality, namely, persons. She was now rejecting the qualitative monism of idealistic personalism, that is, the view that reality is of the nature of mind only. Harkness and Brightman dialogued on this issue, but there is no evidence that he was as rigid as Bowne, who held that mind is the only ontological reality.[104] Brightman himself contended at times that "only persons are real."[105] Yet elsewhere he nuanced this by making the claim that "persons (or selves) are the sole (or dominant) metaphysical realities…"[106] What Brightman insisted upon—and this was not often understood by critics—was a particular understanding of the statement that only persons are real. In a 1928 article he responded to critics, one of whom was Harkness:

> Finally, is it absurd to contend that only persons are real? When I hear this argument seriously urged, I wonder whether the objector has heard of the great historical arguments for idealism; and I wonder whether he understands the personalistic account of nature. *Personalism certainly does not hold that only human persons are real*; nor does it hold that trees and gold and skies are all persons. In Dewey's language (but not in his sense!) personalism holds that trees and gold and skies are all experience; yet not merely human experience, for they exist when no human being is aware of them. Therefore, they are the experience of the Supreme Person. Personalism maintains that this hypothesis fulfills the function of philosophical thought in giving a unified world view, which is more intelligible and truer to the facts of experience than any other account which has been given. Hence, when this particular objection is raised, I want to know whether the objector understands the sense in which personalism holds only persons to be real, and also whether he is able not merely to pick flaws in particular arguments for idealism, but also to present a more intelligible and reasonable view.[107] (emphasis added)

Although Harkness revised her personalism, moving from the idealistic type represented by Bowne and Brightman to a firmer realistic stance, she never left the personalist camp. And yet, based on the line of argument in this book, it did make her less thoroughgoing in her idealism, since she substituted a realistic view of reality. Harkness wrote of both her agreement and disagreement with the Bowne-Brightman strand of personalism:

> I was reared in the personalistic tradition which holds that God and human persons are the only metaphysical realities. Such a view does not, of course, make physical nature an illusion. It makes physical things the acts of God. That is, it regards nature as an eternal system of divine activity; not something God has created, or still creates, but something God causes with consistent regularity. Human persons, being relatively independent real units of existence, are created; physical things are caused. [So far so good. But Harkness continues, and this is where the divergence occurs.] To this view I still assent in part, but only partially. My present view comes closer to a form of theistic realism. I now see no valid sense in which it is possible to say that only persons are metaphysically real.[108]

Remember, Harkness worked with Hocking and Whitehead at Harvard during the fall semester of 1926. By the time she wrote the above statement she was clearly under the influence of Whitehead's philosophy. Although maintaining that Whitehead introduced "confusion into philosophical terminology," Harkness was just as adamant that he "rendered much service by showing that from the standpoint of modern physics an 'actual entity' can just as well be called an 'actual occasion.'"[109] Harkness further clarified her position in a 1938 essay.

> My metaphysical position, stated in the *Recovery of Ideals*, is shamelessly ontic. It is monistic in its foundations and fruition, dualistic in a qualified though not ultimate sense in its theory of God's relation to the world. With the personalists I regard nature as the eternal activity of God. But I do not equate it with an aspect of God's consciousness. Both human and physical nature are the product of God's creative will, and in both there is an interweaving of what Tillich calls freedom and fate, though to escape panpsychism I prefer to use the terms spontaneity and order for physical nature, but not all the juxtapositions of circumstance which arise within the given, uncreated structure of possibilities. God is limited, therefore, both by human wills and the element of chance which emerges within nature and history. There are some circumstances which God cannot prevent, but there are none which cannot be transcended through God's limitless power to enable men to triumph over tragedy.[110]

What Harkness finally opted for, then, is a qualified, not ultimate or metaphysical dualism. Adhering to the idea of a God whose power is qualified, she held that God is limited by human freedom (a divine self-limitation); by the element of chance that emerges in nature and history; and by two other interrelated realities, separate and distinct from human persons, but in interaction with them: events (physical) things and eternal forms (i.e., the essence or cause of things, as mind is viewed in idealistic thought as being the essence of person). Just how to define these realities that presumably exist apart from created persons is a challenge, but one that Harkness tried to address.[111] Harkness' change in perspective has prompted Dianne Carpenter to propose in a two-volume doctoral dissertation that Harkness developed her own "distinctive personalistic synthesis."[112]

The idealistic or typical theistic personalist would pose several questions regarding the Harkness type of personalism. Does the positing of multiple, unrelated realities complicate the problem of explanation? Idealistic personalism holds that events, things, eternal forms, neutral entities, essences, and other allegedly separate but interrelated realities "are simply abstractions from personal experience and instead of being the sources of reality are its pale shadows."[113] In other words, all of these are aspects of some level of mind or self, rather than separate and distinct realities. Should our aim be the production of the most adequate, inclusive, and simplest characterization of the facts of experience? Can impersonal physical realities such as those postulated by the realism camp explain mind or the personal? Is it more reasonable to say that the personal can explain the impersonal, rather than the other way around? Is it more reasonable to introduce multiple realities to explain the facts if one reality, for example, person, seems sufficient and reasonable? Can we better accomplish the task by proposing that nature and physical things are the energizing of the will and thought of God or God's will and thought in action?

In the foregoing discussions on the teleological personalism of George Holmes Howison and the realistic personalism of Georgia Harkness we have considered the views of two thinkers whose personalism takes us a long way toward the type that was systematically developed by Bowne. We saw that both Bowne and Howison made person and freedom capstones of their philosophies. The major difference between the two is that Bowne considered God to be the first cause, and thus the Creator. Howison believed God to be the final cause, and the goal toward which persons strive. God, for Howison, is not the Creator. Since I consider Bowne's to be the most thoroughgoing type of personalism, it must be said that Howison's noncreationist personal idealism comes up short in this regard. Although Harkness studied personalism under Brightman, arguably the chief interpreter of Bowne's philosophy, she deviated from it by arguing that there is not one, but multiple, realities.

In the treatment of each of the less typical forms of personalism to this point (atheistic, pantheistic, absolutistic, relativistic, teleological, and realistic) we have gotten a sense that, while each is in the personalistic family, they each lack some element that characterizes a more typical or thoroughgoing personalism. We also know that this type of personalism is represented in the thought of Borden Parker Bowne. But just what are the essential elements of this personalism that prompts the contention that it is the most typical type?

Theistic or Thoroughgoing Personalism
(Borden Parker Bowne)

In *The Philosophy of Personalism* Knudson rightly characterizes the philosophy of Borden Parker Bowne as "systematic methodological personalism."

> [T]he most distinctive form of personalism is not reached until personalism becomes a philosophical method as well as a body of conclusions. It is this that Bowne has given us, a systematic methodological personalism, in which the whole of metaphysics is organized around one central and all-illuminating principle—that of the self-sufficiency of personality.[114]

Neither Lotze, Bowne's teacher, nor Howison developed personalism as systematically as did Bowne. Although Lotze made mind central and emphasized freedom, he neither stressed the idea of God as person, nor did he make freedom a touchstone of his philosophy as Bowne did. Bowne even stressed the "speculative significance of freedom." We do not find this emphasis in Lotze. Although Howison produced the significant collection of essays *The Limits of Evolution* (1901), this at best provides an outline of his personal idealism. This falls far short of the systematic work of Bowne.

I have pointed out several times that it is questionable whether the Bowne-Knudson type of personalism is the most typical and "normative." Since I challenge Knudson's use of the term normative,[115] I substitute Bowne's own characterization. It will be recalled that in the famous letter to his wife in 1909 Bowne said that he was "a personalist, the first of the clan in any thoroughgoing sense." While I believe this to be a more adequate description of Bowne's personalism, I wonder whether it is consistently thoroughgoing in all of its aspects. I think this concern particularly applies to Bowne's understanding of: (1) The doctrine of God and evil; (2) God and time; (3) his stance on racism and economic exploitation. The first two concerns will be examined extensively in chapters 6 and 7. I will return to the third in chapter 4. But it is important to point out now that Knudson was at best awkward in some of his statements about blacks. Bowne himself did not explicitly address the issue of racism in any of his books, including his classic text on ethics. And although he was troubled by poverty in this country, he was not prepared to make a radical critique of capitalist economy. He denounced Marxism, failing to see in it elements for critical social analysis of capitalism. He did not make the move toward democratic socialism as did Brightman and others of his students. And yet it is conceivable that he might have done so had he lived longer. In any case, because of these and other limitations, we must be cautious about referring to the Bowne-Knudson type of personalism as the most typical, thoroughgoing type. However, it must be acknowledged that it was Knudson—not Bowne!—who maintained that the Bowne type of personalism is the normal or truest type. I will return to this later. For now I assume with Knudson that this is indeed the most typical type of personalism in relation to those types discussed to this point (and more especially in relation to the other types Knudson himself discussed).[116] However, for reasons already noted, I dispense with the designation "normative" for this type of personalism.

The most appropriate designation of this type is Bownean, theistic, or idealistic personalism. Or, simply, personalism. However, like Brightman, Bowne was not big on labels. But the truth of the matter is that Bowne—intentionally or not—was the leader of a school of thought and literally had numerous disciples who were primarily scholars and/or pastors and other church leaders. His scholarly disciples in turn begot disciples, who did the same, until this type of personalism is now in its fifth and sixth generation—the oldest extant American philosophy. And though the fourth through the sixth generations have not yet been productive scholars in terms of writing explicitly on personalism, there is absolutely no question that there is growing interest at least in ethical personalism (with its focus on the sanctity and dignity of persons) in Afrikan American and Hispanic communities.

While many in the European American community are calling for a less pronounced anthropocentric emphasis in ethics, Afrikan Americans are insisting on renewed interest and focus on ethical personalism. Even the most cursory look at the homicide statistics in relation to black males between fifteen and twenty-four years of age makes it easy to understand blacks' desire and need for such an ethic.[117] It is not that Afrikan Americans have no regard for the environment and the plant and animal kingdoms, and it surely is not the case that they systematically destroy nonhuman life forms as has historically been the case with the powerful and privileged in this country. Afrikan Americans simply want to be treated like human beings with dignity and respect, which does not necessarily preclude respect for nonhuman life forms.

Afrikan traditional heritage assures blacks of their inherent worth as persons. This view is supported by the Jewish-Christian principle of the image of God in persons. No wonder Afrikan Americans thirst and crave to be recognized as beings of infinite worth and to be treated as such. In a nutshell, Afrikan Americans want to know what personalism can contribute to solving some of the most serious and deadly problems in black and other communities of oppression. Thus, they are more inclined to an anthropocentric ethic such as we find in ethical personalism.

In addition, Bownean personalism is an appropriate and more acceptable characterization of the type of personalism discussed in this section because, unlike any other before or during his day, Bowne intentionally, systematically, and methodologically developed this personalism that has been so identified with his name since he first publicly announced in 1909 that he was "a personalist, the first of the clan in any thoroughgoing sense." This was not boasting. It was merely Bowne's way of publicly expressing for the first time that something new had occurred in the annals of philosophy and that he had led the movement.

Furthermore, though some of Bowne's disciples diverged sharply from some aspects of his personalism, for example, his doctrine of the nontemporality of God and his "solution" to the problem of evil, all of them—to a person—agreed with the basic outlines of his personalism. Because he is often described as the father of American personalism since it was he, more than any of his contemporaries, who made personalism a going concern, I shall from this point refer to this type of personalism as Bownean, theistic, idealistic, or simply, personalism.

In theistic personalism one can find some element(s) of all of the other types. Even in the atheistic personalism of McTaggart, thought to be the least typical or thoroughgoing type, one can see elements of the Bowne type of personalism. McTaggart's emphasis on reality as a system of selves and persons, God as personal, and his focus on persons as agents are all elements of theistic personalism. We also see in the Bowne type of personalism the strong focus on the nearness of God to persons and the rest of creation, which we find in the pantheistic personalism of William Stern. So significant is the doctrine of divine immanence in Bowne's personalism that he wrote a book on the subject![118] From absolutistic personalism we see, not the more traditional view of an all-embracing God in whom everything is included, but a God in whom all things live and move and have their being; a God who is the fundamental, sole ground of all that is. The Absolute is not the all, but the fundamental cause of the world and all that is in it. The majority of the Bowneans adopted this understanding of the Absolute. We also see in Bownean personalism the influence of relativistic personalism, with its emphasis on freedom and relationality. Reality, according to theistic personalism, is a society of interacting and intercommunicating selves and persons with God as the creative center. In addition, the Bowne type of personalism holds that a thing or person cannot be all that it is capable of being in isolation or out of relation. And finally, we see in Bownean personalism the focus on the primacy of freedom for person and the need to strive toward a higher end, that is, God. This is a chief contribution of Howison's teleological or ethical personalism.

Although we see in Bownean personalism traits found in the other types that have been examined, it would not be accurate to conclude that Bowne actually studied the works of thinkers who represent some of these and then merely appropriated from their thought what he needed. Though well read in the history of Western philosophy, Bowne prided himself on being an independent thinker. McConnell reports that a reviewer in the *New York Tribune* once remarked that Bowne had thought more than he had read. Although the reviewer meant this as a criticism, Bowne took it as the highest compliment.[119] And yet Bowne was a voracious reader. But the point to be stressed here is that, although influenced by the ideas of a number of philosophers, Bowne arrived at most of his conclusions through his own independent thinking. It will also be recalled that he was slow to cite the works of philosophical colleagues. But in addition, Bowne was often scathing and abrasive in his criticisms when he did cite their work. We get the clearest picture of this in his critique of Herbert Spencer's entire philosophical system. To say that Bowne used Spencer's work in his classrooms as a philosophical cadaver is putting it mildly. He finally concluded that Spencer's *New Philosophy* was "an ambitious attempt, and a dismal failure…"[120] Or consider this: "Mr. Spencer has mowed down the 'pseud-ideas' without mercy; but in his enthusiasm has, unfortunately, mowed off his own legs."[121] And then we find this: "In his present position this modern Samson [Spencer] parallels the ancient by pulling the temple on his own head."[122] And this: "In the hands of all its defenders, this philosophy has always taken an insane delight in knocking out its own brains; and, as habit strengthens with age, we shall find it performing this interesting feat with unusual gusto, under the direction of Mr. Spencer."[123] Surely such tendencies did not endear him to some of his philosophical peers, most especially British thinkers,[124] and it did not win him popularity votes. In any event, Bowne did not turn to the works of specific, less typical personalists for his ideas as he was developing his own personalism. He was an independent thinker who arrived at most of his conclusions on his own.

Because personalists, especially Knudson, believed personalism to be the Christian philosophy par excellence, much effort went into uncovering the similarities and differences between Christian or traditional theism, and personalism. Based on the similarities between them Knudson drew the conclusion that this is the most theistic form of personalism.

Personalism has its chief sources in the Augustinian-Cartesian emphasis on the primacy of self-certainty; Leibnitz's focus on spiritual individualism and activism; Berkeley's immaterialism and his view that all of nature is divine language; and Kant's emphasis on the activity of the mind and dualism of thought and object and the idea of the person as an end in itself. But it is to Lotze that we may attribute the "first general and distinctive formulation" of this more typical type of personalism. Lotze, it will be remembered, failed to achieve a thoroughgoing personalism primarily because he did not fully attribute the doctrine of person to God. In addition, he did not, like Bowne, make person and freedom the cornerstones of his philosophy. He therefore failed to develop a systematic, methodological personalism. However, Lotze, more than any of his contemporaries, infused new, invigorating life into theism. He effectively identified the personalistic elements of his predecessors and skillfully wove them into "a new type of theism."[125] But by the time Bowne arrived in Germany to study under him in the early 1870s, Bowne had himself already reached similar conclusions.

Afrikan American Personalism (Martin Luther King, Jr., John Wesley Edward Bowen, and J. Deotis Roberts)

That personalism provides an individual-social conception of reality, persons, and God, and that it gives primacy to the person are two of its most appealing features for Afrikan Americans. Black liberation theologians such as James H. Cone and J. Deotis Roberts have focused on the idea of human dignity and have been chief proponents of the total liberation and empowerment of Afrikan Americans, not so that they may oppress their oppressors, but in order that they will no longer be oppressed.[126] Black liberation theologians and ethicists have been concerned about young Afrikan American males' lost sense of dignity and self-worth, and therefore insist that focusing on their innate dignity must necessarily be the starting point of any theology or philosophy.

Martin Luther King, Jr.

Generally when we think about Afrikan Americans associated with personalism the name that immediately comes to mind is Martin Luther King, Jr. While a Ph.D. candidate in systematic theology at Boston University in the early 1950s, King was much influenced by several well-known personalists.[127] Two of these included his advisors, Brightman and L. Harold DeWolf. The latter wrote of his influence on King: "At nearly all points his system of positive theological belief was identical with mine, and occasionally I find his language following closely the special terms of my own lectures and writings."[128] DeWolf also said that King's most original and creative contribution to the personalist tradition was his persistence in translating personalism into social action by applying it to one of the chief social problems of this country, namely, racism. King also rigorously applied personalism to the problems of economic exploitation and militarism.

King went to Boston University for the express purpose of studying personalism under Brightman.[129] However, once he matriculated, the relationship did not last long, for Brightman died soon afterward. In addition to the influence of Brightman and DeWolf, King came under the influence of Walter G. Muelder, another third-generation personalist. Although he took no courses under Muelder, Muelder mentored him. Muelder also helped clarify for him Reinhold Niebuhr's doctrine of human nature (which King concluded was too pessimistic and left no opening for divine grace) and his critique of pacifism.

King studied under the chief interpreter of the Bowne-Brightman type of personalism, Peter A. Bertocci (1910–1989). When Brightman died, Bertocci provided leadership for the seminar on Hegel's philosophy in which King was enrolled.[130] King was a professed personalist, having defined personalism as "the theory that the clue to the meaning of ultimate reality is found in personality."[131] In addition, King acknowledged in a brief intellectual autobiography that personalism was his fundamental philosophical standpoint, and that it gave him metaphysical grounding for his long-held beliefs in the existence of a personal God and the dignity and sanctity of persons.[132] This is a very important point, for it means that King was actually a personalist (in a minimalist sense) long before he first read books on Brightman's personalism at Morehouse College,[133] and before he studied it in a more detailed way under George Washington Davis at Crozer Theological Seminary, and then under the direction of Brightman and DeWolf at Boston University. Unquestionably, it was his study under Davis at Crozer that prompted King to want to go to Boston University to study with Brightman and other key personalists. Indeed, what Crozer and Boston University actually did was to give King a name and a theoretical framework for what he already believed as a result of his family upbringing and his training in the black church in Atlanta, Georgia. This is a point not often mentioned when scholars treat King's philosophical and theological development. It is a point, however, that James Cone,[134] Garth Baker-Fletcher,[135] Lewis V. Baldwin,[136] and David Garrow[137] all stress in their studies on King.

King scholars such as Kenneth L. Smith and Ira G. Zepp, Jr.,[138] John Ansbro,[139] and Garth Baker-Fletcher[140] do an admirable job of discussing the influence of personalism on King's thought. King was essentially a social personalist in that he, more than any of the personalists, sought to apply the principles of personalism to social problems such as racism, militarism, and economic exploitation. It is fair to say, however, that the precedence for applying the principles of personalism to social problems was actually set by two early personalists: John Wesley Edward Bowen (1855–1933) and Francis J. McConnell (1871–1953). What is important here is that Bowen was an Afrikan American who studied under Bowne.

Four personalistic principles stand out in King's writings and ministry. These include an emphasis on the existence of a personal God, the dignity and sacredness of all persons, the existence of an objective moral order and corresponding moral laws, freedom, and moral agency. I examine King's personalistic social ethics in chapter 9. In addition I provide extensive treatment of the mutual influence of personalism in his life and work in another book presently being written on the Afrikan American as person. Therefore, rather than proceed here with a discussion on the elements of King's personalism, I turn to a brief consideration of the chief personalistic ideas found in the writing of Bowen and the black liberation theologian J. Deotis Roberts. I also treat these extensively in the manuscript on the Afrikan American as person.

John Wesley Edward Bowen

In 1887 John Wesley Edward Bowen (1855–1933) became the first Afrikan American to earn the Ph.D. degree at Boston University. He was the first Afrikan American academic personalist,[141] having studied with Bowne himself. Indeed, Bowne was still in the objective idealism stage of his movement toward personalism when Bowen earned his seminary degree at Boston University and then entered the doctoral program.

During his first year in the Bachelor of Sacred Theology program (1882–83) Bowen enrolled in Bowne's most popular course[142] at the School of Theology on Theism and Ethics. Bowen kept comprehensive notes from that course,[143] a near verbatim account of an early draft of Bowne's third book, *Philosophy of Theism*, published in 1887.

Although he studied with Bowne during the objective idealism stage, Bowen was unquestionably influenced by Bowne's emphasis on the centrality of person, as well as the person's innate sense of dignity and worth. Both of these ideas are prominent in Bowne's *Studies in Theism* (1879) and *Philosophy of Theism*. Bowne had also published the first edition of *Metaphysics* (1882) by the time Bowen enrolled in his class. This means that Bowen very likely studied this book as well. Indeed, Bowen mentions *Metaphysics* in his notes. Even in this book, with its emphasis on objective idealism, Bowne placed heavy emphasis on the primacy of the self and the need for a unitary being that is the independent ground of all dependent existence.[144] Much of the language that Bowen was introduced to during Bowne's objective idealism phase is very nearly the same language we find in the personalism stage that occurred over twenty years after Bowen's first class with Bowne.

Bowen did not write explicitly on personalism. Yet the influence of Bowne in his early writings is very evident. Bowen devoted much attention to the principle of development—a principle that was central in Bowne's ethics and philosophy of religion. Bowen applied the law of development to religion and modern theology, concluding that "the apprehension of religion is a process of growth depending upon the psychological growth of man."[145]

We see the clearest evidence of Bowne's influence on Bowen in an article he wrote in 1897. In it Bowen defends the idea of blacks' need of higher education. Rejecting the stance of those who argued that they needed only industrial education, Bowen argued persuasively that all theories against the higher education of blacks "were the progeny of prejudice and ignorance."[146]

Bowen referred to those against the higher education of blacks as "the children of the dragon's teeth,"[147] a phrase frequently used by Bowne, following Plato. But Bowne meant something different. He used the phrase to describe those "children of sense" who could not seem to free themselves from total dependence on sense and the idea that the real is that which one can experience through the senses.[148] Yet there is some similarity in the way he and Bowen used the phrase. For both men the phrase referred to those who were captive to sense or outward appearance and were not willing to concede that appearance was but one type of reality (phenomenal), but not the causal or ontological type. Bowen implied this when he summarized the rationale that the children of the dragon's teeth used to support their argument that blacks are inferior beings and are thus incapable of higher education. They based their argument primarily on physical traits observable by the senses.[149] Bowen showed that in less than a generation the children of former slaves "laughed to scorn the logic" of the children of the dragon's teeth as they excelled in higher education. Although Bowen did not mention Bowne in his writings, there are a number of other points at which he used language associated with Bowne's philosophy. This is most clearly evident when he gives the reasons that blacks needed higher education.

For Bowen the goal of education was neither selfhood,[150] nor to make places for men.[151] He assumed the selfhood of blacks, and thus insisted that the aim of education was to develop persons into men and women, who would then be able to occupy important places in society. Bowen did not just argue the centrality of selfhood as such. Because of his and his people's experience of racism he was adamant and forthright in lifting up their selfhood. Like other blacks who would study personalism at Boston University in subsequent years, Bowen did not need personalism to create in him his long-held belief in the dignity and worth of his people and the idea that God is personal. Indeed, he resonated with personalism primarily because it provided for him philosophical grounding for his two basic faith claims, that is, belief in a personal and loving God, and the dignity and sacredness of all persons. Bowen assumed the humanity of blacks. This assumption was especially important since many whites assumed that blacks were at best subhuman. Bowen therefore based his argument that blacks needed higher education "on the basis of humanity":

> Whatever is good for man is good for man...There are two questions in this connection that have been clearly and definitely settled for all time, namely, the humanity of all men and the equal right of all men to the opportunities and blessings of life. The humanity of all men contains its corollary, the brotherhood of all men.[152]

Bowen argued that because blacks have the same basic humanity as other persons, their needs and aspirations are similar. These aspirations should be satisfied not because a person is black or white, however, but because he or she is a person. What warrants respect is not the color of one's skin as such, Bowen argued, but one's humanity. "The Negro is a human personality," he wrote, "and, as such, every attribute within him should be cultured, and every aspiration given free scope."[153]

We also find the influence of Bowne's "decided meliorism" in Bowen's writings. The meliorist believes in steady—not necessarily inevitable— progress. Bowne was confident that there would be positive change and progress in the social order, for example. He also believed such change would come only as a result of human endeavor and cooperation with God. However, he argued that the change comes slowly. Bowen's view was similar. He argued, for example, that the so-called "Negro problem" could not be solved in a day or in a generation.[154] Progress would come if persons worked for it in intentional and decided ways. But Bowen was just as convinced that progress would very likely come slowly.

Also like Bowne, Bowen rejected the deistic view of God, labeling it "an old dead philosophic teaching."[155] His belief that afflictions are disciplinary and educative[156] is also reminiscent of Bowne.[157] Indeed, like Bowne, Bowen did not seem to consider the question of why so much discipline seems to be needed, and why it is not parceled out equally. "The school of adversity is a necessary school to educate us," he said. "It seems to be in the very constitution of affairs that affliction is necessary to bring out our virtues."[158] But again, one wonders why so much adversity is needed.

Bowen's was an individualistic approach to solving social problems. This too was similar to Bowne. Bowen placed emphasis on developing "our moral internal resources,"[159] and on the necessity of beginning with the individual. For example, he said that "it is impossible to raise and educate a race in the mass," and that "all revolutions and improvements must start with individuals."[160] Any effort toward solution to social ills must begin and end with the individual. The emphasis must be on personal character development.

Yet, also like Bowne, Bowen argued that where persons are concerned outward physical appearance means nothing. Rather, "the man within is everything."[161] The implication is that the essence of the person is mind, self-awareness, self-directedness, and so forth. These are more spiritual or mental in nature. However, this implies that the sacred is the inward person, which leaves one wondering whether the body too is sacred, a matter to be taken up in a later chapter.

Regarding the matter of race, Bowen could also say explicitly (and unlike Bowne) that "we belong to each other."[162] He further held that one should not have reverence for a person merely because of skin color.[163] Bowen argued convincingly for a concrete, not abstract, "brotherhood" of all persons.[164] He insisted that blacks are the equals of whites and other groups,[165] and that they should never degrade themselves, no matter what others say or do.[166]

J. Deotis Roberts

J. Deotis Roberts, the black liberation theologian who has written most clearly and appreciatively of personalism, provides an instructive, but brief discussion on personalism in *A Philosophical Introduction to Theology* (1991).[167]

Having studied under the British personalist Herbert H. Farmer, Roberts has a good sense of the meaning of personalism. Unlike an earlier discussion,[168] he now exhibits a more receptive attitude toward Brightman's concept of the finite-infinite God,[169] although he still cannot accept it as his own. He points out that even some of Brightman's colleagues at Boston University found the view to be problematic. In any event, there is no question that Roberts was much influenced by the personalism of Farmer as well as his own study of the personalism of key exponents in the United States such as Brightman.

While Roberts does not frequently cite the term personalism in his work, its basic ideas, for example, the affirmation that conscious person is both the highest intrinsic value and is personal, emphasis on freedom and self-determination, and focus on persons-in-community, can be found in nearly all of his books. And to be sure, none of these is inconsistent with what he had already learned through his upbringing in the black church and his study of Afrikan culture. The four personalistic elements that are prominent in Roberts' work include: the dignity of the whole person, God as personal, freedom and moral agency, and persons-in-community.

DIGNITY OF THE WHOLE PERSON

Roberts contends that because of historical and present-day attempts to undermine and destroy the humanity of Afrikan Americans, it is necessary to begin the theological enterprise by declaring the absolute dignity and sacredness of every Afrikan American. As a theologian, Roberts acknowledges the sanctity and dignity of every person. But inasmuch as his own people have historically and contemporaneously been treated like subhumans, he begins by affirming their absolute dignity and sacredness.[170] The latter terms are significant, for Roberts grounds these theologically. That is, he attributes the humanity, sacredness, and dignity of Afrikan Americans to God. Black dignity, he argues, is God-given.[171] Human dignity, therefore, is fundamental.

Throughout much of his writing Roberts stresses the inherent worth of Afrikan Americans without mentioning the term personalism. Yet there is no question that the theme of the somebodyness or dignity of Afrikan Americans is central in his liberation theology. God and God alone created blacks as "somebody."[172] In addition, and unlike many early personalists, Roberts avoids the tendency to place so much emphasis on the sacredness of the mind, soul, or spirit of persons that the sanctity and dignity of the body is undermined. Afrikan Americans' ordeal during and since the time of American slavery only heightens the necessity of emphasizing the worth of the whole person. For Roberts the whole person—soul and body—is sacred.

> Man in black experience is a creature. He is a physical being in need of the goods and services for a dignified and meaningful life...According to black theology, then, we are to be concerned about our bodily life. We believe in the sanctity of the *soma* (body). The body is worthful in its own right because it is a part of God's creation. The fleshly life of man was in God's creative purpose when he declared it "good" and in his

re-creative purpose when the Word became flesh. Just as the Hebrews viewed man as a whole, body and soul, even so our African forefathers affirmed the unity and wholeness of life. A theological view of man emerging out of the Bible and out of our African religious heritage would not present a division in man's life.[173]

Roberts saw this as a complete denial of the Platonic, Cartesian, and Kantian idealistic influence that caused many Western thinkers to place more emphasis on the worth of the mind than on the body. He knows, as every Afrikan American does, that historically and presently it is not just black psyches that are daily assaulted in this country, but their bodies as well. Interestingly, only since the late 1980s have more recent academic personalists been arguing against the early idealistic tendency to deemphasize the significance of the body[174] as it overemphasized the mind.

Regarding the centrality of the dignity of Afrikan Americans, Roberts tends to be much more anthropocentric in outlook than traditional personalists. But clearly his emphasis is on affirming the dignity and sacredness of black personhood and the need for Afrikan Americans to recapture their lost sense of humanity and worth. This has meant focusing on black self-affirmation, self-love, and self-esteem. Roberts and other black theologians maintain that little is more important among Afrikan Americans than the need to learn again how to love themselves and to appreciate their heritage. This is a particularly important point for young Afrikan Americans today,[175] a point I return to in the last chapter.

God as Personal

A second prominent feature in Roberts' work is his contention that God is thoroughly personal. Thus he writes of the humanity of God,[176] the goodness of God,[177] God as Suffering Servant,[178] God who shares the suffering of the oppressed,[179] and the love-wrath of God.[180] The God of Roberts is one who is caring and loving. God "knows each one of us intimately," so much so that God is concerned to know and respond accordingly to all that happens to us in the world. God is love and goodness and is "all-powerful."[181] God is both transcendent and immanent. That God "knows each one of us intimately" suggests Roberts' belief in the individuality and uniqueness of every person, as well as the belief that human persons and God can fellowship together by virtue of their kinship with each other. Intellectually this is a position that is little different from that of traditional theism and the Bowne form of personalism. Indeed, Knudson himself has written:

> To the believer in Christ the personality both of God and man was a matter of unique and vital concern. For him God was in his essential nature a personal Being, a Being with whom he could hold fellowship, and the individual man was a being of infinite worth, an end in himself. These convictions constituted the very breath of his spiritual life...[182]

It may be said that historically Afrikan Americans have taken this double emphasis on a personal God and the dignity of human persons much more seriously in their concrete living than some of those who have written most on the philosophy of personalism. The reason why Afrikan Americans resonate more toward personalism than other metaphysical outlooks is because it focuses on God as the Supreme Personal Being who cares about them. Indeed, as can be seen in the work of Roberts, Afrikan Americans have historically held a view of God that is similar to the theistic absolutism of Bowne.

Since Roberts grounds humanity and human dignity in God and maintains that God is personal, this implies his belief—not different from that of personalists—that only God is fully and perfectly personal. Bowne, following Lotze, held that "proper personality is possible only to the Absolute."[183] Human persons are dependent upon the Divine Person, and as such are always limited and incomplete in every sense.

Roberts maintains that the person is a unitary being. But he means more than the unity of the individual person. Influenced by Afrikan traditional thought, he also means that persons must be addressed in both their personal and social dimensions. Persons can truly achieve wholeness and unity only within the context of the community.[184] This is essentially Brightman's view as well.[185] I return to this communal emphasis of person subsequently.

That Roberts maintains that God is a perfectly unitary being, thoroughly spiritual, and possesses absolute power suggests that his thinking about God is very similar to that of Bowne. There is no question that with the exception of a small number, Afrikan American religious thinkers have generally adhered to the idea that God is omnipotent. In this regard their theism is similar to Bowne's.

FREEDOM AND MORAL AGENCY

Another principle that is central in the work of Roberts' personalism is human freedom and moral agency. Much influenced by his own religious background and Christian existentialists like Blaise Pascal, Søren Kierkegaard, and Paul Tillich, Roberts lifts up the importance of freedom and moral agency. Consequently, he argues that there is much that happens in the world that the clear-thinking person simply cannot hold God responsible for.

In the deepest metaphysical sense God is ultimately responsible for all that happens in the world. This is the extent of personalism's pantheism, that is, that God is responsible for all that happens in the world only in the causal sense. However, on the ethical plane it is not God or some other powerful being, for example, Satan, but we humans who are responsible for moral wrongdoing in the world. This is so because we are self-determined beings who are free within limits to make choices. Certain choices lead to responsible living together in God's world, while others necessarily lead to irresponsible behavior and destruction of person-enhancing and community-making possibilities. For Roberts God has created persons in freedom, and therefore it is we, not God, who make choices for which we alone are responsible. Although created persons are finite and dependent beings, they are still free to make choices, and must accept responsibility for them.[186] Quick to call whites to responsibility for slavery, racism, and misuse of power on a massive scale, Roberts is just as quick to admonish Afrikan Americans not only to be more self-determined, but to accept responsibility for their actions.

NOT PERSONS, BUT PERSONS-IN-COMMUNITY

Brightman contends that personality is "a conscious unity of self-experience," or "a unitary and complex whole."[187] In a fuller discussion he defines personality as "a complex but self-identifying, active, selective, feeling, sensing, developing experience..."[188] But Brightman also stressed the communal or relational aspects of person. It will be recalled that personalism maintains that reality is fundamentally social. The universe is a society or community of interacting and intercommunicating selves and persons. From the time of Bowne there has been evidence in personalism of the fundamental sociality of reality. However, it was students of Brightman, for example, Muelder and DeWolf, who made the communal element central in their personalism. This idea is examined more extensively in chapter 4.

Historically Afrikan Americans have been a communal or family-oriented people. Although there is an emphasis on the personal in Afrikan American experience, just as in personalism, in neither case does personal mean individual or individualistic. This is another way of saying that one cannot truly be an individual or person apart from some group or community. This is what Francis J. McConnell was getting at in *Personal Christianity*. He affirmed both the individuality of persons and their inextricable mutual interrelatedness. McConnell wrote that in Christianity the personal must be understood as "not the individual alone but persons set in relation to one another, which relations are as much a fact as is the separate existence of the individuals."[189] Nels F. S. Ferré (a student of Brightman's) stressed the social or communal nature of persons and the impossibility of getting an accurate sense of individual persons apart from their total social context or community.[190] So once again we see a strong correlation between basic personalistic ideas and the thought of Roberts and other black liberation theologians. Roberts asserts that one simply cannot understand the individual person apart from his or her social context or group. "In order for an individual to be personal, he must act from within some group. Individuals are persons in society,"[191] writes Roberts.

Roberts uses the term persons-in-community to make his point about the social or communal nature of the individual person.[192] As far as I can tell, this is a term that was popularized and systematically developed by Walter G. Muelder.[193] Roberts appropriated the term to highlight the idea that every person is a "psychosocial" being, which means for him that one's self-understanding is always bound up with his social context. He draws out the meaning when he relates this idea to those who are among the systematically oppressed. "Where humans are oppressed, it may well be that social considerations are prior to questions regarding the self. For most individuals there can be no personal fulfillment where the social environment is too hostile."[194] For Roberts community implies more than a group that is functional and works toward the achievement of certain agreed-upon goals. Perhaps even more important is the "affective" character of community, which implies a common "sharing and caring based upon fellow feeling and deep fellowship. *Ujamaa*, 'togetherness,' 'familyhood,' is descriptive of community."[195]

Womanists agree with much that Roberts and other black liberation theologians hold true.[196] The most exceptional and significant difference, however, is that womanists emphasize the dignity and worth of black women in a way and to a degree that has not been done before. Rudiments of the womanist movement antedate the nineteenth century. Womanist thought might also be considered a type of personalism because of the conception of God put forth, the strong emphasis on the dignity of persons, their essential communality, and because of the focus on freedom and self-determination among black women of Afrikan descent.

In addition to the discussion of the more typical types of personalism, it may be helpful to consider explicitly some of the most important principles that inhere in thoroughgoing personalism. A number of these have been mentioned or implied in the eight types of personalism examined. A more explicit consideration of some of the chief traits of thoroughgoing personalism will further clarify the foundation of the subsequent discussions on the nature of person, doctrine of God, and personalistic ethics.

Key Tenets of Personalism

There are several key emphases in theistic personalism that should be more explicitly identified and discussed. When taken together these serve as criteria for determining whether a particular type of personalism under consideration is the most or least typical. Without question we find that each of the following elements are present in the Bowne type of personalism, as well as the realistic personalism of Georgia Harkness. Howison's ethical personalism lacks the element of creationism. Since his personal idealism was not fully developed systematically, we do not find a clear statement on the coherence test of truth or on the synoptic-analytic method. These latter are also missing in Afrikan American personalism, essentially because it has never been systematically developed. Nor do we see in Afrikan American personalism a clear statement as to whether its epistemology is activistic and dualistic. However, the other seven tenets are present.

First, personalism is that philosophy for which person is central both metaphysically and ethically. This means that the Supreme Reality is both personal and Creator. (Person or personal is defined in the next chapter.) It means, further, that because the Supreme Person chooses or wills to create persons, they are of infinite value to the Creator and thus, as a matter of course, should be respected and treated like the intrinsically and infinitely valuable beings they are. This latter point is important. John Wright Buckham maintains that the aspect of personalism "easiest to assent to, yet hardest to realize and live up to, and into, is that belief in the worth of every human self which is essential to faith in personal values."[197] Indeed, some early personalists, for example, Knudson, found it difficult to "live up to, and into" the idea of the dignity and sanctity of blacks. Furthermore, as previously observed, there is even some question as to just where the two chief progenitors of personalism—Bowne and Howison—stood on this matter, inasmuch as neither expressly wrote about blacks' predicament in this country. Any thoroughgoing personalism must not only assert the dignity of a particular group, but of all persons. But in addition, it has been maintained throughout that, at its absolute best, the Bowne type of personalism is fundamentally a way of life, a way of living together with all persons and the rest of creation. What this must mean for a consistent, thoroughgoing personalism is that all persons have inherent, inviolable dignity and sacredness, or none do. This claim can be made because personalism is essentially theistic and maintains that there is one Supreme Person (God) who is creator and sustainer of all. Or as Berkeley and Bowne liked to say, God is that being in whom all persons, all life forms, live and move and have their existence.

Second, personalism is fundamentally idealistic. It contends that all reality is of the nature of mind or spirit. This smacks of Berkeleian immaterialism. That is, according to personalism the real is personal or an aspect or process of some self or person. Although both persons and nature exist, there is but one ultimate order or realm. The objects of nature are aspects or forms of spirit. This is personalism's qualitative monism. Matter and spirit are both aspects of a single unitary process, namely the process of personal will. The eternal reality in the universe is personal. Matter, energy, and their laws are but functions of that reality. They are the result of the energizing of the divine thought and will.

Third, personalism is thoroughly theistic. Proponents believe in a personal God who is the Creator and Sustainer of all of creation. God is both the Creator and that toward which all persons should aim or aspire. God is both efficient and final cause. (Howison maintained that God is only final cause. Thoroughgoing personalism holds that God is both creator and final cause.) Because God is personal, the religious not only pray to God, but expect God to respond to their prayers. This can only be expected of an intelligent, personal being. In personalism we find metaphysical grounding for the biblical belief that in God we live and move and have our being. Indeed, it is only this that personalists have in mind when they refer to God as transcendent. This personal God is infinitely loving, caring, responsive, active, righteous, and just.

Fourth, personalism is creationist. Unlike some other types, for example, the atheistic personalism of John M. E. McTaggart and the teleological personalism of George H. Howison, typical personalism views God as the Creator, and therefore as first cause. Creationism answers the question of how persons enter existence, as well as why they, not the Creator, are responsible for moral evil. Creationism also answers the question of why persons feel such a deep sense of dependence on something greater than they. Creation is a free act of God's will, which is never static, but dynamic. In addition, unlike pantheistic and (some) absolutistic types of personalisms, created persons are not mere sparks or modes of God. These types do not allow the degree of separateness or relative independence needed for human freedom and the corresponding moral responsibility.

Fifth, in addition to viewing all reality as personal, personalism is freedomistic, a point that has been mentioned several times. In fact, the two touchstones of personalism are person and freedom. All being is both personal and free. To be is to be free and to act or have the potential to do so (although it is more than this!). Indeed, to be free is what it means to be a person; to be a person is to be free. This metaphysical claim has important implications for the ethical and political freedom of persons in the world, a point that will be taken up in the discussion on personalistic ethics.

According to personalism we never find being without freedom. That is, being is not first created, and then freedom added to it. The nature of reality itself is freedom. This implies that the Creator does not create persons and then give them freedom. If being is characterized by freedom, as personalism maintains, it seems reasonable to say that persons are actually created *in* freedom. This means that creation and freedom are one rather than two separate acts.

Freedom also has speculative significance, since without it we could not solve the problem of error, or even distinguish between truth and error. Bowne was among the first of his generation to consider seriously the importance of freedom for knowledge, truth, and the dependability or trustworthiness of reason. Discussions about freedom generally focus on ethical considerations. However, Bowne could see that without freedom both morality and reason itself would be "shipwrecked," thereby making moral responsibility and everything else impossible. Bowne reasoned that if we assume that mind is made for truth and that reason is trustworthy, the only way we can explain the fact of error is by appealing to freedom. However, that the mind is made for truth, and reason can be trusted, does not guarantee that persons will always seek truth. There must be a determination or intention on the part of persons to attain truth. That is, one must exercise his or her freedom to act in accord with reason or not. But in either case freedom is a significant factor. One can choose to trust reason, or not. Error results when persons choose against reason and truth.

Sixth, personalism is empirical in the deepest sense. As noted in the discussion on point of departure, personalists always begin with self-experience, and in the final analysis that is where they return. In the quest for truth and knowledge personalists always begin with the raw, uninterpreted data of experience—all experience relevant to a given problem. This is radical empiricism (a term popularized by William James).

By definition and method personalists strive to include all the facts of experience and to bring them before the supreme court of reason. The place to begin is with what is known most immediately, namely, self-experience. For example, everything we know about other persons, the world, and God is arrived at by beginning with experience of the self. Only then do we use the method of inference and analogy to arrive at most reasonable hypotheses about those things. Georgia Harkness helps us on this point.

> Epistemologically, we have no other route to travel except the route which begins in human experience. From what we know about man, viewed broadly, we must infer what we can about God. Some analogical reasoning is legitimate, provided we know where to draw the line against pushing the analogy beyond the evidence. Yet our knowledge could not go from man to God unless creation were from God to man. Metaphysically, God has made man akin to himself.[198]

Harkness means that created persons could not begin with self-experience and ultimately know what they can know about God had God not created them in such a way that there is enough likeness and kinship between them that they are able to get in touch with the universe and the Creator. We can get in touch with God as much as we can because we, like our ultimate reality (God), have thought capability. It has already been established that personalism holds that reality is of the nature of thought, mind, or active intelligence. This is what created persons have in common with God. And for all we know this might not be the only thing we have in common with God, and therefore may not be the only way we and God can communicate.

At any rate, Harkness rightly cautions that in our bid to gain knowledge of ultimate reality we need to be careful when we use the analogical method. We can only go so far in ascribing characteristics to God based on human analogy. For example, on analogy with human persons we can say that God, too, is personal. But we would be mistaken if we conclude that this is all that God is, or that we know all there is to know about what it means to be personal, especially as it applies to God. God may be, indeed very likely is, much more than the personal God we think we know. In a real sense we do not have adequate language to fully describe God.

Seventh, personalism's criterion of truth is coherence. We cannot know absolutely certain truths. That is, truth, finally, is not demonstrable in the absolutely logical sense. At best we can hope to obtain degrees of probable truth that are most coherently interpreted. An extensive discussion of the coherence criterion is undertaken in chapter 5.

Eighth, the method of personalism is the synoptic-analytic method, also taken up more extensively in chapter 5. Personalists seek to be both comprehensive in the inclusion of data, and analytic in the sense that they endeavor to analyze each part, while trying to determine the relation of each to the other, and finally how each is related to the whole (synopsis).

Ninth, personalistic epistemology (theory of knowledge) is activistic and dualistic. This means that the mind is not just the Lockean passive *tabula rasa* or blank sheet on which sense data are written. Instead, the mind receives or takes in data, for example, sensations, but it is also active and creative. The mind acts on what is taken in. In addition, the mind-object relation is dualistic in the sense that my idea of an object and the object itself are not completely identical, although there is a relation between them. This too will be treated in more detail later.

The tenth and final tenet to be considered is that personalism conceives of reality as through and through social, relational, or communal. The universe is a society of selves and persons who interact and are united by the will of God. That the union between persons and God is through the divine will means that persons are not modes of God, and thus retain their individuality. Persons are not made out of God, but are created by God. In personalism, social categories are fundamental and ultimate. From the time of conception to the time of death the individual never experiences self in total isolation. Rather, the self always experiences something that it did not invent or create, but finds or receives through "interaction and communication with other persons."[199]

These are some of the basic traits of personalism. Each warrants much more sustained attention. Although several of these tenets are treated more extensively in later chapters, there is no question that a more thorough examination would be instructive. Because this is an introductory text, such an effort must be pursued in another context.

Conclusion

I have in this and the previous chapter discussed a total of eight types of personalism, moving from the most abstract and least typical to the most concrete, theistic type. The movement has been from atheistic, pantheistic, absolutistic, relativistic, teleological, realistic, theistic, and Afrikan American.[200] The last three types have more in common than they have differences.

By considering a variety of personalisms I have shown how they are limited in relation to the Bownean type. But in addition, I have discussed some of the limitations of Bownean personalism. A more highly social activist oriented personalism, the Afrikan American type, is characterized first and foremost by a strong emphasis on the absolute sanctity and dignity of persons—especially systematically bruised and beaten persons, for example, blacks. All else, including more popular environmental concerns among many liberal and progressive individuals, is secondary. This does not mean, however, that nonhuman life forms are without intrinsic value and thus do not warrant respect. But it does mean that because of the tendency of European Americans and far too many Afrikan Americans to exhibit a low estimate of the value and worth of black personhood, the focus must remain on the personalistic emphasis on the centrality and worth of persons as such. The reason for this is that the Supreme Person (God) has willingly and lovingly called persons into existence and has implanted in every single one a sense of infinite worth and value. Every person has inestimable value to God and, precisely for this reason, ought to be treated with tenderness and respect. Christian theists at their best have believed that God calls for righteousness and justice among persons and has a special concern for the well-being of the systematically bruised and downtrodden.

Now that we have a sense of the origin, meaning, types, and chief traits of personalism, we are better positioned to consider what personalists mean by personality and person. This is important for understanding both the doctrine of God and ethics in personalism. Therefore, I focus next on the idea of person as the chief explanatory principle, and the chief traits of both human and divine person (chapter 4), and finally method and criterion of truth (chapter 5).

Person: The Key to Reality

To this point I have tried to guard against using the terms person and personality interchangeably, although early personalists used them in this way. Indeed, Brightman often did this.[1] The problem is that using the terms interchangeably can be confusing. The reason is quite simple. A personality is actually what a person develops and experiences, and thus they are not the same. And yet, compounding the problem, Brightman frequently used the same definition for personality, person, and personal self.[2] Although he finally conceded that it is better not to use the terms interchangeably,[3] he sometimes did so anyway.

For our purpose I want to continue to use person in place of personality. Therefore, unlike many early personalists, when I use the term personality the reference will not be to a metaphysical principle, but to that which a person makes or develops. A person develops, makes, or learns a personality. Peter A. Bertocci is explicit about the differences between person and personality:

> A personality is learned as a person interacts with other persons. More exactly, a person's personality is his more or less systematic mode of response to himself, to others, and to his total environment in the light of what he believes them to be, and what they actually are.[4]

In a 1950 essay Bertocci wrote:

> Brightman uses the words personality and person interchangeably following traditional philosophical usage. But in a day in which the word "personality" is a dominant concept in psychology, the reader who comes to philosophy with a psychological background will be unnecessarily confused. For in every psychological analysis, personality is basically the product of learning. The person, however, for Brightman and for personal idealism, is the learner; a person develops a personality; personhood is not acquired but original, given.[5]

A person's personality is his or her own unique adjustment and development to his or her own nature and surroundings. The definition that Brightman sometimes gave for personality is one that Bertocci would use for person.

> A personality is a complex but self-identifying, active, selective, feeling, sensing, developing experience, which remembers its past (in part), plans for its future, interacts with its subconscious processes, its bodily organism, and its natural and social environment, and is able to judge and guide itself and its objects by rational and ideal standards.[6]

The experiences of sensing, remembering (in part), imagining, perceiving, judging or thinking, feeling, emoting, ought-ing, and willing are activity-potentials. In this regard Bertocci wrote:

> We must not miss the significance of remembering, for it points to an inexpressibly important fact. Without remembering, the unity of experience would be impossible as we "flit" from moment to moment; without it no man can maintain his self-identity as he grows from infancy onward. Because he can remember, a man can imaginatively visualize what may be but is not yet, and thus he may improve his adjustment.[7]

This is quite different from what he says about personality, namely, that it "is our own more or less unified pattern of adjustment, much of which is hidden from observers, and some of which we ourselves are not aware of."[8] However, the person, with its many activity-potentials, represents a more permanent personal structure characteristic of all persons. Person is given, original, not learned or acquired. Personality, on the other hand, is that aspect of the person that is elastic, and therefore changes and develops. Personality is made, not given. It is for this reason that Bertocci was apprehensive about applying the term personality to God. For him, God is the Supreme Person. I discuss the significance of this terminology in more detail in the personalistic views on God in later chapters.

To Be Is to Act

Personalism contends that being is through and through causal and active. It therefore rejects all notions of lumpish or material being, substituting instead the idea of a world of energy or of causality. It is not being that actually exists, for being as such is an abstraction. Rather, what exists are things or agents. These are the only realities. Influenced both by the physics of his day and the Leibnitzian theory that reality is active, Bowne clarified the emerging personalist view as he sought to show that no object—including inanimate ones—is without activity.

> Underneath the dead rest which the unaided senses show, science discerns the most complex and constant activity. Every thing, even the dead stone and resting clod, is seen to stand in the most manifold relations of action and reaction to every other thing.
>
> …Further, physics makes it plain that things as they appear are not the true subjects of natural activities. Every appearing thing is a function of things which do not appear; and these non-appearing things are the true subjects…Physics further teaches that solidity also is not an ultimate quality of the elements, but is the outcome of their attractions and repulsions…Hence the only solidity of which we know any thing is based upon a dynamism back of it…[9]

At the core of every object is some form of activity or reaction to activity. This activity is constant; unending. Even the dead body that is buried is eventually transformed, returns to earth, and helps give birth to new forms of plant and animal life, which in turn feeds human beings, and the process continues.

The point to be emphasized is that being and activity are inseparable. Activity is coexistent with being.[10] We know of no instance in which being or activity antedates the other. The fundamental nature of being is to act. To be is to act, or to be acted upon.[11] In this, personalism goes beyond Berkeley, who held that to be is to be perceived, as if the object perceived has no activity. By holding that all being is active or causal Bowne believed he was saved from Berkeley.[12] For personalism only that which acts has existence. Accordingly, power of action is the most distinctive feature of being.[13] Being is not a thing, object, or lump that we can picture. Rather, it is "self-centered activity." All being, therefore, is active or processive. Activity penetrates to the very core of being. The passivity of matter is only appearance. The elements of which it consists are perpetually active. "Such rest and inaction as we observe among the objects of experience are but the resultant of an underlying dynamism."[14]

This activity or energy is not picturable. We should not expect to picture fundamental reality, since it is characterized as "concrete and definite principles of action."[15] Reality is of the nature of thought, and therefore can only be experienced and thought. That is, only mind or thought can grasp mind or thought. To perceive another's thought, I must think it. If reality is of the nature of thought I can know this only because I can think it, that is, because I too am of the nature of mind or thought. Knowledge always implies a thinker at both ends of the process. Bowne put it thus: "As speech implies a mind at both ends of the process, so knowledge under our human conditions equally implies a mind at both ends."[16] Thought and reality (things) must have the same laws if there is to be any communication at all between them. "Thought can only speak its own language, and things must be forever unknowable by us unless they also speak thought language; that is, unless they are cast in the forms and molds of thought."[17] We are in trouble unless we assume that the whole of reality is essentially a thought world (whatever else it may or may not be), or "a world which roots in and expresses thought."[18]

Fundamental reality is not simply mind or thought. It is also will or agent. From a theological standpoint we may say that the basic reality is not just a be-er (thought) but a do-er (will). Furthermore, the only be-er that means anything is a do-er. It is not enough to simply know that God is, and that God is thought. God is also active. Therefore, the world is not just idea (as in absolute idealism). Rather, it is idea *plus* act or deed. The world, for personalism, is not merely an idea in God's mind. It is also a form of activity in God's will. The world is both thought and deed.[19] It "is essentially a going forth of divine causality under the forms of space and time, and in accordance with a rational plan." As a be-er, God is eternally active. "The result of God's activity is the phenomenal world...which exists in unpicturable dependence upon the divine will..."[20] It is in the phenomenal world, caused by God's activity, that created persons meet and act together, sometimes with, and too often against, each other.

Personalism's Conception of Reality

Bowne's assertion that he was "a Personalist, the first of the clan in any thoroughgoing sense" was a powerful and suggestive one. For it distinguished his philosophical system from all existing ones. Indeed, for Bowne, personalism was a method, a system that had reached its own conclusions based on one fundamental principle—"the self-sufficiency of personality."[21] We have seen that personalists do not deny that there are other types of personalisms. However, their claim is that the Bowne type is the true, original, or most typical form.

Person is the central interpretive principle. It is "the master principle," or the key to solving all philosophical and social problems[22] as far as human persons can solve them. The purpose, of course, is to be as thoroughgoing as possible in applying this key to philosophy and the problems of life.

All personalists agree that in person we find our best clue to the nature of reality, the universe, and the relationship between these created persons and the rest of creation. Thus the famous phrase "Personality is the key to reality."[23] This phrase does not point to any individual human person, but to the objective structure of reality itself. That is, the phrase "Personality is the key to reality" is a metaphysical statement. It points to the idea that the real is personal or some self or selves. Reality is personal. As a metaphysical principle, person is not identical to the human person, "however true it may be that the personalistic principle is exemplified in human personality."[24] In the human person we find our chief clues to the meaning of the phrase "Personality is the key to reality." This makes sense when we remember that creation is from God to the created, and not from the latter to God. As the ultimate reality, God (Supreme Mind) has created persons in such a way that they have in themselves clues to the meaning of person as metaphysical principle. Human persons can know God (Mind) because they are minds.

Person is the "category of categories." It is that principle without which no other principle matters or can be explained. It is that principle that is capable of explaining every principle but itself.

All other categories and first principles presuppose and require person in order to be or be experienced. Metaphysically person is both the chief category and the one that provides us with clues to ultimate reality.[25] This is not to say that other principles would not exist without person. They might very well exist. But even if they do exist in the absence of person, what difference would it make, and to whom? For how would we know one way or the other? And yet the claim that person is the chief category should not be taken to mean that personalism maintains that there are absolutely no other forms of intelligence in the universe that may be higher than that possessed by created persons. There is, as far as we know, no logical reason to suppose that this cannot be the case. However, we are less certain as to how empirically adequate is the possibility of the existence of such beings. So until there is sufficient empirical evidence to the contrary, it is reasonable to hold that person, not some "higher" principle, is the key to reality and the solution to the fundamental problems of both philosophy and life. We learned from Bowne's transcendental empiricism that it is person that interprets and gives meaning to the categories of thought. These do not explain intelligence or mind, but are explained by it. Ontology, therefore, is interpreted from the side of person rather than the reverse. If the fundamental problem connected with reality centers on how it combines unity with diversity, change with identity, freedom with determinism, and so on, we may conclude that these are all solved through the category of person. It is through self-experience or person that we get our ideas of unity, diversity, change, identity, freedom, and determinism. "In free intelligence itself, which is the source of all the categories, we have at once their living embodiment and their own adequate explanation."[26] Person is the only basis of change in permanence, our only direct knowledge of the union of change and permanence, identity and diversity.[27]

We get our idea of unity and volitional causality from person as well. Can we know anything at all about the world without reference to free, active intelligence? We can know whatever is knowable about reality only through person. Human persons may be incapable of knowing reality perfectly, but since we are akin to the universe, that is, since we and the universe are of the nature of thought or mind, we can, through reason and will, know what we can know about reality. There is a close relation between thought and reality, although these are not identical. To be sure, reality is both other, and more, than thought. Reality is deeper and richer than thought. "Between the two there is an 'indefinable,' an 'ineffable' difference. Reality is deed as well as idea. But how it is constituted we do not know…There is about reality a mystery that the human mind can never penetrate."[28] Because mind or thought is akin to reality it is comprehensible to human persons. However, we must not expect thought and reality ever to be identical. There is no absolute one-to-one correspondence between my thoughts about reality and reality itself. No thought I may have about God, for example, may be said to be perfectly equated with God.

Person Is Essentially Theomorphic

Human persons do not have within themselves the ground of their being. Instead they are dependent upon the intrinsically unitary One. Therefore, they "can be properly understood or comprehended only from the side of the infinite."[29] They get their most important clues to what it means to be a person from themselves. And yet they more nearly approximate what it means to be a person when they examine what this must mean when applied to the Supreme Reality, or God.

The topic now under consideration is intended to get at the metaphysical or philosophical meaning of person. The concern is to determine whether once we free person (as a metaphysical category) of all traits and limitations that are commonly associated with human beings (e.g., the inability to be perfectly and always self-determining, conscious and self-conscious, and rational), we are left with a concept of person that continues to give place both to the scientific data on the subject and that provides a fundamental first principle for interpreting all of reality. When personalists say that person is the key to reality they do not mean person in the strictly anthropomorphic sense. Nor do they mean that the key to reality is to be found in any specific human person that may be the subject of the psychologist. Likewise, personalists do not advocate the view that the universe or reality is perfectly mirrored in the human person.

In what sense can it be said that we find in the human person clues to objective reality? In order to determine the true essence of person (as a metaphysical category) we need to remove all of the limitations that are peculiar to the human person. And yet we are cautioned to remember that some of these "limitations" are characteristics that are germane to what it means to be human persons, and therefore are necessary for their being in this world. But as a basic metaphysical category we need to know just what would be the nature of person were it possible to free it of basic human traits. Personalism maintains that when we have done this we can truly say that in person we have a fundamental first principle of reality.

Brightman endeavored to get at this in the following way:

> Remove desire for victory in war, but leave desire for the highest and best; remove the particular local environment of this or that man's experience, but leave the power to interact with any environment; remove the memories of this man's particular weaknesses and sins, but leave memory as the unifying power binding past and present; remove petty and selfish purposes, but leave purpose as the movement of reality into the future; remove the traits of my partly-integrated personality, but leave the experience of the unity of consciousness as indivisible wholeness—and one then has in personality a clue to universal being, a genuine first principle.[30]

When the more human characteristics are removed, for example, less noble desires and purposes, we are left with a view of person of which it is reasonable to say that this is what is meant when the claim is made that human persons are created "in the image of God." In this sense we may say that the human person is essentially theomorphic. Brightman points out that we think of space, time, and mathematics as theomorphic (not anthropomorphic), even though they are found in human experience. Inasmuch as these are not thought to be purely anthropomorphic despite being found in human persons, Brightman wondered whether it is likewise possible that person is "a universal and cosmic principle" found in created persons. And further:

> [I]s it not at least equally possible that God made man in his own image, and that man is therefore theomorphic, cosmomorphic? To deny any clues to objective reality within man is to deny all science and all objective knowledge. The real issue is whether personality itself is such a clue.[31]

The answer is that we do find in the human person clues to the meaning of objective reality. If God creates persons in God's image, there must be in them clues about the nature of ultimate reality, that is, God, as well as the rational equipment to discern these clues. We can know what we can about God because we are created in God's image. God has made us akin to Godself. Georgia Harkness was instructive when she said that "our knowledge could not go from man to God unless creation were from God to man."[32] God created us to know Godself.

The causal principle involved in the existence of the human person is the Supreme Person. What is needed now is to define person—human and divine—and discuss some of its chief traits. What does it mean to be a person? That is, what are the traits that all persons—human and divine—share in common, and what are the differences?

Definition and Essential Traits of Person

Personalism distinguishes between self and person. It acknowledges the existence of many levels of selves and persons, ranging from the lowly paramecium to the supreme cosmic self or person—God. Implicit in this is the idea that all selves and persons have intrinsic worth, inasmuch as God is considered their fundamental cause. They have intrinsic worth because God thoughtfully and willingly creates and sustains them.

A self, according to personalism, is any conscious being, however simple or complex. A person, on the other hand, is a special kind of self. That is, a person is a self that is not only conscious, but is at least potentially self-conscious, rational, self-directed, and capable of establishing and striving toward the achievement of ideal value. A person is self-aware and can reflect on what that means. One need not exhibit these characteristics in every waking moment. The key is that to be deemed a person the self must at least exhibit periodically the potential of being self-reflective, self-aware, and capable of evaluating and assessing goals.[33] Indeed, it may be more reasonable to say that a person is any member of a species wherein the species has been created with the potential to be self-reflective, self-aware, and capable of achieving ideal value. In the most fundamental sense these are characteristics of the human species. And yet when we get down to specific cases we may wonder, for example, whether the severely mentally challenged are persons. This raises the issue of how they should be treated. What needs to be remembered is that a being given birth by a human being is a human being, no matter how severely mentally challenged. The intention of the Creator is that such a one be a "normal" human being, whether it is or not. This raises the theodicy issue. But since the loving Creator-God is always involved in the creative act we can say that it is God's intention that such a one be "normal." Indeed, part of the way personalism characterizes what it means to be a person has left it open to the criticism that we can be selective about who is a person and who is not. Indeed, as we shall see later, Knudson, and at one point even Brightman, made a major error when considering this very subject. For our purpose suffice it to say that it is God's intention that those given birth by human beings be persons in the fullest sense. Therefore, every human being is potentially a person. That some are severely mentally challenged does not detract from this. But as indicated previously, it does raise the issue of the problem of evil, since God intends for all humans to be persons. This means that even the severely mentally challenged possess infinite dignity because they are created by God. And if we say as I do (following Paul Taylor) that every conscious self is a moral subject to whom duties and responsibilities are owed, especially by moral subjects who are also moral agents by virtue of their level of rational and emotional maturity, we then close the door to the notion that certain human beings, for example, the severely mentally challenged, may be treated as if they are less than persons. In addition, if we remember that one of the key traits of a person is his or her ability to communicate (and not necessarily and always verbally or in other traditional ways), this makes it more difficult to easily deny personhood to the severely mentally challenged and others because they are different in some way from others. I return to this subject in chapter 8.

Brightman and Bertocci did more than most early personalists to clarify the meaning of self and person. In 1940 Brightman surmised that based on known evidence and his own definition of what it means to be a person, there is little reason to deny that certain animals, for example, pigs, dogs, apes, and horses, are at least "elementary persons."[34] That human persons cannot imagine what consciousness would be like to these animals is not evidence against the claim that they may have person-like qualities. But clearly the focus in personalism has always been on unraveling the mysteries of the human and divine person. Although this may raise concerns for some environmentalists, I wonder whether human persons will ever be able to consistently respect the inherent dignity of nonhuman life forms as long as we disregard the dignity of human beings. The most militant and consistent personalism would require that persons, that is, moral agents, respect all life forms because all possess inherent dignity. And yet historically personalism has focused on what has been considered the highest intrinsic value, namely, the human person. This has been its most distinguishing feature. Without implying that humans should have license to disregard the worth of other life forms until we learn how to care for and respect human life, it is quite consistent with the personalist framework to say that persons have much to do in the area of respecting human dignity.

What are some traits of the most minimal or lowest-level self? In the literature on personalism we find a number of chief characteristics. Brightman identifies several of these. Every self—from lowest to highest—is characterized by at least the following:

1. Self-experience. Every self is a complex unity of consciousness and experiences itself as such. "Every item of consciousness is owned, and belongs to a whole." This means that every self not only has or experiences certain activity-potentials, for example, wanting, but actually is its activity-potentials.

2. Qualia. Every self experiences "distinguishable qualities," for example, sense qualities, qualities of feeling. (Qualia are frequently conceived as universal essences, e.g., redness, hardness, sourness.)

3. Time and space. Inasmuch as the world is one of change, every self "must necessarily experience time." It will be recalled that Bowne and Knudson, much influenced by Kant on the point, maintained that God (the Supreme Self) is exempt from this, that is, is not affected by time. In addition, there is a high probability that all selves experience space awareness.

4. Transcendence of time and space. Even the most minimal self is affected by time and has space consciousness. But it also transcends time as a result of its complexity and memory (however dim). There is also high probability that the minimal self transcends space by its ability to aim at spaces beyond itself and by its nonspatial experiences, for example, its experience of itself as a complex unity.

5. Process and conation. Every self constantly changes and is affected by change. In addition, every self strives toward ends (conation). Brightman holds that "to be a self is to experience a desire for future experience, if only the eating of food and the continuance of life."

6. Awareness of meaning. This may be at the vaguest, most elementary level for the least-developed self, but that this self "treats its experiences as signs of further experience" implies an awareness of meaning. This awareness does not necessarily imply self-reflective consciousness, however. To feel conation (the sense of striving toward an end) implies reference to an object beyond the self. "Sophisticated as it may sound," writes Brightman, "the humblest paramecium experiences objective reference in every one of its pursuits and avoidances. If only by 'animal faith,' it reaches beyond itself to something 'meant' whenever it darts toward food."

7. Response to environment. Every self lives in, and is constantly being affected by, an environment. However, since the minimal self does not likely possess awareness of causal relationships and rational potential, it undoubtedly is unable to distinguish between itself and its environment. But it does have an environment that affects it, and it responds, if only instinctually.

8. Privacy. Every self experiences only itself directly. This is the only sense in which Leibnitz's view that "the monads have no windows" makes sense to personalists. This means that what they experience only they can experience and know directly. For nothing outside them can even peer in to see what they are experiencing. For they have no windows! But since the minimal self is devoid of reasoning processes it very possibly is not aware of the trait of privacy and what it means anyway.[35]

But what do we find when we consider the chief traits of that special self known as the person? In general we discover that the previous eight traits of the minimal self are developed to a much higher level.

1. Self-experience is far more complex and highly organized. There is a much greater degree of recognition of what is experienced and the nature of it. In addition, memory of the past and anticipation of the future play a much larger role.

2. New qualia (qualities) beyond mere sensations and general feelings emerge in the person. For example, feelings of moral and religious obligation arise, as well as aesthetic appreciation. One might say, then, that a person is a being who both has moral, religious, and aesthetic experiences and recognizes them as such. A person is a being who can worship. Moral and religious obligation are recognizable by such a being as "imperative norms."

3. Experience of time and space is also more highly developed and extended. There is reflective awareness of temporal and spatial experience. (Again, remember that there is no unanimity of thought in personalism regarding time and the Supreme Person. Bowne and Knudson held to a nontemporal view of God, that is, that God is neither in, nor affected by, time. Claiming the more radically empirical view, Brightman and his disciples held to the temporality of God. I discuss this more extensively in the chapter on Brightman's doctrine of God.)

4. The development of a more complex field of attention and increased sense of memory and its function and familiarity with what is remembered enhances the awareness of time transcendence. This means that the present self is able to recognize the past self and anticipate the future self. But also, it is able to link itself with its present and past self. In addition, space transcendence is enhanced by the person's ability to focus on a multitude of additional nonspatial interests, for example, value experience of all kinds, as well as abstract ideas.

5. Enhancement of the level and quality of conation. It is no longer a matter of mere striving toward some end. The person is able to engage in conscious, intentional, free planning of some goal or purpose, while exhibiting both self-control and control of environment. Unlike the minimal self that only desires, the person experiences self as free—within limits—to control, select, and criticize desires in relation to some ideal.

6. Awareness of meaning advances to the level of conceptual thought and critical reasoning. Brightman cautions that, although once thought to be unique to human persons, this trait is now known to be present to some degree in certain animals, for example, apes, porpoises, dogs, and pigs. "Reflective self-consciousness, as distinguished from mere self-experience, arises on this personal level."

7. Heightened awareness of differentiation of self from its environment. Response to environment is "increasingly a response to a social and ideal environment" at this level. Because the person is self-reflective it freely decides its response to its environment. It is no longer condemned to instinctual or mechanical response.

8. Privacy is transcended by both language and understanding. Knudson exhorts that implicit in person is a degree of privacy, "and this privacy has about it something sacred. In every person there is a holy of holies, which it would be sacrilegious to invade."[36] Only the person is directly and immediately experienced by itself.[37] Because the self more clearly recognizes itself as over against some other object, the possibility of solipsism is not a major problem.

Brightman calls these characteristics of the person "emergent traits of personality," the most important of which are "the consciousness of imperative norms, freedom, and reason." Reason is "the power of testing truth-claims by logical and empirical standards; the principles of deduction and induction"; and, above all, the perception of the relations of parts to each other (analysis) and to the whole (synopsis). Coherence (seeing how things bind together) is the basic principle of reason. The consciousness of imperative norms is the person's experience of his or her "destiny as obligation to pursue the ideal values." The person matures and develops as these ideals become concrete value experiences. Freedom, of course, is the power of self-direction and choice, for example, the power to say yes or no, and the rational ability to act in accordance with one's choice.

The person is not identified with his environment, although he affects and is affected by it. The conscious person is what Brightman called "the Situation Experienced." Anything other than immediate consciousness would be "the Situation Believed-in." In this view the person's environment is the Situation Believed-in, since according to Brightman it is not known as directly as the self, but only inferentially. Although Brightman maintained that the person is no part of her environment (i.e., biological, physical, social, subconscious, logical and ideal, and metaphysical), he was quite aware that the consciousness of human persons cannot exist in this world without the body.[38] In this sense human persons are dependent for their existence on their environment. I need my body to exist in this world. A religious interpretation of this mind-body relationship may be rendered thus: "If…the world of nature and its metaphysical ground be regarded as at least under the control of conscious, value-seeking personality, then man's dependence on and interaction with his environment may be viewed as cooperation with God."[39] This is because God is the ground of all that the person essentially is. That is, the person has the ground of his being not in himself, but in God.

Human and Divine Person

In addition to identifying the traits of the most minimal self and those of the person, what does personalism have to say about the human and divine persons? The traits these share in common include: (1) Sharing in the aforementioned eight essential marks of what it means to be a person. (2) No person can perceive another person by the senses, but infers another person's existence from the data of her own consciousness. Consciousness is not perceptible to the senses. Brightman makes the point:

> From sense data of our own personal datum self we infer the presence of other persons, human or divine. We have no direct sensuous evidence of either human society or divine personality; both can be affirmed only as rational objects of belief based on interpretation of our experience. We do not see other persons; we think them as inferences from our perceptions. For us they are hypothetical entities.[40]

The reference here of course is to person in the metaphysical sense. For personalism acknowledges that the human person is an embodied or enfleshed self.

And yet it should not be difficult to see the implications that not having direct sensuous evidence of persons may have on our thinking about God. God is at least what the human person is at his or her absolute best, but by definition God is much, much more. This implies that there is always an element of mystery regarding God, as well as human persons, since we have to depend so heavily upon inference regarding what we "know" about them. (3) All persons possess an active will, or power of choice, and the way they would organize their own experience is within their control. (4) Every person has experiences not produced by his will, but that he finds (objective idealism). These experiences are given, not made. The will of all persons confronts given factors in their heredity, their sense experience, and their rational nature. These are found by persons, not produced by their will.[41] As will be seen later, this trait looms large in Brightman's theory of the finite-infinite God. As a consistent radical empiricist who tried always to apply to all persons (including the Divine Person) what he found to be reasonably true about the human person, Brightman concluded that the finiteness of God may be attributable to an uncreated, coeternal given content in God's nature—content that God, like human persons, endeavors to control and direct toward the production of the best possible good through will and reason; content that God finds in the divine experience. Bowne's and Brightman's doctrines of God will be taken up in chapters 6 and 7, respectively.

In addition to similarities between the human and Divine Person there are also some important differences. (1) God is the only person who is unbegun and unending. "That something must be unbegun follows from the principle *ex nihilo nihil fit* ("Nothing is made out of nothing"). Had there ever been a time when there was nothing, there would forever be nothing. The mind is hard pressed to imagine some-thing being produced out of nothing. "As surely as there is anything now, so surely there must always have been something." Therefore, unlike in the personal idealism of Howison, persons are not *causa sui* (self-caused). The ground of their being is in God alone. (2) The given in God's consciousness is uncreated, and therefore coeternal with God's will. It is also of the nature of consciousness, and therefore is internal rather than external to God's nature. (3) The Divine Person has no body and no nervous system, at least not in the sense that we human persons do. "The divine personality," writes Brightman, "is the locus and the divine will the energy of the whole physical universe, including the human nervous system." Metaphysically, neither the nervous system nor anything else causes the person. Rather, the nervous system and all else are caused by the Divine Person, that is, by the energizing of the divine thought and will. (4) As noted above, the Divine Person is the creator of other persons. (5) God has experiences that are not known to human persons. This is one of the reasons for the constant reminder that personalism is always aware of the mystery regarding God and other ultimate things. (6) Only the Divine Person is perfectly personal.[42] In light of these differences between God and created persons we may say that God is more than personal, but God is always at least personal. Although our best analogy of what it means to be a person is found in the human person, we need merely to be careful not to transfer to the Supreme Person the "limitations and accidents" of the human person.[43] God is the chief exemplification of what it means to be a person. This means that God possesses perfect consciousness, self-awareness, knowledge, and self-determination.

Because person is the most significant category or principle of personalism, I want to continue the discussion of its chief traits further. As just noted, personalism contends that proper or perfect person exists only in the Supreme Cosmic Person or God, and that the human person "can never be more than the feeblest and faintest image."[44] Only in God do we find perfect consciousness and self-consciousness; perfect self-direction or will; perfect rationality or reason, and so on.

Another Look at Essential Traits of Person

Responding to those for whom it was considered anathema to refer to God as Person, Bowne proposed several essential traits of person: selfhood, self-knowledge, and self-direction.[45] He held that wherever we find these traits we find personal being. These characteristics do not necessarily imply human body or limitation of any sort.[46] In *The Principles of Ethics* Bowne stresses the idea of "an inborn ideal of human worth and dignity." This, too, is a trait that should be included in the essential traits of person.[47] The ideal of worth or dignity, then, increases the essential traits of the person to four. It is not, according to Bowne, the anthropomorphic or physical traits possessed by humans that are essential for personal being. This view and what appears to be Bowne's extreme focus on consciousness would be seen as problematic by both internal and external critics. For it was the tendency of early idealistic thought from the time of Plato through Kant (which influenced early personalism) to stress consciousness to the exclusion of the human body. It was not early personalism's intention to undermine the worth and significance of the human body, for proponents acknowledged that God calls human persons into existence with bodies. Consequently, the body must be part of the essential meaning and worth of the human person. Unfortunately, neither Bowne nor his early disciples consistently made this connection in an explicit way. It will be seen later that the dehumanizing and violent experiences of groups such as Afrikan Americans, Native Americans, and Hispanics make it absolutely imperative that we possess the highest conceivable estimate of the importance and worth of the body and not just the mental aspect of the person.

Second- and third-generation personalists such as Brightman and Bertocci were much more explicit about carrying the discussion of essential traits of personal being further than merely identifying the four fundamental elements: selfhood, rationality, self-direction, and worth. Bowne's concern was to show that the essential traits of personal being do not lead to an "easy anthropomorphism" when the term person is applied to God.[48] "In affirming that God is personal," Bowne writes, "critical thought would mean only to affirm that he knows and determines himself and his activities."[49] Bowne sought to avoid applying to God the limitations of the human person. So instead of saying that God is limited because God is Person, it is more accurate to say something like: The category of person has its chief exemplification in God. Person in its more undeveloped form is found only in created persons. As created and dependent beings, humans do not experience complete self-knowledge, self-control, self-consciousness, and recognition of worth. Indeed, experience reveals that humans possess neither perfect knowledge, perfect will, uninterrupted consciousness, nor perfect sense of self-worth. Therefore, as persons, humans are, even at their very best, incomplete. Perfect person is found only in God, who alone possesses perfect knowledge, consciousness, will, and ideal of worth.

Metaphysically, possession of a body is not the essence of what it means to be personal, although the fact of being female, male, homosexual, heterosexual, Afrikan American, or of possessing other characteristics takes us a long way toward understanding the life-history of a person. But since person is our fundamental reference, such traits of the human person are not, according to personalism, considered the essence of what it means to be a person.[50] However, nonmental characteristics take on much more significance in personalistic ethics, as will be seen later. The exposition to this point is primarily metaphysical. The discussion on ethics will consider how personalism views persons in their individual and societal settings. To a large extent, however, what is said about persons in an ethical sense will be a direct carryover from metaphysical claims about the centrality of person. That is, the metaphysical claims provide the ground for doing ethics and for thinking about persons in an ethical sense.

What should be clear by now is that the metaphysical essence of what it means to be a person has less to do with one's race, gender, class, age, or health. This is a significant point, despite the concern of critics that early proponents of personalism favored the mental aspects of the person over the bodily. And yet the truth is that the early emphasis on the mental aspects of the person made it more difficult to argue in noncontradictory ways for racial, gender, or class superiority on the basis of physical and cultural differences. For the mental traits are spiritual in nature and therefore do not possess physical qualities that enable one to differentiate between persons. When a person is called into existence by God that person is a candidate for rationality, self-consciousness, and morality.[51] This is always the Creator's intention, regardless of biological, racial, economic, sociohistorical, and other factors that may hamper the full development of personhood. God intends that all persons enter the world on equal footing. That there is disparity in this regard is a problem both for the philosophy of religion and sociopolitical ethics. Biological or physical traits become significant factors only in the context of the person's sociohistorical experience or context. That physical characteristics have little metaphysical significance has rich implications for the way we do and think about ethics. Philosophically the idea that person is not essentially body means nothing if it is not transferred to ethics. In principle, the thoroughgoing personalist will never be an advocate of racism, sexism, classism, heterosexism, or ageism. To advocate any of these would contradict the basic principle of personalism that persons as such possess intrinsic dignity and worth because they are called into existence by God, who loves them and imbues them with the divine image. It would also be a contradiction, inasmuch as racism, sexism, classism, heterosexism, and so on, alienate persons from each other and God. Mutuality, or relationality, is a basic element of the personalist worldview. These negative "-isms" are destructive of the communalism and relationality inherent in personalism.

The Communal Nature of Person

Although Bowne did not explicitly include the element of sociality or relatedness in his discussion on the essential traits of person, it is implicit in other things he says about the nature of the person and reality. Indeed, we easily detect the element of sociality in experience. Persons never experience themselves as existing in a vacuum, but always in relationship. One is hard pressed to point to a time when persons have ever been completely alone. Bowne expressed this point in his view that God (Love) greeted us when we came into this world, and God will greet us when we enter the next.[52] Bowne characterizes reality as a world of persons with a Supreme Person (God) at the center.[53] This communal or relational element is basic to what it means to be a person, that is, a being in community who is capable of interacting and communicating.

There is, to be sure, a communitarian aspect in Bowne's ethics. He does not, however, apply the social category to the person in as pronounced a way as did Brightman, Francis J. McConnell, or Martin Luther King, Jr. McConnell acknowledged that the mutual interdependence of persons is as much a fact as each person's separate individuality. "The actual fact is persons existing together—and we doubt as to whether persons could be persons and exist apart from one another."[54] Already, in 1914, McConnell was anticipating what Walter G. Muelder would later characterize as "persons-in-community."[55]

In fairness to Bowne, it should be said that in his discussion on the unity of the World-Ground he emphasized the importance of interaction according to law, which forms an intelligible system. But we cannot even imagine such a system of interacting members without the postulate of a unitary being that is its cause or the fundamental reality. This fundamental reality both causes and maintains the members in their mutual interactions or relations. In this view, nothing exists out of relationship. Indeed, it would be difficult indeed to show how unrelated things can even form a system. "The elements have not their properties or forces absolutely and in themselves," writes Bowne, "but only in their relations or as members of the system. They are all conditioned in their activities, and hence conditioned in their being; for metaphysics shows that conditioned activity implies conditioned being."[56]

Bowne did not explicitly apply this emphasis on interaction or sociality to his discussion of the essential traits of the person, but it is clearly a central aspect of what it means to be a person. No person exists in, or is made for, isolation. Rather, every person is conditioned by every other and cannot be all he can be apart from the others. If, as Bowne contends, all of the members and their activities are conditioned, it is inconceivable that persons can exist at all out of relation. "Its existence is involved in its relations, and would vanish with them."[57] All things, including created persons, are dependent beings.

In a similar vein, Brightman maintains that reality is through and through social. "Every personal experience includes something which the person did not invent or create, but which he received from his interaction and communication with other persons. For personalism, social categories are ultimate."[58] This suggests a strong relational component in personalism at both the metaphysical and ethical levels. We also find this emphasis in the personalism of Howison[59] and Buckham.[60] The latter held that person is the capacity for fellowship. This does not mean, however, that personalism affirms the fundamentality of relationality, as if it has some meaning apart from person. This was earlier identified as an error in Renouvier's philosophy, but it is also a position taken up by contemporary thinkers who are "friendly" to personalism, but are not themselves personalists.[61] Unlike personalists, such thinkers give primacy not to the subject, but to the category of relation. The question for personalism is, What would relation mean apart from a subject or person?

No Fundamental Difference between Persons

The statement that there is no fundamental difference between persons means that in the deepest metaphysical sense persons are the same, posited or created in the same way by same Creator. Theologically we may say that the image of God is equal in all persons, which is to say that there is not more or less of God's image in some more than other persons. The differences between persons are sexual, racial-ethnic, cultural, sociological, historical, and so on. Important as these differences are in actual lived experience (and should never be minimized), they are not essential or metaphysical differences. Indeed, they add richness to the individuality of each person.

In theistic personalism, personhood is given rather than acquired. Personality is acquired or earned. As observed previously, every child is at birth a candidate for humanity, rationality, and morality. In this sense it is God's intention that all persons begin life on an equal footing. Yet, at least one personalist's analysis of what it means to be a person falters at this point. Albert C. Knudson erred greatly in his discussion of who is and is not a person. Writes Knudson:

> But, strictly, "person" is a narrower term. It applies only to selves that have attained a certain degree of intellectual and moral development; a slave is not a person, nor is a child. Personality implies freedom and moral responsibility. It thus transcends the purely psychological or metaphysical plane, and takes on a distinctly ethical character.[62]

Knudson is mistaken. For if his analysis is correct, it makes it possible for any person or group that possesses exorbitant power and privilege to arbitrarily determine who is or is not a person. The privileged and powerful may easily control who may have access to education and other apparatus to attain the level of intellectual and moral development that Knudson refers to. In addition, if Knudson is right, this would mean that sociocultural traits are either equally or more characteristic of essential personal being than self-consciousness, self-knowledge, self-control, and sense of self-worth. Or to make the claim as Knudson does that person is to be reserved for those selves that have already attained a certain degree of moral and intellectual development is just as erroneous and problematic. Who one develops into as a person may depend heavily on whether conditions in a given society are such that one can adequately develop morally and intellectually. What of those, like black persons of Afrikan descent who were forced into dehumanizing slavery, and those whose lives today are still menaced by the consequences of such subjugation? Having been unjustly and systematically denied numerous life-chances, are these to be considered less than persons because some have not developed in quite the same way as those who both subjected them to such treatment and benefit from their exploitation and dehumanization?

At this point Knudson is open to the criticism that he mixes and confuses the ethical and metaphysical levels of argument regarding what it means to be a person. For example, he confuses the term "slave" with a metaphysical category. In the most fundamental sense, no person is born a slave. Slave, then, is a social, not a metaphysical, category. God does not create slaves, but persons. In addition, in the present form of his argument Knudson failed to see that a child is still a candidate for humanity, which is the most any person can be at birth.

In a subsequent book Knudson attempted a revision of his view, although he did not point to his earlier error. He writes:

> Knowledge and moral character are not gifts, they are achievements; and because they are achievements they imply growth. They cannot come into being full-orbed by a creative act. If they did, they would not be personal possessions, they would have no ethical quality, they would

be illusions. Only through freedom can the spiritual life become a reality. We may be, we must be, endowed with the capacity for knowledge, morality, and religion if we are to be spiritual beings. But the capacity is all that can be created; achievement must be ours.[63]

At least there seems to be a clearer recognition that to be a person is to be "endowed with the capacity" for knowledge, rationality, and morality. However, from this passage it is not evident that Knudson clears himself entirely, especially with regard to the earlier claim that slaves are not persons. What of those like Native Americans and Afrikan Americans who are born into a social system that deprives them socially, economically, politically, educationally, and so on, and therefore are not allowed to fully develop some of the qualities of personhood? Are these persons or not? Knudson does not help us very much here,[64] for he nowhere explicitly says that such persons even possess the capacity for knowledge, morality, and religion. There is no question that Knudson was blinded, in part, by racism.

Brightman is much more helpful and convincing in his discussion on who is and is not a person. Having said that a person is one who has the capacity to judge one's own acts by ideal standards, Brightman goes on to indicate the status of infants and others:

> An infant person is not capable of such judgment in the state of infancy; but still he is a person because he is capable of developing the power to judge his values by his norms. It is a repudiation of the ideal of personality to assert that one race, or one economic group, or one cultural group exemplified personality, while all others—Negroes, Jews, Japanese, laborers, the uneducated—are sub-personal and unworthy of respect. To hold such a view is to substitute race or power for personality.[65]

Brightman saw that a being who is essentially rational and moral is not always rational and moral in his everyday behavior. But every such being has the potential or capacity to be rational and moral by virtue of her origin. Every such being is at birth a candidate for morality, rationality, and humanity.[66] God creates him with the capability of developing these capacities. What one needs are the opportunities to do so. That some groups are denied social, political, economic, and other advantages to achieve the highest degree of morality, rationality, and humanity does not diminish their worth as persons in the most fundamental sense. It is clear, however, that from a social, political, and ethical standpoint such persons may feel diminished. Yet it is because of the greatness of person that every conceivable effort must be made to enhance the humanity and worth of every person on the socioethical plane. In the world itself the metaphysical claim of the infinite worth of persons as such means little in the face of the systematic violation and depersonalization of persons, unless all humans and other resources are committed to ending such violations.

Theistic personalism affirms that personhood is given, and that failure (for whatever reason) to achieve all that is humanly possible in the areas of humanity, religion, rationality, and morality does not diminish the sacredness and worth of persons as such. What Paul Tillich said about the criterion for the equality of all persons is pertinent to the personalist view.

> It is their potential rationality which makes all men equal. This potentiality must be actualized if real equality is to be created. But in the process of actualization innumerable differences appear, differences in the given nature of the individual, differences in his given social opportunity, differences in his creativity, differences in all sides of his power of being…But these differences are functional and not ontological, as in the systems of hierarchical thinking.[67]

By definition, then, there is no fundamental or metaphysical difference between persons, regardless of gender, race, class, sexual orientation, and so on. The essential qualities of personhood, namely, self-consciousness, rationality, self-directedness, inherent sense of self-worth, and interaction with an environment, are shared by all persons. Indeed, minimally these traits are what it means to be a person. The differences are sexual, racial, classist, sociological, and so forth, but none of these diminish the sanctity and value of any person. Nor do any one or more of these traits necessarily make one superior to another person.

Personalism as Fundamentally Metaphysical

We have already seen that personalism has an epistemology that is based on the assumption of the trustworthiness of reason, the creative activity of thought, the primacy of the practical reason, and the dualism of thought (idea) and thing (object). Historically, metaphysics has preceded epistemology. Logically, however, theory of knowledge or how we can know anything at all comes before theory of reality. As a philosophy personalism is fundamentally a metaphysics, although some personalists have been more oriented to epistemology, philosophy of religion, philosophical psychology, axiology (theory of value), ethics, social theory, and social action. But all who are thoroughgoing personalists agree that personalism is "predominantly metaphysical."

> The true objective of every systematic philosophy is a theory of reality. Not the knowing process but the object of knowledge is what philosophy as well as common sense is ultimately interested in. Without a metaphysic philosophy remains a mere torso.[68]

Personalism is essentially a metaphysics. But as has been argued throughout, it is not merely a theory of reality to be taught, preached, and written about. It is, rather, a way of thinking about the whole of reality. More importantly, personalism is a way of relating and living together in God's world. So a basic question for personalism must be, What does socioethical living mean in light of a worldview for which person is the central principle or category? It may further be asked, What does such a worldview mean in the face of systematic and massive socioeconomic and other forms of dehumanizing oppression? Indeed, what is required of "responsible" persons and the institutions managed by them in such a world?

Person as the Key to Reality

As indicated by the title of Brightman's last book, *Person and Reality* (edited by Peter A. Bertocci and published posthumously), person is reality. More than any other principle or category, more than any model provided by science, physics, or mathematics, person is the best key to unraveling or explaining (as far as possible) the mysteries of reality and the universe.

> Only as the categories are seen as functions of the category of categories, the person, do the realms whose structure they describe find a coherent interpretation. The person is the model in the light of which the mysteries confronting reason are most illumined.[69]

This is reminiscent of Bowne's transcendental empiricism and his recognition of the need to make the self or person the central explanatory principle. We can explain as much as we can about reality and the universe because of their and our thought structure. Thought and a thinker, as Bowne liked to say, are at both ends of the knowing process.[70] We can learn about the universe because we and the universe are akin to each other, or are of the same quality (i.e., mind or thought). Reality itself is personal and speaks the language of thought. As beings who are "candidates" for rationality or thought, persons are able to make sense of that language. Active intelligence or mind is not, as skeptics assume, a stranger in the universe and thus "without any relation to the nature of things."[71] Rather, the universe itself is a product of mind. Therefore, "there is no reason why our minds should not know it as it is."[72]

Knudson summed up the entire metaphysics of personalism in the phrase "Personality is the key to reality." In this phrase we find the central doctrine of personalism. The category of person explains all categories but itself. How the person is posited or created we do not know. That remains a mystery. Yet the person is the best clue to the meaning of reality and solution to the basic problems of philosophy and life. The meaning of the phrase "Personality is the key to reality," may be summed up as follows:

> It is in personality that individuality finds its only adequate realization. It is personality alone that has the characteristics necessary to a basal unity. It is in personal agency that we have the source of the idea of causality and its only self-consistent embodiment. It is the reality of personality that constitutes the foil to the phenomenality of matter, space, and time and renders it intelligible. From every point of view it is thus evident that in personality we have the crown of the personalistic system, the keystone in its arch, the masterlight of all our metaphysical seeing.[73]

If we wish to know what any of the basic problems of philosophy mean, for example, the meaning of unity, identity, change, freedom, and determinism, we need look no further than personal conscious experience or person. It is in person that we get our best clue to the meaning of unity, identity, change, freedom, and so forth. For example, the person experiences self as one, while it can simultaneously engage in a plurality of things. Or, the person experiences itself as changing while remaining the same. We do not know in a speculative sense how this is possible, but empirically we know it to be the case. Therefore, in the person we find the key to the meaning of the basic problems of philosophy.

I said earlier in this chapter that we also find in the category of person clues to the solution of social problems in the world. Historically many personalists did not make this latter claim expressly, though in principle the idea has always been present. Brightman made it clear, for example, that concern about social problems has a place of prominence in personalism. In 1939 he said that "the ontology of matter is less central for me than the development of a social philosophy of personalism, which I call organic pluralism."[74] This shift in Brightman's personalism arose because of his heightened social consciousness during the 1930s. It might also have been sparked by his earlier conversations with Walter Muelder, then one of his graduate students in philosophy. In the early 1930s Muelder inquired of Brightman as to whether personalism had a social ethic. According to Muelder, Brightman responded that he knew what ethics and sociology were, but he did not know what to make of the combined term, social ethics. In addition, he said that perhaps the closest thing to this in personalism was McConnell's social gospel principles. In any event, Muelder was ultimately instructed by Brightman in 1932 to develop an outline for a course on social ethics.[75] Muelder noticed that not long thereafter Brightman's personal library began to reflect his interest in social philosophy in a significant way.

Since I write as a social ethicist, I think it important to explicitly make the connection between the person and solution to the problems in the world that have generally come about through misuse of human freedom. Inasmuch as human persons are the cause of social problems in the world, much of the solution to these rests with them. However, because of the magnitude of many of these problems today, the only possibility of solution rests in cooperative endeavor with persons and the Supreme Person. Although human persons may not be able to solve these problems alone, it is realistic to say that they can make more meaningful contributions than they have to date. I shall return to this in the discussion on ethics and social ethics in chapter 8.

Following the chief voices in the personalist tradition, I have made many claims, but without stating explicitly personalism's method and criterion of truth. This is the subject of the next chapter. It will not be difficult to see the importance of understanding the method and criterion of truth in personalism for discussions on God, ethics, and social ethics. The discussion on method and criteria of truth also looms large when one considers future directions for personalism.

Personalistic Method and Criterion of Truth

The two basic questions in early personalism were the epistemological and metaphysical questions. That is, How do we come to know things, and What is the nature of reality? We now come to the point of considering personalistic method and means for ascertaining knowledge and truth. It is important to know at the outset that personalism has never claimed to be able to unravel all of the mysteries of being and the universe. Personalism admits that there are ultimate truths such as freedom, immortality, and God that the human intellect is capable only of affirming and recognizing, but is not able to prove or disprove. Human reason helps us to understand ultimate things as far as possible, but it cannot tell us how these come to be. It cannot tell us how persons are created. This is what Bowne had in mind when he wrote in 1882:

> Being is a perpetual miracle and mystery, which logic can never deduce. It is something to be recognized and admitted, rather than deduced or comprehended. We aim not, then, to tell how being is made, or how it is possible, but how we shall think of it after it is made. Not to create, but to understand reality, is the highest possibility of human thought.[1]

This means being willing to criticize our ideas of reality as we endeavor to determine the true nature and connections of things.[2] An underlying assumption is that our notions of reality actually correspond to it. And this, of course, raises the question of how we determine that there is such a correspondence and the nature of the correspondence. Is it a correspondence between thought and thing (or reality), or is it a correspondence between thought and thought?

The human reason is limited, and thus is not capable of solving once-and-for-all the riddle of being. And yet the human mind is so constructed and so akin to reality that it desires to know not only its own origin and nature, but to penetrate and solve the deepest mysteries of being. This has much to do with the inquisitive and active nature of the mind and its ongoing desire for explanation.

What follows is a consideration of what we can know and how we come to know it. Does personalism have criteria or a criterion that enable us to achieve most probable truths? To say with Bowne that "being is a perpetual miracle and mystery" does not mean that the rational faculty can know nothing about it. But it does mean that we need to determine what can be known about it, and how we can best arrive at such knowledge. And yet at the end of our search it will be necessary to admit that some mystery still remains. This should be a constant reminder that human persons do not have within

112

themselves the ground of their being, for that can be attributed only to the infinite being, or God. This is one of the important distinctions between Creator and creatures.

However, personalism contends that if we have faith that our faculties have been made for truth, and if we have been disciplined and determined in our use of reason, there should be less mystery at the end of our search than when we began. That there may also be a heightened sense of wonder may also be a result of our disciplined efforts. The aim of personalistic method is to help us understand reality as far as possible. Personalistic method does not pretend to help us understand where being or reality comes from or how they are posited. In our present embodied, enfleshed form this will always remain a mystery. And yet personalistic method does enable us to make progress toward truth and knowledge. The purpose of the following discussion is to help us understand how far we may hope to go in this regard.

Beyond Psychological Certainty

One may be psychologically certain about nearly anything. But consider what often happens when two persons witness the commission of a crime. When each tells her version of what she saw, each gives a slightly different account. Each insists that the crime happened precisely as she saw it, and that she has described the details of the crime exactly as they happened. Which of the two stories should be accepted as the "true" one? How do we decide? What criterion or criteria do we use? The question that needs to be asked is this: How do we test our truth-claims?

When we make a statement about something, we generally believe we are referring only to that which is the cause of the statement we make. And we believe we are doing so clearheadedly and without any obstructions to our judgment. We do not believe we are simply talking about our own state of mind. For example, we say, "The pen is black," not, "I think the pen is black." "The car is red," not, "I think the car is red." "The room is blue," not, "I think the room is blue." We make our statements as if we are directly in touch with the object of which we speak, or as if what we describe is completely reflective of the object; as if nothing whatever clouds our judgment. We imply that we have complete certainty that the object to which we refer and the idea we have of that object are identical in every way conceivable, or that there is a direct and absolute one-to-one correspondence between them. In other words, we make statements of fact as if they are absolutely true.

When I say, "The car is red," I might well be psychologically certain that this is the case. But psychological certitude cannot be accepted as the sole test or criterion of truth, for the simple reason that too much room is left for error or inconsistency. Anyone who doubts this need only consider the grind that witnesses for the prosecution and defense are put through during a jury trial.

Or consider this. While in my study I hear a ringing sound. Having heard a similar sound many times before, I quickly conclude that it is the telephone. I am psychologically certain that this is the case, and thus at that moment would be willing to wager my life savings that this is so. But upon closer inspection I discover that this time—the first out of hundreds of times—it is actually the doorbell ringing. But I was certain that it was the telephone. The point here is that more than we like to admit, we make statements that we are psychologically certain about as if to imply that what we say must necessarily be the case. When I conclude that the ringing sound I hear is the telephone, the degree of certainty in my mind is equivalent to that which one can only hope to have in mathematics and logic. But if this is truly the case, when I investigate the ringing sound I should find what I actually concluded in my mind, namely that it was the telephone ringing. Yet I discover this not to be the case.

What we are confronted with here is the epistemological question, that is, how do we come to know anything? This leads to the matter of determining the truth or falsity of our judgments and conclusions. In other words, what criteria or criterion may we appeal to as we test our truth-claims about the epistemological object (built up by the mind) and the existent object (that we refer to outside the mind)?

Since the time of Bowne, personalists have devoted considerable time and attention to these and related questions. At an earlier stage of his movement toward personalism, however, Bowne questioned the advisability of spending too much time trying to determine the criterion of truth. For example, he wrote of the barrenness of discussions on the criterion of truth.[3] However, years later he conceded the importance of such discussions and the need for a criterion of truth.[4] This topic receives much attention beginning with Brightman. How, Brightman and his followers asked, can we ever hope to understand anything at all about experience if we have no way of determining what is true and what is not?

Bertocci struggled with this fundamental problem.

> We just cannot take prima facie (psychological) certainty for granted; and we cannot assume that what we have in mind is completely "wayward" or unrelated to what is "in the world." What is needed is a way of ascertaining when we can trust (less than certainty) our states of mind.[5]

In other words, we cannot uncritically assume that what we are psychologically certain about is true. And yet this psychological certainty does play a role in our quest for truth or knowledge. It becomes part of the raw, uninterpreted data with which we begin the search for truth. But psychological certainty cannot stand by itself and must be interpreted, criticized, related to other things we believe to be true, and ultimately orchestrated into the most reasonable hypothesis. On the other hand, it would be erroneous to assume that our psychological certainty (or what we have in mind) is completely unrelated to that which is outside our mind (which caused our idea of it). That is, we cannot uncritically assume that there is no relationship between our idea of an object and the object itself. Although we may not completely understand this idea-object relationship, personalism holds that there is a relationship. What is needed, then, is a way of determining when we can trust our states of mind. Make no mistake about it. There is a relationship between the epistemic object (in mind) and the existent object ("out there"). Our idea of an object and the object itself are not totally unrelated. But we need a way of determining (as best we can) just what is the nature of that relationship. Can we ever be as certain of the exact relationship between what is in mind, and what is in the world of objects, as we sometimes think?

> In spite of our tendency to error, a knowing mind is always in contact, at some point or other, with the actual world. What we know is not merely our ideas, but the real world, our ideas constituting our more or less accurate apprehension of the nature of the real world.[6]

In other words, psychological certainty or assurance is not always trustworthy. Therefore we need criteria or a criterion to determine the truth, falsity, or reasonableness of what is in the mind. This applies to all matters of "fact." Whether it is a claim made about God, good and evil, immortality, the validity of ethical claims, nature, the world, or other persons, we need some means of testing its validity.

Can we ever hope to have complete assurance or demonstrable truth about persons, nature, and God? Of what can we hope? Personalism contends that we cannot expect to obtain absolutely demonstrable truth about such matters. Accordingly, deduction and logical demonstration of ultimate things are impossible. The most we can hope for is the rational interpretation of experience.[7] Personalism maintains this position despite the fact that one may "feel" psychologically sure or certain that what he believes about self, other selves, nature, and God is true.

Augustine and Descartes did much to establish the primacy of self-certainty, which is so important in personalism. But personalism holds that beyond this self-certainty we can have no knowledge that is of the nature "it must be so and cannot be otherwise." That is, we can have no logically certain knowledge about aspects of experience beyond the immediate or momentary self. At best, the most we can establish beyond self-certainty is that a particular view of the facts takes account of more relevant data than any other view.[8] Therefore, when one makes the statement, "The car is red," one cannot be logically certain that this is, in fact, the case. At best one only has psychological assurance that this is the case. What is needed is some means, some criteria or criterion, for verifying the statement.

What generally happens when we make statements about objects "out there," or about anything beyond the datum or momentary self is that we do so in a way to suggest that we are absolutely certain that this is so and cannot be otherwise. Of course, what we actually do in such cases is to confuse psychological certitude (a state of mind one can have even prior to verification) with logical certainty (the awareness of a necessary consistency between our ideas, e.g., as in mathematics and logic). We also seem unaware of reasonable or coherent assertion, or the view that a certain proposition gives the most coherent rendering of all available data and evidence that pertains to a particular problem, and by implication leaves the least data to be explained.

One may have reasonable faith that a car is red. One cannot, however, be logically certain that this is the case. In the case of the red car one needs some test or criterion to help decide the reasonableness of that assertion.[9]

Criteria of Truth in the History of Western Thought

The history of Western thought reveals that there has been not one, but at least a dozen different criteria of truth that have been appealed to at one time or another. Although some thinkers have held that there can be no single criterion of truth for all occasions,[10] personalism contends that the coherence criterion is the most adequate, since it is inclusive of the strong points in other tests of truth.

According to Brightman, there are at least three major groups of criteria of truth. These include:

I. SOCIAL CRITERIA
   A. Custom (less trustworthy than tradition)
   B. Consensus Gentium
   C. Tradition (generally more proven or tested than custom)
   D. Authority

II. CRITERIA BASED ON IMMEDIATE PERCEPTION
   A. Instinct
   B. Sense Perception
   C. Intuition
   D. Feeling

III. RATIONAL CRITERIA
   A. Correspondence
   B. Practical Consequences
   C. Consistency
   D. Coherence

Of these three sets of criteria, personalism places the greatest emphasis on the last group, opting finally for the coherence test. In his discussion of these criteria, Brightman, in typical personalistic fashion, begins with what he considered the most abstract or least concrete set of criteria and methodically works up to what he thought to be the most concrete. Each criterion is discussed and criticized. A determination is then made of limitations and strengths of each. Brightman then shows how the truth of a preceding criterion is preserved in the one that succeeds it. We see this same method at work in Brightman's development of the moral law system (to be discussed in chapter 9), where he moves from the most abstract to the most concrete law. During this period of his writing, Brightman was heavily influenced by Hegel's dialectical method.

Few things are as elusive as truth. There are many points at which personalism can help those who are searching for truth about persons, nature,

God, and the world. Personalism's view of truth, its criterion and method, performs a great service especially for those who desire to give reasons for faith-claims as they try to determine their intelligibility, appropriateness, and extent of moral credibleness in a fast-paced world.

Faith or belief precedes all knowledge. In fact, the whole knowledge process begins and ends in faith. First and foremost we begin the process— whether we are aware of it or not—with faith or trust in reason. It is also important to have faith in the best we know or that is known at the time. And when we come to the end of our search we end with faith in the best we have arrived at by imposing reason and will on that with which we began. We subject all relevant data and evidence to critical reason and interpretation.

It is important to say more about the need to begin the process with faith and trust in reason. Reason must accept itself and its laws or we can make no progress whatsoever.[11] Rather than begin the search for truth with Descartes's methodological doubt, personalism prefers to begin on a more positive note by assuming the truthfulness and trustworthiness of reason and the universe. We assume that reason was made for truth. If we do not begin with such an assumption, there is no need to even pursue truth, since we are defeated at the outset. If we do not assume that reason is trustworthy and can lead us to truth, we merely deceive ourselves in our claim that we are seeking truth. But most important for our purpose is that in the quest for knowledge we do not actually begin with knowledge, followed by faith. Rather, faith comes before knowledge, and opens the way to what knowledge we are able to ascertain.[12] Indeed, according to personalism, we begin and end the process in faith.

In addition, faith is important because we cannot expect to obtain final knowledge of the deeper truths of reality, such as the existence and nature of God, immortality, how God creates persons, the solution to the problem of evil, and so on. In such cases we may need to defer to the practical reason. Said Bowne: "Where we cannot prove, we believe. Where we cannot demonstrate, we choose sides."[13] We also see in this statement evidence of Bowne's religious apriorism. We see more evidence of the fundamental religious orientation that undergirds much of his personalism.[14]

I turn now to a consideration of personalistic method and the set of rational criteria for truth: correspondence, practical consequences, consistency, and coherence. I combine the latter two under the heading systematic consistency and coherence. Personalism takes these rational criteria more seriously than social criteria and those based on immediate perception. After discussion of the method I begin with an exposition of the most abstract of the rational criteria and conclude with a consideration of what personalism holds to be the most concrete.

Analytic-Synoptic Method

Personalistic method endeavors to be both particular and comprehensive in outlook. Its fundamental goal is the development of a "concrete, inclusive perspective on experience and its implications." Indeed, this is essentially the goal of all philosophies.[15] To this end the analytic-synoptic method requires consideration of all relevant data, parts, and facts of experience that pertain to a specific problem. With this method one begins by identifying and analyzing each part to determine the strengths and limitations of each and what each contributes. One is then required to proceed to determine what each fact or part has to do with the other, and ultimately their relation to the whole. However, the process leading to knowledge is not complete once identification and analysis of the parts has been done. According to personalistic method, analysis is a necessary, but not sufficient, aspect in the quest for knowledge. After analyzing each relevant part or fact it is then necessary to determine both what they contribute to the whole and what is unique about the whole. The analytic-synoptic method requires that we know the individual parts, their relations to each other, and their relations to the whole.[16] Although both analysis and synopsis are important in this method, personalism places the weight of the emphasis on the synoptic end.

The quest for truth and knowledge always begins with the immediate, raw, uninterpreted, unintelligible data of self-experience. The aim is to interpret, relate, and make intelligible. From the time of Bowne, personalists have believed that the best we can hope for in the search for truth is the most rational interpretation of experience. In the final analysis, every theory must be judged by its adequacy to the facts.[17] One might espouse, for example, the theory that God possesses absolute power. However, the adequacy of such a theory must be determined in relation to the facts. Of course, if it will not stand up in the face of the best available facts, the theory should either be abandoned or altered.

We begin the process in search of knowledge with a kind of "confused synopsis," that is, with what we find in self-experience at any given moment. From here we proceed to analysis. In the next stage the analysis is tested by its relations to the original whole or synopsis. If inconsistencies are found at any point, the hypothesis should be revised accordingly, or, given up. These stages are repeated until the fullest, most reasonable hypothesis is achieved. Notice that I did not say that the stages are repeated until one arrives at final truth or knowledge, but until one achieves the fullest, most reasonable hypothesis.

In language similar to a metaphor we find in Whitehead, namely, "the flight of an aeroplane," Brightman illustrates the analytic-synoptic method in his analogy of the "arrow of intelligibility."

> One may picture that arrow (1) as starting with the unintelligible given, but aiming at intelligibility; (2) as flying toward the mark of analysis, but discovering that a bull's eye hit is not completely intelligible; (3) then with new aim, as flying back toward the starting point, which then is enriched and transformed by the results of the analysis. This process goes on forever, but the essence of it is that fuller and truer intelligibility is found at the synoptic end than at the analytic end of the flight of the arrow.[18]

What we see here is an initial emphasis on an original, albeit raw and unintelligible, synopsis; movement toward analysis, which in turn enriches the initial synopsis, which gets us closer to the goal of intelligibility. If it is remembered that reality is active or processive, it should not be difficult to see that the process of analysis and synopsis does not cease. The aim is always "fuller and truer intelligibility," which is found at the synoptic rather than the analytic end of the arrow's flight. The arrow's true target "is a synopsis enriched by analysis rather than an analysis that exhausts synopsis and renders it superfluous."

New evidence and data are always emerging and must be taken into account as we strive for an ever richer synopsis. Synopsis means "seeing together"; to comprehend or grasp wholes. Although the parts of the whole must be identified, acknowledged, and analyzed, "synopsis [i.e., seeing whole] is always the goal of thought." Remember, the process begins with a rather "confused synopsis," but a synopsis nonetheless. The aim is a richer, more intelligible synopsis. The emphasis is on inclusiveness or comprehensiveness; seeing things "from all angles in a related whole."

Harkness reminds us that synopsis is not merely "an eclectic but a coherently unified view, an approach in which the defect of each method finds a corrective in due consideration of data available through other channels."[19] Synopsis emphasizes the whole, as opposed to simply seeing all of the parts together or the sum of the parts. The whole has characteristics that are different from either the parts or their sum. Take, for example, the person and her mind-body. Some parts of her mind-body may be identifiably defective. However, when she is considered as a whole person these defects may be minor and insignificant, and may say very little about the person she really is. Therefore, the aim of personalistic method is to form a comprehensive view of experience rather than to focus only on individual parts. Thoroughgoing personalism seeks to avoid making the experiences of one group normative for all others. I now turn to discussion of the criteria of truth taken most seriously in personalism: correspondence, practical consequences, and systematic consistency and coherence.

Correspondence

Personalism maintains that the mind is not capable of transcending its conceptions, and that knowledge consists not of the object itself, but of the conceptions it forms of any object. Knowledge, then, is of the conceptions the mind builds up of an object. The mind has knowledge of an object only through conceptions it has of it. Bowne spoke to this in the first edition of *Metaphysics* when he said that "the object exists for the mind only as it is conceived. Hence a thing can never be more for the mind than a realized conception. However real the outer world may be, the mind can grasp the world only through the conception it forms of it."[20] The mind can grasp the outer world because it is essentially a thought world. In the first place the outer world is a result of the energizing of God's thought and will. But in addition, in order for the mind to grasp it, to have knowledge of it, it must perform various operations on it through the categories of thought. This is how the mind forms conceptions of the outer world and is the only way it can have meaning for mind or thought. But the knowledge the mind has of objects primarily consists in the conceptions it forms of them. What we can know of things in themselves we can know only in their relations to thought. To know any reality at all, it must be in relation to thought. Otherwise we can have no knowledge of it. "It follows that the demand to know things in themselves is absurd, if by things in themselves be meant things out of all relation to thought. Reality as it appears in thought may be known; but reality as it does not appear in thought is unknowable in the nature of the case."[21] If it does not appear in thought, it cannot be known. The mind never grasps the reality itself, but grasps it only through its conceptions of the reality.

This criterion suggests that there is a direct correspondence between our ideas (thought) and reality. I mean by reality those permanent and ultimate things or beings that make up the world. Real things are both dependable and the source or cause of other things or beings.[22] It is important to remember that personalism holds that mind is not a stranger in the universe, and thus has some relation to the nature of things. This means that there is a correspondence between thought and thing, a point that led Bowne to the conclusion that "if the world be the product of mind, there is no reason why our minds should not know it as it is."[23] However, this is not to be taken to mean that there is an absolute one-to-one correspondence between thought and thing, or that such a perfect correspondence exists between my idea of reality and reality itself. Nevertheless, an important truth in the correspondence theory is that there is a relationship between idea and object. Indeed, for personalism the thing-world is essentially a thought-world.[24] Yet there is no perfect correspondence between things and our thoughts or knowledge of them.

Correspondence theorists claim that ideas are true if they are exact copies of reality. For example, the statement "I have a blue notebook" would be true only if it corresponds with a blue notebook in my possession. That is, the statement would be true only if it can be shown that I, in fact, have a blue notebook. To say that Ku Klux Klanners sit in church pews and in my classrooms on a regular basis would be a true statement only if empirical investigation reveals this to be the case. The statement "The church in the United States has always sided with the poor and the disinherited" would be true only if it can be shown that the actions of the church have been consistent with this otherwise fantastic statement. Or the statement "God is all-powerful," would be true if one could verify it.

Correspondence theorists define the true proposition as one that corresponds to a real state of affairs. Accordingly, "truth is the agreement between the statement of fact and the actual fact, or between the judgment and the situation the judgment claims to describe."[25] Such theorists define truth as the correspondence of thought with a thing, a definition that is accurate enough for practical purposes, said Bowne. But in the strictest sense "this definition assumes that we can first know the thing, and then form a conception of it, and can finally compare the thing as we know with our conception of it, and note their agreement or disagreement."[26] Personalism contends that this is not possible. "The thing exists for our thought only in and through the conception; and hence there can be no comparison of thought with thing. What we call comparing our thought with the thing is always a comparing of one thought with another thought."[27] The mind grasps things only through its conceptions of them. Therefore, truth cannot be viewed as a correspondence of thought and thing. Truth would be "the universally valid in our thought of the thing."[28]

Furthermore, the idea of correspondence as the sole criterion of truth is problematic, especially when it is applied to deeper metaphysical issues such as God, freedom, and immortality. The correspondence criterion depends heavily upon the clarity and accuracy of our sense data and their ability to disclose the world or reality as it actually is. It assumes that our sense data are clear and accurate most of the time. And perhaps they are dependable much of the time. But frequently they are not! What do we do when the senses are not as dependable?

Human persons often lose consciousness through sleep, medication, or a blow to the head. The senses are adversely affected by fatigue, alcohol, and other—legal and illegal—drugs, thereby militating against our ability to think as clearly as we might otherwise be capable. In addition, we may be too young, too immature, or our faculties may succumb to old age. Another factor that may make it difficult to make the most of one's faculties is the systematic denial of educational opportunities to particular groups, for example, Afrikan Americans and women. Such opportunities may serve to sharpen their native abilities.

In a related sense there is the question, What of people of other cultures in this and other countries? How can they be expected to see in quite the same way as some other group? Why do they need to? This is a point at which liberation theology, through its principle of the "epistemological break," speaks meaningfully and helpfully. This principle applies especially to those groups that have been forced to the socioeconomic margin, and whose history and existence are all but forgotten by the privileged and powerful. The idea of the epistemological break allows one to focus on commitment and action to liberate and empower the oppressed, rather than to focus primarily on ideas.

Since the way we perceive things is inevitably culturally conditioned and a result of the socialization process, the correspondence criterion will always be problematic. What happens, for example, when persons are socialized in a way that they find it difficult and painful to admit that they and their group are not at the center of the universe? That their attitudes and practices toward other groups have less to do with those groups themselves, than with their own perceptions, greed, selfishness, and so on? Such considerations must leave doubt in our minds about correspondence as the sole test of truth.

With the possibility of so many obstacles to clear thinking, how can the correspondence criterion be considered the only test of truth? Indeed, can we really compare our ideas with reality as the correspondence criterion suggests? Can we be absolutely certain that our idea of an object and the object itself are in perfect one-to-one correspondence? Do we have direct or immediate access to objects outside our mind? Or *in* our mind for that matter? My idea of God is in my mind. What I am immediately in touch with is my idea of God, not with God as object of my idea. Is our knowledge of the object indirect, or known through inference from the sense data that make up the appearance of the object? What is most immediate and accessible to the mind? Is it the object? Is it the idea of the object? If the latter, then we need to be very careful about statements of fact that we make about God, the world, and other persons. Are our thoughts the realities, or completely identifiable with the realities? Does my idea of divine omnipotence necessarily mean that God is, in fact, omnipotent? How do we determine whether our idea of some aspect of reality actually corresponds with that reality? Furthermore, getting back to the notebook referred to earlier, I may have before me a notebook that I declare to be blue. But what of the person who is either color blind, on medication, or the recipient of a hallucinogen that may alter the sense of sight? What of the person who has not been taught the primary colors? And do not forget the previous concern about the socialization process and the differences between cultures. Would the world of objects have a different appearance in such cases? Would it not have a different appearance if created persons had fewer or more senses? One can see the problem that confronts the correspondence theorist. Therefore, another criterion is needed to test the validity of the correspondence between idea and object and to orchestrate other data and evidence that may have bearing.

If our idea of an object is not an absolute one-to-one correspondence with the object "out there," although "it guides us as we interact with reality,"[29] this would seem to suggest that in the search for truth it will always be necessary to consider and coherently organize many types of data and evidence. For example, since it is known that there are many gaps in our knowledge of the historical Jesus, what we think we know about the Jesus of history must be tested in the light of other evidence made available by biblical, historical, and other scholars.

Practical Consequences

This criterion is intended to be a corrective of the correspondence or "copy theory." The pragmatic or practical consequences criterion maintains that what is true is that which works. Therefore, one can determine the meaning or truth of a statement by testing its results or practical consequences.

Charles S. Peirce (1839–1914) and William James (1842–1910) were early American exponents of pragmatism. Both believed that the pragmatic method was at least approximated in the work of Socrates, Aristotle, Berkeley, Hume, and Shadworth Hodgson. In addition, they believed that pragmatism was foreshadowed in Kant's principle of the primacy of the practical reason.[30]

James wrote that "there is absolutely nothing new in the pragmatic method." However, although empiricist in tone, it is "a more radical" and "less objectionable" form of empiricism.[31] Pragmatism amounts to a new name for some old ways of thinking.[32]

The pragmatist, according to James:

> ...turns away from abstractions and insufficiency, from verbal solutions, from bad a priori reasons, from fixed principles, closed systems, and pretended absolutes and origins. He turns towards concreteness and adequacy, towards facts, towards action and towards power.[33]

Peirce described the pragmatic method thus: "In order to ascertain the meaning of an intellectual conception one should consider what practical consequences might conceivably result by necessity from the truth of that conception; and the sum of these consequences will constitute the entire meaning of the conception."[34]

Unlike the correspondence theorist, the pragmatist rejects the belief that ideas are internal copies of existent objects or of the object "out there." Rather, ideas are useful when they can be used to devise plans to help us get things accomplished in the world. On this view there is no such thing as inherently true ideas. Instead, ideas become true or are made true, by leading to satisfactory consequences or results. My idea about how to get from point A to point B becomes true only if the idea leads me to the intended destination. The pragmatic approach may be described as "the attitude of looking away from first things, principles, 'categories,' supposed necessities, and of looking towards last things, fruits, consequences, facts."[35] It is concerned to determine the practical difference our ideas make or do not make. Some of the key terms that characterize the pragmatic approach include: workability; usefulness; results; and satisfactory practical consequences. Ask a pragmatist, What is true? and she is likely to say, "That which works; that which leads to satisfactory consequences is true." On this view, then, the "good" would be whatever promotes a satisfactory life. The true hypothesis would be the one that works.

Pragmatists pride themselves on being thoroughgoing empiricists in their interpretation of experience. This means they work hard at being inclusive and liberal when considering the facts. The pragmatist surveys all facts and evidence relevant to a particular problem. Like personalism, pragmatism rejects all static views of truth, and the claim that one can obtain truth once and for all. No matter how much intellectual arrogance is displayed among persons, we cannot have once-and-for-all truths in human experience. If we work at it diligently, we may be fortunate to obtain bits and pieces of the truth each day. James is helpful when he says that "we have to live to-day by what truth we can get to-day, and be ready tomorrow to call it false-hood."[36]

This way of characterizing truth is not antagonistic to that of personalism. Indeed, the way personalists conceive of reality has important bearing on their conception of truth and how much truth one may expect to obtain. If, as personalism maintains, all being is essentially causal and active or "self-centered activity";[37] if reality is processive or characterized by becoming or development, then the pragmatic idea that we cannot have static, once-and-for-all truths is reasonable. There simply cannot be absolute, final truths in a dynamic, developing world. In such a world we can say with Norman Pittenger that "the world is more like a great adventure than it is like a settled scheme with every detail precisely set forth."[38] In a dynamic, processive world one may not expect to acquire absolute, final truths. And as for the idea of a static universe, Bowne held that it is little more than "a phantom of abstract thought."[39] Pragmatism has done much in the way of bridging the chasm between theory and practice, value and fact, behavior and thought, and therefore it must always be taken seriously in the search for truth. Pragmatism's emphasis on the "instrumental value" and "purposive character" of ideas is quite useful, as is its insistence that ideas should be put to work to enhance the well-being of persons in sociopolitical arrangements in society. The focus on the testing of ideas in order to validate them is also a strong point. However, there are limitations regarding the pragmatic criterion.

When applying the pragmatic or practical consequences criterion it is necessary to consider what may be meant by "workability," "usefulness," or "satisfactory results" in a particular situation. In addition, we should not accept uncritically the notion that "that which works is true." Although a useful idea in physical sciences such as chemistry and physics, for example, one must wonder about the validity of the idea of workability in the everyday experience of persons.

In human experience much that works for privileged groups, for example, works because it is done at the expense of disinherited and oppressed groups, or through indifference and callousness. Furthermore, history confirms the view that untrue and detrimental ideas, theories, and practices have often worked quite well, or, in some instances have had satisfactory consequences for a select group. The idea of white supremacy—a false idea— has worked quite well for many of European descent in terms of special privilege, power, and economic advantage. Ideas that may work well for select individuals may be devastating to society or particular groups. This is often the case, for example, in cut-throat capitalist economies where the worth of persons and nonhuman life forms are defined in terms of profit potential.

Although pragmatism's emphasis on activity or seeking after goals is useful, one must ask whether the goals being sought are those that ought to be sought. Do we need a criterion to determine this? In the case of human oppression one must not fail to ask: Whose goals are being sought, and at whose expense? In a way that pragmatism does not, personalism forces us to ask whether the goals being sought are consistent or in harmony with the idea of the infinite worth and sanctity of persons as such; whether serious consideration is given to the value of nonhuman life forms.

The point of these questions is quite simple. Neither the correspondence nor the pragmatic criterion can be looked to as the sole test of truth. In the case of the pragmatic test we will need some other criterion to help us determine whether what works is consistent with other relevant data and experiences. In addition, we will need a criterion to determine the moral plausibility of pragmatism's goals. "Results (practical consequences) are meaningless unless they are evaluated by a reason which connects them with all the evidence available before the consequences took place."[40] Proponents of the practical consequences criterion would do well to remember that "we are more likely to use this test…in areas where we can more safely live in happy illusion and where we are not likely to be checked by more stringent tests."[41]

The pragmatic criterion can be used quite effectively to one's advantage if it is not checked by a more inclusive and demanding criterion. In personalism that criterion is coherence, for it transcends the limitations of the pragmatic test. But before an exposition of the coherence criterion is given, it may be helpful to make a brief excursus to consider how personalists understand "empiricism" in their quest for truth and knowledge.

Radical or Deep Empiricism

William James called his philosophy "radical empiricism." Mary Calkins was the first to apply the term radical empiricism to personalistic method.[42] Although James's application of radical empiricism was sometimes problematic, he was quite clear about its meaning. "To be radical, an empiricism must neither admit into its constructions any element that is not directly experience, nor exclude from them any element that is directly experienced."[43]

Similarly, personalistic method is empirical in that it always appeals to given experience as its point of departure, and it endeavors to stay close to experience. Personalistic method is radical in the sense that it includes everything that has to do with that experience. That is, it strives to include the whole of that experience, rather than limiting itself to select aspects. In this sense it seeks to be comprehensive and inclusive regarding the facts and evidence. The radical empiricist goes well beyond classical empiricists like David Hume who limited their empiricism to sense experience. This was not truly empiricism, since persons do not merely have sense experiences. Persons also have (and are) other "activity-potentials," for example, willing, remembering (in part), thinking, feeling, wanting, ought-ing, and appreciating. In addition, every person experiences both values and disvalues. Radical empiricism requires that all of these (as well as other relevant data) be included in the search for truth.[44]

We see personalism in its most radically empirical form beginning with Brightman, who consciously sought to be inclusive and comprehensive regarding method. For him this "growing or expanding" empiricism was as much a way of life as living out the entire meaning of personalism at its best. In a way that some personalists did not, Brightman worked hard at insuring that all facts and evidence relevant to a given problem were sought out and included.

It was this stance that constantly led to the broadening of Brightman's own philosophical perspective. He intentionally sought to remain open to voices and experiences that were being suppressed. We get a sense of this in a profound passage in *The Spiritual Life* (1942), which reflects the Hegelian influence.

> In a great spiritual insight, Hegel said that the very idea of the love of God sinks to triviality when "the seriousness, the pain, the patience, and the labor of the negative" are missing from our experience. By the negative Hegel means everything that is left out, the whole area of have-nots. The negative is the lost sheep and the lost son, the share-croppers, the unemployed, the Germans in the days of the Weimar Republic who looked in vain for justice from the rest of the world, the forgotten man everywhere. To consider the negative is indeed labor and pain, but the alternative is forced on us. Either we face the negative and try to cope with it intelligently and unselfishly, or else we neglect it until it rises and rends us.[45]

The "negative" means everything that has been excluded and forgotten, for example, the experiences of pain, suffering, and triumph of Afrikan Americans, Native Americans, and all women. In addition, it means the exclusion of their positive sociocultural, religious, and other contributions from textbooks, classrooms, religious institutions, government, places of employment, and so on. The "negative" means the exclusion of all women and their contributions. It means the exclusion of the experiences of youth, the aged, and the poor.

To use the term "the negative" to symbolize the forgotten or oppressed persons and their experiences is useful in this discussion on radical empiricism. (It must be admitted, however, that despite the significance of the idea expressed by the term "the negative," the term itself is unfortunate since it implies that that which has always been included is of positive worth or value, while traditionally excluded persons are not.) What Brightman calls attention to is the need to acknowledge not only all that has been forgotten, but the importance of their contribution to the whole. It should be added that in an embryonic form this principle is also found in the work of Bowne. We see evidence of it most clearly in his book on ethics.[46] The emphasis on the expansion and inclusion of the traditionally forgotten and excluded is described, for example, in his discussion on development. Bowne's idea of expanding the moral sphere to include duties to human *and* nonhuman life forms previously ignored is important, inasmuch as it anticipates Brightman's use of Hegel's principle of the negative to include the traditionally excluded. Although Bowne was not as explicit as Brightman about what and who he meant regarding the previously excluded, in principle we see in his idea of development and expansion of the moral field openings for an ethic of the oppressed, for example, Afrikan Americans, Native Americans, the plant and animal spheres. I shall return to this matter in chapters 8 and 10.

What Bowne and Brightman had in mind is captured through the use of another term that requires intentionally seeking out and including the forgotten in the work of philosophy, theology, and ethics. The term "deep empiricism" does this quite well. This is the term that David Ray Griffin introduced to describe the empiricism in Charles Hartshorne's philosophy. The term, according to Griffin, "seeks those universal features at the depths of every experience, beneath the fleeting superficialities."[47] Griffin does not entirely have in mind what I take this term to mean, but I think it can be appropriated nonetheless. Deep empiricism, as I use the term, seeks to get to the bottom or depths of experience; to uncover what is deep down under, and has long been out of sight and ignored. Deep empiricism seeks to uncover and to include that which has been forcibly suppressed and forgotten. And by "include" I do not mean to merely add to as an appendage or footnote, but rather to reinterpret the whole of existing experience in light of what has been left out; to alter the entire existing way of thinking and doing things. This, I think, is consistent with personalistic method at its best.

So the empiricism of personalism is a deep empiricism. It aims to seek out and include everything that has been—intentionally or unintentionally—left out. This idea has revolutionary implications for theologians, ethicists, historians, and social scientists. Nevertheless, this discussion would not be complete if I failed to point to limitations in some early personalists' empirical methods.

Some personalists have not been as radically empirical as personalistic method requires. For example, in the areas of philosophy, theology, and ethics, not all personalists have always included the experiences of Afrikan Americans, Native Americans, all women, and other traditionally excluded groups of people. Often there was a hurried reference to these in a sentence or footnote. In Bowne's text, *The Principles of Ethics*, for example, we find no explicit reference to the need to apply his ethical principles to the mistreatment of Afrikan Americans and Native Americans. There is no explicit indication that the principles of good will and the sanctity of persons even apply to these groups. And yet it can be argued that, in principle, Bowne's ethical personalism does apply to these groups. But we must be troubled at his failure to explicitly mention American slavery and the related problems of racism and economic exploitation, as well as the near eradication of the Native American population. We see this same omission in Knudson, who in some ways was more callous than Bowne. In later chapters we will see that it is in the work of Brightman and some of his students, for example, Muelder, DeWolf, Bertocci, and Martin Luther King, Jr., that conscious efforts are made to take seriously the experiences of Afrikan Americans, Native Americans, Asians, Hispanics, and so on. It is in these thinkers that we get a glimpse of radical or deep empiricism at its best.

Systematic Consistency and Coherence

Near the beginning of this chapter we saw that Bowne once wrote of the barreness of discussions on the standard of certainty or the criterion of truth. But he later conceded that "any given item of knowledge must stand or fall, not because it agrees or disagrees with some assumed standard, but because of the evidence with which it presents itself to the living mind in contact with the facts."[48] The aim of thought is to impose reason upon the facts of experience. Critical thought enables us to interpret experience as we move toward intelligibility.

Bowne did not use the term coherence in his discussion, but what he said about the process that leads to knowledge implies the use of the coherence criterion. He also suggests that the ascertainment of knowledge is not an automatic, easy process. We do not begin with knowledge. We begin with knowledge-claims. If knowledge comes at all, it comes at the end of a strenuous, intentional process.[49]

Personalism maintains that coherence is the chief test of truth. This criterion, more than any other, removes some of the needless emphasis on less inclusive criteria such as authority, tradition, custom, and consensus. Although there is some truth in each of these criteria, when considered alone they always come up short and leave many questions to be answered. The coherence criterion, on the other hand, takes into itself the strengths of these lesser criteria and seeks to develop the most comprehensive or synoptic view of experience possible.

Coherence literally means "a sticking together whole," or "to be in harmony with." Thus, the focus of this criterion is on how things bind or stick together. Yet it is not enough to know that things bind together. The mind generally has a need to know how or why things bind together as they do.[50]

Systematic consistency emphasizes relations and connections between ideas, judgments, experiences, and events of life. However, this alone lands us in formalities and abstractions. But we can agree that the truth must at least be self-consistent, although every self-consistent proposition may not be true. For example, the reasoning in the following syllogism is correct, or self-consistent: All women are wealthy; Gem is a woman; therefore Gem is wealthy. The reasoning is correct and the conclusion necessarily follows from the premises. Yet we know that in human experience the conclusion based on such reasoning may or may not be a true one. In addition, one or both of the premises may, in fact, be false. We know, for example, that all women are not wealthy. The aim in syllogistic logic is to avoid self-contradiction in the reasoning process. The emphasis is on the laws of correct thinking, and in this respect the conclusion is "formally" true. But when taken by itself we fall short of truth in actual day-to-day living, a shortcoming that the coherence criterion seeks to transcend.

The coherence criterion focuses on seeing whole and seeing facts in relation, so that no fact is isolated from its context, but rather is seen in relation to the whole. Coherence seeks to interpret the meaning of the facts of experience and to determine their relations with each other and with the whole. In addition, it takes seriously the strong points and contributions of other criteria of truth. Harkness summarizes this idea in a helpful way.

> Fortified with this coherence test, we can now utilize whatever value has been found in the other criteria we have looked at. What is given by authority or custom or tradition must be scrutinized in the light of its ability to take its place in the "vision of the whole." What is generally agreed upon is true, when it is true, because the judgments of mankind

have eliminated the most striking contradictions. Desire and feeling must be tested by their rational coherence with the rest of the experiences of life. Intuition gives us subjective certainty; its objective truth must be tested by a coherent fitting together of all the facts. Consequences must be regarded as important elements in any truth-judgment, but as elements only, not the whole. Sense data likewise afford the raw materials of much of our experience, but this experience must be tested by its ability to harmonize with itself, and with life in its totality. Freedom from contradiction is the final test.[51]

The coherence criterion "places its trust in the consistency or harmony of all judgments." A true judgment, then, is one that is consistent with other judgments known to be true. All elements or parts of a judgment must bind together if it is to be a true judgment. A true judgment is self-consistent throughout. Coherence, then, is more than the mere consistency between ideas and concepts. It forces us to see how ideas are related or connected with each other, with events, and with life experiences. Its goal is to see whole, that is, to form an inclusive and synoptic view of experience. A true judgment must be self-consistent and coherently connected with the best of our judgments. In addition, it must be based upon the most relevant data or evidence we have at a given moment. To be sure, statements must be related in a logical, orderly, and systematic way. But much more is needed to meet the demands of the coherence test. Therefore it may be said that logical consistency is necessary in the quest for truth and knowledge, but is not, by itself, sufficient.

Bowne, following Lotze, often said that life is deeper, richer, broader, and more inclusive than logical consistency. Yet this is not to be taken to mean that experience sometimes requires that one accept logically inconsistent and unsupported beliefs. Precisely because of his fear that the uncareful reader may interpret Bowne's statement to mean that it is all right to adhere to "bad" reasons in support of some truth, Brightman found Bowne's statement to be problematic.[52]

Yet Bowne's repeated reference to the phrase "Life is deeper than logic" was intended to alert us that there is much more to life than mere logic alone. Important as logic is, there are numerous other important considerations that come into play in the arena of life, some of which may not make complete sense to the thoroughgoing logician. Bertocci held that "when we are thinking in mathematics and logic, we are enjoying a holiday from the everyday uncertainties of existence."[53] Such a break from life is equivalent to doing ethics, metaphysics, or theology in the closet (to borrow a phrase from Bowne). For in the closet, as in mathematics and logic, we are shielded from the many contingencies of life. There are no uncertainties to worry about. One does not have to be bothered with the idea of freedom and the capacity of persons to create, co-create, or destroy. How neat it would be to live life in the closet, or to live a life that only requires that one work within the framework of logic and mathematics. No contingencies! If we had only to contend with logic and mathematics it would be easy and convenient to make moral judgments against street people, winos, teen parents, victims of HIV/AIDS, and a growing number of groups forced to the margin of society. If we limit our study of ethics, philosophy, and theology to the security of the class-room, we can easily and callously make judgments of others whom we per-ceive to be just a cut below our socioeconomic status, or who happen to be of a different race or gender.

Make no mistake about it. Logic and mathematics assist us in innumer-able rational and practical ways. But it is in life itself that we actually find the principles by which we live, let live, and die. Bowne said that the law that the logician lays down is this: "Nothing may be believed which is not proved. The law the mind actually follows is this: Whatever the mind de-mands for the satisfactions of its subjective interests and tendencies may be assumed as real in default of positive disproof."[54] When the mind has a deep enough need to believe, it may do so even when there is not sufficient evidence to support such belief. The rules of life are not nearly as exact as those in logic and mathematics, and in this respect life really is deeper than logic. Life, with all of its contingencies, uncertainties, and unpredictabilities is richer, fuller, and more morally challenging than logic and science alone.

To live out one's life on some mythical planet called Vulcan with little use for anything but logic might be meaningful in one's dreams. However, it may be doubted that a person, created in freedom by an all-wise, perfectly good and just God, would truly enjoy living the totality of her life on such a planet. She may be turned on by the rigor and vigor of logic; may even enjoy brief holidays from the contingencies of life. But she will always be reminded that human persons have been created in such a way that the rigor and vigor of logic alone will be insufficient to enable them to live life to the fullest.

The most adequate criterion of truth, then, makes room not only for logical consistency, but for the whole of the facts of experience. Coherence is such a criterion. It includes, but goes beyond logical consistency. Brightman affirms that "coherence means inclusive systematic consistency." It is inclu-sive in the sense that all facts of human experience that are relevant to a given problem are taken into consideration and systematically and imagi-natively related in an orderly, significant way.

Throughout this discussion I have repeatedly referred to the need to consider all facts. Indeed, the personalistic principle of respect for persons requires respect for facts—facts of self as well as those beyond self and one's own group. If we take this seriously we must conclude that there is need to consider the facts as reported by every person and group, rather than those of a single group that controls power and privilege by virtue of race and/or gender.[55] This is the type of concern I had in mind earlier when I introduced Griffin's concept of deep empiricism. There are important implications in this for those individuals and groups such as Afrikan Americans, Native Americans, and women, whose history, culture, and other pertinent facts have been so long excluded or not taken seriously. Personalism maintains that one cannot seriously claim to adhere to the ideal of respect for persons if he does not give as much weight to respect for facts, which is necessarily implied in the principle of respect for persons. This means that the principle of respect for facts must be extended not to some, but to all persons and groups. "Respect for some at the cost of others," writes Brightman, "is not respect for personality, but respect for that which differentiates one person from another."[56] If genuine respect for persons means respect for all persons, and respect for persons necessarily involves respect for the facts, it follows that the facts of all persons and groups must be respected.

Inasmuch as created persons are not omniscient, we know only in part. In a dynamic, developing, processive world we will never know all there is to know, for the data and facts of experience grow daily and are always forthcoming. There will always be more data to interpret and relate to what is already "known" to be true. There will always be more hypotheses to alter. Therefore, the coherence criterion does not lead to final, static results, and it most assuredly does not lead to absolute truth. However, personalism maintains that it does a better job than other criteria of truth. Yet the truth is that coherence is a "principle of constant reorganization, a law of criticism and growth, rather than a closed system."[57] Since it is a principle of becoming and development, coherence cannot be fully applied. Yet it always stands ready to receive and interpret new data, and to alter an existing hypothesis in light of them.

Some Criticisms of the Coherence Criterion

An important element in the coherence criterion is inclusiveness. Yet critics often point to this as its chief limitation. It is said, for example, that since created persons are finite, one may ask how it is possible to ever know every aspect of experience. Obviously this is not possible. Personalism therefore places emphasis upon knowing every "known" aspect of experience at a given point. The finiteness of human persons means they will never attain "a completely coherent account of all experience."[58] Those who make claims to complete coherence may be suspected of pretense or self-delusion. Brightman admonished that "coherence can never be fully applied until all thinking about all possible experience has been finished…"[59]

Another criticism that has often been lodged against the coherence criterion is that it does not lead to certain, final truth. However, as indicated previously, the world is of an evolutionary, developing, or processive character. In addition, there is constant growth and development in the sciences and other fields of knowledge, and there are differences of opinion, all of which make it impossible to have knowledge of the logically certain kind in any final sense in the realm of human experience. For personalism, then, it is not a real criticism to say that coherence does not lead to final truth. It is simply a fact. The coherence criterion leads, at best, to hypotheses that may be viewed as having degrees of "probable truth." Personalism, therefore, views knowledge "in terms of reasonable probability."[60]

A third criticism that has been raised against the coherence criterion is that the inability to attain to final truths may lead to skepticism. Yet this need not be the case. After all, we are finite, limited beings, capable of knowing only in part, no matter what criterion of truth we appeal to. Brightman responds to this criticism in the following way:

> Our apprehension of truth is growing; but it does not follow from this that the present stage of knowledge is worthless and untrue. The view of a distant star through a telescope does not mean that the view with the naked eye is not really a view of that star. It is simply a less adequate, less coherent view.[61]

Although I only see the star with my naked, unaided, weak eyes, I *do* see the star! That I see the star more clearly and adequately with the aid of a powerful telescope does not diminish the fact that I see the same star with my naked eyes, although less clearly. Just as there is a relationship between the unaided view of the star and the clearer, more adequate view, the point is that the levels of truth we are able to attain are related to truth. At any stage in our search for truth it may be said that we do not have a perfect conception of the truth. But if we take the coherence criterion seriously, we may say that it is possible to ascertain the most empirically adequate, or "epistemically reliable" view of the truth at this particular juncture in experience. Our knowing faculties are limited and conditioned, which means that we are necessarily confined to a limited apprehension of knowledge. However, as Bowne maintained, even "a limited knowledge may be true as far as it goes."[62] Therefore, we may at least trust what knowledge we have. If we cannot, then no truth whatsoever is possible. We may say that we have done all that we can do to orchestrate the best of the relevant facts and data into a coherent, systematic, and symphonic whole. We cannot, however, have absolute, final truth. But some truth we can attain, and we are obligated to grasp as much of it as we can. Only God, the Omniscient One, can have absolute truth. Personalism concludes that it is reasonable to be guided by the coherence test until a better one comes along. If we could bring ourselves to stop thinking in terms of an absolute, perfect criterion that will open the door to final truths, we would be in a better position to achieve the levels or degrees of probable truth that we can attain. We must either accept most reasonable hypotheses based on the best we can know at a particular moment, or we must settle for despair and frustration at the failure to acquire absolute truth. McConnell tells us that terms like "absolute infallibility" have only intellectual significance, "and rather barren intellectual significance at that."[63] In addition, Bowne concluded against the idea that we can ever hope to obtain demonstrable truths. We must settle for "a rational interpretation,"[64] of the facts of experience.

That we cannot have logically certain truth about reality need not discourage our search for truth. In such a quest we must "use every possible source of information," and "connect all bits of data at all relevant to the problems we are facing."[65] It may be that coherence is the best we can hope for, for in the end it asserts that "there is only one road to truth-finding, and that is the road of taking everything into account and seeing everything in relation to everything else, as far as a human being can."[66] The great challenge of truth-finding is to orchestrate the whole of experience, striving to see the connections and relations between ideas and experiences, and trying to eliminate as many contradictions as possible. In the final analysis, truth is what coheres or binds together best.

The challenge before us is that we allow no single aspect of experience to dictate arbitrarily to any other part. Each part must have its day before the supreme court of reason; each must be seen in relation to the others, and ultimately to the whole. Yet the results may never be viewed as final. Thought and reality are not identical, and therefore "thought must always hold its results [about reality] humbly and open to correction, with the awareness that there is infinitely more beyond the best thought of the present."[67] We can never say that we have truth about reality once and for all.

In the quest for truth we must remain open to, and be willing to examine, all relevant facts. We must work hard to get rid of as many contradictions as we can and to arrive at the most coherent view of the evidence. And we must have the courage to follow the facts wherever they lead, disregarding no facts or evidence because they lead to a view that is contrary to what we previously believed. Bowne provides an instructive word for all who are genuinely interested in truth and knowledge.

> Come and let us reason together and look at the facts together, must be the scholar's motto; and he must always aim at adjusting his thoughts to the facts, and never at adjusting the facts to his thoughts.[68]

The next four chapters introduce the reader to two substantive issues in personalism. Chapters 6 and 7 each provide a different perspective on the doctrine of God. This will lay important foundation for understanding personalistic ethics and social ethics, which are discussed in chapters 8 and 9. In the final two chapters attention is given to some challenges and next steps for personalism.

6

Borden P. Bowne's Theism

It is not an overstatement to say that personalists in the Bowne-Brightman tradition have espoused some of the most orthodox as well as the most unorthodox and creative ideas about God. There is no uniform doctrine of God among personalists. Neither is there unanimity of thought regarding a number of other philosophical issues, for example, time and its relationship to God and the world.[1] It can be said, however, that theistic personalists in the Bowne-Brightman camp do reject the view of an all-embracing Absolute.

The mainstream of personalism adheres to the view of a God who is omnipotent, omnibenevolent, omniscient, and nontemporal. This is the view of Bowne, although he defined the divine attributes differently from traditional views. For example, omnipotent and Absolute did not mean for Bowne that God can literally do all things. It means, rather, that God can do all things that are doable. As a being of supreme intelligence and integrity, God cannot do the ridiculous, nonsensical, irrational, or unintelligible. To speak of God as Absolute (in Bowne's sense) means that God is limited by nothing beyond Godself. In addition, it means that God is that Being upon which all else is dependent and has its existence.[2] So we need to be clear that although Bowne did not hesitate to speak and write of God as the Absolute, he was by no means a metaphysical absolutist like Mary Calkins, who defined metaphysical absolutism as "the doctrine that the universe is fundamentally a single, individual, and all-including being."[3] This all-including being is not the God of the Christian faith, however. But when Bowne refers to God as the Absolute, he has in mind a God very similar to the God of Jesus Christ. Furthermore, it will be recalled that in chapter 2 Bowne was scathingly critical of metaphysical absolutism or absolute idealism.

The view of philosophers and theologians that God is "a kind of absolute metaphysical being," completely devoid of moral attributes such as love, goodness, and involvement in creation,[4] was rejected by Bowne. The God of Aristotle, for example, was deemed to be problematic. Aristotle's God essentially set all things in motion and then removed Godself from involvement in creation. Accordingly, God's major activity is thinking God's own thoughts and merely enjoying Godself, while showing no concern for persons, the rest of creation, and the destiny of the world. For Bowne, Aristotle's God is not the God of the Christian faith. It is, rather, the God of reason. This God is metaphysically conceived and has primarily a "metaphysical function."[5]

Too often the God of philosophy, even when it has moral qualities, possesses them in only abstract ways. Bowne had little patience with any view of the Absolute whose "holiness consisted mainly in making rules for men and in punishing their transgression."[6] Bowne had not a little contempt for this despotic deity who merely ruled over, but displayed no obligation to, created persons and the rest of creation. Such a God, he believed, is not worthy of worship. The more thoroughly religious conception is that God is supreme reason, supreme righteousness, and supreme goodness. A supremely good God would necessarily care for and love the entire creation, much as a loving parent would care for and love her children.

Brightman, like Bowne, recognized that the human mind is limited, and that in the quest for ultimate truth it inevitably comes up short. Mystery remains. However, as his thinking matured, Brightman was more willing to press the mind further in the direction of a more reasonable explanation for the existence of suffering and pain. More than Bowne he insisted on pushing the mind beyond seeming limits. Often when faced with troublesome or difficult metaphysical issues, Bowne took a more religious-faith line rather than strictly adhering to consistent, thoroughgoing philosophical radical empiricism.[7] It sometimes appears that when reason, the facts, and following empirical method suggested a conclusion that was different from his faith stance, Bowne would settle for his faith. In a moment we will see that this seemed to be the case regarding his doctrine of God and evil as well as his conception of God and time. In these matters the facts and his own method suggested the opposite of what he concluded. In other words, it seems that Bowne sometimes appealed too quickly to human ignorance. One such instance is his treatment of the problem of evil.[8]

Brightman, himself an adherent of theistic absolutism in the early part of his career, relinquished this view when he surveyed the history of the evolutionary process and saw all of the destruction alongside the more positive occurrences. He seemed to take more seriously than Bowne the tragic elements throughout the history of human experience. He consciously sought to understand these in light of his earlier view that God was both omnipotent and omnibenevolent. Indeed, Walter Muelder and Laurence Sears maintain that Brightman, more than Bowne, faced "more squarely the dysteleological and the evil in nature and in man."[9] His attention to empirical fact in the physical and biological sciences, his determination to force reason beyond the point where Bowne stopped, and his allowing reason greater creativity in an attempt to see whether the amount of suffering and pain in the world can be made to cohere with the idea of a God who is "all-powerful" led Brightman to reject the traditional view of God as Absolute. Brightman proposed, instead, the provocative hypothesis of the "finite-infinite" God. He believed that personalism in its most thoroughgoing sense leads one to this hypothesis. Not many in the personalistic school follow this line of thought, but there are some notable exceptions, for example, Bertocci, Muelder, John Lavely, S. Paul Schilling, and Harkness.[10] But clearly, personalistic theistic finitism is the minority perspective.

This exposition of the doctrine of God in personalism focuses primarily on the views espoused by Bowne and Brightman. Generally the work of other personalists is a continuation and/or development of the insights of one or the other of these men. My discussion of their views is not intended to be exhaustive, but to indicate some of the main components of each man's theism. I point to what appear to be strengths and limitations in each view, followed by suggestions for improvement. Brightman, in some ways, took the problem of evil more seriously than Bowne. He did not resort as quickly as did Bowne (following Lotze) to the argument that it is impossible, from the standpoint of human reason, to solve the theodicy problem.[11] I will attend to Brightman's response to the problem of evil in chapter 7.

I begin with a discussion on Bowne's argument for theism. I consider his stance on the classical arguments for God's existence, a discussion of both the metaphysical and ethical attributes of God, and the problem of evil.

Bowne's Argument for Theism

We will need to remember that according to Bowne the theist cannot demonstrate or prove the existence of God with absolute logical certainty. Indeed, the attempt to provide such proof is not even the basic aim of theism. Instead, the fundamental aim of theism is to show that although God is that postulate that cannot be proved, without the assumption of God the problems of metaphysics, epistemology, ethics, and life cannot be solved.[12] Bowne was in complete agreement with those who held that science and philosophy, reason, and morals depend on God, "the only foundation of truth and knowledge."[13]

Although Bowne was convinced that there are limits to human reason and that philosophical speculation admits to no solution to the problem of evil and other ultimate questions,[14] he never undermines the importance of logic and metaphysics. To be sure, these do not give us all that we need in practical life, but they do not deprive us of making practical postulates, as long as we are aware that they are practical in character, and thus are not demonstrable. For Bowne "nothing can warrant us in contradicting logic and metaphysics, and no such contradiction can escape final destruction."[15] Therefore, we should always be willing to proceed with logic and metaphysics as far as they take us. Beyond that, particularly in areas of ultimate concern, for example, freedom, God, and immortality, we will have to resort to "the realm of practice and probability." The intellect cannot decide once and for all in such matters, and therefore must yield to belief.[16]

Metaphysics opens the door to belief in a first cause or ground of all things. But this alone is not sufficient for those who desire to worship God. Epistemology shows that reason or intelligence can avoid shipwreck only on the assumption of the existence of God, who is the cause of idea and object and provides the solution to the dualism between the two. But the God that epistemology leads us to is not the God of Christian faith. To reach this God it is necessary to resort to "the demands of our moral and religious nature, or on some word of revelation, or on both together."[17] Thought can lead us to belief or faith, but by itself it cannot lead us to positive faith or faith in a personal, caring, and loving God.

According to Bowne, the work of logic and metaphysics comes rather late in the whole process. A great deal of actual living has occurred long before critical reflection enters the scene. In any event, even the work of logic and metaphysics falls well short of absolute, demonstrable truth. "In every department our knowledge is patchwork, and rests on assumption."[18] Bowne was influenced by William James's idea of "the will to believe" in this regard, holding that when we have followed logic and metaphysics as far as they can take us and we still fall short of complete demonstration, we then have the right to believe what we have the deepest need to believe. For example, we have the right to believe in the existence of the God of Christianity, even in the absence of absolute proof. It is important to remember that in principle it is crucial in Bowne's personalism that reason be strained and pushed to its limits before resorting to this. The knowledge we come to about reality and God may be imperfect and inadequate, but it is not totally false and irrelevant.[19] A God who loves and cares for all creation would reveal something of Godself to intelligent beings, even while retaining an element of mystery. Bowne came to this conclusion in his first book. Some of his views changed at various points in his development, but not this one.

> Though, to be sure, we now see through a glass darkly, yet the image there discerned must not be wholly distorted. As we think of the infinite to come, it becomes plain that there is much in the Infinite One which we can never hope to understand, but upon which we can only gaze; yet must not all be wrapped in shadow; something must pierce through to the sunlight and the clear blue. In contemplating Him we shall ever be as men watching in the darkness of early dawn, with a deep sense of awe and mystery pressing upon us; still there must be some glow upon the hill-tops and a flush in the upper air. There must, indeed, be a solemn silence that reverence may bow low and worship; but there must also be a voice which we can trust, bidding us be not afraid. The absence of either of these elements would lead, I believe, to the decay of all true religion. In the God who commands our reverence and our loving worship, there must be mystery, and there must be manifestation.[20]

Bowne always insisted that "though belief has a highly complex genesis which admits of no very clear presentation," it is the business of logic and reason to hold it accountable. There is no question about the tendency of humans to believe certain things about reality and God, but this alone does not prove that we have the right to believe. "Hence, after the genesis of a belief has been described its truth remains an open question. It is therefore the province of logic to go through the luxuriant growths of credulity and cut down such as cannot prove their right to exist."[21] Our deepest beliefs are a matter of life. Logic does not object to this, as long as it is remembered that such beliefs are not demonstrated or proved. Regarding the deeper issues of life, the whole person enters the argument, not just the rational faculty.[22]

This difference between what we can expect from logic and metaphysics and what actually occurs in life regarding our deepest beliefs is important. In his argument for theism, Bowne intentionally made this distinction. In addition, he began with the argument from intelligibility, showing that though this leads to the idea of a Supreme Mind or Intelligence, it is not the God of religion. He then argues that to get to this God it is necessary to consider religious and moral-ethical ideas. The God of philosophy "appears as the principle of knowing and explanation," but is rather detached and uncaring. To say that philosophy leads to the view that God exists is a positive step in itself. Yet this God is not worthy of worship. As for the deepest questions of thought, for example, whether God exists or not, we may never expect to come upon the line of no resistance for reason, but our hope must rest with the line of least resistance.[23]

The Argument from Intelligibility

From the standpoint of logic, Bowne believed that the most convincing evidence for theism is the intelligibility of the universe, that is, the fact that the universe is knowable. He considers five arguments for the intelligence of the world-ground. The least important, or commonsense arguments, are inductive, and thus can be arrived at by conclusions drawn from observing particular facts. The commonsense arguments include the argument from order, from teleology, and the argument from finite intelligence. Wherever we observe the facts of order, purpose, and intelligence it is not uncommon to raise the question of authorship. The more important arguments for theism, however, are speculative. These include the arguments from epistemology and metaphysics. Epistemology shows that to know things we must think them or "form thoughts which truly grasp the contents or meaning of the things."[24] We are at an impasse if we do not assume "that the thing world is essentially a thought world, or a world which roots and expresses thought."[25] All of nature is characterized by thought. "Nature is speech, not existence. If nature expresses the thought of a thinker beyond it, it is quite credible that we should find thought in it."[26] Metaphysics, on the other hand, shows that the categories of mind have no existence apart from intelligence.[27] It is active intelligence that interprets and gives meaning to the categories of thought, for example, the notions of being, unity, identity, causality, space, time, and purpose.

If the universe were not intelligent, we (intelligent beings) would have no way of getting in touch with it—no way of unraveling any of its mysteries. That we have been able to read the universe at all is evidence that it is a product of thought. We can know this because we are also products of thought. Bowne was adamant that thought can only speak its own language, and in order for us to know anything at all there must be thought at both ends of the knowing process.[28] Thought can grasp nothing but thought or thought relations. All of this assumes, of course, the trustworthiness of reason itself. Any evidence of intelligibility in the universe, then, is a clue that it is intelligible to mind in every respect.

But in saying that the universe is intelligible and that this is "the decisive argument for theism," Bowne did not mean to convey the idea that it is fully intelligible to the finite mind. What he means is that finite mind could not even know the universe is there were it not through and through intelligible. Forever is not enough time to unravel the mysteries of the universe. Indeed, in many instances much that we would like to know about the universe may remain a mystery to finite mind throughout eternity. The point Bowne wants us to grasp is that there is a message there, and because of the nature of reality and mind we are capable of deciphering at least some of the message. We can get in touch with the universe only because we share the common trait of intelligence. That our minds can know anything at all about the world and its objects is indicative that everything is founded in thought.

In the attempt to prove theism Bowne stressed the decisiveness of the argument from the intelligibility of the universe. However, he warned that we should not expect this (or any) argument to prove too much. The argument from intelligibility shows only that Mind is back of all things. The argument tells us nothing or very little about the moral-religious nature of such a Mind, or whether it even has such a nature. To conclude that the intelligibility of the universe points to Intelligent Mind that is the fundamental cause of things does not point to the God of Christianity, for example.[29]

The argument from intelligibility points to theism, but not to theism in the fullest sense of a God who is worthy of worship. Although intellectual factors are important in the argument for theism, other factors, for example, religious and moral, are necessary if we are to arrive at a reasonable conception of the God of Christian faith. But clearly for Bowne the place to begin, and the most significant factor, is the argument from intelligibility. Bowne did not desire to force conclusions about the nature of God beyond intelligence. In terms of anything else said about divine attributes, (in principle) he held the line on the need to allow the evidence to inform what we think about God. This is an important methodological consideration for Bowne, and at every step it is important to ask whether he himself is consistent in this regard. This is especially important in his doctrine of God and the problem of evil. Does he, for example, allow the facts, especially what he often refers to as "the dark things," to inform his way of thinking about God and evil?

In his empirical method Bowne uses the analogy from finite to Infinite Intelligence. What is important here is that Bowne was never totally dependent on the analogy from finite intelligence. Rather, he tried to relate this to all relevant and supporting evidence. To do otherwise would leave the door open to abstract constructions that have no foundation in experience. For example, it would become possible to make the claim that the true explanation of the universe is found not in intelligence or nonintelligence, but "in the inscrutable transcendental," a phrase that sounds good but had no real meaning for Bowne.[30] All explanation must be in terms of intelligence. Bowne writes that "X Y Z may be a very profound truth in the realm of the inscrutable, but in the realm of intelligence it is only a meaningless group of letters."[31]

It is highly possible that God may have attributes that have no analogy on the level of finite intelligence. For example, if intelligence has only to do with methods and procedures for discursive reason and shifts from imperfect to more perfect insight, if it has only or primarily to do with inner and outer relations, then we would have to conclude that there may be something higher than intelligence (especially as the term is applied to the Infinite Person). If, on the other hand, intelligence is viewed as essentially the power to know (which is its essential meaning), there is less difficulty thinking of God as Intelligence. "This power to know," writes Bowne, "is not a limitation but a perfection."[32] In addition, the Infinite Reason is intuitive rather than discursive.[33] By definition God does not have to figure things out by appealing to methods and procedures. God's knowledge is direct and immediate.

Bowne did not begin his exposition of theism by considering the full religious conception of God. At the start his was the more humble task of showing the intelligibility and unity of the world-ground. Metaphysics affirms both of these, but it is important to remember that at this point we are a long way from a complete theistic view.[34] Bowne was consciously methodical in his effort to arrive at a view of a God who is more than a metaphysical entity of some sort that is completely out of touch with created persons and the rest of creation. He first sought to establish the existence of the One of philosophy, and to show that it is a unity, or is one rather than many. The next step was to determine the nature of the God of religious faith. Before proceeding with a discussion of this I want to take a slight detour and comment briefly on Bowne's view of the classical arguments for the existence of God.

Classical Arguments for the Existence of God

In his discussion of the classical arguments for the existence of God, Bowne was careful not to force the "positive argument from design"—the only argument for God that has some merit—to prove more than either it or the evidence is capable. For, in his view even this argument does not prove with absolute logical certainty that God exists. Although the evidence presented in this argument is such that one may reasonably conclude that God exists, this is all one can say. The God it points to is at best the God of philosophy or speculative thought. It is not the personal, loving, caring God of religious faith.

Yet Bowne shows us the value of approaching God methodically, and one can easily see that ultimately this must lead to a much broader idea of God. We discover some formal things about God through reason alone, for example, God's unity, eternity, and omnipotence. But through faith, belief, and daily practice we discover a God who is more than intelligence, reason, or will. We find instead a God who cares about created persons and the rest of creation. Bowne effectively opened the door to the idea that it is possible to find the Great Lover or Companion of created persons and creation in a number of ways, and that one's view of God is likely to be fuller and richer if one remains open to all possible avenues to God. In this regard Bowne did a great service.

Bowne was influenced by Immanuel Kant in several ways, including his dualistic epistemology, his emphasis on the activity and creativity of mind, his emphasis on the primacy of practical reason, and his rejection of the classical arguments for the existence of God.[35] He pointed out, however, that Kant (as well as John Stuart Mill) was at least sympathetic toward the argument from design.[36] Clearly rejecting the ontological and cosmological arguments, Bowne also exhibited sympathy for the teleological argument, although not in its classical form.

Bowne rejected the piecemeal approach of the classical form of the teleological argument that this, that, or some other item is the result of design, and therefore there must be a designer. What Bowne preferred, but did not name, is what Bertocci, following Frederick R. Tennant, called the "wider teleological" argument for God.[37] This is a much more comprehensive argument from teleology. Bowne's name for it is "the positive argument for design." It attempts to show that many processes in nature are determined by ends, and that "there is concurrence of many factors in a common result."[38] The emphasis is on mutuality or relationality, or how things affect and determine each other. The starting point is not mechanism or purpose, but our conception of how things work together, according to law, to form an intelligible system.[39] What we need to determine is how such a system is possible and, as Bertocci maintains, "to understand what is buried in this conviction that things interact as parts of a dependable causal system."[40] Once we understand that intelligence purposely works toward ends in orderly, dependable ways, it is reasonable to conclude that unitary cosmic Intelligence is the ground both of the interaction of the orders of nature and of intelligence that seeks to understand and depend on nature and its laws.

Bowne affirmed the essential sociality or relationality of reality. This means in part that nothing can achieve its true end in isolation. "The notion of interaction implies that a thing is determined by others, and hence that it cannot be all that it is apart from all others."[41] Since the activities and properties of a thing are conditioned, the thing cannot exist apart from relations. "Its existence is involved in its relations, and would vanish with them."[42] Things are what they are in relation. It is not difficult to conclude from this that persons are what they are, finally, in relation or community, a point that also has rich implications for ethics and social policy.

Metaphysical Attributes of God

Bowne highlights and discusses two classes of divine attributes. The first group comprises the more formal metaphysical attributes: unity, unchangeability, eternity, omnipresence, omniscience, and omnipotence. The second class includes the more concrete, worship-inspiring ethical attributes. The metaphysical attributes "aim to tell what God is by virtue of his position as first cause." The ethical attributes have to do with the moral nature or character of God and God's more intimate relation with created persons and the rest of creation.[43]

But just as in his discussion of the teleological argument, Bowne was not hasty in the conclusions he drew about God as he considered the metaphysical attributes. Each attribute must be carefully related to the evidence, and care must be taken not to force conclusions. This is why Bowne did not move too hurriedly from the evidence for teleology in the world to the existence of the God of religious faith. However, he believed that the consideration of the metaphysical attributes brings us to a closer understanding of a real living God.[44] Yet at the end of the discussion we still will not have reached the richest religious conception of a God with moral-ethical attributes. To achieve this end it will be necessary to consider the divine character or ethical nature.

Even in the discussion of the metaphysical attributes we get a sense that we are moving in the right direction, since, for the first time, Bowne instructs us that he will be using "the terms, God and world-ground, as interchangeable."[45] Bowne was convinced that there is a point beyond which philosophy cannot take us regarding the nature of God. An element of mystery always remains. He allows us to appeal to "the worship and adoration of religion" in such cases, but he cautions that it is not a procedure that the careful thinker will resort to quickly and easily. Indeed, prior to dependence on ethical and religious demands, Bowne is vigilant in his efforts to lay the epistemological and metaphysical basis for our thought about the divine attributes and God's relation to created persons and the world. However, procedurally he did not hesitate to rely upon the moral-ethical and religious contributions toward the development of a fuller, richer, worship-inspiring idea of God. I now turn to consideration of the metaphysical attributes of God.

Unity

If a thing is a unity, it is at least uncompounded, indivisible, without distinction of parts, and implies that there is but one fundamental existence.[46] The chief exemplification of real unity in experience is the conscious self, which experiences itself as a complex unity. Bertocci contends that "any other model for unity is only makeshift until we can make our way to the unity exemplified in persons."[47] We will see in chapter 7 that this insistence on unity in the world-ground has important implications for Brightman's hypothesis of the internal rational and nonrational givens within the divine nature. If the world-ground is truly indivisible and not compounded, this would seem to close the door on critics who maintain that by locating the given within the divine consciousness Brightman effectively set up a dualism therein.

Unchangeability

The meaning of unchangeability where God is concerned refers to "the constancy and continuity of the divine nature which exists through all the divine acts as their law and source."[48] Bowne's treatment of this attribute reminds one of the ambivalence in his thinking about time. No one has done as thorough a job of examining the problem of change (and time) in Bowne's thought as José Franquiz Ventura, a student of Brightman's.

By suggesting that the problem of time and God is the most serious difficulty in Bowne's view of change and identity, Franquiz Ventura reveals the ambivalence in his thinking regarding time. For example, Bowne sometimes suggests that time is relevant to God and that God is in time. At other times he contends that God is beyond time.[49] Yet elsewhere Bowne writes of the impossibility of reaching "the ideality of time by eliminating change from being,"[50] and even more dramatically:

> Change can never be eliminated from the world of experience, and this world of experience can never be in any way looked upon as a manifestation of a changeless order beyond it. Hence change is real, and if the reality of change implied the reality of time, time also is real, not merely for our experience but for things in themselves.[51]

Although there is considerable evidence of ambiguity in Bowne's treatment of time, Franquiz Ventura concludes from a thorough study of relevant passages in Bowne's writings that in most cases he opts for the ideality of time. In other words, God is beyond time.[52] Bowne did not adequately solve this problem, but it is evident that he was at least aware that a serious problem existed. He could see the problem with an unchanging soul substance in light of a changing world. Having gone on and on about the nontemporality of God and the idea that God is not conditioned by time, Bowne then makes the assertion:

> This is easily admitted for God as the absolute person, but a difficulty arises when we consider him as the founder and conductor of the world-process. This fact seems to bring God into a new relation to time. This process is a developing, changing one, and hence is essentially temporal. Hence the divine activity therein is also essentially temporal. The divine knowledge of the system in its possibilities may be non-temporal, but the divine agency in a knowledge of the actual system must be temporal, because the system is temporal. There is succession in the process and there must be succession in the realizing will.[53]

But Bowne just as quickly rejects this view, claiming that epistemology does not allow us to subordinate consciousness to change. "Consciousness itself is the fixed background on which change is projected and without which it is nothing."[54] So Bowne was at best ambivalent in his view of God's relation to time. It should be pointed out that one of Bowne's great fears was that by acknowledging that God is temporal, one would have to conclude that God develops and evolves. Bowne, of course, was having none of this, claiming that "the notion of an evolving, developing God does not commend itself to speculative thought."[55]

So Bowne finally removed God from all change and time. "Nothing will meet the case except the conception of the absolute person, which freely posits a changing world-order without being himself involved in the change."[56] In the end Bowne concludes that "the only changelessness we need is not the rigidity of a logical category but the self-identity and self-equality of intelligence."[57] What change does exist in the world exists only for created persons, not for God.

Eternity

Already in the discussion on unchangeability there has been reference to the problem that eternity raises with respect to time and God. Bowne did not want God to be considered limited in any way regarding eternity. Bertocci has characterized the issue quite well: "If the thrust of omnipresence is to reject limitations in the here and there of spatiality, the thrust of eternity is to deny the now but not then suggested by time."[58]

Bowne contends that in the most minimal sense eternity has to do with "unbegun and endless duration of existence." This means that God is unbegun and unending, changeless amid change, and consequently never affected by change. God, then, is nontemporal. As in the case of some of the other attributes, Bowne seemed to have a better sense of what eternity is not with respects to God, than what it actually is. God is unconditioned and, therefore, not subject to time. God remains changeless in the presence of change, even though this seems like a contradiction.[59] Bowne was concerned because it appeared to him that if God changes, God cannot be in full possession of Godself. It was difficult for him to see how such a God could be viewed as dependable. Change, he contended, has meaning only for the unchangeable. Bowne believed this point to be grounded in sound epistemology and metaphysics.

Although he did not adequately solve this problem, Bowne suggested both where we must look and what real changelessness entails. We must look to active intelligence or the self. True changelessness is found only in the self-identity or self-equality of person.[60]

Omnipresence

In *Metaphysics* Bowne suggests that as a category of mind space is a principle in being; being is not in space. To conclude that being is in space would mean that space is "a self-existent reality," a view that would lead to the conclusion that there is not one, but at least two fundamental beings. So, as in the case of time, Bowne concludes that space is phenomenal or ideal (though as we have seen this conclusion is more problematic regarding time). "If space be a real objective existence, then the infinite, or rather God, is in space, and possesses bulk and diameter."[61] Bowne could see that if something exists in space it possesses volume and, therefore, cannot be a unity. He is adamant about the implications of a real space for God and the issue of omnipresence.

> But such a conception applied to the infinite cancels both its unity and its omnipresence. That which is omnipresent in space cannot be extended in space, for such extension would imply merely the presence of the being part for part, or volume for volume, in the occupied space.

Philosophy cannot reconcile the necessary unity of the infinite with existence in space, and theology cannot reconcile its conception of the non-spatial mode of the divine existence with existence in space. But if space be real it must be infinite, and God must exist in space, and the indicated conclusions must follow.[62]

The metaphysical reality of space would bring into question the unity of the world-ground as well as "the unity of all principles in one fundamental being." Space, then, is a form of intuition, not a mode of existence. Things are not in space and space-relations, but only appear to be.[63] But Bowne is careful to point out that if we admit the subjectivity of space, we must also concede that there is something beyond ourselves that determines our spatial experience. "This objective factor may be conceived in two ways. We may regard it as a non-spatial system with which we are in interaction; or we may regard it as God himself, who is reproducing in finite thought the order which exists in his infinite thought."[64] Apparent reality, for example, the paper on which I am writing, exists spatially. However, "proper ontological reality" does not exist in space and has no spatial predicates.

As an attribute of the world-ground, omnipresence has always been important for believers. Christians, for example, have always claimed that God is everywhere at once and at all times. The attribute, then, has to do with God's relation to space. The only way the claim of divine omnipresence makes sense is that the world-ground not be regarded as corporeal or anthropomorphic in any sense whatsoever. It is not "stuff or raw material, but cause or agent. It is not something out of which the world is made, but the agent by which the world is produced."[65] Therefore God is not something extended in space, which would greatly complicate the matter of omnipresence. For how would it be possible for an extended being to be everywhere at once, and capable of meeting the needs of the total creation? In addition, an extended being would bring into question the unity of the world-ground, since "in every such being it will always be possible to distinguish different parts which are either actually separate, or are held apart and together only by the forces in them."[66] Extended being cannot be every place at once, but it is quite reasonable to suggest that this is possible for an agent or causality. "Omnipresence is real only as the entire being is present at any and every point; as the entire mind is present in each and all its thoughts."[67]

As immanent in all things, God is omnipresent. Since God is not an extended being in space, it is inconceivable that God ever has to take leave from any given place in order to get to some other place. God does not have to cease one activity in order to start another elsewhere. God needs no "media" in order to do what God needs to do in the world. Instead, God's "activity is rather immediately and completely present." Similarly, if created persons desire to get in touch with God, say through prayer, "neither the prayer nor the person need go wandering about to reach and find God; for we live and have our being in him; and he is an ever-present power in us."[68] Elsewhere Bowne writes that God "comprises all reality in the unity of [God's] immediate activity, and hence is everywhere. For by omnipresence we can mean nothing more than this immediate action upon all reality."[69]

Omniscience

To understand the meaning of omniscience something more than mere "etymologizing" will be needed. In the largest sense the word means knowledge of all things, past, present, future, necessary, and free.[70] However, there must be a limitation on this meaning in light of human freedom. The meaning of omniscience must not be so broad as to also include divine foreknowledge of the specific free acts of created persons. If humans are indeed free (and metaphysics shows that to be is to be free), a free act is only a possibility until it is actually performed.

Bowne contends that just as the omnipotent God can do all that is doable, the omniscient God can only know all that is knowable. Human freedom is a limitation on divine foreknowledge. Although it must be conceded that an infinite and omniscient God may have ways of knowing and knows things that are inscrutable to us, the contention that such a God can know which specific choice we will make prior to our having made the selection raises questions about the divine integrity. God can, however, know the full range of choices or alternatives before us. But if we take the idea of freedom and the idea of God's love seriously it cannot be said that God knows in advance the specific choice we will make. In this regard Bowne would not disagree with William James's analogy of what I will call the cosmic chess player.

James, also concerned about the issue of human freedom in relation to divine foreknowledge, imagines that there are two chess players seated at a table. The one is a master chess player, an expert. The other is a novice, playing perhaps for the first time. On the surface it would seem that the expert knows every single detail about the game of chess, but in fact she does not. What she knows, however, is sufficient to guarantee victory. She knows in advance the full range of moves the novice may make. In addition, she is confident that no matter which move is made she can counter it, thereby assuring victory. But what she does not know ahead of time is which of the many alternative moves the beginner will make before he actually makes it.[71]

According to Bowne's doctrine we may say something similar about God and created persons. God knows all that is knowable about past, present, and future, and certainly all that is expressed in the order of nature. But because of freedom, God's knowledge of the future is limited to the vast range of choices open to humans. God cannot foresee the actual choices that will be made prior to the selection. Indeed, if God did know and did nothing to prevent choices that would lead to tragedy and unnecessary suffering, this would logically bring into question God's goodness and love.

But in his discussion of divine omniscience Bowne raised an interesting question. How, he wondered, is it possible for God to comprehend the "totality of physical experiences" attributable only to created persons? In other words, does God know precisely what I am thinking or experiencing even as I am thinking or experiencing it? This question is all the more significant when it is remembered that personalism maintains that one of the chief traits of person is privacy. In any event, the question of what God knows is a puzzle (and an irresolvable one on all but the theoretical plane), since Bowne held that "the thing itself is realized only in immediate experience."[72] Bowne concluded that if we are neither willing to ascribe experiences such as pain to God, nor to deny God's knowledge of such experiences, we must fall back on the view that God has "modes of knowing" that we cannot comprehend. The question Bowne raised is an important one, since many religious persons believe that God knows and experiences their suffering and pain.

Omnipotence

Bowne's is an absolutistic theism. As absolute or omnipotent God is restricted or limited by nothing in or outside of God's nature. Since Bowne was familiar with much of the philosophical thought of his and the previous generation, he was aware that some philosophers maintained that though God is able to do the "doable," God is "limited by some necessities, probably self-existent and eternal, which cannot be transcended."[73] But he rejected this view as being incommensurate with both the religious experiences of individuals and with speculative thought, since such a view implies a weak or subordinate God.[74] But just as Bowne rejected the idea of a God limited by "necessities of reason, or eternal truths," he rejected the idea of a God that can do all things, including the impossible and the ridiculous. In addition, and in keeping with the attribute of unity, Bowne contended that if God were limited, the eternal truths and necessities of reason would have to be internal to the divine nature. We will see in the next chapter that Brightman recognized this, too, and therefore located the limiting factors within the divine nature. The purpose of this was to avoid metaphysical dualism, or the view that there are multiple fundamental beings.

Bowne acknowledged that there are self-imposed limitations in the divine nature. These at least include the creation of free finite beings, and God's own goodness and reason that are eternally coexistent and integral to God's being. These self-imposed limitations are not viewed by Bowne as inconsistent with divine omnipotence. Indeed, these, in a sense, merely enhance God's omnipotence. God, according to Bowne, is absolute or omnipotent by virtue of being the self-existent cause of all things. That is, God is that being upon whom all living things depend for their existence. Similarly, that all of creation is dependent upon God for its existence is what Bowne means by divine transcendence. That God is the ever present power in and through which creation has its being is what he means by divine immanence.[75]

Only when Bowne considers God in relation to time and the problem of evil does his doctrine of divine omnipotence become seriously flawed. This is especially the case regarding the theodicy question. Bowne admonished that there is no evidence that God's power is limited by other than human freedom and by the laws God imposes upon Godself. God is, in this regard, "bound" by Godself.[76] But this, like human freedom, is a divine, self-imposed limitation. One may wonder, as Brightman surely did, whether this alone is sufficient to account for the existence of nonmoral evil. Indeed, we may agree with Bowne when he says that the God that is worthy of worship must at least possess the perfection of wisdom and selfhood. But that such a God must also possess "perfection of power"[77] is a point of contention and will be taken up in the next chapter.

Ethical Attributes of God

Bowne did not consider suffering, pain, and evil in his discussion of the metaphysical attributes of the world-ground. Indeed, although the metaphysical attributes are important, he argued for the primacy of the moral-ethical attributes of God,[78] for he considered these to be the most worship-inspiring. Consequently, when he did get around to considering pain and suffering in the world, he was most concerned to vindicate the moral nature and goodness of God, since the religious conception of God is that of a God who is worthy of being worshiped.

Bowne's focus, then, was not on the raw power of God, but on the goodness and love of God. Bowne was much more concerned to present a God who is self-sacrificing and the greatest of burden-bearers (as symbolized in the incarnation). So it is not power, or even benevolence, but "boundless love issuing in mysterious self-sacrifice" that is the most worship-inspiring trait of God.[79]

Empirical Grounding of Moral Nature and Goodness

Consistent with personalistic method, Bowne grounds the moral nature and goodness of God empirically. We need merely consider human persons' possession of a moral nature, the structure of life itself, and the course of human history to effectively ground the goodness of God.

The presence of a moral nature in human persons implies the existence of a moral creator. "He that formed the eye, shall not he see? He that giveth man knowledge, shall not he know? So also, he that implanted in man an unalterable reverence for righteousness, shall not he himself be righteous?"[80] If we deny moral will to God we do so at the expense of making God inferior to created persons in whom God has bestowed a moral nature. Just as we cannot deduce intelligence from nonintelligence, the personal from the impersonal, we cannot arrive at the moral from the unmoral.[81] The moral nature in human persons points to moral character in God.

The second aspect of the empirical argument for the moral nature of God centers on the structure of life, in which we find numerous stimuli in moral directions. "Both nature and experience inculcate with the utmost strenuousness the virtues of industry, prudence, foresight, self-control, honesty, truth, and helpfulness."[82] These traits point toward life, while their opposites lead to destruction of values. Bowne argues that even when failures have been accounted for, "the nature of things is still manifestly on the side of righteousness."[83]

Not only do we find evidence for goodness in the structure of life, but in society as well. In the best sense society is "a moral institution with moral ends." Bowne takes account of individuals who are selfish, greedy, and power-hungry in society, and whose behavior diminishes the good that others may gain through organized society. This notwithstanding, he contends that persons cannot live together in life-enhancing ways if society is not based fundamentally on moral ideas. Without such ideas society is susceptible to legalized injustice and oppression, the consequence of which is nothing short of "social earthquakes and volcanoes" that rock, and ultimately destroy, the foundation of society.

The third element of the empirical argument for God's goodness seeks its clues in the course of history. Indeed, the historical argument does not lead to a conclusive view of either the goodness or the evilness of nature. The facts support the existence of both. "Over against the good in nature we should put the evil; and this would hinder the affirmation of goodness. But over against the evil we should put the good; and this would not allow us to affirm a fundamental malignity."[84] Arguing that the religious mind cannot be satisfied with the idea of a basic malignity in history and the nature of things, Bowne appeals to faith in the ideal, and suggests that what appears in the immediate context to be conflicting facts (e.g., the existence of both good and evil in nature) amounts to little more than something we do not presently understand, while "perfect insight" and knowledge would reveal that both have their place.[85] It is not logic that forces this conclusion, but "an act of instinctive self-defense on the part of the mind, whereby it seeks to save its life from destruction."[86] The conclusion that both the intellectual and moral order are universal is based not upon logical demonstration, but faith.

In addition to these considerations, Bowne grounds divine goodness by considering both the good we find in human experience and the moral character of some of the world's greatest and stellar personalities. Any good that human persons do is at least "a faint type of a goodness more august than our own."[87] The highest revelation of God's goodness is found not in nature, but in the noblest persons, that is, in "the pole-stars of the race." I think of the eighth-century prophets, Jesus Christ, David Walker, Marie Stewart, Angelina and Sarah Grimké, Mahatma Gandhi, Martin Luther King, Jr., Malcolm X, Clarence Jordan, Fannie Lou Hamer, Oscar Romero, and Mother Teresa. We cannot but think that in germ these most truly represent the divine character.[88] This points to the view that essential goodness is at the very center of the universe, and that in the final analysis God's goodness and purpose will be vindicated.

God is no "monster of the moral universe"; no selfish, despotic, imperial governor over human persons. Bowne opposed the older theology of his day, much of which was based on the then-prevalent view of political absolutism.

> a great deal of our theology was written when men believed in the divine right and irresponsibility of kings, and this conception also crept into and corrupted theological thinking, so that God was conceived less as a truly moral being than as a magnified and irresponsible despot.[89]

For Bowne, this was bad theology, and the ethics that followed from it were worse. "God, like the king, could do no wrong, and the clay was forbidden to protest at anything the potter might do."[90] Bowne substituted the idea of God as Parent for that of the older view of the absolute monarch who is an impersonal, imperial governor over humanity and the rest of creation. "The deepest thought of God is not that of ruler, but of father; and the deepest thought of men is not that of subjects, but of children" of God.[91] As Divine Parent, God is forever near to human persons, bears with them, and seeks "by all the discipline of love and law to build them into likeness to and fellowship with [Godself]."

If God's nature is truly love and goodness, there must be evidence that God acts with love and goodness in the world. Rejecting the philosophers' conceptions of God as metaphysical perfection, Bowne stressed the idea of God as both ethical and as involved with creation.[92] God, on this view, acts in feeling and loving ways toward creation.

God's Heavy Moral Obligation

Any serious consideration of the moral-ethical nature of God requires that God abide by moral-ethical standards. Although the chief criterion of this is not found on the human plane, it is here that we get clues to its meaning. The best and highest moral-ethical standards among created persons provide clues to what this may mean for God. It at least means that if God is goodness and love, God must do (in the world) what these require. Therefore, if God is Creator and has called persons into existence without consulting them and placed them in a world in which they may—indeed do—suffer all manner of pain, God is responsible for caring for them. Bowne observes that

> from an ethical point of view, [God] is the most deeply obligated being in the universe. And having started a race under human conditions he is bound to treat it in accordance with those conditions. God is bound to be the great Burden-bearer of our world because of his relations to men.[93]

If humans have held among themselves that the strong ought to bear the burdens of the weak, surely God must be the great burden-bearer and fellow-sufferer. "In the moral world he that is greatest of all should be the servant of all."[94] As the most heavily obligated being in the universe, God is as bound by moral principles as human persons. By calling persons into existence in a world with "fearful possibilities of good and evil," God put Godself under obligation to concretely love and care for all persons. Every person belongs to God's family and therefore has infinite value for God. Because persons are so highly valued and loved by God, God is heavily obligated to care for them.

God and Evil

Bowne was impressed with "the order and grandeur" of the physical world, but he recognized that suffering and pain were present everywhere in the world. He believed God to be Absolute in the sense of being the independent ground and cause of the whole of creation. And although he believed that he adequately grounded the goodness of God, Bowne was aware of the difficulty this raised in the face of massive suffering and pain. Indeed, the problem becomes more acute, he maintained, the more the evidence points to a God who is Absolute. For questions inevitably arise as to the purpose of such suffering and pain and about the character of a God who would allow such evils to exist.

When Bowne examined history and evolutionary process he saw evidence of much pain, carnage, and waste. Yet he did not see this as being inconsistent with the moral nature of God. Instead, Bowne vindicates God's goodness. What he failed to see, however, is that this alone did not account for the existence of massive nonmoral evil. Indeed, he devoted little attention to anything but moral evils. In addition, Bowne did not always mean by moral evil the suffering and pain that results from the human misuse of freedom. He often included evils that have nothing to do with human freedom, for example, natural disasters. This tendency seemed only to further obscure his treatment of the problem of evil.

Having established the goodness of God, Bowne refused to consider seriously any challenge to God's power relative to the existence of evil of any sort. Although he too easily dismissed any consideration of theistic finitism, Bowne was clearly aware that for some thinkers this was a viable option. He observed, for example, that the great empirical evidence of suffering and pain causes one to wonder whether in the nature of things there exists "a positive malignity" that produces "contrivances for the production of pain, distorting, thwarting, destroying."[95] However, convinced that God is good, and that given enough time and knowledge it will be seen that all things—including evil of all kinds—have their place in the scheme of things,[96] Bowne dismissed the idea of an inherent intractable element in the nature of things that militates against the achievement of God's purpose in the world.[97] In addition, Bowne had no patience with theories that limited either God's power or goodness in order to account for the existence of nonmoral evil.[98]

Bowne essentially explained away the problem of evil. If it can be shown that the world is an arena for moral opportunity and development, the problem of evil is effectively or practically solved for us. Indeed, he asserts at both the beginning and end of his discussion on evil and suffering that this issue admits of no speculative solution. The problem of evil is that "before which all human wisdom is dumb,"[99] and it is therefore more reasonable to admit "that we have no sufficient data for the speculative solution of this problem."[100] The solution lies beyond the reach of human reason. Knudson expressed well the stance that was Bowne's (and Bowne's teacher, Lotze) regarding our inability to solve the problem of evil.

> The wiser and more scientific method is frankly to confess our ignorance and retain our faith. As Lotze puts it, "Where there appears to be an irreconcilable contradiction between the omnipotence and the goodness of God, there our finite wisdom has come to the end of its tether, and we do not understand the solution which yet we believe in."[101]

We will see in the next chapter that Brightman ultimately challenged the failure to push human reason further, and insisted on the need to take much more seriously not only the facts of nonmoral evil and suffering, but the contributions of the developing biological sciences, dynamic treatments of evolution, the pragmatism of William James, and so on. In addition, Brightman insisted on consistency in drawing inferences about God from created persons. For example, if an analysis of the human person reveals the presence of rational, volitional, *and* brute factors, and if we take this to be the nature of persons as such, we must be willing to apply this to the Supreme Person, although by definition we must not assume that there will be a perfect one-to-one correspondence. But because rational, volitional, and brute fact content are essential traits of person, we cannot refuse to apply these to the Divine Person. This would be a violation of personalistic empirical method. But as we shall see, according to Brightman's mature theism, the hypothesis that there is brute fact content in the divine nature opened the possibility for a radically different and unorthodox conception of God that seems to take evidence and facts more seriously than does the absolutistic theism of Bowne.

However, we would be mistaken to conclude that the issue of an inherent defect in the nature of things was of no importance to Bowne. For he introduced the subject in several of his major writings. But he either did not know what to do with this, or he lacked the courage to follow in the direction this idea seemed to point. Here Bowne was less the radical empiricist and more the orthodox theologian and Christian. Clearly raising the same concern Brightman raised nearly three decades later regarding the power of God and the existence of evil, Bowne concluded that nothing can rock the absoluteness of God. The more traditional, orthodox Bowne insisted that all that happens in nature and the world "represent the moral judgment and wisdom of the Almighty."[102] We have to be willing to see the longer view of things, he argued. What appears evil today may later be seen to have its place in the moral order. For example, Bowne makes much of the point that character is made through suffering, and that the goodness of the world consists in its infinite perfectibility.[103] Suffering and pain in the world clearly had for Bowne strong disciplinary and character-making potential. Indeed, for Bowne the soul of persons is made perfect through suffering and struggle.[104] And yet the final word must be that regarding some aspects of the problem of evil Bowne violated his own method by refusing to alter his doctrine of God in light of some of the evidence and facts. One wonders, for example, how his view of God and evil would have been different had he pursued his suspicion that there just might be an inherent defect in the nature of things that makes it difficult for God to achieve the divine purpose in the world.

Ongoing Progress through Cooperation

What we find in Bowne's absolutistic theism is an adamant, "indefinite," or "decided meliorism."[105] Persons and the world have been created in such a way that the conditions are always ripe for perfectibility. "God's great provision for maintaining that practical optimism without which life could not go on, is found in the inextinguishable hopefulness of humanity."[106] However, the difficulty of achieving the kingdom of righteousness is due only to the unwise use of freedom. The fault lies in human nature, not the nature of things.[107] Yet Bowne was confident that things will change for the better if persons—human and divine—work together cooperatively. What he did not adequately explain, however, is why progress often comes—if at all—at such great cost and sacrifice in human values, as well as values in the plant and animal kingdoms.

Bowne was aware that many would not be satisfied with his conclusions about God and evil, and that none of his considerations remove the fact that there seems to be an overwhelming amount of evil that persons have to contend with in the world. Indeed, it is not just the quantity of evil that confronts persons, but there is also the matter of the sheer devastation that results from certain types of evil. In addition, there is the matter that the consequences of some human choices far exceed the choice made. But here again Bowne concludes that it is misuse of human freedom, and that only, that is responsible for evil and suffering in the world.

Bowne's theism finally points to the idea of a God whose nature is "holy love"; who is transcendent in the sense that all things are dependent upon God; and who is immanent in the sense that God's is the ever present power in and through which all things exist. Indeed, love, according to Bowne, roots deep in life itself, and is the source of all life and creation. It is "the essence" of God's nature.[108]

Consequently, in the end, Bowne, the adamant meliorist, insists that progress will be continuous not inevitably, but because of cooperative endeavor between persons and God. Persons must be intentional about this. That is, they must make the decision to work together with God to achieve the best possible good despite evil and suffering. For if, as Bowne argued, goodness and love are at the center of reality and the universe, these will have the last say. The most reasonable thing for intelligent beings to do is to strive together, cooperatively, to ensure such an outcome.

Adequacy of Bowne's Theism

What we do not find in Bowne is a satisfactory explanation—or even consideration—of evil and suffering whose cause is beyond human freedom. In addition, Bowne's insistence on the ideality of time and thus the nontemporality of God seems to contradict his argument for the goodness of God, since he believed that a good God must act out this goodness in the world. In part, at least, we know that God is good by observing what God does and has done in the world. If God is not affected by time one wonders, How is it possible for God to really care about creation? Or, how is it even possible for a God who calls persons into a world of time not to be affected by time? Bowne himself was troubled by this, as is indicated by the many inconsistencies in his statements about God and time.

Bowne's doctrine of God might have been more empirically adequate had he taken more seriously his very hurried reference to the idea that there is an inherent intractable element in the nature of things that works against the achievement of God's purpose in the world. On this point his empirical method breaks down. Using personal, conscious experience as his starting point, Bowne, unlike Brightman, believed the two chief elements in the person to be reason and will. He did not introduce brute fact content (e.g., appetites and emotions) as a third major factor. (Brightman would do this later and develop his controversial theory of the finite-infinite God.) Bowne was surely aware of the existence of brute fact content in human persons. But rather than follow consistently his philosophical method and infer the existence of an analogous content in the divine nature (which proves troublesome to the divine will and reason), Bowne reverted to his faith and concluded that no matter how much suffering and pain exist in the world, "we are in our Father's hands, and…, having brought us thus far on our Godward way, he may well be trusted to finish the work he had begun."[109] By turning so quickly to faith or belief, Bowne violates his empirical method and his test of truth or knowledge, namely, "positive adequacy to the facts" or "rational probability."[110] His doctrine of God and evil does not meet this test.

Near the beginning of this chapter I cited the claim of Muelder and Sears that Bowne did not take as seriously the dysteleological and devastating evils as did Brightman. And yet there is evidence that Bowne did ponder the idea of the existence of evils that seemed to be irreducible to good, or that are good for nothing. One even gets the sense that he wondered whether such evils had any disciplinary or soul-making value whatever. In *Studies in Theism*, for example, he wrote of evils that appear to be "overdone in connection with man."

> There are frightful evils which develop nothing, but rather crush out both faculty and possibility. They also reproduce themselves, and like some malignant venom spread from man to man, and from generation to generation, poisoning soundness and blighting life with death. The laws of heredity and of social solidarity are leagued for human ruin. By the former the sins of the fathers are visited upon the children unto distant generations: by the latter, whole classes of men are handed over to ignorance and destitution of all that makes up a truly human existence. It is hardly possible for multitudes to be human beings, owing to the miserable arrangements of society.[111]

Bowne did not pretend that any of these things were good. They were evil and destructive. Indeed, in his very first book he raised the theodicy question, but said that such a problem is forced on us not by reason, but by the senses, and these "furnish no solution." Said Bowne:

> The clearer the proof of a supreme intelligence, the darker and more perplexing does the moral problem of the world become. The whole creation groaneth and travaileth together in pain. From the very beginning, nature has been "red in tooth and claw with ravin." On every side

we see the most prodigious waste of faculty, of happiness, and of life. "Of fifty seeds she often brings but one to bear." Generations and races of men seem born, only to be beaten and pelted by want and misery. A positive malignity, even, seems to exist in nature, producing contrivances for the production of pain, distorting, thwarting, destroying... What must be the character of the being who can even permit such disorder in his empire?[112]

Yet—and this is where the observation of Muelder and Sears is on target—Bowne was still able to conclude that the cause of such evils is not a result of some inherent intractable element in the nature of things, but a result of human contrivance. He concluded that "the chief ills under which man suffers are the results of his own doing."[113] Bowne had moral evil in mind. But what he did not consider was the cause of nonmoral evils, for example, natural disasters, incurable disease, and so on, that destroy massive numbers of innocent persons.

At any rate, Bowne's theory of God might also have been strengthened had he developed more fully an idea he introduced implicitly, but did not develop. He implied the idea of dipolar theism or the view that God has two natures. In one instance he writes: "In his absolute, self-related existence, God is timeless," and "in his absolute self-knowledge and self-possession God has neither past nor future."[114] The implication here is that God possesses another nature in addition to God's absolute, self-related existence. This implies that there is an aspect of God's nature that is absolute or perfect.

Elsewhere the implication of dipolar theism is clearer still when Bowne writes that "while God in his absolute existence must always remain a fathomless mystery to us, we come nearest to the truth when we think of the Father, the Son, and the Spirit."[115] Here he implies that God has an abstract nature (absolute existence) and a more concrete nature that enables our close communion with God.[116] The latter may be taken to mean that God is in time and thereby affected by and affects all of created existence, most especially persons. On the other hand, God's abstract nature (to which Bowne refers) is beyond time.[117]

Indeed, persons would not come close to God in God's "abstract, self-related existence." It is not this aspect of God's nature that we find most worthy of worship, for it sounds more like the metaphysically perfect, uninvolved God of the philosophers. This view of God Bowne himself combatted with all his might.

However, as "Father, Son, and Spirit," God is forever near created persons and the rest of creation, a point Bowne made most poignantly in his discussion on the incarnation and atonement. He held, for example, that through Jesus Christ God became subject to human limitations and conditions and thereby "assumed our nature and lived our life."[118] In this way God was able to live among us and to witness and experience suffering and pain firsthand. It is this aspect of God's nature—not the former more abstract side—that enables us and God to encounter one another and to affect, and be affected by, one another. This is the side of God's nature that cares for and loves us. It is here only that we experience God as "holy love" (which is how Bowne finally characterized God). Here God is affected by all that is not God, and conversely, affects all that God has (and has not) created.

Had Bowne developed this into a full-blown dipolar theism he might have seen more clearly the limitation of the more traditional, simplistic responses to the problem of pain and suffering in the world. For example, this would have enabled him to preserve both the goodness and power of God with some intellectual integrity. Not only did he not have the language to do this in his traditional monopolar theory of God, but he was not able on the issue of evil and suffering to push himself to follow the evidence where it seemed to be pointing. This, too, was a violation of personalistic method.

Bowne knew the complexity of the problem of evil, but his treatment of it did not lead to the most reasonable hypothesis. His repeated claim that the theodicy question has no speculative solution was made before he allowed himself to push reason further than he did. In the final analysis, Bowne was not willing to dispense with the more traditional God of his faith. Rather than subject this idea of God to honest philosophical scrutiny, he chose to hold it close to his chest. However, a maturing Edgar Sheffield Brightman did not hesitate to diverge from his teacher's treatment of the theodicy issue. Indeed, in Brightman we find both a controversial and creative doctrine of God and evil. Brightman's personalism aggressively and creatively responds to radical evil and the nature of God.

Edgar S. Brightman's Theism

Unlike some of Bowne's disciples, Brightman was quite an original thinker in his own right. Because of his unending commitment to following truth wherever it led; his insistence that all of the relevant evidence and facts be brought to bear on a problem; and his insistence that the evidence not be forced to fit existent theories, Brightman went beyond his teacher at several points. Some examples will illustrate this.

First, Brightman felt compelled to supplement and correct Bowne by the use of more empirical facts through both the biological and psychological sciences, and by bringing to bear on ultimate problems, for example, the theodicy issue, a bolder, more creative, concrete, and imaginative use of reason. In addition, Brightman wanted personalism to be informed by more of William James's pragmatism and his emphasis on doing and action. He also wanted more of Hegel's emphasis on including and harmonizing opposites as far as possible, and including what has historically been left out, that is, "the negative." Third, Brightman embarked on "a renewed study of Darwin and later evolutionary theory, especially Edmund Noble's *Purposive Evolution*."[1] Fourth, he was also influenced by an article by Joseph A. Leighton, "Temporalism and the Christian Idea."[2] In this article Leighton developed the view that the universe is not static, but is essentially processive, creative, dynamic, and developing. From this Leighton concluded that God is limited by the temporal structure of God's experience. Since Brightman agreed with this he developed the hypothesis that God cannot be a being of "finished perfection." The combining of these and other elements along with his awareness of the presence of tragedy amid beauty led Brightman to reject his earlier adherence to Bowne's absolutistic theism. In its place he substituted his controversial hypothesis of the finite-infinite God. To the degree that he was willing to draw the conclusions that the facts and evidence seemed to warrant regarding the problem of evil, it may be argued that Brightman took the tragic in experience much more seriously than did Bowne. Brightman, unlike his teacher and other absolutists, was not as concerned about saving the theological reputation of God in the face of facts that do not cohere with the idea of an omnipotent, omnibenevolent God.

And yet there is no question that Brightman agreed with much of Bowne's theism. Fundamental differences with Bowne lay at two points. The first has to do with the doctrine of time. In the discussion on Bowne's theism we saw the ambivalence involved in his treatment of change and identity. This particular issue is important because of its bearing on time, eternity, and God. Bowne concluded that time is ideal or merely a form of experience. Since he maintained that it has no ontological or metaphysical existence, this means that for Bowne God is not in time. And if God is not in time, God is therefore not affected by time. However, the fundamental question that Bowne failed to answer was how it is possible that an unchanging

God can create other beings in time, be immanent throughout creation, initiate actions toward human and nonhuman life forms, and respond to creation, without also being affected or changed. Brightman takes Bowne to task for this unempirical view of God and time and argues instead for the temporality of God.

Brightman differs from Bowne on other points as well. However, for our purpose I want only to call attention to his rejection of Bowne's absolutistic theism and the belief that this is consistent with the existence of nonmoral evil and suffering in the world. It will be recalled that Bowne was aware of what he referred to as "the darker facts" of experience, but he was not willing to push the argument regarding divine omnipotence in the presence of such facts to its logical end. He was aware of the existence of theories of divine finitism, and one gets a sense from reading his book *Theism* that he chose not to press the argument of whether there is consistency between divine omnipotence and certain types of evil and suffering because he feared that God's reputation might be jeopardized. What will become clear momentarily is that Brightman, unlike Bowne and the majority of his followers, displayed both more courage and a deeper commitment to radical or deep empiricism, with its emphasis on including all relevant facts when endeavoring to solve a problem. Brightman was willing to follow the evidence wherever it led, including the deepest places in hell. Even if the evidence pointed to an unpopular hypothesis such as that of the finite-infinite God, Brightman was convinced that in the interest of truth one should adopt it until the evidence proves the need to revise or drop it.

The Problem of God and Evil

Brightman took the idea of radical empiricism seriously. For him, the radical empiricist must necessarily take into consideration all the facts of experience that may have relevance to a given problem one is trying to solve. Brightman did not hesitate to point out that radical empiricism means including all of those elements or factors that have previously been left out. We saw in chapter 5 that the term he used (following Hegel) to designate such facts is "the negative." Therefore, regarding the problem of God and evil, he went well beyond Bowne. Bowne gave considerable attention to divine goodness but failed to give adequate attention to the facts of evil and how these may be made to cohere with the idea of an all-powerful, all-loving God. Brightman devotes considerable attention to divine goodness as well. However, he insists that the goodness of God must be considered in light of the facts of nonmoral evil in the world. Both good and evil are significant facts of experience, but it is not enough to simply acknowledge this as Bowne did. It is also necessary to seriously consider what this means in light of the traditional view of an omnipotent and omnibenevolent God.

Brightman meets the traditional dilemma regarding God's power and goodness in the face of, massive suffering and pain head-on. It should be remembered, however, that he too began his career as a theistic absolutist. He came under the influence of Josiah Royce's absolutism early, having adhered to it in its entirety for several years before being "swept" off his feet by William James's book *Pragmatism*.[3] But when Brightman began his career he was still devoted to theistic absolutism.

Because of his reading of Edmund Noble and other evolutionary theorists, James, and Hegel, coupled with some painful personal experiences of tragedy, Brightman grappled with the dilemma of divine power and goodness in a way that many had not. It had special meaning for him. The dilemma may be put in the following form: Either God wishes to take away evils, but is powerless to do so; or God has the power to eliminate evil, but is not willing to do so. If God desires to remove evil, but is not able to do so, at least this protects the divine goodness, although a degree of God's power would be sacrificed. On the other hand, if God has the power to eliminate evil, but either does not want to or is selective about it, God's goodness is brought into question, although the divine power remains intact. Brightman wanted to adhere to the principle of being consistent in personalistic method. For him this meant staying close to the facts of experience and drawing the appropriate inferences regarding the divine attributes. Because he wanted a doctrine of God and evil that is coherent with all known facts, he finally concluded that one has to choose one horn or the other of the dilemma, that is, divine goodness or divine power. And yet his revised doctrine of God essentially views God as the most powerful being in the universe, and as perfectly good, loving, and just.

According to Brightman the solution to the problem of evil turns on the relation between goodness and power in God.[4] Although he once adhered to the idea of divine omnipotence even when the facts warranted no such belief, Brightman later came to believe that God desires to eliminate evil, but is hampered by an uncreated, eternal, internal factor called the nonrational Given. Although the world is an evolutionary moral order characterized by law and regularity, Brightman came to believe that a God who is truly good would desire to eliminate evils for which persons are not responsible, and that an all-powerful God would be able to make this a reality. The fact that such evils not only exist, but proliferate, cannot be doubted without making oneself appear stupid. A God who is both omnipotent and omnibenevolent would, pure and simple, put an end especially to nonmoral evil.

Overview of Brightman's Doctrine of God

Brightman once believed that the natural evils in the world are parts of a world of soul-making[5] or of the best possible world. He believed that physical evils that could not be explained in terms of some morally good purpose were similar to natural events that scientists were unable to bring "within the province of causal law." The remedy, he held, was deeper and richer experience and study. This was another way of saying that if we only knew enough we would be able to see that physical evils once thought to have no morally good purpose do, in fact, have such a purpose. This was not unlike part of Bowne's explanation for the existence of evil.

During the early part of his scholarly career Brightman defended the traditional absolutistic conception of God. According to this view, God's nature is essentially exhausted by will and reason. In this too, Brightman was clearly a student of Bowne. But by 1925 there were already signs of his uneasiness with this conception of God. Part of this had to do with a tragedy suffered by a loved one.

Jannette E. Newhall has written of Brightman's marriage to Charlotte Hulsen in 1912 and his experience of watching her die a slow death from facial cancer in 1915.[6] Brightman himself referred to this experience when he wrote of "the ravages of an awful disease [that] swiftly took a loved one away."[7] In addition, he wrote of other inexplicable tragedies that struck various other people who were dear to him. There was no way to make sense of such experiences on the basis of the traditional view of a perfectly powerful and loving God.

Brightman was forced to seriously reconsider his stance not only on the basis of speculative thought. Personal experiences of almost unbearable tragedies, in addition to his critical and intensive study of evolution, led to the first formulation of what he called the doctrine of the finite-infinite God.[8] Also during this early period Brightman paid a debt of gratitude to Hegel's notions of "the true is the whole" and the dialectic (the search for completeness and coherence). Dialectic implies that all reality is characterized by opposition and contrast. This principle, according to Brightman's empiricism, applies to all persons—human and divine. In fact, the nature of consciousness itself contains opposition and tension. These can be overcome only through constant struggle and persuasion. There were other significant influences on Brightman's thought during this period, but what is important is that as a consistent and deep empiricist, he was willing to alter his earlier doctrine of God in light of newly discovered facts and experiences.

Unlike many of his contemporaries and predecessors, Brightman was not content to draw conclusions about God that were inconsistent with the evidence. Instead, he wanted to be true to synoptic method and the coherence criterion by following the evidence where it seemed to point, and then drawing the most reasonable conclusions. In addition, Brightman believed person to be the fundamental explanatory principle. From this he concluded that all inferences about God must be drawn from our understanding of person. This was indeed the stance of a radical empiricist or militant personalist of a different genre. In this regard it may be said that Brightman's revised doctrine of God is the outcome of a consistent and thorough application of personalistic method. This is why he could diverge from Bowne's more traditional conception of an omnipotent God who was primarily will and reason. Brightman's further examination of what it means to be a person—human and divine—led him to the conclusion that there is a third element besides will and reason, namely, a brute fact content. He called this the nonrational Given, which is uncreated, coeternal, and within the Divine Person. This is truly illustrative of radical empiricism at its best. Any truth about the ultimate reality or God must, accordingly, rest on a theory of the person taken as a whole.

A closer examination of the nature of the person revealed to Brightman this third aspect, that is, brute fact content. It is this content that is the basis of his theistic finitism. All experients (persons) have at least three properties according to Brightman: action, form, and content.[9] These three properties approximate will, reason, and the nonrational Given, respectively. These are "inseparable," integral elements of consciousness. Appealing to the analogy of the human person, Brightman writes:

> Our experience of activity would be evidence for the cosmic will of God; our experience of "form" would be evidence for his uncreated eternal reason; and our experience of brute fact would be evidence for his uncreated nonrational content.[10]

The Given is the new element in Brightman's doctrine of God. As a radical empiricist he believed he was only adhering to personalistic method by inferring the existence in God of this new element that is part of what it means to be a person at the human level. If indeed it is true that in person we find the clue to the meaning of reality, then one must at least inquire as to what it may mean relative to ultimate reality if we find the equivalent of brute fact content in created persons. Brightman did not hesitate to explore what this might mean regarding God.

When Brightman reexamined the facts and the emerging new evidence he became critical of the absolutistic conception of God. He maintained that if one is not able to understand just how some evils can be employed to produce good, one should have the courage to admit that these may be evils that are totally irreducible to good, or what Brightman at one time called "surd evils." Evils of this type have no instrumentality whatsoever toward the attainment of good.[11] Later, however, Brightman espoused the view that some good—however imperfect—can be derived from evil of whatever sort. He sent a letter to L. Harold DeWolf expressing this change.

> My statement on p. 246 [of *A Philosophy of Religion*] that "if there be any truly surd evil, then it is not in any sense an instrumental good" was unfortunate, although I intended the context to show that I was not committing myself to belief in that extreme type of surd evil. I should have written something like this: "If there be any truly surd evil, then it is not in any sense an intrinsic good, and it can be an instrumental good only in a very imperfect sense."[12]

So for all intents and purposes, Brightman relinquished the idea of surd evil, claiming that if there are such evils, some good, however imperfect, may be derived from them through persistent struggle and cooperative endeavor.

Unable to reconcile nonmoral evil and suffering in the world with the idea of an omnipotent and perfectly good God, Brightman became convinced that a new hypothesis, more consistent with the facts, was needed. So he proposed the theory that there is a coeternal, internal, nonrational element in God's consciousness that acts as a "retarding factor" in the divine will. The power of God's will to achieve God's ends is therefore limited by what

Brightman named the nonrational Given. But since the inexhaustible good will of God is grounded in experience, God, according to the new hypothesis, is finite-infinite. That is, the power of God's will is limited by the nonrational Given, but God's love, justice, goodness, and moral character are perfect and unchanging. In addition, God's will and reason are always urging, persuading, and molding the nonrational Given in the direction of best possible goods. Analogically, this is what happens when created persons are at their best and intentionally strive to achieve the best. The difference, of course, is that because God's nature is love, God is always striving toward the achievement of the best.

Brightman, wanting to account for what seemed to be senseless evils, for example, the long and excruciating suffering that persons victimized by incurable disease often have to endure, attributes this to the lack of rationality in the internal nonrational Given in God's nature. He came to see that the problem (unlike what Lotze, Bowne, and Knudson believed) is more complex than the presence of an inherent limitation in human rationality to account for the failure to understand how some evils can produce good. Religious revolters against reason like Søren Kierkegaard held that the limitation of the human intellect is what causes persons to conclude that there may be some evils that are strictly nondisciplinary and irreducible to good.[13] But for Brightman—who once held a similar view—this was no longer an adequate response. Nor could he any longer believe that most human misery is due merely to the misuse of human freedom. Unlike Kierkegaard and Bowne, Brightman sought to penetrate the purposes and being of God by human reason,[14] recognizing that reason can only take us so far. But he was convinced that it can take us farther than Bowne thought.

Brightman believed the hypothesis of the nonrational Given can be grounded in human experience. In addition, he held that it may be likened to a retarding factor that makes it difficult for God to achieve ideal value (much as the appetites in humans can retard and thwart our ability to achieve our highest ideals). At the same time the nonrational Given causes the evil of incurable disease, imbecility, and other forms of nonmoral evil and suffering. Since the nonrational Given is of the nature of consciousness (i.e., is both internal and integral to God's nature), Brightman maintained that his new theory escapes some of the problems of metaphysical dualism that are inherent in finitistic theories such as those espoused by William James and William P. Montague, which contend that the uncreated coeternal aspect that God's will struggles against is external to the divine nature. Brightman believed that by placing the limiting factor within rather than outside of God's nature leaves fewer questions unanswered. Questions may be raised in either case, but Brightman maintained that his theory is the path of least resistance for reason, and thus is the most reasonable view.

Brightman's goal was to propose a theory of God that more consistently adheres to the facts. He therefore distinguished between the "expansionist" and "contractionist" theories of God. The former points to a God who is absolute, while the latter calls attention to the immanence of God and God's sharing in human suffering. Brightman, in true Hegelian fashion, sought to see divine expansionism and contractionism in dialectical tension. The expansionist view, seen in isolation, tends to protect the divine dignity at the expense of sacrificing a God who is immanent, caring, and loving enough to work toward eliminating human suffering and misery. To consider the contractionist position in isolation protects God as lover of all creation, but at the expense of God's dignity. Believing there to be some truth in each stance, Brightman sought to preserve both the dignity of God (divine transcendence) and the love of God (divine immanence). He maintained that his theory of the internal nonrational Given makes it possible to preserve both. This was Brightman's version of dipolar theism, although he did not use this terminology to describe his position.

Brightman renounced Aristotle's concept of the deity as *actus purus* (pure actuality). This is a being in whom all potentialities have become actual, and all possibilities are perfected.[15] Such a being is "completely self-determined with no potentiality for further development." The Aristotelian doctrine implies that God has done all that needs to be done in the world and in human affairs. However, one need not look far to see that the facts of experience suggest otherwise. Experience is as wide as the content of consciousness, and truth is the most coherent interpretation of that vast range of experience. So all relevant facts regarding the problem of God and evil must be given their day in court. But once the truth-seeker has given a coherent rendering of the facts, she must have the courage to draw the conclusion that seems to follow from the evidence, and then live accordingly. The truly empirical thinker must be empirical in every aspect of experience. Writes Brightman:

> It is strange, but true, that many philosophers, who are intelligently empirical in their attitude toward the physical world and toward most moral and social experience, become abstract, remote, and artificial when they talk about religion.[16]

This commentary is given further weight because many who still cling tenaciously to the absolutistic view of God insist that though created persons are free, God possesses perfect foreknowledge. Such persons are also adamant that God has only self-imposed limitations, the chief of which is human freedom. They imply that divine self-imposed limitations are sufficient to account for the existence of nonmoral evil and suffering. It is precisely at this point that Brightman diverges from theistic absolutism.

The absolutist fails to adequately account for the existence of "nondisciplinary evil" in the world. If God has none but self-imposed limitations, it is conceivable that God would be able to eliminate evils that seem to have little or no disciplinary value. None can deny the continued existence of such evils in the world. What, for example, may be said to be the disciplinary value of the natural disaster that indiscriminately takes the lives of thousands of innocent children, women, and men? That such evils continue unabated, according to Brightman, suggests: Either God can eliminate them but will not; or God desires to do so but cannot.

Contrary to popular misconception, Brightman's hypothesis of the finite-infinite God is not that of a weak God. The power of God's will is limited to effect God's purposes, though God is infinite in goodwill, beauty, and love. God, accordingly, does not possess "all power" in the traditional sense. However, God continues, in Brightman's theory, to be the most powerful being in the universe and thus is able to achieve ideal good through the cooperation of created persons. God's power is sufficient to achieve God's purpose in the world. In addition, Brightman could see that the claim that God possesses all power is a contradiction, since experience shows that other beings in the universe—not least of all created persons, as well as nature—possess some power as well. God, according to Brightman's theory, possesses what Charles Hartshorne terms "unsurpassable power." This is not, however, the same as saying that God possesses all power. God's power is sufficient to God's tasks in the world, and is surpassed by no other power.

Brightman's doctrine of the finite-infinite God is not popular among most personalists. Nor is the doctrine to be identified with personalism as such, since finitistic personalism is but one of several forms of personalism. In addition, there are non-personalists, for example, Plato, William James, H. G. Wells, and William P. Montague, who were also theistic finitists. Yet there are those outside the personalist tradition, for example, Henry Nelson Wieman and Bernard Meland, who do not hesitate to say that "there is nowhere a fuller facing of the problem of evil which lies at the door of personalism" than Brightman's doctrine of the finite-infinite God.[17] Because there is no evidence that the main outlines of Brightman's theory have been adequately disputed, his remains a viable way of understanding the problem of God and the continued existence of nondisciplinary evil in the world. A fuller account of the theory of the finite-infinite God is therefore in order. But before proceeding with this I want to briefly note some further evidence that led Brightman to adopt this hypothesis.

Evidence for the Finite-Infinite God

Reviewing the intellectual climate of the late nineteenth and early twentieth centuries, Brightman determined that there was considerable protest against the then-prevailing idea of an absolute, unchanging, static God—a God who was neither involved in nor affected by the day-to-day events in the world. Brightman discovered four factors of that period that, taken together, preempted the older, more abstract view: (1) evolution, which stressed change and becoming; (2) a new concern for time and growth, especially as represented in the work of the French philosopher Henri Bergson; (3) the emphasis of voluntarists upon the significance of human will and initiative or activity; (4) the process philosophy of Alfred N. Whitehead.[18] The last years of the nineteenth and the early years of the twentieth century, then, were characterized by an emphasis upon change, growth, creativity, and process or development. These were all emphases in the work of Bowne as well, but as we saw earlier, there was an element of ambivalence in his discussion of time relative to God. Bowne was simply not able to come to terms with the idea of a developing God, which, in his view, must be the case if God is affected by time. It would be left to Brightman to show what aspect of the divine nature is probably affected by time and change.

What are some other facts that point to theistic finitism? One of these pertains to several objections to theistic absolutism, each of which points to finitism, since it takes the opposite view. In the first place, absolutism appeals to ignorance. It contends that surd evils are inexplicable and that we must be honest and acknowledge our ignorance, while retaining the faith that through immortality we will somehow discover what we presently do not know.[19] What the absolutist fails to explain, however, is that if we are indeed ignorant, how is it possible that we possess any knowledge at all? If we are ignorant, we have no right to suggest that "surd evils are real goods." The theistic finitist maintains, however, that although persons possess imperfect and often inadequate knowledge, we do possess some knowledge. The Brightmanian theistic finitist always seeks evidence in present experience and knowledge (or what is "known" to be true) and proceeds from that point.

Second, those who claim that God is perfect and possesses all power tend to ascribe surd evils to God's will. If (as the absolutist claims) God's will is omnipotent beyond human comprehension and faces no conditions it did not create and approve, then the ultimate source of all surd evils must be in the divine will. The finitist wonders why a God of infinite love and goodness would will such evils into existence. In addition, it is no consolation, Brightman contends, to say as Martin Luther did that if God's omnipotence could be comprehended by reason, there would be no need for faith.

Third, theistic absolutism tends to make good and evil indistinguishable. It views all "apparent" evils as goods. But the finitist asks: If this is the case, what can we know about values at all? The only response the absolutist can give is that it is our limited knowledge and foresight that causes us to conclude that specific instances of evil are, in fact, evil rather than good. In this view all evils that appear to the human psyche to be irreducible to good must nevertheless be judged to be good. But the finitist retorts: If it can be said that what seems evil is really good, it may also be said that what seems good is really evil!

Fourth, theistic absolutism seems to paralyze moral endeavor, thereby making it impossible for free beings to participate in the creative struggle with God to conserve and increase value in the world. Absolutism effectively removes all incentive and desire for moral reform and transformation in persons because of its denial of the reality of time and its belief in a timelessly perfect world. Brightman held that if "what happens in time is reduced to the level of phenomenon or even illusion," efforts to make changes in the time order lose their "militant cast."[20] The absolutist seems to imply that the world is already perfectly good. But this does not square with the facts of experience. The finitist wants to know: If the world is already perfectly good, then why sweat over trying to change it? What is there in such a world that warrants changing? How does one change for the better that which is already perfect? The point, the finitist claims, is that the facts of experience reveal that there is indeed much that needs changing in the world. The absolutist who implies, on the one hand, that the world is perfect, but works diligently to change various things in the world on the other, is involved in a contradiction. The fifth objection is that theistic absolutism tends to neglect some aspects of experience. Rather than begin at the point of present conscious experience and move to the unknown (e.g., the existence of other persons, nature, and God), it more often begins with the unknown or with preconceived ideas, and then proceeds to the known. In other words, absolutism often tends to be unempirical. It is "a theory founded on an *a priori* faith, which in turn grows out of desires found in certain types of religious experience."[21] Radical empirical method requires that we begin with the known and proceed to the unknown. The failure to consider all knowable aspects of experience makes absolutism unempirical. The primary limitation of absolutism in this regard is its tendency to treat religious desires as absolute and *a priori*.' Rather than consider all of the relevant facts, the absolutist is content with the a priori faith that these facts will be explained at some distant time in the future.

Brightman believed his finitistic theism to be more empirical than absolutism, since it is based on all facts that can be known in experience rather than merely those of one's own arbitrary choosing. Herein lies the major difference of opinion between absolutism and finitism. "The absolutists neglect or explain away the harsh details of experience in the interests of their rationalistic faith growing up out of the concrete rough-and-tumble of experience."[22] The theistic finitist always begins with the facts of personal conscious experience. The movement is always from known to lesser known, and as far as possible preestablished conclusions are rejected.

Characteristic of Brightman's method and the Hegelian influence on him, it follows that there are also points of agreement between theistic absolutists and finitists. Both agree that: (1) God is a person or eternal conscious spirit; (2) ideals are objective, and God's will is eternally disposed to the realization of ideal values; (3) God is worthy of worship, and goodness is more fundamental than power; (4) persons worship God not because God's power compels them to, "but because the eternal will of God is eternally loyal to those ideals which impart value to existence"[23]; (5) God is responsive to created persons and the creation, and is therefore conscious both of Godself and of all other happenings in the world; (6) in some sense God is guiding the cosmos; and (7) both agree that God is limited by the principles of reason, and the freedom of creatures like us who may choose to do less than the "best possible," thereby contributing to the temporary thwarting of God's purpose in the world. There is a difference, however, in the way the absolutist and finitist view these two divine self-imposed limitations. The absolutist contends that both freedom and the principles of reason are approved by God and are in themselves sufficient to account for all suffering and pain in the world. The finitist, on the other hand, maintains that these two limitations taken together fail to adequately explain the ongoing presence of nondisciplinary evil in the world. Brightman's finitism requires that something more be introduced in order to provide a reasonably adequate explanation for the continued existence of such evil.

Similarities and dissimilarities notwithstanding, Brightman was adamant that the two schools of thought (absolutism and finitism) propose fundamentally different solutions to the problem of evil, and "imply fundamentally different practical attitudes in many concrete situations."[24] At bottom the absolutist believes that all evil is willed by God, and ultimately sees evil as good. The finitist insists that there are some evils neither willed by human persons nor by God, for example, natural evils, incurable disease, imbecility. The divine goodness and character requires that God forever struggle against, persuade, and shape such evils in ways that produce the best possible good. Evil is not willed by God, according to the finitist. As noted earlier, however, Brightman did finally concede that some good—however small or imperfect—may be derived from evil of any sort.

The theistic finitist is one who believes that the eternal will of God is eternally confronted by uncreated obstacles (in addition to divine self-limitation), either external or internal to the divine nature. If the obstacles are external, we are confronted with the question of metaphysical dualism, of which Bertocci appropriately asks:

> If there are two different realities co-eternal with each,…the question arises: How comes it that once God turns his attention to this matrix supposedly indifferent to himself, he finds it so amenable to his persuasion that the present orderly universe exists…?[25]

From the time of Bowne, personalists have seen the difficulty of postulating the existence of two ultimate realities, particularly when they seem to have nothing in common. The existence of two or more such entities is a contradiction in what we claim to be a universe (rather than a multiverse). There can be no universe where there are two or more unrelated ultimate realities. If these realities are able to interact at all, it is likely to become evident that the one is superior to, and therefore in control of, the other in some way. But it is questionable that they can interact at all if there is no likeness between them, that is, if they are not made of the same basic quality. However, if the obstacles to the divine will are internal (which is the most empirically adequate view according to Brightman), we have a version of personalistic idealism,[26] and thereby escape the problem of metaphysical dualism.

Brightman considers other evidence that points to a finite God. For example, he includes a more in-depth discussion of the empirical nature of (1) finitism; (2) evolution; (3) the principle of dialectic with its emphasis on the idea that everything in experience is confronted by something that stands over against it, and that all conscious experience is a union of conflicts, tensions, purposes, and thoughts and that there is always a striving from lower to higher; (4) dysteleological surd evil; and (5) discussion of the belief among most religionists that the most worship-inspiring characteristic of God is God's goodness and love, as opposed to divine power. Goodness, Brightman

maintains, is more fundamental than power, and is therefore more fundamental to the finite-infinite God hypothesis. Power as such is not
worship-inspiring. For Brightman "only the power of the good is adorable,
and it is adorable because it is good rather than because it is power."[27]

Just what does Brightman mean by finite-infinite God? What are some
of the key traits of the Given? What are some criticisms of the Given? Because of the importance of the idea of divine perfection for believers, I shall
devote some attention to this idea near the end of this chapter.

Characteristics of the Finite-Infinite God

Brightman's first systematic formulation of his theory of the finite-infinite
God appears in his book *The Problem of God* (1930). A second, more concise
and cogent version appears in chapter 3 of *Personality and Religion* (1934),
under the heading "The Finite-Infinite God." This is the best available introduction to Brightman's theory of God.

Not able to reconcile the traditional horns of God's omnipotence and
omnibenevolence in the face of evils that God did not create and for which
divine self-limitation could not account, and believing that the only way he
could sacrifice God's goodness was to adopt an atheistic stance, Brightman
concluded that the most reasonable way of explaining the existence of such
evils was to introduce the idea of a God whose power is limited by coeternal,
internal, nonrational factors that are in opposition to the divine will. More
will be said about these factors in a moment.

Brightman's hypothesis of the finite-infinite God suggests that God retains enough power to ultimately achieve the divine purpose in the world.
What Brightman actually did, without explicitly saying it, was to redefine
the term omnipotence. More traditional understandings of the term caused
many people to become "lost and embrangled in inextricable difficulties." It
will be recalled that even Bowne rejected the idea that omnipotence means
the ability to do anything and everything. Rather, it means the ability to do
all things that are doable. Interestingly, we find that even in his doctrine of
the finite-infinite God, Brightman maintains that God has sufficient power
to do all that is doable, even as God possesses absolute and perfect goodness. God does not possess all power. Yet all life depends on God for its
existence, and in this sense God is, even for Brightman, omnipotent or absolute. Brightman's preferred language, however, is that God is the most powerful being in the universe, and quite capable of achieving God's purpose.
That God is not able to achieve the divine purpose at this precise moment is
not the point, according to Brightman. Rather, the point is that a close look
at history, evolutionary development, progress in the sciences, biblical and
other spiritual accounts of God's workings in the world, and so on, more
than adequately supports the hypothesis that God is working out God's will
in the world.

God, Brightman contends, is finite in power and infinite and perfect in
goodness and love. This, he believed, is the best or most reasonable way to
reconcile the existence of nondisciplinary evil and suffering in the world

with the idea of an infinitely good God whose power is surpassed by no other being in the universe. One merely makes a mockery of self and logic, in addition to becoming embrangled in all kinds of metaphysical difficulties when he or she insists in the face of nonmoral evil that God must necessarily and simultaneously possess all power and perfect goodness.

Brightman's conception of God gives ample consideration to both the transcendence and the immanence of God. The idea of divine transcendence often over-emphasizes the dignity of God so much that human suffering and conditions of massive and systemic oppression are entirely overlooked or ignored. This idea comes dangerously close to the deistic view of a God who created the world, set all things in motion, and then left it to fend for itself. The idea of the immanence of God, on the other hand, seeks to explain human suffering by the divine life and suggests that God not only shares in human suffering, but that God also participates in solving the problems of human suffering. A temptation of adherents of the divine immanence theory is to make God so much a part of human existence that one loses the sense of the holiness of God.

Brightman believed it possible to preserve something of both the transcendence and immanence of God in his theory of the rational and nonrational Givens within the divine consciousness.

> The conception of a God limited by the Given within his own nature, yet wresting meaning from it by the achievements of his rational will, seems to account more adequately than other ideas of God for the paradoxical assertion of religious experience that its object is both a Mighty God [transcendence] and a Suffering Servant [immanence]. It places the Cross in the eternal nature of God.[28]

It will be helpful to further characterize the nonrational Given that presents such a challenge to God's will. From where did Brightman get the idea of the nonrational Given?

The Rational and Nonrational Givens

As noted previously, the idea of the nonrational Given is the new element in Brightman's theory of God. The concept is arrived at through analogy with the human person. This is a significant place at which Brightman's personalism is at once more empirical and thoroughgoing than Bowne's. Brightman took a critical look at personal conscious experience and concluded that there is present in it not only reason and will, but a third factor. Therefore, personal conscious experience always has in it a "predominantly passive" and a "predominantly active" aspect, and each always occurs in conjunction with the other and is inseparable from it.[29] Both aspects are given, and therefore not willed or created by the person. The person finds these in her or his consciousness.

The passive element has two forms. One is sensation, for example, emotion, appetite, pain, pleasure, impulse, desire, instinct. Elsewhere Brightman characterized these as "brute fact content," all of which "are problems, starting points, capable of functioning either as obstacles to the will or as instruments for it."[30] Brightman equated this aspect with the nonrational Given.

The second element in the passive aspect of consciousness is reason or the principles of reason. The laws of reason "cannot properly be said to do anything; we perceive them and acknowledge their validity, but they do not think for us. Hence, they are relatively passive."[31] The element of reason is equated with the rational Given.

The other aspect of consciousness is the active side, or will. It is the will that acts on the passive experiences and works with or against the laws of reason. Together will and reason are capable of refashioning and shaping the brute fact content. "Our activity is directed on the content of sensation, and is subject to the limits of rational possibility."[32]

Brightman's reason for looking again at the nature of consciousness was to determine whether there was something in the nature of things that could account for nondisciplinary evil. Using the method of analogy, he then inferred the existence of a nonrational Given in God's consciousness.[33]

> Creative activity, complete and unerring reason, and a content of experience which includes the whole range of divine sensation—all suffering, all obstacles to reason and purpose: such would be the structure of God's experience if it bears any analogy to man's. Then his creative will would always act under the conditions which are presented by the passive factors in his experience, namely, the given unchanging principles of reason, and the given eternal facts of divine sensation.[34]

Brightman and Bowne were in agreement regarding the presence in persons of will and laws of reason. The new element (in the divine nature) proposed by Brightman is sensation. Bowne was aware of this element in human persons, but he did not draw from this the inference that as Person there must be a similar element in the divine nature. Indeed, Bowne also used the analogical method in his reasoning about created persons and God. But he seems to have believed that attributing sensation to God's nature would be a case of pushing the analogy too far. At any rate, Brightman recognized that there is no perfect correlation between the nonrational Given in created persons and that in the Divine Person. He was aware of the limitations of the analogical method. But as a radical empiricist seeking to be consistent with personalistic method, he believed it reasonable to infer from his analysis of persons the existence of the equivalent of sensation or brute fact content within the divine nature.

According to Brightman there is sometimes such a tremendous challenge to the rational Given (reason) that the achievement of ideal good is frustrated or hindered at a given moment, even though the will may ultimately be victorious. Mindful of the limitations of the analogical method, it may be said that analogically this is also the case with the rational and nonrational Givens in God's nature.

Just as sensation limits the will and reason of man, yet presents problems which can be solved in rational terms, so The Given limits the will
and probably the foreknowledge of God, without limiting his goodness
or his rationality or his power so to mold The Given as to derive value
from it.[35]

Although God's struggle with the nonrational Given is eternal, God is
never baffled (as we humans are), and therefore can always bring meaning
and value out of the most dreadful evil. Brightman might have said (more
explicitly at this point) that since we and God have business with each other,
we can—when we work together cooperatively—bring meaning and value
out of evil situations (even though the evils have no intrinsic value). If God
achieves value without the assistance and cooperation of created persons, it
cannot be seen to have the same meaning or worth as when it is a joint ven-
ture between us and God.

Traditional theists will find it difficult to accept Brightman's view. Such
is the case with many in the personalist tradition as well. Yet the conception
of the nonrational Given within God's consciousness seems to adequately
account for much of the evil and suffering in the world. According to
Brightman, the nonrational Given both accounts for the existence of nonmoral evil and gives reason for continued activity and striving to achieve
value amid difficulties.

Therefore, despite the difficulty some may have in accepting this doctrine of God it seems reasonable to conclude that since God has to face internal limitations, such a God is likely to be even more sympathetic with the
limitations and sufferings of created persons. That God is eternally confronted
with the nonrational Given also renders greater significance to the temporal
nature of experience, while not impinging on God's dignity. The presence of
the internal nonrational Given means that God's willing occurs within rational limits. Although God, in such a view, takes the temporal process more
seriously than other views, God's transcendence remains unchallenged. There
is, within the divine nature, then, the mysterious and nonrational, along
with the moral and rational. These combined make God more worthy of
worship.[36]

As a "retarding" factor within God's nature, the nonrational Given causes
difficulties for God in the achievement of ideal value. At the same time it
causes evil and suffering in the world. Because the nonrational Given is of
the nature of consciousness, Brightman contends that it escapes the problem
of dualism that is inherent in theories of finitism that locate the limiting
factor(s) outside the divine consciousness. When Brightman writes that the
nonrational Given is "a conscious datum or perception, analogous to human sense experience," it should be remembered that this is analogy only.
We must be careful to avoid transferring to God limitations that belong only
to created persons. The Given is the "name which describes the total complex of eternal factors in the divine nature which he did not create and with
which he always has to deal in the eternal activity of his perfectly good will."[37]

The Given is an integral part of the total complex conscious experience of God.

The eternally active will of God is always confronted by the Given. The Given is composed both of the uncreated laws of reason and the uncreated brute facts of experience such as sensations, desires, horrendous suffering and pain, the forms of space and time, and all else that may be sources of nonmoral evils. The uncreated necessities within God's consciousness "have no reality apart from the unity of the divine personality."[38] This is a crucial point to remember when trying to understand Brightman's doctrine of the Given. It should also be remembered that from the time of Bowne, personalism maintained that the person is a self-identifying, complex unity and thus is indivisible. The person is not just an entity composed of numerous disconnected parts that may be dissected by a scientist. The person—human and divine—is a complex unity, and thus a whole. This point is consistent with the analytic-synoptic method that seeks to analyze all parts, relating them to each other, and ultimately relating the parts to the whole. The Given, then, is but one aspect of the total divine Person, and must be considered from the standpoint of the whole unity of the Person God is, rather than in isolation. The Given is a distinguishable, but inseparable, part of God's consciousness.

Brightman highlights several other traits of the Given. Because it is of the nature of consciousness it is an integral element within the divine nature. It therefore follows that since there is no unconscious matter within God, the Given is a conscious experience of God, as is every aspect of personal experience. It should be remembered that personalism holds that all persons are "through and through conscious."

The Given is also complex. It stands for the total, uncreated, eternal nature of God. This includes rational and nonrational elements within God's nature, for example, moral law, reason, and eternal brute fact content.

Another important trait of the Given is that it is eternal and uncreated. If this were not the case, it would be the product of divine creation, since something must account for its existence. If God created the nonrational Given, one would have every right to wonder why a good and loving God would have created such an obstinate obstacle to the achievement of ideal good in the world. It was Brightman's intention to be a consistent radical empiricist. He was always looking to, and taking seriously, the facts of experience. Because he looked to the human person as the model for analogy with the divine, it seemed reasonable to him that the nonrational Given would have to be coeternal with God and would always be present in divine experience.

> There seems little ground...to believe that [the nonrational Given] will be entirely eliminated. There is more ground to hope that it may be raised to higher and higher levels, and that it may enter into increasingly beautiful and holy creations or the endless future of advances.[39]

That the nonrational Given must be uncreated if God is not to be held responsible for evil seems reasonable enough. However, Brightman's contention that there is little ground to believe that God will ever eliminate the nonrational Given, and that God does not have sufficient power to ultimately destroy it, is likely to be problematic for many believers.

The Given is also internal to the divine nature. This, according to Brightman, is the best way to explain the fact that God has both difficulty expressing divine purpose and yet has a great deal of persuasive power to form and shape the nonrational Given in ways to produce the best possible good. Locating the nonrational Given within (rather than outside) God's nature may still present problems. However, the contention of some finitists that the limiting factor is actually external to God's nature raises many more questions than it answers. It certainly does not tell us how God is able to control it as much as God apparently does if the limiting factor is external.

Critical self-analysis reveals that something slows and retards the achievement of ideal value among persons. On analogy we may reasonably infer that something similar happens within the divine nature. At least we may infer this if it is our intention to be consistent with personalistic method. God knows what ideal good is, but it is clear that it has not been consistently realized in immediate contexts in the world. This implies that something is hindering its realization. However, on the whole, it appears that God is working out God's purpose in history.

Finally, the Given is controlled by the divine will. For Brightman this "implies subjection and guidance, but not creation."[40] Although all of these traits of the Given are uncreated, internal aspects of the divine consciousness, God still persuades, shapes, and ultimately uses them in the service of ideal good. Indeed, God can persuade and shape the Given as much as God does precisely because as a limiting factor it is within the divine nature. "Every obstacle and delay is real; The Given causes the world to be other than it would be if God were strictly omnipotent; it explains the presence of the horrible evils and distortions."[41] All obstacles and delays are patiently faced by the divine goodness, and God is able to bring meaning and value out of them all.

The Given consists then of both eternal necessities approved by the divine will and those not approved. The former acts as an instrument to the attainment of ideal good, while the latter acts as an impediment or obstacle. "God's control of The Given means that he never allows The Given to run wild, that he always subjects it to law and uses it, as far as possible, as an instrument for realizing the ideal good."[42] God's control of the nonrational Given means that no defeat or frustration is final, "that the will of God, partially thwarted by obstacles in the chaotic Given, finds new avenues of advance, and forever moves on in the cosmic creation of new values."[43]

Having already established that God's will is characterized by infinite and inexhaustible goodness, it may be said that any defeat—though real in the life of individuals in the world—is but temporary for God. In addition, some good, however imperfect, can be wrested from evil when God and created persons work cooperatively to oppose and overcome it. The control God exercises over the nonrational Given then consists in transforming it and seeking new avenues of creativity.

Some Internal Criticisms of the Given

Critics within and outside the personalist tradition have questioned various aspects of Brightman's theory of the finite-infinite God. I shall first present the responses of three internal critics. One was a teacher and colleague of Brightman's; another was a colleague who taught at the University of Southern California; and the third was a former student.

ALBERT C. KNUDSON

Both Brightman and Knudson studied under Bowne. In addition, Brightman studied under Knudson. Later they were colleagues at Boston University.

Brightman said that Knudson and Edwin Lewis were the most significant and careful critics of his theory of the Given.[44] Knudson characterized Brightman's hypothesis of the finite-infinite God as a "subtle and refined form of the Manichean theory of natural evil."[45] It differs from classical Manicheism in that it locates the limiting factor within the nature of God, rather than holding that there are actually two forces, eternal and unrelated to each other, one good, the other evil. Brightman's theory, according to Knudson, sets up "a dualism of nature and will within God."[46]

Since God is conceived as a unitary being (a trait common to all persons) as having one undivided consciousness, and as one whose will is the only source of the world, Brightman's theory is monistic. But Knudson contends that it is "monistic-dualistic," since God's will is limited by aspects of the divine nature and therefore is hampered in making the world better than it is at any given moment. Yet Knudson believed that Brightman's "monistic-dualistic" hypothesis was presented in the "most original, complete, and attractive form," and the introduction of limiting factors within the divine consciousness is "new in the history of theistic idealism."[47]

Knudson contended that Brightman's theory is similar to that of Leibnitz, who also held that God is limited by the laws of reason. But Knudson was careful to point out that Brightman's was not just a supplement to the Leibnitzian theodicy. Knudson conceded that Brightman's introduction of the nonrational Given into the divine nature as an eternal, internal force with which God's will and reason eternally confronts is a novel idea. Much of Knudson's critique of Brightman's hypothesis focused on the nonrational Given. According to Knudson there are two decisive problems with Brightman's theory (numbers 1 and 2 below), although he pointed to five additional areas he considered problematic.

1. By introducing a conflictive element into the divine consciousness Brightman "compromises the divine unity and so fails to meet the rational demand for a basal monism." Knudson understood the nonrational Given to be a conflictive element that is over against and apart from God's will.[48] This, Knudson held, implies the existence of two separate natures, so that the Supreme Person cannot be considered a unity.

2. The limitation of God's power is effectively a limitation of God's goodness as well. This makes God less than worthy of worship. Knudson was more concerned that the limiting of God's power implies an inability to actually achieve good. "For the goodness in which religion puts its trust is not simply a goodness of intention but a goodness linked with power, an 'objective' as distinguished from a merely 'subjective' goodness."

3. As the Creator of all there is, God must have known beforehand "the evils that would inevitably result from his delayed and hampered creative activity." Having known this in advance, why would a good God have proceeded with creation since there was no necessity to proceed? To have done so implies that God approves of creation, and thus of the evil in it.

4. It is dogmatic and inconsistent with both the scientific spirit and true religion to suggest that there are surd evils, that is, evils irreducible to good. We cannot rightly claim from empirical observation (as Knudson thinks Brightman did) that much of the suffering in the world has an "absolutely evil and irrational character." Given more time and knowlege, it may become evident that there is no incompatibility between suffering and pain and the goodness of God.

5. The theory of the nonrational Given implies that God is more like human persons than is supported by the evidence. That is, it is "an unduly anthropomorphic conception of God." Like Bowne, Knudson saw reason and will as the two chief elements in persons—human and divine. In addition, he did not see it as problematic that nonrational, given factors were introduced into the consciousness of humans. But to infer the existence of an analogous trait in the divine nature he held to be sacrilege. He believed Brightman to have introduced into the divine consciousness "something akin to an inherited human weakness, a kind of Adamic nature."

6. From where did the nonrational Given come, and why? "If The Given were an integral factor in personality [and for Brightman this was precisely the case], or if it were an essential part of an ultimate rational whole, we might accept its existence without further question." Knudson saw two concerns here. The nonrational Given is not rational, nor is it an essential aspect in person. "Both God and the world, so far as we can see, would be better off without it." Knudson wondered whether the nonrational Given would ever get completely out of control. Does God's control of it increase or decrease in efficiency? He further wondered whether the nonrational Given increases or decreases in its ability to resist God's will. Will God ever tire of struggling against it? Does this not raise questions about the future of believers and the world?

7. There is nothing in the nature of the nonrational Given that gives reason for the existence of specific kinds of evil as a result of its

resistance to God's will and reason. What is there about the nonrational Given that necessarily causes a limitation of God's power at any particular moment? "The Given is merely a symbol of the vague and abstract idea of a limiting necessity, to which God is forced to submit. It throws no light whatsoever upon the concrete evils of life."[49]

Brightman responded to Knudson in his article "The Given and its Critics."[50] As to whether the nonrational Given permanently thwarts God's achievement of the divine purpose, Brightman said this depends on how we conceive divine purpose. Does it mean something to be achieved once-and-for-all? Furthermore, "thwart" is not the best term, since it implies permanent defeat. "The divine will would be thwarted only if the increase of value were to cease, that is, if God gave up the struggle. Despite The Given, no suffering or disaster is final." In addition, the processive, active nature of reality itself implies an ongoingness, so that there is no point at which it can be said that God's purpose is completed. The goal "is not the end of the struggle," but "eternal life which lifts the struggle to ever higher planes."

Brightman said that Knudson's objection that the denial of divine omnipotence implies the absence of moral perfection does not hold up, since empirical observation reveals that there is always something that is not what it ought to be, and therefore of which God cannot approve. Brightman maintained that even Knudson would have to grant this. But if this is the case, it has to be asserted that there is a limitation on divine achievement. This is a refutation of Knudson's demand for "perfect objective goodness" in God.

To the criticism that he sets up too sharp a distinction between the divine nature and will, Brightman responded that Knudson refutes his own criticism "in principle" through his "admission that the divine nature does limit the will." Yet Brightman was aware that Knudson's reference was to reason (the rational Given), while his own view called for an element in God's nature (the nonrational Given) that is neither "ratified by God's will," nor willed and approved. But for Brightman the more important concern was not God's approval of uncreated isolated aspects of the divine nature. Rather, what was most significant was God's approval of the divine Person as a whole, "for his nature as a whole is the progressive control of The Given, not ratification of it."

In addition, Brightman took issue with Knudson's criticism of the existence of surd evils, or evils that seem to have no disciplinary value. Here Knudson, following Bowne, suggested that it is only due to humans' insufficient knowledge and inability to see the whole picture when it is claimed that certain evils are absolutely irrational and irreducible to good. For Knudson, given a choice between affirming divine impotence and human ignorance, he would opt for the latter. Brightman rejected this alternative.

> The choice is not between divine impotence and human ignorance, but rather between two faiths for us ignorant mortals. We must choose between the faith that God's will does not produce the evil in question,

yet can make all things work together for an increasing good, and the faith that God produces both the evil and also a perfectly ideal outcome from it.[51]

RALPH T. FLEWELLING

Flewelling was a student of Bowne's shortly before Bowne's death. He did most of his writing on personalism at the University of Southern California and was the founder and editor of *The Personalist* in 1922. Flewelling maintained that Brightman's way of presenting the idea of the finite-infinite God amounted to no solution to the problem of evil at all, since it implies that God is responsible for evil.

Flewelling did not reject Brightman's theory entirely, however. In fact, he suggested several ways Brightman's hypothesis might be strengthened. First, the nonrational Given must be viewed explicitly as a self-limitation "for a creative purpose." This is clearly not what Brightman had in mind, since for him the nonrational Given is an uncreated, internal limiting factor that is over and above the self-limitations of the necessities of reason and freedom. Second, Flewelling proposed that the purpose must be of such importance as to outweigh whatever suffering and pain occurs. Third, to avoid objections to the theory of the finite-infinite God there must be a way(s) that the individual can solve the problem for oneself, thereby attaining "the highest capacities of selfhood and self-possession." This, Flewelling thought, would present more opportunity for character-making in human persons. Fourth, the theory must reveal more clearly that God shares the suffering and pain of created persons who are victims of evil. This, Flewelling held, serves to complete God's own experience.[52]

Flewelling's last three suggestions are in line with what Brightman included in his theory. However, Flewelling's most problematic suggestion is the first, namely, that the nonrational Given be viewed as a self-limitation, rather than a coeternal, internal limiting element within the divine consciousness. Unfortunately, he did not say enough about this to help us understand why he had a preference for this. It does appear, however, that by making the Given a self-limitation, God is effectively not limited at all. For Flewelling writes: "Here lies the secret of 'the given': the Cross is the solution of the problem of evil. By that complete self-limitation which for the Holy is perfect freedom, God escapes limitation. The Cross of Christ would be an inexplicable offense against humanity unless He who voluntarily hung upon it were also God."[53] Flewelling was also concerned that Brightman's view of the nonrational Given leaves the door open to the charge of internal dualism in the divine nature. But this might not be of such great concern if one remembers what is meant by person. As a complex unity, there is no aspect of the person that is divisible. The nonrational Given is of the nature of consciousness and therefore is an integral aspect of the total personal consciousness of God. The nonrational Given is not a foreign, unrelated element in God's nature. It is, rather, part of the fabric of the divine consciousness, as indivisible as any other element.

A Brightmanian response to Flewelling's criticism that the finite-infinite God amounts to no solution to evil would be that while God is responsible for evil in the sense that God's moral nature obligates God to solve all problems irresolvable by created persons (since God called persons into existence) such divine responsibility does not necessarily mean "that [God] created the terms of the problem."[54] God, Brightman held, may be controller or persuader of the Given without being responsible for having produced evil.

S. PAUL SCHILLING

Schilling was a student of Brightman's and essentially agrees with his doctrine of God. He found that the real problem is that Brightman referred to the nonrational Given with language that left his view of it open to the criticism that it sets up a self-contradictory relation within God's nature. Schilling suggests that viewed in the right sense a nonrational aspect within the divine consciousness presents no problem of disunity or dualism.[55] What is needed is the application of more positive language in describing the nonrational Given, thereby avoiding the misleading connotations that seem to imply a dualism within the divine nature. Unless Brightman's terminology is qualified or replaced, there is no way to avoid the criticism that the nonrational Given implies "opposing tendencies of various kinds that are hard to reconcile with our human experience of a unified cosmos and religious experience of one God."[56]

Schilling took a close look at the etymology of the terms impediment and recalcitrant—terms that Brightman frequently used to characterize the nonrational Given. Schilling found that application of the former to God "intimates that because of it he is somewhat at odds with himself, lacking in harmony of aim and execution."[57] To postulate the presence of an impeding factor in the divine nature implies a hindrance, obstruction, blocking, or preventing God's normal functioning. This, Schilling held, is suggested by the Latin term *impeditus*.

The Latin verb *recalcitare*, on the other hand, means "to kick back, or strike with the heels." Therefore, "to be recalcitrant is to be obstinate, disobedient, or stubbornly rebellious; to resist restraint or defy authority."[58] Schilling concluded that "a God who must suppress a recalcitrant element in his own being hardly qualifies as the Ground of the universe we experience or the ultimate Source of healing and wholeness in the personal and social life of fragmented human beings."[59]

Brightman would have appreciated Schilling's contribution. However, to those who insist that his theory sets up a dualism within God's nature he would say that "we must choose between accepting an eternal malicious Satan and an eternal nonmalicious but problematic resisting force that produces a tension and a drag within the divine nature."[60] Surely the idea of an eternal Satan running loose in the universe threatens the unity of the ultimate rule of goodness much more than the view of a "resisting force" within God's nature that God's will and reason can persuade to higher good.

External Criticisms of the Given

Other critics have suggested that the nomenclature Brightman employs to characterize the limiting factor within God's nature, namely, the nonrational Given, implies a Giver. But one need merely remember that for Brightman the nonrational Given is a coeternal, uncreated, integral part of divine consciousness. Therefore, by definition it does not imply a Giver. Critics have also objected to the view that the nonrational Given is analogous to sensation. Here the rejoinder may be that just because sensations within humans often arise from external stimulus, this does not necessarily mean that the nonrational Given within divine consciousness arises in the same way. The nonrational Given in human persons does imply an external world. "But if God is to be God, his Given controlled by his will explains the world. The content of the Given is analogous to sensation without its having an analogous cause."[61] It is important to remember that the method of analogy has its limitations, especially when we begin making claims about God based on human experience. So it is crucial to be careful not to read more into or out of the divine nature than can be supported by the evidence. There are several other criticisms that have been directed at Brightman's view of the finite-infinite God, but for our purposes I want to note just two more.

First, some critics have claimed that religious experience demands a God who is perfectly powerful and perfectly good. Brightman conceded that religious experience is one of several ways of finding God. However, experience does not support the contention that the God that religious experience finds necessarily possesses the attribute of perfect power. In addition, there is no universal agreement as to the nature of the God found in religious experience. It may be that the most we can determine from religious experience alone is what William James suggested, namely, that "God is the natural appellation, for us Christians at least, for the supreme reality...We and God have business with each other; and in opening ourselves to his influence our deepest destiny is fulfilled." But religious experience itself does not provide indisputable evidence for a perfectly powerful God.[62] The most we may glean from religious experience is the idea of a power that is greater or wider than the religious experient, and who is friendly to both that experient and ideal value.

Second, the most acute and serious criticism made against Brightman's doctrine of God is that it sets up a dualism within the divine consciousness. We saw in chapter 5 that personalists are epistemological dualists, that is, they believe that idea and object are not one and the same. Instead, there is a dualism between them. But this is quite different from the charge of metaphysical dualism, which is the accusation against Brightman's theory of the nonrational Given. Brightman himself rejects metaphysical dualism, claiming that his view does not undermine the "assertion that the unity of personality contains complex experience which is controlled, although not originated, by God's creative will."[63] But, given a choice between a dualism of God and Satan, and a monism that prescribes all that is—especially evil—to the will of God, Brightman would most assuredly opt for dualism.[64]

Brightman himself may have unwittingly contributed to leaving himself open to this criticism. His use of certain language to characterize the challenge that the nonrational Given presents the divine will may well be the culprit. The use of such terms as "impediment" and "recalcitrant element" does tend to imply that there are two fundamental forces in the universe—one God and one the force represented by the nonrational Given, which impedes and obstructs God's efforts to achieve God's will in the world. The implication is that God literally struggles with a being that is completely foreign to, and outside of, the divine nature.

If we suppose for a moment that Brightman's view does lead to metaphysical dualism, there would indeed be what critics say is a division of power in the universe. They would have every reason to wonder how it is possible to be assured that God will always be able to control what Brightman refers to as "recalcitrant elements" in God's nature. Brightman's response, however, is that "an eternal Satan threatens the unity of the ultimate rule of goodness far more than does an antithesis within the divine nature which divine power can always lead to higher and higher syntheses."[65] The idea that the nonrational Given is internal and integral to the divine consciousness led Brightman to conclude that "divine self-control is more credible than divine creation or tolerance or conquest of Satan."[66]

Brightman's radical empiricism prompts the view that the basic structure of God's experience is similar to that of human persons. We saw in chapter 4 that all persons—human and divine—share the basic traits of what it means to be person. All persons are a unity of active will (without which it would not be possible to pursue ideal value); reason or rational principle; and brute fact content. The latter may be likened unto those experiences that are not produced by the will, but are found to be present in every moment of consciousness. Consciousness, therefore, is a complex unity within which are found distinguishable but inseparable functions. The nonrational Given within God's nature, then, is so inextricably interwoven into the being of God, along with God's reason and active will, that there is less need to worry about a dualism within the divine consciousness. Personalism stresses the unity, and consequently the indivisibility of consciousness—including the divine consciousness. Much of the credibility of Brightman's theory of the nonrational Given turns on this point. If one fails to understand the meaning and significance of the unity and indivisibility of person, it will not be possible to avoid the conclusion that the idea of the nonrational Given sets up a dualism within the divine consciousness.

Bertocci argued that the nonrational Given does not set up a dualism in God's nature. Persons are not only complex unities, but they also experience control.

> If the nonrational Given were not as interwoven into the very being of God as are his will and reason, then there would be point to the fear that it might stand "outside" the will and reason of God and thus be unresponsive to the volition and thought of God. But Brightman's view

is that in the unified Person, the phase which we distinguish as "content" rather than form or activity is responsive to control by rational will and as such must be within the framework of the laws of God's nature.[67]

The nonrational Given is an integral part of God's nature. It is distinguishable from the rational Given (i.e., will and reason), but not separable from it. All consciousness—human and divine—is at once rational form and nonrational content. Since "the nonrational Given is a phase of God's total unity, and not made of different stuff," it may be easier to understand how it is possible that God controls or persuades the nonrational aspect of the divine consciousness.[68] God is not always able to completely control the nonrational Given. But it does not necessarily follow that this content is not within the framework of the divine consciousness. Created persons are not always able to control their appetitive nature, but that nature remains within the overall framework of their consciousness.

But a question that continues to loom large is whether or not the nonrational Given will ever get out of control and simply run wild, wreaking total havoc and destruction in God's world. After all, God is finite precisely because God is not able to completely control the nonrational Given in every moment. On the surface such a view is likely to be very disheartening to the religious woman or man. Will the Given get out of control, run wild, and end up controlling God? In keeping with personalistic method, the answer must be that we cannot know this in any a priori sense or with absolute logical certainty. But a close scrutiny of the facts of evolution, history, the sciences, the order we detect in the universe, the ongoing experience of increase in ideal value, and the interaction and cooperation of persons with themselves, nature, and God suggests a high degree of probability that this will not happen. These "are the basic grounds for believing that he who has controlled the nonrational Given may be expected to continue and improve his control."[69] We cannot prove this through intellect alone, but having followed reason as far as it can take us, we may then resort to faith to support our belief that God will not lose complete control of the nonrational Given. We have a right to believe this, although we are without absolute proof. The course of human history, of the value already achieved over evil, and of the best evidence available presently justifies the right to believe that God will continue to control the nonrational Given.

At least two things must occur if one is to develop an accurate understanding of Brightman's theory of the nonrational Given. First, there is need to understand his radical empiricism and his insistence that we begin the quest for knowledge about God, the world, and other selves at the point of personal conscious experience. What we know about God and the world is inferred from self-experience. Second, one needs to understand personalism's doctrine of the unity and indivisibility of person. Failure here will likely lead one to accuse Brightman of setting up a dualism within the divine consciousness.

Divine Perfection

Some critics have held that Brightman's God is not perfect, and therefore is not worthy of worship. It is true that Brightman's God is not perfect if this means static completion.

But Brightman takes temporalism (time) too seriously to be left vulnerable to this criticism. The only thing perfect about a God who is in time and affected by time is God's will to good, love of humanity and creation, and God's knowledge of all that is knowable. God is always engaged in creative struggle with the nonrational Given. So there is no place for a static perfection. All persons are affected by, and aware of, time in every moment of experience. God's principles, purposes, and goodness do not change. But as Person, God too is always a "concrete synthesis of change and identity." To be person is to be affected by time and change. As Person, God must know change. The idea of divine, creative will would have neither meaning nor anything to do if God were not affected by time.

Brightman renounced Bowne's view of the ideality of time. This led to rejection of the idea that God is once-and-for-all perfect, or perfect in the sense of being complete or unchangeable. God's perfection, rather, is a growing perfection. It is not immutable and eternally complete. God's perfection may more reasonably be characterized as "inexhaustible perfectibility." That which is completely and permanently perfect cannot truly be affected by time. There is no empirical evidence to support the idea of such existent perfection.

However, Brightman did not adhere to the view that God was evil at some point and is only now becoming morally perfect. God's good will, reason, and knowledge have always been perfect. Yet experience and a quick look at the world shows that God has not done all that needs to be done. God's moral nature requires God's involvement in a world so full of pain and suffering. If God is involved in the affairs of human persons, God is affected in some way(s) even as God affects what is going on. God therefore cannot be viewed as perfect in the classical sense. Too much remains to be done, and no person—human or divine—can seriously engage this world without both impacting and being impacted by it.

The etymological meaning of the term perfection is *completion*. The idea of a God who is "timelessly completed" may be religiously satisfying to many, but "is as far above human comprehension as it is above concrete imagination; and it is so remote from the facts of experience as to be incoherent (although doubtless consistent) with them."[70] We humans do long for perfection, but such a longing cannot be coherently fulfilled through the idea of a timelessly perfected, completed deity.

In effect Brightman redefines perfection, suggesting that the traditional meaning of the term be replaced with the notion that God's perfection consists in God's endless perfectibility. This is consistent with what we know from experience, namely, that there is much that needs to be done in the world. There continue to be numerous evils to be overcome by God and God's co-helpers. In the idea of the "ideal of inexhaustible perfectibility" we have a conception that is applicable to God and meets the religious needs of created persons. Although God's will is limited by the nonrational Given, God's goodness and perfectibility are "infinite in the sense that beyond every stage of the universe there lies a better one ahead, and every achievement of divine control of the Given is a promise of still more creative achievement further on."[71] God's perfection, then, is a growing perfection. It is never quite finished or completed, but is forever reaching new levels of perfectibility.

Brightman points to four reasons that the divine perfection must be regarded as growing perfection. First, in a growing, developing world there is always more for God to do. Indeed, the present world situation supports this contention. In addition, the nature of person as conscious, ongoing activity points toward the attainment of infinite purposes. Second, the nonrational Given would be dealt with on higher levels as the movement of evolution seems to suggest. Third, the reality of time implies that "increasing purpose" runs through time. God's work is always expanding. Fourth, the creatorship of God suggests that God's creative will is inexhaustible, and that God "will always devise loftier and nobler cosmic dramas."[72] God is not perfect in any final, completed sense, but "is an infinite series of perfectings." God works creatively in history. Although struggling with the nonrational Given, God remains the most perfect being we know. God is always both able and willing to bring meaning out of what appears to us meaningless.

God's will is always guided by perfect love for creation. All experience bears witness to the healing power of nature, and therefore of God, since nature is the manifestation of God's will and thought. God's purpose and will to good are indivisible. This is revealed in experience by the rationality of physical laws, the onward march of evolution, the humanly independent but divinely guided, and so on. What we know of experience and history suggests the existence of a God who is true to divine purpose, despite isolated instances of God's purpose being frustrated in the world.

8

Chief Elements
in Personalistic Ethics

This and the next chapter focus on an aspect of the meaning of personalism in the concrete existence of persons in the world. That is, the emphasis is on ethical personalism, the view that persons are the highest—not the only—intrinsic values. Ethical personalism holds that persons possess infinite worth or dignity. Although thinkers such as Immanuel Kant argued that persons are ends in themselves by virtue of being persons, the type of personalism espoused in this book grounds the dignity and sacredness of persons in God. In other words, persons possess inherent dignity not merely because they are persons, but because they are summoned into existence, loved, and sustained by God. Persons possess inviolable worth because they belong to God, who imbues in each of them the image and fragrance of God.

I do not pretend that all has been said that needs to be said about metaphysical personalism, or that it has no relation to ethical personalism. As a theological social ethicist who takes personalism seriously, I contend that every reasonable social ethic is grounded in a metaphysics or theory of reality, and most specifically in a sound conception of God (a subject addressed in chapters 6 and 7). At some point every theological social ethicist is forced to consider the *why* or the ground of thinking about and doing social ethics. Inevitably the social ethicist must consider the nature and ground of reality and what that reality requires of created persons in their interpersonal and corporate relations in the world. If one happens to be a theistic social ethicist, one must consider what is required of persons in interpersonal and group relations in light of one's doctrine of God.

The present chapter considers some of the fundamental elements in personalistic ethics. Although much attention is given to these elements as they appear in Bowne's writings on ethics and theism, all of these may be found in some form in the ethical writings of five generations of his disciples. Therefore, a primary question that this chapter raises is: What are some of the basic elements that undergird personalistic ethics, and what distinguishes it from other ethical systems? The next chapter focuses on how personalists make moral decisions. But presently attention is given to the essential tenets of personalistic ethics. I begin with a brief discussion of Bowne's ethical theory.

Bowne and Ethical Theory

Bowne was at his best when constructing the principles of ethical theory. By principles I mean those laws that ought to govern and direct conduct at the individual, interpersonal, and collective levels. One of Bowne's students went so far as to say that the best of Bowne's many books is *The Principles of*

Ethics (1892).[1] Another contended that Bowne was a forerunner of what came to be known as axiology or the systematic study of value theory.[2]

In *The Principles of Ethics* we find a text that has important implications for Christian social ethics that is difficult to rival even today. Bowne did not intentionally write as a Christian ethicist. He was always the consummate philosophical moralist. However, unlike many of his contemporaries and successors, Bowne made a conscious effort to apply ethical principles to blood-and-guts issues of everyday living, for example, child labor practices and the rights of women. He accomplished this despite his failure to explicitly apply personalistic principles to some other social issues. For example, there is the glaring, indeed embarrassing, omission of explicit criticism of racism and racial discrimination in his writings on ethics.

For Bowne the aim of ethics was to impose reason on all of life for the purpose of raising life to the moral and spiritual plane. Bowne was not simply interested in espousing lofty ethical principles and ideals, or simply developing what he considered the most reasonable ethical system. He was always careful to point out that the moral always finds its field in the arena of life. It is not an abstraction that is divorced from human experience. Persons engage in moral behavior in the marketplace or in the hustle and bustle of human experience. We discover the subject matter for ethics and solutions to ethical problems, not in the closet, not in the classroom, or the sanctuary, but in the everyday contingencies and uncertainties of life.

In the area of ethics one senses in Bowne a desire to get on with the business of doing and living ethics where it counts most, namely in the everyday world of lived experience. As a philosopher, and not a social ethicist (in the sense that Walter Muelder is a personalistic social ethicist), Bowne clearly recognized the importance of sound ethical theory, critical reflection, and the need to revise both theory and practice in light of such reflection. In addition, he did not make the mistake of ethicists in times past and present. That is, his inclination was not to first spend month after month engaging in critical ethical reflection in the classroom, the privacy of his study, or with a group of experts in ethics, and then (and only then) begin the tough process of trying to determine just how to apply well-worked-out theories to the pressing social issues of the day. Instead, Bowne, anticipating present-day liberation theologians and ethicists, preferred to work out his ethical theory through actually engaging social issues. In this way much of his ethical theory emerged from encounter with the concrete social situation. It is true, however, that he unashamedly began his discussion on ethics by considering three basic presumptions: the sanctity of persons, the primacy of good will, and the centrality of human freedom. The latter, of course, implied moral responsibility.

But having said this, I want to point out that Bowne was not a social activist in the sense exhibited by the lives and works of Gandhi, Martin Luther King, Jr., Fannie Lou Hamer, Oscar Romero, or Mother Teresa. Indeed, Francis J. McConnell reminds us that Bowne's was an individualistic ethic in the sense that he had little understanding and appreciation for the role of institutions in both the cause and solution of social problems. Bowne was always coming back to the individual person, and at bottom believed that the moralization of more and more individuals would lead to the solution of social problems and the establishment of the common good. Only in some of his disciples, for example, McConnell, Brightman, Coe (and their students), do we see a deep sense of appreciation for the depth of sin in human beings and the potential destructiveness of institutions, as well as their potential for justice on a large scale.

Bowne was a philosopher, a personalist, who understood better than most that any philosophical system that is based on the centrality and ultimacy of person cannot in its ethical theory begin the work of ethics anywhere other than with persons, and particularly among those whose personhood is being diminished by socioeconomic and political forces of evil. This, in part, is why Bowne was always adamant that although we may have a conception of the basic principles of ethics and claim to adhere to the primacy of good will (love), for example, it is another matter altogether to concretize or actualize such a profound principle in human conduct. This brings us back to the earlier point that the true laboratory for any ethicist is the field of life itself. Here is where ethical theory that makes sense comes into being and is worked out. Bowne was adamant that the point is not to first work out an ethical theory and then try to force it on a concrete situation. Initial theory informs the situation, but the social context also speaks to and shapes theory, even when the theorist is not aware of it or refuses to acknowledge it.

To a large extent what we see in Bowne's ethics is an effort to take seriously the elements of truth in two schools of thought: the formalist or intuitionist school, and the experience or consequences school. Roughly speaking, the former is an effort to grapple with both Kantian principles and those of utilitarian thinkers such as John Stuart Mill and Jeremy Bentham. From Kant, Bowne took the idea of good will as the absolute disposition in morality. From Mill and Bentham he accepted and applied the emphasis on concrete application and testing of attempts to actualize good will.

Throughout Bowne's ethics there is a tension between good will and its concretization. In personalistic ethics it is never enough to point to the ideal of good will. Because person is at the center of this ethic, it is imperative to determine the concrete nature of good will in the actual experiences of persons. Experience shows that we are often aware of what the common good ought to be, but we have difficulty realizing it when we try to achieve it. Bowne struggled long and hard with this.

> After having decided that the common good as conditioned by moral principles must be the aim of social action, the practical question of the best mode of realizing that good remains entirely open…Ethics of course must emphasize the moral spirit and ideas which should underlie social development, but it cannot dictate its forms.[3]

When we consider ethical principles in abstract thought only, or apart from the arena of life, we discover that our principles may be very clear. The problem comes, however, when we attempt to apply these in concrete situations. The basic principles of ethics do not provide specific directions on how to apply them in the lives of persons and groups. For this there is need to turn to human experience and the work and contributions of the behavioral and social sciences, social and political philosophy, and so on. For Bowne, at least, the chief difficulty lay not in determining the ideal in ethics, but in finding the best way(s) to apply it or to bring persons into harmony with it. The real challenge for the ethicist in the personalist tradition does not lie in developing abstract ethical theories and principles for hypothetical beings. Such a task would be relatively simple to accomplish. The real challenge, on the other hand, is to develop and work out ethical theories and principles in the context of living human beings who are victimized and crushed by existing social problems. The personalistic ethicist, then, would want to know the meaning, for example, of good will in the face of the racism, sexism, classism, and heterosexism of individuals, groups, and institutions.

I have primarily talked about Bowne, but in ethics as metaphysics, philosophy of religion, and epistemology, nearly six generations of Bownean personalists accept the fundamental outlines of his thought, although, as noted previously, several of them, especially Brightman, made improvements by breaking new ground, rather than uncritically adhering to some of the commonly accepted personalistic party lines. But in the final analysis, personalists have endeavored to be thoroughgoing in their personalism. At every point person is the central category in personalism. When we consider this in the discussion on ethics we can see the revolutionary tenor of personalistic ethics. For it means, on the one hand, that nothing we do can be considered either appropriate or morally credible in light of the personalistic credo if it demeans any person. But in addition, personalistic ethics means that an ideal like the "realm of God" on earth could be a reality if we would develop a profound sense of the dignity and sacredness of every person and consciously discipline ourselves to live this out in all that we do. This would mean that persons are more important than things, more important than political and economic systems, which in fact exist for persons, and not the other way around. Furthermore, it means that all socioeconomic and political policies must be developed and implemented with the aim of making the most, not of the greatest number, but of *all* persons. A more profound sense of the dignity of persons also means that persons should respect and care for other life forms throughout the creation. For there have always been in theistic personalism what may be referred to as openings for the development of an ecological ethic. It has never been the intention of personalists that the focus on the centrality and sanctity of persons precludes respect for the dignity of nonhuman life forms. I shall return to this later in the present and final chapters, since there are critics both within and outside the personalist tradition who have claimed that early personalists focused so heavily on the centrality of persons that they failed to consider seriously the dignity of nonhuman life forms and the environment.

Personalism introduced several principles that inform the way that proponents think about and do ethics. And yet there has always been an emphasis on the need to constantly work in the concrete situation to allow it to inform both theory and practice in personalistic ethics. In this chapter I consider how personalists have thought about ethics, social ethics, and moral principles. I primarily discuss two major areas of personalistic ethics. First, basic principles of ethics, which must be conditioned by what Bowne often referred to as "extra-ethical conceptions." Although I essentially have Bowne in mind in this discussion, it should be understood that the same emphases appear in the work of all personalists in this tradition who specialize in ethics. Second, I examine the importance of moral laws or principles (to be discussed in the next chapter). Most thinkers who have written on the moral law system in personalism tend to begin with Brightman, inasmuch as he was the first to actually formulate a system of moral laws. However, I begin with Bowne's influence, since it can be shown that his book *The Principles of Ethics* is actually a forerunner to Brightman's book *Moral Laws* (1933). I now consider what I believe to be the most distinctive feature of personalistic ethics.

Extra-ethical Conceptions

I begin with a discussion on extra-ethical conceptions, since Bowne held that each of the basic principles of ethics must be conditioned or informed by these assumptions. Although no personalist before now has said so explicitly, in addition to the centrality of person these extra-ethical assumptions or conditioning factors are the most distinctive features of personalistic ethics. The reason this claim is made is quite simple. Personalism as an ethical system shares with other types the emphasis on principles such as duty, the good, virtue, love, and justice. However, personalism stands alone in stressing the primacy and worth of the person and the need for all ethical principles to be conditioned by the highest conceivable estimate of the value of persons as such. Personalistic ethics begins and ends with this primary focus on the centrality of the person. It never loses sight of this fundamental point.

Personalism maintains that the chief aim of ethics is the moralization or spiritualization of the entire natural order. That is, ethics is concerned about raising the natural or the everyday world to the moral or spiritual plane. This is done most effectively by imposing reason on experience. "The natural must be raised to the plane of the moral; but the moral must find its field in the natural,"[4] that is, in the everydayness of human experience.

Personalistic ethics focuses on the centrality of good will in the moral life. Accordingly, good will is the only "fixed and absolute" in ethics. "The law of love and the loyalty to what we conceive to be right are of absolute and inalienable obligation."[5] As an inner disposition, good will is an absolute duty. Therefore, no outside authority—human or divine—can absolve us from this duty.[6] This idea is captured in Brightman's law of autonomy[7] and developed in a more systematic way than we find in Bowne.

The emphasis on the primacy of good will is evidence of a strong Kantian influence in personalistic ethics. As Kant influenced Bowne's epistemology (for example in his emphasis on the active, creative nature of thought, and the primacy of the practical reason), he also influenced his ethics. The emphasis on good will is evidence of the Kantian formalism in personalistic ethical theory. Bowne made it quite clear that the central element in all ethics is good will, and that much more needs to be done in terms of the intelligent, persistent, creative, and radical application of it in the social order. But I want to postpone further discussion of this principle for the moment. Instead, I want to return to what Bowne referred to as "extra-ethical conceptions."[8]

Bowne wondered whether ethics is a self-sufficient science based solely on moral insight or intuition, or whether ethics really makes sense at all if its principles and insights are not conditioned and profoundly influenced by some deeper "ideal conceptions" or assumptions.[9] According to personalism, all ethical principles, for example, the duty of good will and justice, must be conditioned by some inner, ideal conceptions. Good will is absolute as a disposition, but the contents of this principle must be thoroughly conditioned by "an inborn ideal of human worth and dignity."[10] And, of course, consistent with the conclusion that epistemology and metaphysics necessarily eventuate into theism, personalism holds that ethics can be formed only by resorting to theistic conceptions. In other words, "theism is a necessary postulate of ethics."[11] This means that ethics finds its fundamental source in God. One works toward the actualization of good will, for example, because God requires it.

So, now, what are these extra-ethical conditioning factors that should inform all that we think and do in the field of ethics? Essentially they have to do with three factors: our conception of the origin and destiny of all life; a profound sense of the sanctity of persons as such; and the highest conceivable estimate of the worth and value of nonhuman life forms. As we will see, the last two assumptions are integrally linked with what may be described as the teleological-developmental component of personalistic ethics. This important element has to do with expanding the moral field to include the heretofore left out or excluded. This principle, it will be seen, has profound implications for race, gender, and class issues as well as for ecological concerns.

Conception of the Origin and Destiny of Life

Ethics is not merely based on our moral disposition. At its best, ethics should appeal to and be conditioned by our conception of the origin and destiny of life. This means that at some point we are forced to address the question of the source of morality and ethics. In personalism that source is the Personal God in whom all persons live and move and have their being.

We may see the value of ethical principles such as the duty to do love and justice, but how or whether these get actualized is dependent, to a large extent, on how we think of the cause and destiny of persons and nature. If we have a mechanistic or materialistic view of reality and existence, for example, one wonders why it would even be necessary to treat human and nonhuman life forms with dignity and respect. According to the mechanistic view, what we do or fail to do should, in the long run, be of little consequence, since necessity will have the last word. In necessitarian systems of thought there is little room for creativity and novelty in ethics. Indeed, one might say that there would be little, if any, room for ethics at all, since choice, in such a system, is negated. Without freedom of choice there is no such thing as ethics.

However, if the cause or source of life is Purposive Intelligence or a Creator who is Parent of all persons, it is possible to view all persons as possessing infinite dignity and worth. This is one of the points at which personalism is influenced by Christian principles.[12] Not unlike both Christianity and Kant, Bowne held that there are at least three assumptions we inevitably come to when we attempt to think the moral problem through: (1) the existence of a moral order; (2) belief in a future life; and (3) the existence of a perfectly good, moral world governor who assures the ultimate victory of goodness.[13] Therefore, Christianity merely strengthens the personalistic faith in this regard. In addition, theistic personalism affirms that it is precisely God, the source of the origin and destiny of created persons, who is the basis of the view that human beings possess inalienable dignity and worth. Persons have worth because they were created by the One God who is Love, who has created us for love. Bowne said it best when he wrote that in Christianity "we are told of a God whose name and nature are love, in whom we live and move and have our being, and who is carrying all things on to an outcome of infinite goodness."[14]

The level of goodness we commit ourselves to is dependent upon and conditioned by our perception of the meaning and destiny of life. In order to realize our highest aims for human and other life forms, we must depend "on something beyond ourselves, ultimately, on the essential structure and meaning of the universe."[15] In other words, our highest ethical aims for self and neighbor are necessarily conditioned by our metaphysical and theological conceptions. What we think about God and the origin and destiny of created existence will have much to do with the way we think about and do ethics. "Our conception of what social relations ought to be must be affected both by our theory of value and by our metaphysics, and hence, manifestly, by our religion."[16] Our way of perceiving the cause and destiny of reality and the world profoundly affects both our ethical theory and our conduct.

Profound Sense of the Sanctity of Persons

No philosophical or ethical system is based on as profound a sense of the preciousness of the person as personalism. The deepest, truest aim of ethics is the achievement of the common good and making the most of persons. But whether or not this is possible is dependent on our awareness and acknowledgment of our innate sense of the sacredness and dignity of self and other persons. Bowne believed this to be an "inborn ideal," and if the highest aim of ethics is to be realized, it will be necessary to condition all ethical principles and conduct by it. This is the second extra-ethical conception. Since persons are thoughtfully, willingly, and lovingly called into existence by God, they all possess "an inextinguishable claim to...reverence."[17] Correspondingly, our estimate—high or low—of the worth and sacredness of persons and nonhuman life forms necessarily conditions and influences the way we treat them. Our conception—high or low—of persons and the rest of creation has much to do with our ethical conduct toward them.

Although the practical outcome of conduct depends much on the unfolding of the moral ideal and strengthening the sense of duty, the application of good will and the formation of corresponding moral codes, and the expansion of the moral field to include all that has previously been excluded or left out, for example, particular groups of persons, nature, and the animal world—all of these are conditioned by a low or high conception of the worth of persons and the world.

> Our conceptions of the worth and significance of humanity, and our general theory of things must have a profound influence upon our theory of conduct. The formal principles of action may remain unchanged, but the outcome will be very different. Thus, a low conception of the sacredness of personality or of the meaning of human life will result in corresponding action. If it does not produce inhumanity, it will certainly tend to indifference.[18]

In other words, we treat our own personhood, that of others, nature, and the animal kingdom with disrespect because we have a low estimate of their worth. We do this despite the lofty ethical principles we espouse. Interestingly, and in a similar vein, ex-slave and abolitionist Frederick Douglass (1817?–1895) also wrote of the need to presume that humans possess the highest qualities, implying the importance of maintaining the highest possible conception of the value of persons.[19] Based on this line of thought, Afrikan Americans, Native Americans, Hispanics, women, children, and the poor are mistreated and demeaned because of the generally low estimate oppressors have of their worth.

Bowne observed that as great a thinker as "the divine Plato," who "wrote wonderfully about the just and the good," defended infanticide[20] and the killing of the aged and helpless. In addition, Plato believed women to be the weaker gender, although he wrote of the equality of women.[21] The great Aristotle had a much lower conception of women, criticizing Plato's view, and placing women on the level of children and slaves relative to rational capacity. In addition, Aristotle agreed with Sophocles that women would do well to speak as softly and infrequently as possible.[22] "In essence Aristotle maintains that woman is a mutilated or incomplete man..."[23] Similarly, Aristotle, "whose ethics has abiding value for all time," defended slavery as rational and right.[24] Furthermore, the ethical systems of both Plato and Aristotle made it possible for adherents to consider as morally permissible those communities in which the best was reserved for the few, while the masses were condemned to partaking of second best. The point of all this is that one may be quite adept at developing lofty ethical theories, but if there is no corresponding high conception of the worth of persons, it is possible to do as Plato and Aristotle did.

> The trouble in these cases was not in their ethical insight, but in their philosophy of man, or in their conception of the worth and destiny of the human person. Apart from some high ideal of the worth of man, there will be no high effort for his improvement, and no inviolable sacredness in his rights.[25]

A low estimate of the worth of persons frequently translates into commensurate behavior, as will the highest conceivable conception. In the case of Plato and Aristotle, Etienne Gilson contends that neither had "a sufficiently high idea of the worth of the individual as such."[26]

What personalists have insisted on, however, is that the inviolable worth of persons be placed at the center of ethics. It does not matter how grand our theory of justice and fairness, love and benevolence, if these are not conditioned by the highest possible ideal of the worth and dignity of persons as such. If we consider that any person or group, animals or nature, have no rights or fewer rights than we ourselves possess, we will very likely treat them accordingly. But the converse is also true. All of history and present-day experience bears this out.

High Estimate of Nonhuman Life

The third extra-ethical conception is important, especially in light of the criticism that personalism has no ecological ethic, or that its heavy emphasis on the dignity of persons somehow precludes the intrinsic dignity of nonhuman life forms. Critics have claimed that if persons only are real (as some early personalists held), and if everything exists in, of, and for persons, this opens the door to a kind of license to rule over and violate all other life forms and the environment. Critics say that a person-centered or anthropocentric philosophy only encourages such mischief.

On the contrary, personalism encourages nothing of the sort. As pointed out in chapter 4, it is important that one understand the sense in which personalists contend that reality is personal and persons only are real. This claim does not undermine the value and worth of other areas of creation. It simply means that all existence is personal or an aspect or experience of the personal. Howison made this point when he said that "the only thing absolutely real is mind,…all material and all temporal existence take their being from mind, from consciousness that thinks and experiences;…out of consciousness they all issue, to consciousness are presented, and presence to consciousness constitutes their entire reality and entire existence."[27] But this does not deny that objects in nature have both a reality and value of their own. In addition, it should be remembered that personalists maintain that all things are the result of God's thought and will in action. God is the cause not only of created persons, but of nature and all its objects. Implied in this is the idea that all existence has value since caused and sustained by the Supreme Personal Will, and therefore should be acknowledged and respected. Personalists do maintain, however, that persons are the highest intrinsic values. But there is nothing inherent in this claim that necessarily diminishes the value of other areas of creation. No personalist in the Bowne tradition has ever espoused the view that animal life and nature are to be trampled on and destroyed at whim by insensitive, arrogant, and greedy persons.

In addition, Bowne's view of miracle has bearing on how we think about the worth of human and nonhuman life forms. To be sure, Bowne was at best ambivalent about the significance of the miracles of biblical history, maintaining that their importance diminishes almost daily, and that they can never be demonstrated through speculative thought.[28] Rather than try to find God in physical miracles, Bowne preferred to seek God's presence and involvement in the development and unfolding of the normal life of persons and their interactions in society and history. Yet both Christianity and personalism insist on the free relation of God to the world, and therefore at least leave the door open to belief in biblical miracles, without deciding the question of fact one way or the other.[29]

Bowne was actually contending against the idea that miracle is a radical departure from the order of law. So he rejected the deistic view of an absentee God, and the idea of an independent, self-propelled nature, which makes God unnecessary in the continuing scheme of things. In the deistic view there are no unnatural (and therefore no divine) events. There is no need for God, since all physical effects are traceable to physical antecedents.[30] Bowne believed all events are natural, but he meant something different than that of the necessitarians of his day. Their view excluded God. But in Bowne's personalism God is absolutely essential if anything is to make sense at all. Therefore, according to personalism, there is no mutual exclusivity between the natural and the supernatural.[31] God and nature are not different and antithetical powers.

The order of law in nature represented, for Bowne, the general form of the free causality of the supernatural, that is, the administrator or cause beyond the natural law. Bowne argued for a Supreme Living Will realizing its purposes under the form of nature. Nature is an order of phenomena, discoverable without appeal to metaphysics, but it gives us no insight into causality. There is no metaphysical nature, but only natural events that occur in an order of law. It is merely a rule according to which the Supernatural realizes its purposes.

God, for Bowne, is immanent in nature, an idea he believed solved the problem of miracle. Accordingly, nature is not causal or self-running as claimed by deistic thinkers. Instead, it is the phenomenal form of divine causality. Nature expresses order and uniformity, but gives us no clues as to cause and purpose. All events are natural in the way they occur. Since theistic personalism includes God in this process, events in nature are not only natural in the mode of occurrence, but they are supernatural in causation. "The commonest event, say the falling of a stone, is as supernatural in its causality as any miracle would be; for in both alike the fundamental reality, or God, would be equally implicated."[32] In other words, every event is supernatural in its causality and is as miraculous as any conceivable miracle. God is implicated in all that happens in the world. This, according to personalism, is the miracle. That human persons can act at all, and with volition, that God is closer to us than we are to ourselves, is the miracle. Since all events have a supernatural root, all things or events are miracles. "The most familiar event proceeds as directly from the divine will as the most extraordinary and miraculous. But the supernatural cause is orderly, i.e., natural, in its manifestations."[33]

Bowne introduced the terms *supernatural natural* and *natural supernatural* to make the point. The supernatural natural means that the natural eternally roots in the supernatural (God). All that happens in the order of law has its cause in the supernatural or the divine immanence. The natural supernatural, on the other hand, points to the idea that the supernatural proceeds in orderly, uniform ways.[34] Yet there is an important caution to keep in mind. Neither nature nor anything else can bind or limit God as the divine purpose is being worked out. God is the absolute source of all finite existence and, according to the Bowne strand of personalism, is "bound by nothing but his own wisdom and goodness."[35] Whatever God's wisdom and goodness dictates, God does. If they call for uniformity and change, there is uniformity and change.

I think this discussion effectively makes the point that Bowne's view of miracle has bearing on the way personalists think about areas of creation other than persons. Inasmuch as personalists believe God is the fundamental cause of all things and events in nature, there is always a miraculous element present. This is no less the case regarding the environment and the animal kingdom. Because of the origin or source of these, they have both rights and value in themselves, which created persons are obligated to respect.

More pointedly, early personalism conveyed the view that animals and nature have value and rights that are not dependent upon their utility for human beings. Instead, they have value and rights in themselves. Those who contend that early personalism had no ecological or environmental ethic must give pause in light of this stance.

> We may not inflict needless pain upon the animals, but, except in this respect, we regard them as having no rights. We enslave them, or exterminate them, at our pleasure; and any effort for their development we may make rests mainly on self-interest. This action on our part rests upon an implicit assumption concerning the relative insignificance of animal life. Or, rather, it should be said that only such an assumption can justify our action; in practice no justification has ever been thought of or desired.[36]

Not only is there need to condition ethical principles and conduct by a profound sense of the sacredness and worth of persons, but it is necessary to see that our estimate—whether low or high—of the value of the animal world and the environment will influence the way we treat them as well.

Personalism maintains that persons pay far too little attention either to their duties to animals and the environment or to their rights. When Bowne wrote of the need in ethics to more broadly expand and increase the moral sphere he did not merely have persons in mind. "He did not," writes McConnell, "think of man as necessarily the peak of all creation, or the universe as necessarily made for man alone."[37] One implication of this is that Bowne acknowledged the intrinsic worth of nonhuman life forms. The most explicit and forceful passage in his work that points to this concern for the value of nonhuman life follows.

> Long ago it was declared that the merciful man regardeth the life of his beast; but in general the dealings of man with the animal world have been a revolting round of brutalities. Here also there is room for extending the moral area, not less for the sake of man himself, than for the sake of the animals. Macaulay is supposed to have made an exquisite hit when he declared that the Puritans were opposed to bearbaiting because it pleased the spectators, and not because it gave pain to the bear. No better reason could be given for suppressing the sport than its brutalizing effect upon the spectators.[38]

Bowne could see that such a view made a mockery of the worth of animals and animal rights. There was no real consideration or compassion for the animals themselves—no recognition of their intrinsic value. The primary focus of Macaulay (in the above quote) was on the effect that the practice of animal torture might have on persons. The rights of the animals were at best of secondary concern, and Bowne clearly found this ethically unacceptable.

Personalistic ethics stress the moralization of the whole of nature. This implies that both human and nonhuman life forms are to be brought under the control of right reason, or developed in accordance with it. "Moral progress can be made only as the good will is informed with high ideals, and is guided by the critical reason."[39] Accordingly, we will more nearly approach what Christianity speaks of as the realm of God if we are diligent in our efforts to moralize all life forms.

> The perfect development of the human kingdom upon earth involves no less than the development and harmony of the animal kingdom and even of the vegetable kingdom, with their mischievous and destructive elements removed or controlled as far as may be, and with all their possibilities unfolding under the guidance of human intelligence. The direction and nature of terrestrial life are coming more and more under human control; and if there were in man a disposition to fulfill his commission "to dress and to keep" the world in which he has been placed, it would not be difficult to turn the earth into a garden of the Lord.[40]

There will be significant progress toward the development of the whole of creation only as the good will is informed both by the highest ideals and the highest conception of the human, animal, and plant kingdoms. A realist in this regard, Bowne was quite aware that the complete moralization of these realms of life was a long way off. Much work still remains to be done.

These three extra-ethical conceptions—one's worldview or the origin and destiny of life; a profound sense of the absolute dignity of all persons; and the need to have a high estimate of the worth and value of nonhuman life—must, in personalistic ethics, condition the application of all ethical principles and conduct. Indeed, failure to do this can lead to all sorts of unacceptable or unreasonable ethical practices. On the other hand, if good will is consistently and vigorously informed by these conditioning factors, we may more nearly approximate the ideal of the realm of God. In addition to the need to apply the extra-ethical conceptions as factors that condition ethical principles, there are three prominent ideas to be considered in personalistic ethics. These include the centrality of good will, the radical and creative application of good will in concrete ethical situations, and the developmental aspect. A brief consideration of these will bring to closure the discussion on some of the basic elements in personalistic ethics.

Centrality of Good Will

In personalistic ethics the emphasis is on the will or intent, the source of moral activity. This means that the good will is at the center of morality.[41] The greatest need in ethics is the unqualified, impartial will to do right. If we possess the will to do the right thing, we will generally be motivated to find a way(s) to do it. But without the will to do so there is little hope that the right thing will be done. "Just as Dr. Bowne conceived of the thinking person as furnishing the clue to the universe, he conceived of the moral will as the only element which would make personal life worth while."[42] Without the will to do right, the moral life reverts back to the natural plane. Therefore, the will to do the right thing is a very important factor in moral development, and is "the only sacred thing."[43]

The good will is an absolute disposition of the moral life and is the most significant factor in the achievement of the moral ideal.[44] From a moral standpoint, no person can be compelled or forced to do right. Civil law may, on threat of punishment, compel one to abide by the law, but such obedience is not a result of moral intent. If one does not have the will to do a thing, but is forced by civil law to comply, it cannot be considered moral. In addition, the good will is still absolute as a disposition, whether we comply with its dictates or not. In personalistic ethics this claim sets the tone for everything else in the moral-ethical arena. A necessary companion of the centrality of good will is its application in concrete situations. The situation itself will have much to say about the best ways to apply good will and the best form(s) it may take.

Radical Application of Good Will

No personalist is content with only the recognition that good will is absolute as a disposition. Although it has authority, good will has neither the power nor the might to insure that it will, in fact, get acted out in ways that will lead to the common good and the enhancement of persons. Indeed, we may say that if good will had power and might as it has authority, it would rule the world.[45] Yet, even if it had power and might, we would be left with the matter of how best to apply good will in concrete ways. One may act from good will, but this is only one of two essential steps. The other is the specification of good will into concrete actions.[46] An important implication here is that the moral disposition needs the assistance of the social sciences, legal experts, politico-economic theorists, social workers, and so on.[47] This is an interesting point, for it is precisely what Walter Muelder proposed when he pioneered in personalistic social ethics. Muelder stresses the interdisciplinary nature of social ethics. Bowne did not develop a systematic social ethic. Against critics he maintained that his ethics pointed more in the direction of social ethics than individualistic ethics.[48]

From the time of early personalism, morality had a double aspect: one subjective and one objective. The former is concerned with motive, intent, disposition, or "the spirit of the agent." The objective aspect has to do with the concrete application of principles and the consequences of the act(s) performed. "In concrete ethics there is need for both the good will *and* the appropriate manifestation of it. As life develops, the fitting forms of action are gradually recognized and become customs and conventions."[49]

Since personalism stresses the centrality of person and demands the highest conception of the sanctity of persons, it follows that the social ethicist in this tradition will have little patience with timid, conventional, nonsacrificial ways of addressing and solving social problems that undermine the dignity of persons. There is no indication in early personalistic ethics that this should be the case, for at every point we see what amounts to an adamant meliorism. There was clearly a sense that things would get progressively better. The problem was that the focus tended to be on slow development. Or, perhaps more accurately, Bowne's reading of history convinced him that changes in society and human relations tend to come about slowly. So he got into the habit of emphasizing this. For example, when he wrote of the need to extend the moral field to include beings who had traditionally been excluded, he was careful to point to "the gradual extension" of the law of duty over all life.[50] However, in principle one can also quite easily draw the conclusion that there should be radical, indeed, revolutionary application of good will whenever a person or group is being trampled underfoot, and particularly when the culprit is an entire socio-politico-economic system. This is a point I shall develop more fully in the final chapter. For now suffice it to say that any who are serious about the extra-ethical conditioning factors previously discussed will have to be willing to take radical and creative steps to protect, defend, preserve, and enhance the dignity of all persons. The doctrine of what it means to be a person and the belief that the origin of persons is attributed to a loving and just God demands such a response. It is never enough to merely possess good will and be inwardly committed to applying it. If conservative application of good will is as far as one is willing to go, then what, finally, is the point? Would not all the fuss about the infinite worth of persons and the primacy of good will be viewed by critics as little more than talk?

In any event, personalistic ethics maintains both that the greatest need in ethics is the impartial and unselfish will to do right, and that next to this "is the serious and thoughtful application of intellect to the problems of life and conduct."[51] In addition, because of the processive, active nature of reality and experience, it is important to remember that righteousness or the good cannot be achieved once and for all—whether at the individual, interpersonal, or collective level. The will to do right must be present on every level, and must forever reaffirm and adjust itself to new conditions and contexts.

Teleological-Developmental Aspect

Muelder uses the phrase "teleological developmental ethic" to characterize Bowne's ethics.[52] This is not a static, finished ethic. Rather it is goal oriented in that it seeks the greatest common good as well as the moralization of all life. One need only read Bowne's book on ethics to see that this is an accurate description. Four characteristics of this teleological-developmental ethic emerge. The first three of these have already been introduced and discussed. (1) Consequences have declared themselves, which means that we can learn from these and allow present and future forms of good will to be altered accordingly. (2) Knowledge has increased. This, too, will influence new practices and the formulation of moral codes. (3) The meaning of life has deepened, and, in corresponding ways, the application of good will must deepen. (4) The ideal of humanity has enlarged.[53] Those committed both to the common good and making the most of persons will have to alter the concrete forms of good will in light of these developments.

Also significant in this teleological-developmental ethic is the emphasis on the extension of the moral sphere, which has a triple focus. First, it requires that more and more persons and their actions be brought under the head of duty, and that we recognize that "we owe duties to beings who have hitherto not been included within our ethical sphere."[54] A second emphasis regarding the extension of the moral sphere requires an increase in practical wisdom in order that moral principles be applied in more fitting forms. These two aspects necessarily imply a third, namely, that all life forms be included in our ethical sphere. Bowne made it very clear that "there is room for extending the moral arena, not less for the sake of man himself, than for the sake of the animals."[55] What we actually see in personalistic ethics, then, is the driving force of the law of development.

Because of the law of development and the emphasis on the need to expand the moral sphere to include all that has been left out, we can say that in principle the personalistic ethic has always been against all forms of exclusionary practices regarding the rights, dignity, and worth of all persons, animals, and the environment. Bowne was not as explicit in this regard concerning the racism of his day, but such a practice has no place in ethical personalism. Indeed, personalists do not even define person in race-, gender-, or class-specific terms. Whatever else it may mean to be a human person, we may say that wherever there is self-consciousness, self-knowledge, self-directedness, and a sense of innate worth, we are in the presence of a person(s). Bowne's emphasis was on the moralization of the entire life of individuals, society, and nature. He stressed "the inclusion of at least all human beings within the sphere of moral relations,"[56] although he clearly intended to also include nonhuman beings.

Having considered some of the basic principles of personalistic ethics, I now turn to the method used in making moral judgments. Most of the laws involved in this appear implicitly in Bowne's ethics, but were later systematized by Brightman. Some of Brightman's followers then made their own special contribution to his "moral law system." This is the subject of the next chapter.

Personalism and Moral Laws

In addition to the six basic principles of personalistic ethics discussed in the previous chapter, we need to consider the moral law system that was first developed by Brightman and enlarged in various ways by some of his students and then also by theirs. As will be seen, enlarging the moral law system does not necessarily mean expanding the number of laws. Since the moral law system is a regulative one and therefore is not dependent on a particular culture, it was Brightman's intention that the system be relevant and meaningful in any culture. Muelder's commentary at this point is instructive.

> In the personalistic system the moral laws are intentionally regulative, not prescriptive or culturally substantive. To be regulative means to state what all persons ought to do in making moral choices. They are rational, not arbitrary or conventional. They are not prescriptive like the Ten Commandments or codes of law. They are not principles of applied ethics like the principle of "informed consent" in medical ethics. They are not like the traditional natural law of the Roman Catholic Church which mixed church law with universal rational principles. They are not heteronomous, that is, they are not handed down from an external authority either divine or human…[The moral law system is one of] testing whether persons have been reasonable in making choices among values according to some standard and with ideal goals.[1]

However, cultural differences may require certain adaptations of the respective laws. This chapter is an exposition not of each of the eleven (or more) moral laws, but of the system itself and the forms it has taken. Before presenting the system of moral laws in outline and discussing Brightman's presentation of it, it is appropriate to note the influence of Bowne.

Bowne's Contribution

As noted in earlier chapters, there are essentially two touchstones in personalism: person and freedom. We have already discussed the nature and significance of person but have said little about freedom. Bowne, aware that freedom is important in ethical practices, sought to show that freedom has not only ethical significance, but speculative significance as well. The fact of freedom must be determined, not by ethics, but by psychology and metaphysics.[2] Bowne established this conclusion in his books *Metaphysics*[3] and *Theory of Thought and Knowledge*.[4] In these texts we find that freedom is both a fundamental assumption in rationality or reason and is the only solution that saves it from destruction. So in *Metaphysics*, Bowne writes that "the question of freedom enters intimately into the structure of reason itself."[5]

In Bowne's personalism, freedom has both speculative and ethical significance. It enters intimately into both the rational and the moral consciousness, and it alone saves them from shipwreck. Ethics requires responsibility for our acts, and responsibility presupposes freedom within limits to choose and embark on our acts. If there is no freedom, there can be no responsibility. Indeed, without freedom there can be neither reason, nor moral life, nor science. "The denial of freedom must in logic result in denying all proper responsibility and merit or demerit."[6] According to Bowne, ethics need not concern itself with the "ultimate foundation" of freedom, for metaphysics has already established its place in the nature of things. This would include the moral consciousness as well.

In the course of his argument in *The Principles of Ethics*, Bowne contends, following Friedrich Schleiermacher, that the three fundamental principles of ethics are duty, good, and virtue. And, of course, good will is at the center of all morality. At several points in the text he uses the term moral law, although his intention was not to present a system of moral laws. He did not, for example, list and develop moral laws. Yet in the course of his discussion he anticipated all of the laws that Brightman included in his own moral law system over forty years later.

As noted above, the term moral law does appear periodically in Bowne's book on ethics.[7] He basically attaches the same meaning to the term as Brightman, namely, that a moral law is a universal law. Yet we should understand that nowhere did Bowne say that his purpose is to present a "system of moral laws." This was, however, Brightman's purpose. Bowne did not endeavor to name, systematize, or show the interrelatedness of moral laws that appear in embryonic form in his work.

This notwithstanding, we do find in Bowne's book many passages that point to the later appearance of the system of moral laws developed by Brightman.[8] Interestingly, Bowne's wording and that of Brightman regarding the description of a particular law are strikingly similar at some points. One need only do a cursory reading of chapters 4 and 5 of *The Principles of Ethics* to reach the conclusion that, in one form or another, Bowne appeals to at least ten of the moral laws that appear in Brightman's systematic formulation. In addition, Bowne implies and applies a law not included in Brightman's system, namely the Law of the Ideal of Community. The addition of this law to the moral law system was made in an explicit way and developed by two of Brightman's students, L. Harold DeWolf and Walter G. Muelder.

The laws included in some form in chapters 4 and 5 of Bowne's book include: The Logical Law, the Law of Autonomy, Law of Consequences, Law of Ideal of Control, Axiological Law, Law of Specification, Law of Individualism, Altruistic Law, Law of the Best Possible, Law of the Ideal of Personality, and Law of Ideal of Community.[9] But as indicated previously, it should be remembered that Bowne did not set for himself the task of developing a system of moral laws, and therefore did not introduce the laws we find in his book in any set order. Second, unlike what we find in Brightman's system, there is no indication in Bowne that these laws necessarily follow, precede, or include each other. However, I think we can say that since Bowne believed the good will to be at the center of moral life he, like Brightman, essentially began with formal laws. Like Brightman's Law of Autonomy, the good will is, for Bowne, an absolute disposition for the moral life.

Because of Bowne's contributions, it is no longer appropriate to begin a discussion on moral laws in the personalist tradition with Brightman's formulation of the moral law system. But like so much in the philosophy of personalism, the idea of the moral law system had its beginnings in the work of Bowne. That Brightman gave name and systematization to these laws does not diminish the importance of this point. Brightman was a member of this school of thought and did not hesitate to take its chief ideas as his own. However, neither was he apprehensive about imposing his own sense of creativity and imagination, nor of moving the insights of Bowne in new directions when warranted by experience and the evidence.

Brightman's Systematic Formulation

At several points Brightman was more creative, imaginative, and courageous than either his contemporaries in the personalist tradition or his teacher, Bowne. The move he made from theistic absolutism to theistic finitism is but one instance. His empiricism was more radical and inclusive regarding the doctrine of God. In addition, Brightman was not hesitant to push the personalistic argument to what he believed to be its logical end in other areas as well. For example, Muelder and Sears contend that Brightman, more than Bowne, "develops more fully the formal problems of axiology."[10]

Brightman's major contributions to personalism were in the areas of axiology and philosophy of religion. Although both Knudson and Flewelling wrote texts on personalism,[11] these did not go far beyond the basic insights of Bowne. This was not the case with Brightman. It is in this sense that it can be said that he was the foremost interpreter of Bowne's personalism. Upon Brightman's death this mantle was passed on to his student, Peter A. Bertocci.

Brightman's book *Moral Laws* (1933) does not make explicit reference to the influence of Bowne's ethical writings, although against Bowne and Schleiermacher, he maintains that the three principles of ethics are duty, good, and law. He substitutes law for virtue. Yet one wonders why Brightman failed to mention that the moral laws appear in germinal form in Bowne's work on ethics.[12] Perhaps we can find the answer in Brightman himself.

In one of his early essays, "The Tasks Confronting a Personalistic Philosophy," Brightman takes issue with those thinkers who denigrate the idea of philosophical schools of thought and the tendency of philosophers to follow a particular great philosopher or philosophical tradition. The two thinkers he had in mind were James E. Creighton and Josiah Royce.[13] Both men were concerned that joining a particular school of thought would foster a tendency to accept uncritically all that that school espouses. In addition, they expressed fear that this would discourage critical thought and original contributions to the philosophical enterprise. Brightman understood this concern, and conceded that it was an important caution. He agreed with Royce in this regard.

A philosophy merely accepted from another man and not thought out for one's self is as dead as a mere catalogue of possible opinions. The inevitable result of the temporary triumph of an apparently closed school of university teachers of philosophy, who undertake to be disciples of a given master, leads to the devitalizing of the master's thought, and to a revulsion, in the end, of opinion.[14]

Brightman was less impressed with Creighton's attack on schools and labels, however, since his greater concern seemed to be that of catapulting his own school to preeminence. No philosophical school, Brightman maintained, exists in a vacuum. They have all been influenced by the ideas of great thinkers. "How can one survey the history [of philosophy] without seeing that it is no record of the individual insights of unique individuals, but the cooperative labor of free men not too free to learn from others?" In a real sense all philosophy, since its appearance in the earliest civilizations, is eclectic, or built on insights that have gone before. As original as Whitehead's process philosophy was, for example, even he did not hesitate to say in his great work *Process and Reality*: "The safest general characterization of the European philosophical tradition is that it consists of a series of footnotes to Plato."[15]

Where I think we see an answer to the concern about Brightman's failure to note the influence of Bowne on his system of moral laws is in both his positive view concerning philosophic schools and the need to share ideas, and the caution that no school or thinker be deified.

The personalistic school has, then, perfect right to be loyal to its own insights, to acknowledge, with pride and gratitude, its debt to Bowne, in short, to be a school; but it must avoid the pitfalls that beset the school. Bowne must not be erected into the St. Thomas of Methodism. The open-minded temper must be preserved. The problems of philosophy must be attacked in new ways, and confidence in the possibility of philosophical progress must not falter. The relations of personalism to all contemporary movements of thought must be investigated, and vigorous polemic against all forms of impersonalism continued as need arises.[16]

Thoroughgoing personalism requires both an open mind and a critical spirit. In addition, Brightman held that whenever one has thoroughly and critically examined the chief insights of a great thinker or school and decides that she or he will join that school of thought, the ideas of that school become one's own—they belong to every member of the school. Therefore, when one ventures to break new ground or to introduce a new emphasis (as Brightman does at several points), it is not necessary to indicate that the germ of the idea appeared in the work of another member of the school. I think this perspective is the best way to understand Brightman's failure to connect his work on the system of moral laws with Bowne's text on ethics.

The following is an outline of Brightman's system of moral laws.

I. The Formal Laws
   1. The Logical Law
   2. The Law of Autonomy

II. The Axiological Laws
   3. The Axiological Law
   4. The Law of Consequences
   5. The Law of the Best Possible
   6. The Law of Specification
   7. The Law of the Most Inclusive End
   8. The Law of Ideal Control

III. The Personalistic Laws
   9. The Law of Individualism
   10. The Law of Altruism
   11. The Law of the Ideal of Personality

The moral law system is regulative, not prescriptive. That is, it does not tell us what moral choices to make. Rather, the laws are intended to guide our choices or help us to make responsible moral choices. It is essentially a method for making moral judgments. Because it is a system, its use requires effort and intentionality on the part of those who would use it. For in order to be most useful the moral law system must be seen in its totality, and one must be cognizant of the place and role of each law, as well as their interrelationship with each other and the entire system. Before proceeding further, I want to explain briefly the terms *law* and *system* as used by Brightman.

Although Brightman opted for the use of the term law in the title of his book and refers to each of the eleven principles as laws, there is evidence that he was not completely satisfied with the term. For example, at numerous points in the book he uses *law* and *principle* interchangeably.[17] Bertocci contends that since the term law is confusing, causing some to conclude that Brightman was suggesting descriptive laws, some of Brightman's students substituted the term principle.[18] Because of his own discomfort with the term law, Brightman would likely have welcomed the change, which, according to DeWolf, "is a salutary one."[19] Bertocci and Richard M. Millard make the change from law to principle in their formulation of the moral laws in *Personality and the Good* (1965). DeWolf also has a predilection for the term principle.[20] The reader may be wondering why the term law was troublesome for Brightman. I think the clue lies in his (and other personalists') way of conceiving reality as dynamic and active.

Brightman was thoroughly committed to the personalist frame of reference. All reality, in this view, is active or processive. The term law has a tough time fitting neatly into such a conceptuality, since the term itself implies something that is static and unchanging. It also implies the ability to tell us what to do once and for all. Brightman was bothered by this throughout the writing of *Moral Laws*, and therefore was not consistent in his use of the term law.

The term principle, on the other hand, is a much more fluid and flexible term that does not bring to mind the idea of unchangeability and permanence. It is thus a more reasonable one in a philosophical system that stresses the processive and active nature of being. Thus Brightman's claim: "The laws which are presented in this book are principles of rational development, not rigid prescriptions of specific acts which are supposed to be eternally right."[21] The term law has about it an air of rigidity, a notion quite out of character in personalism. Also, Brightman considers ethics to be a normative science, and therefore there is no room for "fixed and unchangeable conclusions." A normative science has built into it the principle of progress. The word principle is amenable to progress. With this understanding in mind I will, like Brightman, use the terms law and principle interchangeably, although the preference is for the latter term.

In order to adequately comprehend Brightman's work on moral laws it is necessary to understand and keep in mind at all times his use of the word *system*. Failure to do this may lead one to the hasty conclusion that more and more principles need to be added. Though it is true that Brightman, consistent with personalist methodology, leaves the door open to improvement of the system of moral principles,[22] improvement may or may not mean increasing the number of principles. By introducing the word system Brightman hoped to avoid the tendency to merely appeal to isolated principles when in the process of moral deliberation. The mind itself is not chopped up or segmented in this way, but experiences itself as whole, or as a system. The point of the moral law system is to see the principles in relation to each other and as a whole.

Indeed, this is consistent with personalism's synoptic-analytic method. The system of moral principles is to be viewed as a synopsis (whole), whose parts contribute significantly to the system itself, although no one or more isolated principles explain the whole system. Each principle has a significance of its own. Yet the entire system has properties that are different from those of the individual principles that make up the system. Furthermore, any appeal to a single principle will leave one feeling that something fundamental has been left out. For example, if one merely appeals to the Law of Individualism with its emphasis on the idea that the individual is the basic moral unit, he or she is not likely to be comfortable with this, since there is the matter of the good for the neighbor, group, or community to be considered. Or, one may choose to appeal only to the Logical Law, which requires only that one choose values that are logically consistent. The issue of the type and quality of values is not important here. What is important is consistency. One committed to a life of crime, for example, is required only to consistently will criminal activity. Brightman makes the point well.

> It must be granted that some of the laws, taken by themselves, are as truly laws of evil as of good. If one wishes to be maliciously and successfully evil, one will have to obey the Logical Law; his will must be consistently evil. The Law of Consequences is observed by the prudent

sinner as much as by the thoughtful saint. The Law of Individualism is very dear to egoist and lawless lover of "personal liberty." But these considerations are only proof of the central contention…that the moral laws are to be taken as a system.[23]

System has to do with relationality, connectivity, and wholeness. To understand what the system of moral laws intends, one has to know what each individual principle requires, its relation to preceding and succeeding principles, what each contributes to the entire system, and what the system itself requires of those who appeal to it. This is what Brightman means when he writes of "the organic structure of the System of Laws," and that "each Law is connected with all the others and needs the others for its completion."[24] The good or evil of an act must be judged not in light of isolated principles, but in light of the whole system to which each of these belongs.[25]

This should bring to mind personalism's criterion of truth, which is based on the systematic orchestration of all relevant facts and data in an attempt to see the whole. The moral principles can best be understood through their relation to the whole system. For example, one of the moral principles, the Axiological Law, is based on the fact that all persons choose values. Brightman's fundamental concern throughout is that "no single value can stand alone, and that the only strictly intrinsic value is the whole system of coherent values, or, stated more empirically, that the highest intrinsic value is the experience of a person whose values are harmonious."[26] DeWolf points out the importance of understanding that what Brightman presents is a system, not a disconnected, unrelated set of moral principles.

> There is a genuine interdependence among all the principles. Every principle after the first is rationally inferred, directly or indirectly, from the Principle of Consistency combined with observations of experience. On the other hand, every principle excepting the last is elaborated and interpreted by those which follow. The first takes account of the least empirical data. The last is the most comprehensively inclusive of human experience and makes the most inclusive moral demands.[27]

Brightman's aim was to develop ethics as a normative science, the chief attributes of which are "universality and progressiveness." The principles of a normative science must apply at all times and in all places. The principles cannot, then, be culture specific. They must be applicable to all persons everywhere.[28] Progressiveness means that the principles should be open both to improvement and subsequent criticism.[29] In fact, the idea of progressiveness is built into Brightman's system of moral principles. We see it most clearly in the Law of the Best Possible, which is a principle of development or improvement. In his commentary on this principle, Brightman writes that "every real moral achievement in our experience enlarges our powers to some extent, and, as we grow, the best that we could do today is surpassed by the best of tomorrow."[30] The Best Possible is not static, but dynamic. It grows; it is progressive. The Law of the Best Possible "means constant improvement, wherever improvement is possible."[31]

It is the Hegelian influence that led Brightman to present the moral principles as he did. As in the case of Knudson's presentation of the six types of personalisms,[32] and Brightman's discussion of the three categories of criteria of truth,[33] the movement is from the most formal or abstract to the most empiricial or concrete moral laws. In the treatment of the Axiological Laws Brightman applies this technique in his discussion of the movement from empirical values (value-claims) to ideal values (true values).[34] This method is reminiscent of Hegel's dialectical movement from thesis, to antithesis, to synthesis. This method had a significant influence on early personalists. According to Muelder, the Hegelian influence on Brightman was especially acute, though he was critical of some areas of Hegel's thought.[35]

The moral law system of Brightman is composed of three sets of principles: formal laws (logical consistency, law of autonomy); axiological laws (axiological law, law of consequences, law of the best possible, law of specification, law of the most inclusive end, law of ideal of control); and personalistic laws (law of individualism, law of altruism, law of the ideal of personality). Each category, and the laws in them, presupposes the law that came before and anticipates or points to the principle that follows in the line of progression toward the most concrete law in the system. Each principle beyond Logical Consistency includes more content than the one that precedes it. Brightman sums up the contribution of each set of principles to the system. "The Formal Laws deal solely with the will as a subjective fact. The Axiological Laws deal with the values which the will ought to choose. The Personalistic Laws are more comprehensive; they deal with the personality as a concrete whole."[36] In the Personalistic Laws the emphasis is on the person and persons-in-relationship as the subjects of the preceding principles. The Law of the Ideal of Personality is, for Brightman, the summary principle of the entire moral principle system. It states: "All persons ought to judge and guide all of their acts by their ideal conception (in harmony with the other Laws) of what the whole personality ought to become both individually and socially."[37]

Earlier it was observed that, consistent with personalistic methodology, Brightman constructed the system of moral laws in a way that the door would always be open for improvement. "Doubtless," he asserted, "the laws here defined can and will be improved."[38] Improvement may mean adding more principles to the system (which some Brightmanians and their students have done). It may also mean the addition of richer empirical data that further legitimates the existing laws of Brightman's system while drawing out more implications of each principle (which is essentially the approach of Bertocci and Millard). The point to keep in mind is that Brightman was aware that the system of moral laws may warrant improvement. This is the case primarily because reason never knows all there is to know at any given moment, and the evidence and data of experience are always forthcoming. However, it was not Brightman's intention that it be easy to add additional principles. Such additions must be based upon reason and evidence that the existing system of moral principles taken as a whole excludes some emphasis or area of experience. In other words, Brightman intended that the burden of proof be on those who contend that more laws should be added.

According to Bowne the ideal good for persons "involves the perfection of individual life and of social relations." Ideal good is attainable "only in and through the co-working of the community."[39] Bowne saw no theoretical inconsistency between duties to self and to community. Indeed, ideal good for the individual emerges and develops only in and through the community.[40] Yet Bowne recognized that in actual day-to-day living there are conflicts between individual and community. We see a similar concern in Brightman.

In the discussion of the Law of Altruism, Brightman observed that there is no theoretical inconsistency between the requirements of the Law of Individualism that stresses the idea of the individual as the moral unit, and the cooperative endeavor of individuals working together in community. "But the theoretical consistency of the two does not imply practical consistency. There is a conflict between the realization of values which satisfy the personal interests of the individual and the achievement of the most valuable forms of community life."[41] The system of moral laws points to the ideal of the highest happiness for both the individual and the community. But herein lies the rub. Often the values of the individual conflict with those of the community. It is precisely at this juncture that some of Brightman's students maintain that his system requires explicit communitarian principles.

L. Harold DeWolf and Walter G. Muelder

DeWolf accepts Bertocci's and Millard's substitution of *principle* for *law*, since the latter implies what Brightman did not intend, namely rigid prescriptive statements of particular acts and what the moral agent ought or ought not do. So DeWolf calls them "principles of moral decision."[42] Muelder, on the other hand, retains Brightman's use of the term law.[43] Another point of refinement for DeWolf is the renaming of some of the original principles. For example, the Law of Specification becomes the Principle of Situational Relevance.[44]

The chief addition to the system of moral laws is the attention that both DeWolf and Muelder give to communal or societal influences on the individual. To be sure, Brightman's analysis of the influence of individuals on each other and their obligations to each other was second to none. However, he did not place enough emphasis on the mutual obligations of individual and community. Nevertheless, such obligations are clearly implied in Brightman's Laws of Altruism and Ideal of Personality. But because all persons affect and are affected by the community, DeWolf and Muelder see a need to be explicit about the mutual obligations of individual and community. They therefore saw a need for Communitarian Principles, an idea first suggested to DeWolf by one of his graduate students, Glen Trimble.[45] But it should also be noted that this communal emphasis was present in the work of Bowne (although not as fully developed as it could have been) and McConnell.[46]

Muelder contends that the ideas included in the three Communitarian Principles (Principle of Cooperation, Principle of Social Devotion, and Principle of the Ideal of Community) are consistent with what is implied in Brightman's system. But both he and DeWolf conclude that "it was important to recognize explicitly that 'Groups have distinctive traits and generate distinctive problems.'"[47] As noted in the previous chapter, this was also a limitation in Bowne's ethics. It is not difficult to understand how Muelder arrived at this conclusion. Muelder has a strong history, social science, and philosophy background. In addition, there was a rigorous treatment of Ernst Troeltsch's category of historical wholes and the idea of "the Individual Totality" in his doctoral dissertation. All of this was supplemented by years of social activism. Therefore, Muelder could easily see that groups of whatever size have properties that the individuals in them do not. In this regard Muelder was also influenced by Hegel's doctrine of the organic nature of reality (though he, like Brightman, rejected Hegel's absolute identification of the individual with the group or the state that invariably opens the door to totalitarianism).

Delineating six traits of Troeltsch's concept of "Individual Totality," Muelder holds that, "Within larger totalities are smaller units of meaning and value with their own identities while participating in the whole."[48] There is always ongoing mutual interaction between the smaller units and the larger totality. An example would be a given Protestant denomination within Protestantism, and the latter within Christianity. Another of the traits of "Individual Totality" is the category of "Common Spirit," which stresses the relationship between individual and community. The idea of the common spirit can be grounded metaphysically. Personalism, after all, contends that reality is through and through social. We saw this in chapters 3 and 4. Brightman himself recognized that metaphysically, person is essentially social.[49]

At any rate, experience teaches that persons develop and interact in and through community, a point that led Muelder and DeWolf to conclude in favor of communitarian moral principles. "The communitarian conception of human nature became a cornerstone of my developing ethic," writes Muelder. "I argued, in effect, that personality is a *socius* with a private center."[50] The individual is necessarily a part of the community and influences, and is influenced by, it. However, the individual is never completely defined by it. In addition, although a person-in-community, one always retains her or his unique sense of individuality. Although influenced more by the personal idealism of George H. Howison, John W. Buckham also stated expressly that "the person is a *socius* and finds himself only in relation with other persons. Personality is in its very nature relatedness, and yet, uniqueness."[51] Muelder did what Brightman failed to do. He gave express, systematic treatment of the idea of the sociality of person relative to the moral law system.

Through his studies of church history, biblical studies, personalism, philosophy, and the work of Ernst Troeltsch, Muelder intentionally sought to deepen and develop Christian social ethics and to go beyond what he believed to be a too individualistic emphasis in personalistic ethics.[52] As it turned out, Muelder was a major pioneer in developing the discipline of social ethics. He recalls that during his graduate student days at Boston University he "was brash enough to ask Brightman whether personalism had a social ethic."[53] Brightman's response implied that he did not know what a social ethic was. He could only point to the social activism of Francis McConnell, who, in Brightman's view, was not a social ethicist, but rather a proponent of the Social Gospel. In any event, in 1932 Brightman gave Muelder an independent study assignment to work out an outline for a course in social ethics. One year later Brightman offered his first course in social philosophy. He was apparently impressed with Muelder's query and subsequent outline, for Muelder noticed that his personal library in social philosophy literature grew immensely thereafter.

Personalism has had at least an implicit social ethic from the time of Bowne. But because it views the person as the basic moral unit and therefore always begins there, it is quite possible that the significance—both positive and negative—of the group or social institutions for individual behavior and development may not receive adequate attention if there is not explicit emphasis on communitarian principles in the ethical system. The tendency might be, as in the case of Bowne, to insist that the social question will be solved only as more and more individuals are moralized (a common view among many evangelicals during the nineteenth century and the early years of the twentieth).

At times Bowne seemed totally unaware that institutions as such actually existed. His emphasis was always on the individuals within them. Bowne's student Francis J. McConnell went well beyond his teacher in this regard. This might have been because of both his labors as a college president and the many years of ministry as a bishop in the Methodist Episcopal church that gave him a great deal of insight into the dynamics between individuals in their interpersonal relations and their behavior in groups. In addition, unknown to those critics who have accused early personalists of advocating a purely individualistic ethic, McConnell was deeply influenced by the social ethicist Reinhold Niebuhr.[54] In any event, McConnell said that Bowne "would lay such stress on the fact that individual human beings are the only realities concerned that he would now and again understress the other fact that when individuals meet together in group contacts, their conduct is different from that which marks them as unrelated individuals."[55] Bowne did not seem too concerned about the fact that groups have properties that the individuals comprising them do not, and that the group is not merely an aggregate of individuals. He did not read much in the area of social theory. Such limitations left him vulnerable to the criticism that "he did not always make clear his own understanding of the part played in human life by social groups functioning as groups rather than as mere assemblies of individuals."[56]

In a more systematic and forceful way than McConnell, Muelder sought to correct these limitations in the work of earlier personalists. Taking seriously all the work that personalist predecessors had done in ethics, he went on to determine the nature and role of groups in efforts to obtain both the individual and the common good. So he developed a view of social ethics as an interdisciplinary field. Such a characterization complicates the matter of definition, but it appeared the only way to conceive of social ethics that would be up for the task. It had to take moral principles seriously, as Muelder showed in his book *Moral Law in Christian Social Ethics* (1966). But it also had to be an active, involved social ethic that sought to realize the responsible society, making use of "middle axioms" (a term first proposed by J. H. Oldham in 1937). These are provisional definitions and stand midway between ethical principles and actual directions or courses of action.[57] Middle axioms are more concrete than principles, but less specific about particular ways to proceed in the concrete situation. Muelder addressed this tension in an earlier volume on social ethics, *Foundations of the Responsible Society* (1959), making it clear that social ethics also had to converge and be conversant with other disciplines and their methods.

> A sound scholar in Christian social ethics ought to be well-grounded in Bible and theology, in philosophy, in history, and in the behavioral sciences. This is a big order and requires a vigorous community of scholars and scholarship. Science, philosophy, and theology all converge in the methods of social ethics…Christian social ethics must be thoroughly and intelligibly inter-disciplinary. This means that it masters the language, concepts, and methods of the contributing disciplines. Social ethics must concentrate on communication, for it defines the area where ideals become relevant in social situations.[58]

The methodology of the social sciences has a prominent place in Muelderian social ethics. The social sciences provide much important empirical data on existing social problems, enabling us to know whether there is in fact a problem, for example, poverty, and the extent of its seriousness. The theological social ethicist, essentially looks at the problem in light of what ought to be in accordance with the love ethic and the common good.

Finally, both Muelder and DeWolf emphasize the idea of *persons-in-community*. DeWolf preferred the term *persons-in-relationships*, but both stressed the same idea. Persons are born into community, nurtured by it, and influenced by it in numerous ways. But persons also influence the community in many ways. Both persons and their groups affect the community. Although Brightman seemed cognizant of this in his system of moral laws, Muelder and DeWolf are among his students who concluded that he did not place explicit enough emphasis on the communal or relational element. According to Muelder and DeWolf, the communitarian principle, which is only implied in Brightman's moral law system, needed to be made explicit. They therefore expanded the system by adding communitarian principles. Yet, one fourth-generation personalist is not satisfied that even this is enough, and therefore proceeds to add even more moral principles.

Paul Deats, Jr.

Paul Deats, Jr., is Walter G. Muelder Professor of Social Ethics, Emeritus, at Boston University. He has primarily been influenced by the more philosophical strands of the personalism of Brightman, Muelder, Schilling, McConnell, and Lavely than the more theological contributions of Knudson and DeWolf.[59] Like many other people, Deats discovered that he was a personalist when he arrived at Boston University as a Ph.D. candidate in 1952 at the age of thirty. Though exposed to the teachings and works of several third-generation personalists, he was most influenced by Muelder's approach to social ethics.

In the volume of lectures and essays edited by Deats and Carol Robb in 1986, *The Boston Personalist Tradition in Philosophy, Social Ethics and Theology*, Deats acknowledges that he was a "closet personalist" until he initiated the seminar on personalism in 1980 that led to the publication of this volume.[60] Having persuaded John Lavely to co-teach the seminar, he credits Lavely as having been his tutor in personalism. It was during this period that Deats delved into the literature on personalism and began conscious reflection on his own debt to Boston Personalism. He began "to affirm [his] identification with the tradition"; to come out of the closet![61]

Having been a student of Deats's when I was a doctoral candidate at Boston University in the seventies, I can affirm that prior to completion of my formal work in 1979, he had not acknowledged publicly that he was a personalist. I took three classes with him, and there was no time that he explicitly identified himself with personalism. It was no secret that he had been a student of Walter Muelder's. I did not suspect, however, that Deats was familiar with the literature of personalism until I was working on my dissertation on Brightman's concept of the finite-infinite God. It was during my dissertation defense that I discovered his knowledge of Brightman's doctrine of God—knowledge that did not merely come as a result of his having read my dissertation.

In any event, by 1984 Deats was ready to exit the closet with his personalism. But even prior to this, on the occasion of his installation as Walter G. Muelder Professor of Social Ethics in 1979, he indicated in his installation address his debt to Muelder's role as a pioneer in social ethics, but then added:

> Muelder has a strong understanding of the social nature of personality and of the organic character of society, but as I read the communitarian laws, I do not find sufficiently explicit the full range of "participation in the community." Even in the moral laws, the focus is on the moral agent making up his/her mind. How does the moral agent discover that the mind is made up wrongly and requires change? How does participation and conflict not only contribute to the group, but enable the agent to learn how to make up and change his/her mind? How does one do justice both to integrity and to consensus? Recognizing convictions and working through conflict to consensus are neglected but necessary components of an adequate ethic.[62]

Impressed both by this omission and "Brightman's insistence that the method [of the moral laws] itself requires continuing revision," Deats saw the need to add two more laws. Following Muelder's formulation of the laws, he adds another category that he calls "Laws of Praxis." These include: Law of Conflict and Reconciliation ("All persons, in their own lives and in the lives of groups to which they belong, ought to accept conflict in the course of seeking to formulate and achieve the ideals of personality and of community, and to work through conflict—with others, 'friends' and 'enemies' alike—toward consensus, justice, and reconciliation"), and Law of Fallibility and Corrigibility ("All persons ought to expect to make—and suffer—mistakes, failures, and defeat, without being overcome by these experiences or losing hope. When mistakes are made, and repentance is acknowledged, and forgiveness asked, the way is opened for resources, human and divine, to be made available").[63]

The rationale Deats gives for the inclusion of his two principles is similar to that given by DeWolf and Muelder when they added the Communitarian Principles, namely that something was implied in Brightman's formulation that should now be made more explicit, and the best way to do this is to add more principles. But there is a crucial difference. DeWolf and Muelder were concerned about Brightman's failure to include in an explicit way in his system of moral laws a category that is absolutely germane to personalist conceptuality, namely, the social or communal principle. Only by adding a category of principles that emphasizes this would it be possible to avoid the oft-made criticism that personalism is fundamentally an individualistic ethic. This criticism was easily made of Bowne and may have been appropriate regarding Brightman in the early part of his career. Both men were always committed to social issues, but there was lacking in their ethical thought an understanding of the nature and role of groups in interaction with individual persons. Although Brightman became much more cognizant of such matters after he began teaching social philosophy, it was DeWolf and Muelder who supplied the principle that would do much to remove the stigma that personalism is fundamentally an individualistic ethic that has no relevance to systemic problems and their solutions.

In order to effectively add more principles to the system of moral laws, the rationale will have to consist of more than the idea that some point is not made explicitly enough in the existing system. By adding the Laws of Praxis, especially as presently formulated by Deats, one gets a sense that the emphasis is on the "how" or details of cooperation, social devotion, and community. It sounds more like a middle axiom than a universal ethical principle. It was not Brightman's intention that the moral laws be thought of in this way. To be sure, the claims Deats makes in his principles are adequately grounded in experience and should be included in any discussion on the system of moral laws. However, presently it seems that they are not germane to the system itself. This was Bertocci's assessment of the principles added by Muelder and DeWolf. As implied earlier, I think the Muelder-DeWolf additions are nuclear to the system and are firmly established.

J. Philip Wogaman

Unlike most fourth-generation personalists, J. Philip Wogaman has been very productive in a literary sense. Influenced primarily by Muelder and DeWolf, Wogaman has been a prolific writer in the area of Christian social ethics. However, he does not in these writings reveal his own affiliation with the Boston Personalist tradition. Although he either mentions the term "personalism" or the names of Muelder and DeWolf (summarizing the views of the latter two men at some points) in many places in his books,[64] he does not explicitly identify himself as a personalist. However, those who are familiar with personalism will not miss its influence on Wogaman's work. There is no indication that he intentionally tries to distance himself from personalism. Rather, like Paul Deats, Jr. (prior to 1980), he tends to be a "closet personalist." Perhaps this has something to do with "the unpopularity of personalism," a point to be addressed in the next chapter. Nevertheless, and also like Deats, Wogaman exhibits deep appreciation for Muelder and DeWolf. He dedicated *Faith and Fragmentation* (1985) to "two of my great teachers, Walter G. Muelder and L. Harold DeWolf, in gratitude for their wisdom, support, and friendship through many years."[65] Yet one not familiar with the Boston Personalist tradition would not likely connect either Wogaman or his two teachers with that tradition since he makes no reference to it.

But clearly, Wogaman is a personalist in the Bowne-Brightman tradition who has made significant contributions in Christian social ethics. I was first introduced to Wogaman's work in one of several ethics courses I took with Muelder while in graduate school. Perhaps the text that personifies the influence of personalism on his thinking is *A Christian Method of Moral Judgment* (1976). (The book has since been revised and given the title *Christian Moral Judgment*.[66]) One familiar with the moral law system of Brightman and his students will readily recognize that the method Wogaman employs is fundamentally based on the moral law scenario. He calls his method of Christian moral judgment "methodological presumption." This is the method of arriving at moral judgments even in the absence of certainty by making an initial presumption "of the superiority of one set of conclusions and then testing that presumption by examining contradictory evidence."[67] The method begins, then, by admitting initial biases or presumptions and then proceeding with the critical examination of other relevant data and facts.

Wogaman is quite clear about the need for criteria for any adequate Christian ethical methodology. He points to four of these, all of which are detected in personalistic methodology and the moral law system. First, it is necessary that we be tentative regarding all moral judgments inasmuch as we are not omniscient, nor are the data of experience all in at any given moment. So we must give our initial presumption tentative approval, recognizing that after all testing and critical analysis it may be necessary to replace it with another. Second, since (in this case) the method is Christian, there is need to be faithful to the central affirmations of the Christian faith.

Third, there must be "a basis for investing judgments and actions with whole-hearted commitment and seriousness without abandoning tentativeness." And finally, there must be a way(s) of clarifying moral dialogue that leads to an understanding of why certain acts are preferred over others.[68] Like other personalists, Wogaman takes as a given the idea that one will not arrive at certainty in moral judgments; yet whatever method of moral judgment chosen should at least minimize the morally weakening effects of uncertainty. An adequate method of moral judgment must "permit us to act with certitude if not with certainty."

Wogaman believes that upon reflection it can be shown that in the process of moral judgment everyone begins with certain initial "biases or presumptions" that are, in that moment, deemed superior to all others, thereby placing the moral burden of proof on all other options. Wogaman urges that we freely admit these biases into the process at the outset. The initial presumption(s) is then tested by other, and often contradictory, evidence. If, after this testing, it is found that uncertainty remains about the contradictory evidence, the judgment is made on the basis of the initial presumption.

In Wogaman's view methodological presumption is "peculiarly useful" when one has to make moral judgments even when uncertainty reigns. The method itself seeks to balance the seriousness of ethical perfectionism with its emphasis on moral principles and situationalism and the emphasis it places upon the particular moral situation, the unique values inherent in every specific situation, and the importance of allowing the situation to inform the judgment to be made. This is not unlike the moral law system of Brightman, which seeks to do this through its emphasis on universal moral principles. The Law of Specification in the moral law system, for example, is a situational principle and was formulated by Brightman as follows: "All persons ought, in any given situation, to develop the value or values specifically relevant to that situation."[69]

There are, according to Wogaman, five types of presumptions and their subtypes: positive presumptions, negative presumptions, ideological presumptions, polar presumptions, and presumptions of human authority.[70] In addition, Wogaman observes that there are moral presumptions that are Christian specific. These include: positive moral presumptions, which stress the positive direction God would have us take (e.g., acknowledging the goodness of created existence, the value of individual life, the unity of the human family in God, and the equality of persons in God);[71] negative moral presumptions, which point to human finitude and human sinfulness and indicate human limitations in traveling in the direction God would have us take;[72] polar presumptions (or dialectical values), which include: individual/social nature of persons, freedom/responsibility, subsidiarity/universality, conservation/innovation, optimism/pessimism.[73] Polar presumptions are values that are in dialectical tension. They are not opposites in the sense of not having anything to do with each other. Neither are they intended to suggest that either pole cancels out the significance of the other. On the contrary, each needs the other. Polar values belong to each other, although they may have the appearance of being contradictory.[74] It is not a matter of either-or, but more like both-or-neither. Both polar values are needed if either is to continue to exist and have real meaning in moral judgment. Wogaman contends that "one value cannot be meaningful in the total absence of its apparent opposite."[75] We may recall this same kind of emphasis in the moral law system. Regarding the Axiological Principles, Brightman holds that no value can stand alone or makes complete sense when viewed in isolation. The emphasis must be on values in relation, or as Brightman says, harmonious values.[76] In Wogaman's case, as in Brightman's, each value must be included, even though we may not know in the moment how any two values should be related.

Before pointing to the other two sets of presumptions Wogaman proposes, namely, those of human authority and ideological presumptions, I should say a brief word about his view of one of the positive presumptions, namely, the presumption of equality of all persons before God. In the most fundamental sense all persons are equal. So, concretely, there must be a strong presumption for the equality of treatment that all persons receive from socioeconomic, political, and other societal structures. "Equality cannot merely exist on the 'spiritual' plane; existential equality is an important condition of spiritual recognition of equality."[77] This is not meant to suggest that any person or group should have absolute equality in all matters in the world. Nor does it mean that all persons have equal talents or inherited physical qualities. Such equality can, however, be affected in one way or another by the distribution or maldistribution of material goods in society. The real point of all of this is—as Bowne would put it—that no person is to be used as fuel to warm society,[78] and whenever any two or more persons meet any place in the universe they owe each other respect and good will. The latter is "the first and primal duty in a moral community," and implied in this duty of good will to each other is the essential equality of all persons and "the implied recognition of the sacredness and inviolability of the moral personality."[79] Because we are beings of divine parentage and divine destiny, we have inestimable reverence and sacredness. In this rich, fundamental sense, all persons are equal.

Where Wogaman falters in his discussion of the presumption of equality of all persons is when he implies that human equality and worth can only be demonstrated through theological statements. The questionable passage follows.

> Those philosophers who challenge any inherent worth or property of man as a ground for the equality of persons are not incorrect. Human value is not a property of man qua man. In Christian perspective, it is solely a gift of the Father's love. Apart from faith in a source of human worth transcending human life itself, it is dubious whether either human value or human equality can be demonstrated philosophically.[80]

Like Bowne, Wogaman contends that the only way to account for the dignity of persons is to look to a source or Creator of such. This is the view of all theistic-creationist personalists. Yet one must wonder with Walter Muelder whether there is anything about being human and person that is of intrinsic value in itself or that makes each person worthy of infinite respect whether we conceive of ourselves as having derived from an infinitely loving personal God or not. Is the value of the human person dependent solely upon the Creator? In other words, does a person have absolute dignity only because she or he is created by God? Does the atheist necessarily and fundamentally deemphasize the worth and value of persons? Muelder presents much for us to think about in this regard.

> To base the worth of human life exclusively on God's valuing it is extreme since it denies all inherent features of personality and regards human value as only extrinsic or relational. If all moral subjects (viewed apart from God) are only value ciphers, then relational attributes do not confer anything. There is intrinsic value in being a creature capable of making value choices. Kant's second version of the categorical imperative expresses the explicit ethical view in contrast to a wholly derivative type of religious view: "Act so that you treat humanity whether in your own person or that of another always as an end and never as a means only." The capacity to be a moral agent (person) makes us worthy of respect by all. Yet Kant was reared in the Christian West, and historians of morals have pointed out the role of Christianity in establishing the idea of the sacredness of personality.[81]

Yet Muelder would be the first to remind even philosophers that Christianity so emphasized the sacredness of persons that it can be said that with its appearance the book on the worth and dignity of persons was signed and sealed forevermore. We may grant (against Wogaman) that not all roots of human worth are theological (or Christian). However, it is important that philosophers be reminded that often principles like person emerged long before they were taken up by philosophy and given credence from that vantage point.

Like the moral law system of Brightman and others, Wogaman's method of methodological presumption or "moral burden of proof" requires that all of the presumptions be seen in interrelationship and as a whole. One who uses this method must have in mind each of the presumptions, the contribution each makes, the relation of each to the other, and finally how they relate to the whole. The final two categories of presumptions that Wogaman includes are Presumptions of Human Authority, particularly those most likely to reflect insight into things Christian (e.g., Community of Faith, Tradition of the Faith, Tradition of the Faith community, Technical and Factual Expertise, Civil Society); and Ideological Presumptions.

There is much more that can be said about Wogaman's method and his overall contribution to personalistic ethics. Were Brightman alive today he would not object to the way Wogaman has appropriated and adapted the system of moral laws. Though Wogaman does not seek to improve the system in the same way as others (by increasing the number of principles), his is the most creative application of the system to date. Openings for this type of creativity are built into personalist conceptuality.

Peter A. Bertocci and Richard M. Millard

The Bertocci-Millard formulation of Brightman's system of moral laws appears in their massive and instructional volume *Personality and the Good: Psychological and Ethical Perspectives* (1963). The authors were in close collaboration throughout the writing of this text, but by virtue of division of labor Millard wrote part 4, "Principles of Ethical Choice."[82] Here he elaborates extensively upon the system of moral laws as Brightman originally presented it. The authors do not see a need to "improve" the system by adding more principles. Instead, their improvement is in the form of adding more empirical data, thereby enriching each principle through more concrete illustrations. Indeed, Brightman was hampered in this regard since he wrote *Moral Laws* in a relatively brief period while he had several other major manuscripts in process or had just completed the writing of them.

As noted earlier, it is Millard and Bertocci who point explicitly to the ambiguity of the terms "law" and "principle,"[83] and who substitute the latter term. Similar to Brightman, they insist on the need to view this system of moral principles wholistically or as "interpenetrating." The system "cannot be used 'in part' without serious loss of value."[84] Since their formulation primarily differs from Brightman's in the ways I have suggested, I will forego extensive discussion of it. The tendency has often been to refer to Brightman's formulation and those of DeWolf and Muelder. Wogaman does this, for example, when he writes: "The starting point of Muelder's ethics is the moral law formulation first developed by Edgar S. Brightman and later refined substantially by L. Harold DeWolf and by Muelder himself."[85] "Refinement," for Wogaman, apparently has only to do with expanding the number of moral laws. No reference is made to the Millard-Bertocci formulation of the system. Thus it is appropriate to at least mention their treatment of the moral law system. When Brightman left the door open for improvement and/or refinement of the system of moral laws he did not necessarily have in mind the addition of more principles. He might well have meant doing what Millard and Bertocci did, namely to draw out the deeper meaning of the system and each of its laws and to enrich each through adding more empirical data.

Martin Luther King, Jr.

It would not be appropriate to end this discussion on the moral law system in personalism without pointing to its influence on the fourth-generation personalist Martin Luther King, Jr. (1929–1968). A number of King scholars contend that he was first introduced to the term personalism during his student days at Morehouse College.[86] He studied Brightman's personalism under George Washington Davis while a student at Crozer Theological Seminary.[87]

During his graduate studies at Boston University, King was a student of Brightman's before the latter's sudden death in 1953. King wrote of

Brightman's strong influence on his character development.[88] In addition, he wrote of his desire to do doctoral work at Boston University because he had been influenced philosophically by a number of its faculty members, and "more particularly Dr. Brightman." King went on to say: "For this reason I have longed for the possibility of studying under him."[89] Since King also studied under DeWolf, who became his major advisor when Brightman died, there is no question that he was familiar with the moral law system. Indeed, in at least one research paper in which he was treating the significance of freedom, he cited a passage in Brightman's book *Moral Laws.*[90]

King was influenced by personalism's doctrine of the personal God of love and reason[91] as well as personalistic ethics with its emphasis on moral laws and the inherent sense of the dignity and worth of persons. It is important to remember, however, that these were beliefs that King took with him to seminary and graduate school. King's wife makes this point in her book *My Life With Martin Luther King, Jr.*[92] It is of interest to note that King scholars like David Garrow[93] and Keith D. Miller[94] mistakenly deemphasize the importance of personalism as a major influence on King. This notwithstanding, King believed in a personal God and the sanctity of persons long before he heard the term personalism and formally studied it.[95] Indeed, King himself implied as much in *Stride Toward Freedom* (1958). Personalism, he said, "strengthened me in two convictions: it gave me metaphysical and philosophical grounding for the idea of a personal God, and it gave me a metaphysical basis for the dignity and worth of all human personality."[96] The phrase "strengthened me in two convictions" implies that personalism primarily provided a philosophical framework for his long-held belief in a personal God and the sanctity of persons—beliefs he held before he was formally introduced to personalism. But once introduced to it he became "wholeheartedly committed" to it.[97] Indeed, Garth Baker-Fletcher further substantiates this point in his penetrating study of King's theory of dignity.[98]

One who both knows the moral law system of Brightman and has read King's writings will be able to see his appropriation of these principles. What one should not look for in King, however, is explicit reference to or naming of the individual laws, although there is clearcut evidence that his ethical reasoning is influenced by them.

Both Walter Muelder and John Ansbro have addressed the subject of the moral laws in the work of King. Although Kenneth Smith and Ira Zepp, Jr., considered the influence of the existence of an objective moral law on King's thinking—which was present in embryonic form in his senior year at Morehouse College[99]—they did not examine his appropriation of the moral law system as such.[100] A brief consideration of Muelder and Ansbro in this regard will be instructive.

Muelder on King and Moral Laws

In 1983 Muelder read a paper at Morehouse College entitled "Martin Luther King, Jr., and the Moral Laws." Muelder was not merely concerned with the influence of Brightman's moral laws on King. He went further to show that King was also influenced by Muelder's and DeWolf's Laws of

Community. Although these laws are implicit in Brightman's Altruistic Law and the Law of the Ideal of Personality, Muelder and DeWolf were of one accord in the view that this mere implicit focus on Laws of Community in Brightman was a limitation. They came to this conclusion because experience itself reveals that we are not persons in isolation. Rather, we are persons-in-community, and this point, they believed, should be expressly stated in the moral law system.

Also implicit in the original moral law system of Brightman is an opening for a law that more explicitly expresses the need to provide the ultimate ground or reason for the moral law system and for endeavoring to live a morally responsible life individually and collectively. So in his own version of the moral law system, Muelder added the Metaphysical Law. He argued that each of the moral laws (Brightman's original eleven plus the Laws of Community [which include the Law of Social Devotion, The Law of Co-operation, and the Law of the Ideal of Community] and the Metaphysical Law) had a significant place in King's moral deliberations. As can be seen, then, Muelder's version of the moral law system adds four laws to Brightman's eleven, giving us a total of fifteen.

Muelder essentially supports his claim that King was influenced by the moral law system by doing a thorough exegesis of King's book *Why We Can't Wait*, which is the story of the Birmingham, Alabama, movement for civil rights in 1963. (My own examination of others of King's books, e.g., *Where Do We Go From Here: Chaos or Community?* and *The Trumpet of Conscience* reveals King's use of the moral laws in moral deliberations.) Muelder succeeds in showing that King's own writings reveal "the regulative function" of the moral laws in his decision-making process. As for the aim of the moral law system, Muelder points out that it is "a system testing whether persons have been reasonable in making choices among values according to some standard and with ideal goals."[101] Muelder names each of the fifteen moral laws and points to specific passages in King's book that reflect his appropriation of a specific law. One example will suffice.

The Law of Individualism states: "Each person ought to realize in his own experience the maximum value of which he is capable in harmony with moral law." This law conveys the idea that the person is the fundamental moral unit or agent who is to obey moral laws. Following Thomas H. Green and Brightman, Muelder observes that all values are in, of, by, and for persons.[102] Said Muelder: "The law of individualism is the principle of human dignity and of personal realization. The law states a normative self-image."[103] This idea supported King's insistence that everybody is somebody because they are called into existence, loved, and valued by God. King's aim was to heighten the sense of somebodyness in his people, and thus he saw the need for one to have self-love before one can properly love others. To support this view Muelder turns to a passage in King's book: "The old order ends no matter what Bastilles remain, when the enslaved, within themselves, bury the psychology of servitude…In the summer of 1963, the Negroes of America wrote an emancipation proclamation to themselves." Muelder does similarly regarding each of the moral laws he identified in King's book.

Ansbro on King and Moral Laws

John J. Ansbro published *Martin Luther King, Jr.: The Making of a Mind* in 1983. He included an eleven-page discussion on the influence of Brightman's moral laws on King. Although Ansbro's approach is similar to that of Muelder, unlike him, he focuses on the original eleven laws of Brightman. In addition Ansbro points to at least a couple places in King's books (e.g., *Why We Can't Wait* and *The Trumpet of Conscience*) to show how he applies the moral laws. However, he does not, like Muelder, pay close attention to any particular writing of King's for this purpose, and yet, Ansbro does a good job of showing how King applied each of the laws in his work. Like Muelder, he names and defines each of the laws, explains what it means, and then proceeds to show how King applied it. For example, the Logical Law states: "All persons ought to will logically; i.e., each person ought to will to be free from self-contradiction and to be consistent in his intentions. A moral person does not both will and not will the same ends; this property of a moral person is called his formal rightness." This law calls for consistency with reason and willing consistently. This is the only way one can maintain respect for one's inner life. If one arrives at the conclusion that persons have inherent worth and should be respected, one should always will those actions that are consistent with this belief. But this willing has to be applied universally, or to every person everywhere. According to Ansbro:

> In his application of this Logical Law King maintained that a person convinced of the sacred value of human personality should consistently will this value in all his intentions, and thus oppose every act of discrimination and injustice that degrades personality. He recognized that he could not be morally consistent if he demanded that there be respect for human life in the ghettos and did not publicly denounce violence on an international scale.[104]

King's appropriation of the Logical Law contributed to his ultimate public stance against the war in Vietnam, which he publicized at Riverside Church in New York City in 1967, exactly one year before he was assassinated.[105]

Ansbro conveys the sense that because King's experience was different from that of Brightman, he could not accept some aspects of Brightman's treatment of the moral laws. For example, agreeing with the Law of Specification ("All persons ought, in any given situation, to develop the value or values specifically relevant to that situation"), King rejected part of Brightman's commentary on it. Brightman had written that there are at least two types of responses to situations: passive and active. The former type tends to give in to the situation and adjust to it. The latter type will generally "rebel against the actual situation in the interests of the ideal" and press for reform or transformation of the situation.[106] Brightman went on to say that "the merit of the passive type is its respect for fact and for the personalities of others." The merit of the active type is one's commitment to improving the situation.[107] For Brightman both types of persons may be considered good. The passive type clearly did not appeal to King, since he and his people had been victims of racism, discrimination, and economic exploitation since the time of American slavery. For King the only type of response to dehumanizing and person-destroying conditions is the active type that protests and seeks radical transformation.

> Confronted with segregation, King could not accept Brightman's assertion that the passive type of individual respects fact and the personalities of others when this type adjusts his attitude to the situation and refuses to adjust the situation to his attitude. King contended that the passive acceptance of the evil of segregation constitutes even a disservice to the segregator since it allows him to continue in his error. In actively opposing segregation he could attempt to adhere consistently to both the Law of the Best Possible and the Law of Specification.[108]

In at least one other instance Ansbro suggests that King appropriated the moral laws differently than Brightman. Although King appealed to both the Law of Individualism and the Law of Altruism, Ansbro suggests that he identified more with the latter law, which implies that there was in King's ethics a stronger other-regarding sentiment. The Law of Individualism points to the idea of the individual as the basic moral unit and the importance of self-love. It expresses what Bowne meant when he said that no person should ever be used as fuel to warm society. King accepted the validity of the Law of Individualism but seemed to place less emphasis on it than did Brightman. According to Ansbro, King "was convinced that *agape* may at times demand even the suspension of the law of self-preservation so that through our self-sacrifice we can help create the beloved community."[109] King did not believe that such self-sacrifice necessarily precludes self-respect and self-love, but that the individual may well grow in this regard, having sacrificed all for the redemption of others. Ansbro rightly concludes that more than Brightman, King's application of the Law of Altruism was more open to self-sacrifice.[110]

Near the end of his student days at Morehouse College King decided that he would enter the ministry and that he would commit himself to a life of service to others. Therefore, he did not need personalism to convince him of the moral obligation to launch a full-scale assault against segregation and all forms of injustice. What personalism and the moral laws did do, however, was to reinforce that commitment and provide the metaphysical basis for his long-held belief in the personal God of love and the inherent dignity of persons as such.[111]

Reasonableness of Adding More Moral Laws

There are two final matters to be addressed before bringing this chapter to a close. One pertains to the matter of adding more principles to Brightman's original eleven. The other has to do with the viability of a method of moral judgment like Brightman's, inasmuch as it seems that one has to remember a great deal when engaged in moral deliberation. How does one remember so many laws when, on the spur of the moment, she or he has to make a responsible moral judgment?

As for the first, I concur with Bertocci that in the final analysis we must leave the door open for critical discussion regarding the issue of adding more laws to the original moral law system of Brightman. Furthermore, if one has a thorough and accurate understanding of the system as Brightman conceived it, it will be difficult to make the case for increasing the original number of laws—even though Brightman intentionally left open the door for improvement. Such improvement may involve adding more principles (as Muelder, DeWolf, and Deats did) or further refining the original ones (as was the case with Millard and Bertocci). There was a time when, as Bertocci's student, I agreed with him that the addition of the Laws of Community introduced by DeWolf and Muelder was not necessary since these are implied in Brightman's formulation. Two things have caused me to alter my position.

In the first place, I later studied more closely DeWolf's and Muelder's rationale for the need to give explicit attention to communitarian principles. At the same time I was taking a closer look at the personalist frame of reference and the way it views reality, namely as active and social through and through. Personalists are quite explicit about both this and being thoroughgoing and consistent in the way the moral laws are applied. Sociality is one of those basic laws. Consistency requires that this idea be applied not only to the way personalists think about fundamental reality, but to the way they think about ethics as well. Adamant about the centrality of person, personalists are just as insistent about the communal nature of reality. Consequently, we are not simply persons, significant as such a claim is! Instead, it is truer to say with Muelder that we are "persons-in-community," or with DeWolf, that we are "persons-in-relationships." Indeed, this is one of the two points at which Muelder goes beyond Brightman in ethical reflection. That is, in Muelder there is an intentional movement "toward an historical communitarian view of human personality." Muelder wanted to erase the tendency of critics to say that personalism is based on a purely individualistic ethic. Even though the individual is the fundamental moral unit, she can only be an individual in community. Therefore, rather than focus on individualism, Muelder shifted the focus to communitarianism.

> Personality is viewed by me not only as experience, but experience is understood as social or communitarian. The self is not an individual experient who *has* a social environment which influences the self; the self *is* its social experiences (which comprise its identity) as well as its uniquely private experience.[112]

The second thing that influenced my decision to agree with Muelder and DeWolf that communitarian laws should be explicitly expressed in the moral law system has to do with developments that have been taking place in liberation theologies. For example, one finds in such theologies a strong emphasis on collective and structural forms of evil that undermine the worth of persons. This convinced me that the social question can never be adequately addressed by merely working to convert individuals. This is so because of the complexity of the issues themselves and the fact that social structures have properties that will not respond in significant ways to individualistic approaches. In addition, liberation theologies have seen more clearly than most theologies the interrelatedness between individuals and society, as well as the destruction that societal systems can wreak upon human beings. These theologies tend to stress the communal or relational nature of persons rather than the individualism of persons. As we have seen in the earlier discussion, Muelder developed an excellent sense for this through his study of history, Troeltsch, Hegel, and personalism. My study of liberation theologies confirms this communal emphasis.

Bertocci has argued that the additions made to Brightman's system of moral laws by Muelder and DeWolf are not really necessary. He "wonders whether these principles are nuclear to the system or articulations. It seems that the system itself does not require these specific corollaries."[113] Although I initially thought that Bertocci's concern might be applicable to DeWolf's second ontological principle, the "principle of ethical adaptation to ultimate reality" (or what Muelder calls the Metaphysical Law): "Every person ought to form all his ideals and choices in relation to his conception of the ultimate reality which is the ground of ethical obligation,"[114] it is now clear to me that logical consistency will drive the mind to consideration of the ground or source of the moral laws. In addition, I do not see that Bertocci's concern applies to inclusion of the communitarian laws, inasmuch as these are grounded in personalistic metaphysics. Nevertheless, the concern Bertocci raised should at least protect against any easy addition of laws to the moral law system in the future.

The second matter that warrants comment is the large number of laws one has to remember and appropriate when trying to apply them to moral judgments. "Is it realistic," some may ask, "to expect an ordinary citizen to remember all of these at the precise moment when moral judgment is required?" My response is that it is not too much to expect of most persons, and especially when we remember the role that habit plays in much of what we do. When I first studied Brightman's system of moral laws with Bertocci he urged me to read William James's *Psychology* (The Briefer Course). Since I, too, was wondering whether it was a bit much to expect that most persons would be able to remember each of Brightman's laws, I was helped a great deal by James's chapter "Habit." Much like learning to tie one's shoes, to ride a bicycle, or to swim, whenever we develop a habit of doing something it becomes automatic. I mean by this that we are then able to perform an act without conscious attention or will. James illustrated the process.

> If an act require or its execution a chain, A, B, C, D, E, F, G, etc., of successive nervous events, then in the first performances of the action the conscious will must choose each of these events from a number of wrong alternatives that tend to present themselves; but habit soon brings it about that each event calls up its own appropriate successor without any alternative offering itself, and without any reference to the conscious will, until at last the whole chain, A, B, C, D, E, F, G, rattles itself off as

soon as A occurs, just as if A and the rest of the chain were fused into a continuous stream.[115]

Like anything else that is new to us we may, through initial, conscious effort of attention, will, and effort, internalize the moral laws to the extent that an appeal to them will become automatic. When this happens, and when one is confronted with a situation that requires moral judgment, all one has to do is think the first principle in the system, namely the Logical Law, and this will automatically call up or trigger the others. Habit is, as James said, "the enormous fly-wheel of society, its most precious conservative agent."[116] Habit allows us to perform many tasks with little thought and expenditure of energy and effort.

At various places in this book I have pointed out that personalism has never enjoyed the popularity of some philosophical systems. Indeed, this has been the case even in the United States, despite the fact that it is the nation's oldest extant philosophy and still has disciples. Although the philosophy of personalism found its way to many parts of the world as a result of Brightman's travels and teaching, there have not been huge numbers of professional philosophers who have been thoroughgoing, systematic personalists. Most have at best been minimal or reluctant personalists, and therefore have not committed themselves to following the personalistic argument to its logical conclusion and then doing what it requires in day-to-day living. Therefore, the next two chapters examine some reasons for this phenomenon of "unpopularity," and then propose some next steps for personalism if it is to remain a viable philosophical option in the twenty-first century.

10

The "Unpopularity" of Personalism

Personalism has never been a dominant philosophy in this country. However, a case can be made that most religious people in the United States are at least near-personalists, in the sense that they believe in a personal God who cares about persons and the world. In addition, they at least give lip service to belief in the sacredness of persons. It would be a considerably less defensible stance, though, to say that most persons in this country are thoroughgoing, systematic personalists in the sense that Bowne and Brightman were. Indeed, personalists in this category comprise a very small minority.

Many in the personalist camp are what Paul Deats, Jr., described as "closet personalists."[1] They are either not aware that they are personalists, or they are apprehensive about acknowledging it publicly. Brightman said that "partial" or "near-personalists" are "those who, accepting in large measure a personalistic foundation, for some reason hesitate in the presence of a personalistic conclusion, and either deny the existence of a personal God, or somehow shuffle or evade in the presence of the problem."[2] Closet personalists very likely comprise a large group, but thoroughgoing personalists are few indeed.

Personalism has never experienced the level of sustained popularity of its greatest rival and greatest potential ally—process philosophy. Indeed, there is no evidence that the very term *personalism* has been popular among large numbers of people in the United States. What Knudson said in 1927 is applicable today. "Many who might be classed as personalistic in their philosophy or at least as near-personalists, still avoid the term so far as they themselves are concerned."[3] Knudson, like Brightman, hoped for a renaissance in personalistic philosophy, believing that its popularity would increase significantly in ensuing years. Both men were confident that this would happen. Knudson believed personalism to be "steadily gaining in favor, and bids fair before long to have a well-established place in philosophical usage."[4] Flewelling, also a student of Bowne's, and the founder-editor of *The Personalist*, held a similar view.[5] In 1959 Johannes Hirschberger believed personalism to be "an important movement" in the United States. He cited both Boston University and the University of Southern California as the two centers of personalistic studies.[6]

According to Brightman, at least four things need to happen before the renaissance in personalism can occur. First, persons who are philosophically inclined must persist in consciously trying to make sense of the most perplexing philosophical problems. Ideas are important no matter what we do. Second, personalists will have to write, teach, and lecture on personalism and not allow social and other circumstances to discourage them from es-pousing the personalistic faith. Failure to do these things is one of the chief reasons for the "unpopularity of personalism" today. People simply do not know what personalism is. I shall pursue this point momentarily. Third, institutions of higher learning need to devote much more attention to phi-losophy in general. And fourth, more pastors need to read voluminously in philosophy and learn to think critically.[7] This would also enable ministers to more adequately ground their theological and ethical claims and pro-nouncements. By taking philosophy or metaphysics more seriously we can say, for example, that God as causal agent supplies the dynamic for ethics—for linking the gospel narrative with what is happening in God's world.

However, the hoped-for resurgence of interest in personalistic philoso-phy that Brightman and others anticipated has not occurred. Indeed, in 1960 a symposium on "The Renaissance of Bowne" was hosted by four third-generation personalists: Peter Bertocci, Walter Muelder, Richard Millard, and John Lavely, all of Boston University. Although correct in their contention that Bowne "has never been sufficiently appreciated as a seminal thinker," they were too optimistic in their belief that "there are hopeful signs that scholars throughout the land are 'rediscovering' him."[8] These third-generation personalists gave no concrete evidence of these signs. One could argue, of course, that from the mid-1950s one of the most famous personal-ists, Martin Luther King, Jr., was creatively and courageously applying the basic tenets of personalism to the struggle for civil and human rights. But beyond his dissertation, King seldom referred to Bowne in his speeches, ser-mons, and writings.

At any rate, I intend in the present chapter to address what I believe to be some of the reasons for the "unpopularity" of personalism. I will also address some areas in which personalism may be improved, and thereby made a more viable philosophy. These considerations will point in the di-rection of a new personalism, that is, one that builds on the strengths of the Bowne-Brightman type of personalism that is the subject of this book. But one final preliminary comment is in order.

I am a fifth-generation personalist. I am not merely associated with this tradition because of my graduate work with two outstanding third-generation personalists, namely, Bertocci and Muelder. I am all the more affiliated with personalism because of the many affinities it has with my Afrikan American religio-cultural heritage. When I was a youngster, my fam-ily, church, and pre–high school experiences emblazoned in me the "spirit of personalism," although I had not heard or seen this term before my days as a seminary student. I was a personalist (at least a near-personalist) long before I first heard or saw the term in print. I have always believed in a personal God who loves and cares, especially for the beaten and crushed among humanity. Belief in the dignity of all persons—particularly Afrikan Americans—and the sacredness of all that God creates was instilled in me at an early age at home. This belief was reinforced at church and the black elementary and junior high schools I attended.

In chapter 1, I observed that there are at least a dozen types of personalisms. The type that informs my work has variously been referred to as Bownean, Orthodox, "Normative," Typical, Theistic, Boston Personalism, Personal Idealism, or simply, Personalism. Personalism is fundamentally a metaphysics, a way of thinking about reality and how all things hang together. It is in the deepest sense a way of life; a way of living together in a world in which all life forms depend for their existence and destiny on a God whose nature is love, and whose acts of creation are acts of love.

Many in the personalist tradition find it difficult to publicly acknowledge that they are personalists. This chapter will, among other things, consider some reasons for this apprehensiveness. This is not intended to be an exhaustive treatment of the issue. However, it is my hope that what is said here will cause "closet personalists" to leave their safe haven and begin contributing to the still-hoped-for renaissance in personalistic philosophy. In what follows I consider five concerns critics have raised that have contributed to the unpopularity of personalism. In each case I show that the criticism raised is based on a fundamental misunderstanding of theistic personalism. On the other hand, in several instances it will be seen that legitimate concerns are raised that can only serve to strengthen personalist conceptuality.

Against Metaphysical Personalism

From the appearance of Bowne's first book, *The Philosophy of Herbert Spencer* (1874), he was aware of the unpopularity of metaphysics. "I have not much expectation of a speedy revival of metaphysical study," he wrote, but "still I do hope that intellectual buffoonery may not always pass for profound wisdom, even if it does call itself science."[9] He had no doubt that it was "extremely fashionable...to decry metaphysics as a useless study."[10]

At the writing of the first edition of *Metaphysics* (1882), Bowne believed the subject of metaphysics was still in ill repute. "That works on metaphysics are always useless, and generally absurd, is the profound conviction of many." It is a conviction arrived at through "hearsay, and party-tradition."[11] By the time Bowne wrote the revised edition of *Metaphysics* in 1898, he observed that metaphysics was gaining in popularity, since the emerging view was that "metaphysics underlies all thinking and all science." (He had also said in the first edition of that work: "There is an immanent metaphysics in all thinking and in all science." Apparently it took some time for more people to begin to accept such a claim.) All persons appeal to a metaphysics, whether implicit or explicit, to which they turn for justification of their beliefs.[12]

Wolfhart Pannenberg also refers to the topsy-turvy career of metaphysics in his book *Metaphysics and the Idea of God* (1988). He writes that the dominant trend over the past two centuries has been in the direction of the unpopularity of metaphysics in both philosophy and theology, though there have been notable exceptions, for example, Nicolai Hartmann, the English Hegelians, Alfred N. Whitehead, Charles Hartshorne, and so on.[13] He might also have included the Boston Personalists. Pannenberg contends, not unlike Bowne, that the rejection of metaphysics cannot be successful in the long run.

Metaphysics, then, has not always been popular, although there have been periods when it has gained in popularity. This has been the trend of particular systems of metaphysics as well. In the case of personalism there is no question that personalists in my generation were developing at a time (from the 1960s) when there was a moratorium on metaphysics. It was not popular to work at, or appeal to, metaphysics. During that period the emphasis, in part, was on logical positivism. There also seemed to be a resurgence of interest in pragmatism, existentialism, and similar philosophies that avoided unduly abstract speculation. In addition, liberation theologies were emerging, and proponents made it clear that their chief conversation partners were not metaphysicians, but social and political scientists, radical economists, and so on. Since personalism is fundamentally a metaphysics, liberationists and others at best ignored it. However, would-be personalists within these groups failed to see that their distrust of metaphysical personalism did not necessarily place them entirely outside the personalist camp. That is, the problem was not—then or now—with ethical personalism, the view that the person is the fundamental moral unit and is the highest—not the only—instrinsic value. In principle, at least, no one seemed to have difficulty with the idea of respect for persons. The concern, rather, was with metaphysical personalism with its emphasis on the view that reality itself is personal. Many professional philosophers have simply not been able to bring themselves to accept the idea that God is personal.

Although Bowne and Brightman contributed much toward the development of ethical personalism, they were primarily metaphysical personalists who sought to be thoroughgoing in applying the basic principles of personalism to the chief problems of philosophy and life. Personalism was for them a general way of seeing the world and how all things relate or hang together. And, of course, personalists are willing to concede some things, but not their most basic idea that reality is personal. The whole system of personalism is built on this principle. The solution to the problems of philosophy, theology, ethics, epistemology, and the world is rooted in the theistic principle or belief in the existence of a personal God.

Although it is fair to say that some of the well-known personalists, for example, Walter G. Muelder, were more intentionally ethical personalists in the sense that they primarily identified themselves as ethicists, there is no gainsaying the fact that underlying their basic ethical principles is the view that reality is personal. One need not be a metaphysical personalist in order to be a proponent of ethical personalism. However, one will have a difficult time adequately grounding his or her belief in the absolute dignity of persons if one cannot see some ultimate reason for respecting and loving persons. For example, Martin Luther King, Jr., was quite clear about this. One should love self and other persons precisely because God, who is love, chose to create them. And having created persons, every one of them has infinite worth because God loves them. King said that "every man must be respected because God loves him. The worth of an individual...lies in relatedness to God. An individual has value because he has value to God."[14]

In any event, it should be clear to the reader that this first concern of critics is more general in nature. Even in Bowne's time it did not apply specifically to his earlier objective idealism and later personalism, but to metaphysics as such. Nevertheless, the next four criticisms have been raised specifically against personalism.

Individualistic Ethic

Metaphysical personalism places much emphasis on self or person. This has caused many to conclude that personalism is a purely individualistic philosophy with a corresponding ethic. Even Walter Mueller, the premiere social ethicist in the personalist tradition, once asked his teacher, Brightman, whether personalism has a social ethic.[15]

But it is precisely here that critics have erred in their understanding of personalism. Personalism is concerned with whole persons-in-relationship, that is, with persons in all of their concrete, blood-and-guts, daily problems. As noted above, even those Bowneans who have done their work primarily as ethicists ground their ethical principles in the metaphysics of personalism. Reality, for them, is personal. But when personalists refer to the personal they do not mean the individual alone, or that the individual somehow exists in a vacuum and is neither related to other individuals nor to other areas of creation. Yet, if one is not familiar with the metaphysics of personalism, it is easy to conclude (albeit wrongly) that personalism is a purely individualistic philosophy and ethic.

Since the time of Bowne, personalists have thought of reality as personal-communal, social, or relational. In *Personalism* (1908), for example, Bowne concludes that criticism and analysis lead to the idea of "a world of persons with a Supreme Person at the head."[16] Elsewhere he affirms the essential sociality or relationality of all things. He writes that "the notion of interaction implies that a thing is determined by others, and hence that it cannot be all that it is apart from all others."[17] A thing cannot be all that it can be in isolation. Not only is there a plurality of persons in the world, but each exists in community or in relation. Therefore, when the personalist says that reality is personal she or he is not talking about an individualistic or privatized way of thinking about persons in the world. The emphasis is unmistakably on the significance of the person as such, but the person is not separate from all others. Rather, we are all persons-in-relationship. Indeed, it is questionable whether a person can even be a person apart from others.

The point to be lifted up here is that personalism has always recognized that individuals do not exist in isolation in the world. We are what Mueller characterizes as persons-in-community.[18] Indeed, long before Mueller coined this phrase, McConnell was expressing (more emphatically than Bowne!) the relational nature of reality and persons.

Trying to dispel the idea that personalism is individualistic in its emphasis, McConnell stressed that the personal does not mean the individual alone or in isolation, "but persons set in relation to one another, which are as much a fact as is the separate existence of the individuals."[19] In this sense the individual person is unique, but not separate. In addition, she or he is able to develop fully only through communal relations. Therefore, the more basic fact is "persons existing together."

Similarly, Nels F. S. Ferré (a third-generation personalist under Brightman) has written that, inasmuch as created persons are God's creatures and children, they are "by nature more of a socius than of an individual."[20] No person is an individual if by this is meant that she or he is not necessarily related to others. According to Ferré, "the origin, content and function of consciousness are social in nature." To treat the individual apart from his or her total sociocultural context is at best a "methodological abstraction."

> The individual, therefore, is real as a center of consciousness, of experience, of choice, or of satisfaction, but he is never real apart from his social background in origin and function. Knowledge is basically a social fact.
>
> We cannot, therefore, accept any personalism in which the discreteness of the individual is strongly stressed, except for hortatory purposes.[21]

John W. Buckham (1864–1945), a personalist who was more influenced by the personal idealism of Howison, shared this perspective when he said that the person "finds himself only in relation with other persons. Personality is in its very nature relatedness, and yet, uniqueness."[22]

Harold H. Oliver has written on the subject of "relational personalism." One must applaud his contributions, especially his desire to exorcise from personalism outmoded, idealistic baggage.[23] He is critical of the nineteenth-century idealistic concept of the person in early personalism, since the focus seemed to be too much on the mind side of the mind-body relation. In addition, Oliver makes the claim that early personalists paid little attention to the relational nature of persons. But it is strange indeed that he has not been able to locate the relational-communal emphasis in the personalism of Bowne, Brightman, and other early personalists. Instead, Oliver looks to Eastern views of selfhood and the contributions of Erazim Kohak.[24] He finally concludes that "both Whitehead and Buber proposed views of reality more universal in scope than those of the Personalists."[25] Oliver therefore claims to be more influenced by these two men in the development of his own relational metaphysics, and lists as its basic principles: "(1) that experience is all there is; (2) that experience is a unity; (3) that experience consists exhaustively of relating; and (4) that mutuality is the prime feature of being."[26] The fundamental emphasis is on relation.

Oliver does make a concession from his earlier treatment of "the relational self" as a radical alternative to traditional Western concepts of self, including perspectives of early personalists. He now believes that Bertocci's discussion and analysis of "person" in *The Person God Is* (1970) is very near his view of "the relational self." Oliver seems to imply that we do not see the emphasis on relationality and mutuality in discussions on the self until Bertocci's mature thought on the subject.

It must be conceded that neither Bowne nor Brightman worked out the fuller implications of a relational metaphysics. On the other hand, it should also be affirmed that from its inception personalism was, in principle, a relational metaphysics. There is no gainsaying the contribution that Oliver is making toward the further development of a personalism that is both more intelligible to today's generation, and lifts up the significance of relationality in the world. But he goes too far when he claims that the notion of relationality is absent in the first two generations of personalism. Indeed, the four fundamental principles of a relational metaphysics that he proposes sound like something right out of the early works of Bowne and his disciples.

If one has understood the type of personalism discussed in this book, it will be seen that its theory of reality is social, or relational, not individualistic. Therefore, there need not be the fear or suspicion that personalism's ethic is individualistic and nonrelational. Although it is true that there is no strongly identifiable social ethic in Bowne (as we understand social ethics today), we do find in his work a precommunal ethic or a framework for developing a social ethic. Ethical personalism is based on the principle of the person as the moral unit. This is not to be taken to mean that personalism has no concern for the relational character of reality and implications for social ethics. Ethics can be personalistic without being individualistic.[27] Indeed, authentic personalistic ethics are social! Furthermore, one must wonder whether in Oliver's strong focus on mutuality the person somehow gets lost or whether the integrity of the person can be maintained. What happens to respect for the person as such in Oliver's position? If one concludes that mutuality or relationality is fundamental, it is conceivable that one may conclude that the intrinsically valuable is not the particular individual in relationship, but the relationship itself.

Popularity of Other Philosophies

A third reason for the unpopularity of personalism is that there are other, more popular, theologies and philosophies in major seminaries, colleges, and universities today. In the Introduction we saw that there was a radical decline in the significance of philosophical idealism after the two world wars. During this period existentialism began to emerge and take center stage. We found that the attempt by some thinkers to revive the absolute idealism of Josiah Royce failed, and with that, idealistic philosophy has not recovered to any significant degree.

Process or panpsychistic philosophy is an example of a popular philosophy today. What is interesting here is that historical works on personalism reveal that, despite differences, there are many points of convergence with process philosophy. One might say that the two are at least "soulmates." In fact, one could say, following Knudson, that what we now know as process philosophy is a type of personalism.[28] Both philosophies essentially contend that being is active, processive, or dynamic. Both are influenced by the philosopher Leibniz, with his strong emphasis on the active or processive nature of reality. According to Leibniz, "in the smallest portion of matter there is a world of creatures, living beings, animals, entelechies, and souls."[29] Leibniz called these monads. Each monad—from the lowest to the highest—has its own internal power.

This leads to the idea so prominent in personalism and process philosophy that to be is to act or be acted upon. However, neither personalism nor process philosophy has much use for the Leibnizian idea that the monads are windowless, for this would mean that they cannot see outside themselves and are therefore not able to interact in a meaningful way. Yet as was pointed out in chapter 4, Brightman saw in this the importance of the trait of privacy relative to person, while also insisting on the person's ability to interact and communicate with others. "No person can experience any other's consciousness directly; yet every private person can communicate and interact with others."[30] Whitehead's way of responding to Leibniz's windowless monads was to say that every actual occasion feels and thus prehends every other. Each is related to the entire universe.[31]

Both personalism and process philosophy elevate the worth of nature, although as will be seen under the next subject heading, personalism was late in treating this in a more explicit, systematic way. Both elevate freedom to a place of supremacy, thereby contending that, in the most fundamental sense, to be is to be free. But finally, it is significant that metaphysical personalism antedates process philosophy, which is not to say that herein lies its superiority. Yet, before Whitehead developed his process philosophy, Bowne had already written several major texts in which he systematically and methodically developed the philosophy of personalism. A key way in which personalism differs from process philosophy is that it makes the additional claim that process as a first principle necessarily implies a more fundamental first principle, namely, active intelligence or mind. How else can the claim be made that reality is essentially processive? To speak only of process would be an abstraction. However, I think John Lavely makes a more important point about the relation between these two philosophies.

> What is clear is that the affinities between and the common motifs of personalism and panpsychism are such that both positions have more at stake in reenforcing each other than in repudiating each other... Jointly panpsychism and personalism may be the last best hope of metaphysics.[32]

In a comparative study of Brightman's personalism and Whitehead's panpsychism relative to value theory, Wilbur Mullen noted that both provide "a fruitful metaphysical ground for the development of a rich and commendable theory of values," and that value considerations are prominent in their entire systems of thought.[33] Both men stress the "axiological function of God" and the idea that, as the source of values in the universe, God both conserves and increases values. Mullen concludes that there are points at which personalism and panpsychism can come together in a higher conception of what is true.

A fruitful synthesis of the thought of the two men might begin by more emphasis on organic relatedness in Brightman's personalistic pluralism, while Whitehead's concept of God could move more profitably in the direction of Brightman's clear-cut theism. Perhaps also more equality of emphasis on the aesthetic would enrich Brightman's axiology and lessen what is considered to be an excessive concern in Whitehead's thought.[34]

In addition, it was previously pointed out that personalists have not exhibited the courage to publicly espouse their position, which means that personalism does not get the hearing and attention it rightly deserves. As far back as 1921 Brightman pointed to the need for personalists to avoid being silenced because other philosophical perspectives have gained in popularity. Instead, he challenged them to be productive scholars—to write and teach about personalism on a frequent and regular basis.

In addition, there are those who contend that personalism is not an original philosophy. For example, William James pointed to what he considered a major limitation in Bowne's personalism, namely, its eclecticism.[35] However, it may be argued that this is not what is most significant about personalism. Rather, its most outstanding feature is the prominence it gives person and the metaphysical, epistemological, and ethical insights it gleans from this category. Robert Neville also points to what he considers the unoriginality of personalistic philosophy.[36] The problem with this latter criticism, however, is that it essentially applies to all Anglo philosophical systems in the West! All have consisted of what Whitehead characterized as "a series of footnotes to Plato."

On the other hand, one can find something original in both personalism and process philosophy. Both are original in the sense that they took certain basic ideas from past thinkers and orchestrated them in such a way that a new way of thinking about and doing philosophy emerged. For example, in the case of personalism the chief idea is that the category of *person* is the fundamental principle of explanation. Yet, when one considers the basic ideas that characterize personalistic metaphysics and epistemology, it will be seen that it is not a single idea that gives personalism its originality and distinctiveness as a worldview. For example, personalistic epistemology is based on four fundamental principles, each of which can be located in the thought of an important thinker in the West. These principles include: the dualism of thought and object, the creative activity of thought, the primacy of the practical reason, and the trustworthiness of reason. But Knudson showed that no single one of these, viewed in isolation, is unique or "peculiar to personalism. But taken together they constitute a distinctive body of doctrine."[37] I think a similar claim can be made regarding process philosophy.

Personalism need not be an unpopular philosophy merely because process or other philosophies are having their day in the sun. It is essentially in the hands of proponents of personalism to determine its fate. It is completely consistent with the personalist tradition for present-day exponents to look carefully and critically at other philosophies and appropriate their truths toward developing a higher, fuller synthesis in personalism. Doing this need not necessarily preclude retaining personalism as one's fundamental point of departure in the quest for truth and knowledge. Rather than wilt in the face of other philosophies, it is crucial for personalists to stand their ground and confidently proclaim the need for a philosophy based on the principle of respect for persons as such, especially in today's world.

Absence of an Environmental Ethic

A fourth reason for the unpopularity of personalism may be due to the strong emphasis that more recent theologians and philosophers place on environmental ethics and the value of nonhuman life forms. Indeed, in some circles there seems to be nothing less than a radical movement away from stressing the dignity of persons. Such a shift must concern the systematically and massively oppressed who have never been respected as persons, and are now being told in essence that "quality of life concerns," for example, the environment, should be treated with respect and cared for as much as they. An effect of this, too often, is the depersonalizing and instrumentalizing of persons. This is a particularly troubling idea, and one I shall return to in the next chapter. For now, suffice it to say that early personalists failed to work out the full implications of their metaphysical and ethical principles that at least provided a basis upon which to develop a more ecocentric ethic, or one in which emphasis on the dignity of persons does not mean a diminishing of the value of other life forms. Indeed, the outline of such an ethic was present even in the works of Bowne, a fact that has eluded most critics. A better understanding of the Bowne-Brightman type of personalism would point one to the conclusion that emphasizing respect for persons does not preclude respect for the dignity of nonhuman life forms.

In his article "Can Personalism Provide a Theoretical Basis for an Environmental Ethics?" John Howie asks whether personalism can "provide a warrant for considering nature of intrinsic or inherent worth." Howie is concerned that personalism, like Christianity, has so elevated the worth of persons that the door is left open for the exploitation and destruction of the environment and natural resources. He seems to think that one's focus on the dignity of persons necessarily implies that she or he has no sense of the value in other areas of creation. And this, he contends, could provide a license for the indiscriminate abuse of the environment.[38]

From the time of Bowne, personalists have often said that everything in the world exists in, of, and for persons. Understandably, the novice may interpret this to mean that persons are considered to be the pinnacle of all creation. Such a view may lead to the idea that persons may literally use (and misuse) other areas of creation as means to enhance their own good regardless of the consequences for nonhuman life forms. From here it is a short distance to the conclusion that as long as we respect the dignity and sanctity of persons we may do whatever we like to nature, the environment, and the animal kingdom. That is, we can abuse them in any way we want, for after all, these things exist for use by persons.

In addition, the early personalist claim that "persons only are real" may be misleading to the uninformed. For among other things it may imply that created persons are the crown of creation or that the universe exists only for them. But the contrary is true. McConnell, for example, maintained that Bowne "did not think of man as necessarily the peak of all creation, or the universe as necessarily made for man alone."[39]

Brightman gave a helpful response to those who were critical of the idea that persons only are real.

> Personalism certainly does not hold that only human persons are real; nor does it hold that trees and gold and skies are all persons. In Dewey's language (but not in his sense!) personalism holds that trees and gold and skies are all experience; yet not merely human experience, for they exist when no human being is aware of them. Therefore, they are the experience of the Supreme Person.[40]

This is an important statement, and is indicative of Brightman's thoroughgoing idealism. The affirmation that person is the ultimate reality did not mean for early personalists that there were no other realities. Nor did it mean that these other realities have no value in themselves.

It will be recalled from chapter 1 that Bowne, in opposition to Berkeley's subjective idealism (the view that physical objects are little more than a series of presentations or ideas in the mind and, thus, are not real) held that there are at least two levels of reality: phenomenal and ontological. All aspects of nature or the world have phenomenal reality, since they can be experienced. But these realities do not depend on themselves for their existence. Instead, they are caused by a power behind them, namely, the energizing of God's will and thought. But it is important to observe that what is implied in this view is the significance to God of phenomenal objects. For since all of creation is the manifestation of God's thought and will, and since God's nature is love, God willingly, thoughtfully, and lovingly creates all things. Thus, all creation has intrinsic worth or value, although all does not have the same value. If God is the Creator, then all that has been created has value infused into it. And if all is valuable to the Creator, then especially those creatures endowed with the potential for rationality, humanity, and morality must proceed with caution in the way they relate to each other and to the rest of creation. This is a reasonable conclusion that one may draw from early personalists.

Though present-day critics like Oliver and Neville find the mind-centered Cartesian and Kantian idealism of early personalists distasteful, it is important to be aware that Bowne and Brightman rejected the idea of a bifurcation between persons and the world of nature. They rejected dualistic personalism in favor of idealistic personalism. Brightman characterizes both types.

> Dualistic personalism...holds that the Supreme Person has created a world of nature or matter which is impersonal and unconscious, as well as the world of persons. Idealistic personalism holds, on the contrary,

that matter itself is a form of spirit, being the very will and experience of God in action in one of its realms. Dualism holds that matter and spirit are utterly and irreducibly different…Idealism holds that matter and spirit are both aspects of a single unitary type of process, namely, the process of personal will. For the idealistic personalist, the whole of nature, as revealed in our sense experience, is truly what Berkeley called it, a divine language, which symbolizes to our minds the purpose and the reason of the divine mind.[41]

Brightman's thoroughgoing idealism led him to the view that all matter or physical nature is but the functioning or activity of God's will and thought. If this is so, according to Brightman, there is no real relation between matter and spirit as such. Rather, it is a relation between spirit and spirit.

Nothing truly impersonal exists; the "impersonal" is simply an incomplete or abstract way of viewing what is really personal when fully understood. On this view, a pebble, which is apparently impersonal and which, of course, has no personality of its own, is understood to be nothing but the energizing of the will of the cosmic person; all nature is the ongoing of the conscious activity of God.[42]

This, for Brightman, is the more coherent view and is more consistent with what is meant by universe. The more coherent interpretation is that this is one world, the whole of which belongs to, and is loved by, the Creator. If nature, for the personalist, is but the energizing of God's will and thought, then one's disrespect for nature is also disrespect for God and all members of creation. It seems that Brightman was on to something, although he failed to draw the full conclusions from the foundation he was laying. Although he struggled in a later work to deal more systematically with the issue of metaphysical dualism,[43] Brightman nowhere explicitly talks about the dignity of nature and the environment. Yet throughout his work as well as Bowne's, we find—at least implicitly—a basic respect for nature, the environment, and the animal kingdom.

In 1928 McConnell raised the concern that his colleagues in the personalist tradition were not always careful to "take due account of the non-human reference of many, many features of the world in which we live."[44] He seemed to recognize that areas of creation other than persons have value in themselves. He implied that his colleagues in the tradition had been derelict in acknowledging this point. It was Bowne, however, who laid the metaphysical and ethical foundations for an environmental ethic in personalism.

In *The Principles of Ethics*, we find Bowne constructing a teleological developmental ethic. This ethic requires that persons not only respect themselves and other persons, but that they respect the environment and the animal kingdom. Personalism contends that reality is relational. On the ethical side this means, minimally, that moral agents have responsibilities to self, other selves, and the rest of creation. A further implication is that neither we nor other areas of creation can be all we can be if we engage in abusive practices.

Personalism acknowledges the value of all life, and thus would be in agreement with environmental ethicists like Paul W. Taylor who distinguish between moral agents and moral subjects. Because every living being is at least a moral subject, each warrants moral consideration and is owed responsibility. On the other hand, every living being to whom responsibilities are owed and who possesses the capacity and power to choose between right and wrong, good and bad, and has the power to actually consider the implications for their choices and actions are moral agents.[45]

Moral agents always owe responsibilities to moral subjects (who may or may not be moral agents). The mentally challenged and the mentally insane, for example, are moral subjects to whom moral agents owe responsibilities and ought not take advantage. The mentally challenged lack one or more of the capacities of moral agents, for example, the ability to make responsible moral judgments, the power to critically consider the reasons and implications of their judgments and actions, and so on. In an unpublished paper Howie writes: "Just as there are, biologically speaking, human beings who are not moral agents, there are other living beings that are moral subjects even though they are not moral agents."[46] But, as we will see below, this perspective is not foreign to personalist conceptuality.

Howie goes on to distinguish between an anthropocentric and ecocentric outlook and opts for the latter because of its emphasis on "the community of living things, together with the necessary inert ingredients including water, soil, and air."[47] This means that persons, along with all other living and inert things, are "members of a biotic team or community" and thus should not exploit or use the other members solely for their own benefit. However, it will be seen that since the time of Bowne, personalists have always been against the indiscriminate misuse and destruction of the environment and the animal kingdom. Yet it is also true that Bowne was not always consistent in this regard, since he sometimes wrote of the subordination of nature to human service.[48] But in principle there is no question that Bowne's personalism supports the dignity of both human and nonhuman life forms.

Bowne's emphasis on expanding the moral field to include all that has been left out is significant because he held that nature and the animal kingdom have been forgotten and thus need to be included in our moral field. Regarding these nonhuman areas of life, Bowne writes that "there is room for extending the moral area, not less for the sake of man himself, than for the sake of the animals." He was clearly against animal and environmental abuse.

> Macaulay is supposed to have made an exquisite hit when he declared that the Puritans were opposed to bear-baiting because it pleased the spectators, and not because it gave pain to the bear. No better reason could be given for suppressing the sport than its brutalizing effect upon the spectators.[49]

Here Bowne was contending against a purely anthropocentric outlook regarding nonhuman life. He saw clearly the need for human regard and respect for the dignity and rights of animals rather than merely focusing on how our treatment or mistreatment of animals affects us. However, Bowne saw a need to moralize the environment and animal kingdom, although he would have these come "under human control." Yet he accepted the biblical charge that persons are "to dress and to keep" the world in which they have been placed. Unfortunately, Bowne was a man of his time in that he was not completely able to avoid referring to the need for nature to "be subordinated to human service." As can be seen, he did not entirely escape the language of "conquest" and "control over"[50] the nonhuman areas of creation.

Early personalism did provide a theoretical basis for an environmental ethic that requires a deep respect for nature and animals. The most outstanding woman in the personalist tradition, Georgia E. Harkness, also made a significant contribution to environmental ethics. Harkness did not hesitate to remind persons that they ought to be good stewards and love the world, not because of its instrumental value for persons, but because it is God's creation and is loved by God. Like Bowne she insisted on the need for the highest conceivable estimate of the worth of the environment and the animal kingdom. Harkness urged persons toward "a shared concern for the earth and all its resources," and believed that without it persons "are not likely to work with God in a shared enterprise to use them for human good."[51] The key to her environmental ethic was her belief that God has "intimate regard" for the entire creation. Outside the Bible, Harkness knew of no literature that more explicitly portrayed God's love for creation than James Weldon Johnson's sermon "The Creation," in *God's Trombones*.[52] Harkness was outraged over the abuse of natural resources and declared this "a sin against God" and a robbing of God.[53] Appealing to the biblical account of creation, she concluded that "man's lordship over the earth is a gift of God in trust, not a natural right and not something man has earned."[54] Although she too used "subordination" language in her references to humans' relations with nature and discussed the subject in terms of the potential good that nature could provide for persons, Harkness rejected all theories and practices that encouraged the wanton destruction of plant and animal life. She grounded her view both biblically and metaphysically. Thus, once again, as with Bowne, the theoretical framework for an environmental ethic was present.

In addition, there is no better chapter in personalistic literature on the significance and worth of the natural environment and the respect and moral responsibility it is due than DeWolf's treatment of the subject in *Responsible Freedom* (1971). DeWolf writes of the biblical requirement that we not only work, cultivate, and keep the land, but more importantly, that we keep, guard, protect, and preserve it. His interpretation of the creation event in Genesis is that nature is "good in itself." In addition, he agrees with the view of Albert Schweitzer and Jonathan Edwards that we ought to have "reverence for life" and "reverence for being," respectively.[55] DeWolf writes of the environment as an "object of wonder and respect," and quotes approvingly Gerhard von Rad's interpretation of Old Testament hymns with respect to creation.

> Since it was so wonderfully created by Jahweh and is so wonderfully preserved, it has splendour of its own, from which praise and witness issue: in other words the world is not only an object which calls forth praise but is at the same time also the subject which utters it.[56]

The animal and plant kingdoms have value of their own, and therefore must be respected in their own right. This implies an acknowledgment of the dignity of nature, animals, and other nonhuman life. We see evidence of this need from the time of Bowne.

Meaning of Person

A fifth criticism is the claim that personalists have yet to provide an acceptable definition of their basic principle, that is, the person or the personal. Of particular import is the criticism that personalists have been too much influenced by Descartes's mind-body dualism in their treatment of the person. Likewise it is claimed that early personalists were too much influenced by the Kantian view that the real self, and consequently that which warrants the deepest respect, is the inner self—not the body. This is potentially the most damaging of the criticisms. Indeed, John Lavely criticizes his teacher, Brightman, on this point. "I have heard Brightman insist emphatically that a person's body is no part of his mind."[57] Lavely concludes from this that for Brightman the real person is essentially identified with mind, while the body is little more than an external environment on which the mind depends. Mind, a "Situation Experienced," is for Brightman, more fundamental than the body, a "Situation Believed-in."[58]

Although Brightman was adamant that mind and body are not one and the same, he clearly concedes that there is an intimate relationship between them. Each affects the other. Indeed, he would not have disagreed with John W. Buckham, who held that there is such an intimate, integral relationship between mind and body that it is difficult to know where the body ends and the mind begins.[59]

The influence of both the Cartesian mind-body dualism and the idealism of Kant and Hegel caused Brightman to speak and write about mind and body in hierarchical fashion. The great emphasis on mind caused him—whether intended or not—to suggest the superiority of mind over body. It is not difficult to see how such a view can have serious implications for social ethics. If the real person, for example, is mental or the inner self, why worry about the well-being of the body? Why engage in actions to free the body of unnecessary pain and discomfort caused by socioeconomic oppression? Brightman's thoroughgoing idealism regarding the mind-body relation prompted him to propose that the body is part of nature, and nature is the energizing of God's will. Therefore, as an expression of the Supreme Mind, the body is little more than a conduit for the interaction between God and the created mind.[60]

From the time of Bowne, personalists have recognized the need to refine the model of person. Lavely contends that the concept of person "needs to be freed from what I call the Cartesian flaw. The resulting asymmetry between the human and the divine needs to be confronted."[61] The Cartesian flaw has to do with too sharp a dualism between mind and body, and the corresponding tendency of personalists in the Bowne-Brightman camp to place too little emphasis on the importance of the body for thought and other processes. We particularly see this limitation in Brightman's more rationalistic treatment of the self. Jack Padgett makes the point well.

> Also the fact remains that one's particular bodily organism is more intimately and causally related to one's mind than the sun. My body is experienced as mine in a way that the sun or the air we breathe are not. However, on Brightman's view, the body's response to the self's purpose occurs through the direct activity of God and not through the direct interaction of mind and body. [This is Brightman's thoroughgoing idealism at work, but it unfortunately undermined the importance of the body.] Such a dichotomy between mind and body seems unnecessary and unwarranted. The unity and identity of the self is sufficiently complex that bodily functionings play their part and should be incorporated into self's unity and identity.[62]

In addition to this critique by Padgett (a personalist), Oliver and others would like to see personalists cease their dependence upon the idealism of Kant in their treatment of the person.[63]

To be sure, views of the person elaborated on by early personalists need to be reconsidered in light of present understandings and experiences. Oliver, Lavely, Kohak, and Thomas O. Buford are making significant contributions in this regard.[64] In addition, there is need to look more closely at Bertocci's later work on the person,[65] since he, more than any of his contemporaries in the tradition, tried to clarify the meaning of person and the mind-body relation. For Bertocci any adequate metaphysics would seek to provide a reasonable explanation of the relation of both the body and the unconscious to the person.[66]

The criticism that early personalists, by focusing on the Kantian and Cartesian strands of idealism, tended to emphasize the mind side of the mind-body relation is a valid one. This emphasis opened the way to an undermining of the significance of the body. However, it should also be pointed out that this is not a recent concern, even among personalists. Indeed, three personalists, two in the Bowne-Brightman camp (Nels F. S. Ferré and L. Harold DeWolf), and a Frenchman (Emmanuel Mounier), raised concerns about the idealistic view of the person in the 1950s. Moreover, King stressed the need to view the whole person—mind and body—as sacred.[67] As will be seen momentarily, DeWolf did the same thing.

Nels Ferré, a student of Brightman's, wondered whether "we have suffered too long from an abstractive idealism" in our efforts to understand the relation between mind and body. Ferré wanted nothing to do with that part of idealistic thought that made mind superior to body, thereby implying that the body is less worthy or valuable. The body is as much a part of the self as is the mind.

> Purpose and self-perpetuation,…also involve intrinsically bodily aspects. Human beings, at least, express purpose and perpetuate their lives through material media…The body is our way of being related to the world outside. It is a means whereby we declare our intentions and effect our purposes…The body…is the medium of communication from self to others, and from others to self.[68]

Likewise, DeWolf questioned the traditional idealistic view of the relation of mind and body and the tendency to subordinate body to mind. He implied that the creation of the human mind and body are not two separate divine acts, which might suggest that there is a chronological order between the two such that one is superior to the other.

> It may be that the creative activity of God which gives being to the new soul is the very same as appears spatially in the development of the fertilized ovum into the lively new-born body. In any event there is apparent the closest kind of correlation between the development of the body and that of the soul, both as to temporal sequence and as to quality.[69]

Thus it seems reasonable to conclude that it was not God's intention that one of these be superior to or more important than the other. DeWolf goes on to suggest that the body is important in communication as well as the moral and religious development of the person. The body therefore is not an evil, but a good thing, and is as worthy of care and respect as the mind or soul. DeWolf then turned to the Bible, more specifically 1 Corinthians 6:13–20, to support his contention that the body, too, is sacred.

> Nowhere in literature is there a more emphatic and exalted assertion of the rightful sanctity of human bodies than the passage in which Paul depicts them as "members of Christ." He seems even to imply that the body is rightfully so sacred that a sin against it is worse than a sin of the soul in which the body is not involved.[70]

DeWolf has the distinction of being the first personalist to explicitly refer to the sanctity of the body.

At any rate, this emphasis on the importance of what may be viewed as the embodied self, rather than the more mental self of classical idealistic thought, is an example of an internal critique in the Boston Personalist tradition—a critique that occurred long before the more recent criticisms of Oliver, Lavely, Padgett, Kohak, and Neville.

The French personalist Emmanuel Mounier (1905–1950) also made a significant contribution to this issue in his book *Personalism* (1952). Mounier opposed any type of idealism that disembodies the self, or "reduces all matter (and the body) to a reflection of the human spirit, absorbing it into itself by a purely mental activity."[71] Mounier held that no Christian or personalist speaks of the body with contempt, and that to do so is contrary to the best in these traditions, according to which mind and body are fused in existence. "Man is a body in the same degree that he is a spirit, wholly body and wholly spirit...There is nothing in me that is not mingled with the earth and the blood."[72] He held further that "my embodied existence, far from depersonalizing me, is a factor essential to my personal status...I exist subjectively, I exist bodily are one and the same experience. I cannot think without being and I cannot be without my body..."[73]

If the person is truly an embodied self, it is not difficult to conclude that "the flesh and the spirit are one;...when you mortify the one, you have mortified the other."[74] There are not many who know the significance of this better than those who are systematically crushed and depersonalized because of race, gender, class, sexual preference, health, or age.

In the final chapter I introduce what I call *militant personalism*. Under this heading I consider several aspects of Afrikan American sociocultural and religious experience that may contribute to the emergence of a new, more active and vibrant personalism. One of the most crucial of these contributions is that of black women's ways of thinking about the dignity and worth of the human body. I then turn to the Afrikan and Afrikan American emphasis on we-centeredness rather than I-centeredness. This is followed by an examination of the view that any viable personalism for today and tomorrow will have to develop a preference for the poor and the oppressed. This leads to the idea that a militant personalism will have to get beyond meliorism in ethics, since the poor and the oppressed live under such urgent conditions. But this will also mean an increased emphasis on the dignity of all life forms, since personalism at bottom is relational.

11

Toward a New Personalism

Militant Personalism

It is important that personalists not be forced into silence because other conceptualities are more popular at the moment. Metaphysical personalism is not popular today. But the truth is that neither is ethical personalism, which focuses on the principle of respect for persons. Far too many people give only lip service to the idea of respect for persons. To support this claim one need only consider the present level of poverty, homelessness, unemployment and underemployment, institutional racism, sexism, classism, ageism, and militarism in this country and other parts of the world. Surely these would not exist to the phenomenal degree they do if the attitude and behavior of persons reflected a basic respect for persons as such.

Today there is no sustained emphasis on the prominence of persons and their inherent dignity and worth. Rather than the rule, it is more often the exception that persons are treated like beings imbued with the image and fragrance of God. It seems to me that one of the reasons for this is the failure of personalists to proclaim more forthrightly the need to elevate the significance of persons, a stance that does not necessarily preclude acknowledgment of the intrinsic value of other areas of creation.

I think this calls for a personalism that is at once more militant and aggressive than what we have known before now. To this end I want to suggest several ways the personalistic argument may be enhanced and enlivened if we include emphases of Afrikan American experience. The method of personalism is comprehensive and is characterized by what I have referred to as deep empiricism, the view that all relevant data should be admitted in the quest for truth and knowledge. Therefore, it is quite appropriate to consider and include that which has been traditionally and systematically left out. While a good deal more has been left out than what I shall include in this prolegomenon to a new personalism, there is no question that Afrikan American experiences were given very little positive consideration during the first two generations of personalism. Although this began to change with the appearance of the third generation, much more needs to be done. I want to consider several points at which the personalistic argument may be strengthened. Integrating these matters can point only to a more militant personalism.

Sanctity of the Body

Because of the long history of massive, systematic destruction of black bodies through both legal and illegal means, a focus on the sanctity of the body must necessarily be central to a new personalism. Historically Afrikan Americans rejected the idea that there is a dualism between mind and body and believed the entire cosmos to be sacred. This, and the faith that God is personal and loving, led long ago to the view that all persons have infinite value and thus warrant respect. However, in truth this statement must be qualified, inasmuch as patriarchy and sexism have been major problems and contradictions in black communities at least since the eighteenth century. It is most assuredly counter to the stated claim of the sacredness of all persons, including their bodies. In addition, black women have been and continue to be victims of physical and other forms of abuse both in and beyond the black community. Those who genuinely accept the principle of the sanctity of every person's body do not abuse, participate in, or allow (through silence or indifference) abusive practices to be perpetrated against persons' bodies. One of the saddest commentaries on the male gender in this and every other country is its systematic efforts to dehumanize and desecrate the image of God in *all* women, regardless of race, class, religion, and so on. Historically and contemporaneously, men of all races and classes—but for a few outstanding exceptions—have in practice tended to disrespect and deny the sanctity of women's bodies. One womanist-personalist sums up the matter of mind-body dualism in the black community this way:

> I don't think it is accurate to say we have always rejected the mind-body dualism. Heck, sexism presupposes the dualism—the male mind and body are superior to anything female. Sexism sees body parts, not the person.[1]

With this qualification in mind, it may be said that partly because of their understanding of the biblical emphasis on the worth of the entire person—mind and body—blacks historically believed that the body is as sacred as the mind. This view was reinforced as a result of slavery, lynchings, discrimination, and other inhumane practices against the Afrikan American's mind-body. In this regard, the idea of the sanctity of the body took on even more significance for blacks since it was and continues to be threatened by the wedded forces of sexism, white racism, and economic exploitation. So historically, when black preachers and other leaders talked about the sanctity of the person, they were not just referring to the worth of the inner self. They meant the whole self—mind and body. This was all the more important since whites worked so hard to teach them to hate themselves and everything about themselves. This is why there were such elaborate efforts during the black consciousness movement of the sixties and seventies to reinstill in blacks their lost sense of dignity and worth.

When people are not in touch with their sense of worth the tendency is to turn to self-destruction and destruction of others. Few recognized this as clearly as did Malcolm X, who sought to help the black masses regain their sense of worth. For Malcolm, the worst thing white racism did was to cause his people to hate themselves. His basic aim was to teach them to love themselves. Malcolm once responded to an interviewer: "It is true that Negroes kill Negroes, but this is because the white man himself has taught Negroes to hate Negroes. The Negro hates another Negro because this was taught to us during slavery, and the Negro hates everything about himself." What Malcolm wanted more than anything was for blacks to once again learn to love, respect, and appreciate themselves.[2] Malcolm knew what any good psychotherapist knows, namely, that before a person can be restored to sound mental health, it is necessary for one to feel good about oneself, and a good deal of this has to do with loving one's physical self. But this self-love is precisely what was taken away from many Afrikan Americans.

> By making our people in the Western Hemisphere hate Africa, we ended up hating ourselves. We hated our African characteristics. We hated our African identity. We hated our African features. So much so that you would find those of us in the West who would hate the shape of our nose. We would hate the shape of our lips. We would hate the color of our skin and the texture of our hair.[3]

Afrikan Americans have known the importance of loving the inner self, while not pretending that there is no relationship between the mental self and the bodily self. The concern that Jack Padgett, Harold Oliver, John Lavely, and others raise about the failure of early personalists to highlight the significance of the body is an important reminder. If personalism is to be a more viable philosophical and theological option, it can learn a good deal from Afrikan Americans about the worth of the body. Indeed, relative to this issue, both personalism and black men can learn much from black women.

Afrikan American women have done more than any group in drawing attention to the significance and value of the body. Although a particular group of these women, womanists, have been concerned to lift up the experiences and unsilence the heretofore muted and silent voices of black women, they would be the first to say that the emphasis on the worth of the body generally applies to all persons—female and male. Women of Afrikan descent focus on the worth of the black woman's body because historically and presently it has been devalued by all men, as well as by the familial, socio-economic, political, and other structures of this society.

At any rate, the womanist writer Alice Walker knows that hatred of oneself can lead to attempted suicide and worse.[4] Not only did Walker attempt suicide during a period when she thought little of herself as a person and a woman, but she has worked hard to keep before the American public the fact that large numbers of young black women all over this country commit suicide. Walker has done much to show that the best remedy for self-hatred among women of Afrikan descent is learning anew to love their whole black selves—mind and body—and everything it means to be black and woman. In addition, her concern has been "the survival whole of my people."[5] And when Walker talks about the spiritual survival of Afrikan Americans she does not mean survival of an inner spirit only, since for her there is no dualism between spirit and body. Spiritual survival has to do with the well-being of the entire self.

None have written more poignantly and poetically about the dignity of black women than Maya Angelou. In her poem "Phenomenal Woman" she proudly describes the outstanding beauty of ordinary black women.

Pretty women wonder where my secret lies.
I'm not cute or built to suit a fashion model's size
But when I start to tell them,
They think I'm telling lies.
I say,
It's in the reach of my arms,
The span of my hips,
The stride of my step,
The curl of my lips.
I'm a woman
Phenomenally.
Phenomenal woman,
That's me.[6]

Only the woman who truly loves herself can speak these words with passion and conviction and live what they mean.

Other womanists, for example, Audre Lorde (1934–1992), stressed the need for black women to learn to love themselves "as Black women." But this goes well beyond the proclamation that "Black is beautiful." For Lorde, loving self has much to do with the pursuit of empowerment to serve self and other black women. But most importantly, self-love is necessary in order to recapture the lost sense of love of self.

> I have to learn to love myself before I can love you or accept your loving. You have to learn to love yourself before you can love me or accept my loving. Know we are worthy of touch before we can reach out for each other.[7]

In addition, Lorde was quite adamant about the need for black women to learn "to mother themselves," for it is often to mothers that we attribute the traits of tenderness and loving care. This means establishing authority "over our own definition" and over how black women will grow and develop; affirming "my own worth" by doing whatever is necessary to ensure survival in a hostile environment; being tender and kind to self even in the face of temporary failure; "learning to love what we have given birth to by giving definition to, learning how to be both kind and demanding in the teeth of failure as well as in the face of success"; being self-assertive in defining who black women are and will be; and "laying to rest of what is weak, timid, and damaged."[8]

Lorde knew well the importance of unashamedly and unabashedly naming and defining oneself. Therefore, she once proudly proclaimed that she was "a forty-nine-year-old Black lesbian feminist socialist mother of two, including one boy, and a member of an interracial couple."[9] Lorde named herself because she recognized that each of these traits was an important part of who she was as an integrated whole person. Each part belongs and contributes to her wholeness. She learned to love each aspect of herself and came to see them as compatible with, and belonging to, each other.[10] The different parts of her are distinct, yet they interpenetrate. In addition, none of these traits would mean anything if they were not also parts of her bodily self. She not only had experiences of each aspect of her self, she was these experiences, as she was each of the traits she named.

Not only have people of Afrikan descent generally been taught to hate themselves, or at best to undermine their own worth, but black women have received at least a triple dose of such teachings from the white community in general and far too many black men. They are mistreated because they are black, because they are women, and, when they are without economic means, they are mistreated because of their socioeconomic class. This is why Lorde and others have insisted on the need for black women to learn again to love themselves just because they are persons, women, and black; to learn anew how to be gentle and nice to each other. Lorde said it best:

> We have to consciously study how to be tender with each other until it becomes a habit because what was native has been stolen from us, the love of Black women for each other. But we can practice being gentle with ourselves by being gentle with each other. We can practice being gentle with each other by being gentle with that piece of ourselves that is hardest to hold, by giving more to the brave bruised girlchild within each of us, by expecting a little less from her gargantuan efforts to excel.[11]

Lorde stressed the need for black women to learn to be caring and compassionate toward themselves, rather than to merely be these things for others. She called them to "self-value and self-love."[12]

If we listen and hear, we may learn from Lorde and other womanists that persons are, first and foremost, integrated selves, which means that all parts of who one is must be accepted by the self and allowed to contribute what each can to one's wholeness, empowerment, and liberation. This is a stance that is particularly relevant today in the face of the deadly phenomenon of "self-imposed genocide" within the ranks of young Afrikan American males. All that Lorde says about the need for black women to learn again how to love, appreciate, and respect themselves as full-fledged human beings may be easily integrated into a vibrant and militant personalism that can provide a framework for the total liberation and empowerment of the entire Afrikan American community.

Toni Morrison provides another womanist perspective on the prominence of the idea of the embodied self and the need—especially for blacks—to love their bodies. In her classic work *Beloved*, we find the character Baby Suggs urging her people to love and cherish their flesh, even though others did not, and instead did all they could to demean, disrespect, and destroy it.

> "Here," she said, "in this here place, we flesh; flesh that weeps, laughs; flesh that dances on bare feet in grass. Love it. Love it hard. Yonder they do not love your flesh. They despise it. They don't love your eyes; they'd just as soon pick em out. No more do they love the skin on your back. Yonder they flay it. And O my people they do not love your hands. Those they only use, tie, bind, chop off and leave empty. Love your hands! Love them. Raise them up and kiss them. Touch others with

them, pat them together, stroke them on your face 'cause they don't love that either. *You* got to love it, *you*!…This is flesh I'm talking about here. Flesh that needs to be loved.[13]

The body is not something sinful; not something to bemoan. Rather, it has a sacredness of its own and should be loved, cared for, and treated tenderly. And most importantly, one need not wait for the approval or support of others in order to begin loving one's body. Nor should it matter that others love your or my body. What matters first and last is that you love your body, and that I love my body. As Morrison says, *"You* got to love it, *you*!"

I introduce these ideas of womanist writers because in recent years they, more than any others, have written and spoken eloquently and passionately about the ongoing need to recapture the sense of self-love and self-dignity, among Afrikan Americans, and most especially Afrikan American women. In light of the phenomenon of black-on-black violence and murder among young black males in recent years, which is reaching genocidal proportions, this focus on the love, respect, and tender care for both mind and body among Afrikan Americans is significant. For it is absolutely clear that persons who do not love themselves will not love and respect others. Bowne had this principle in mind over a century ago when, writing on personalistic ethics, he said that there is a vast need for extraethical factors, for example, the highest conceivable estimate of the worth and value of persons as such, to condition ethical principles such as love and justice. Bowne concluded that this, more than anything else, will determine how persons treat self and other persons. A low conception of the value of persons (or of particular persons) will lead to the worst possible behavior toward persons. A high estimate of the worth of persons, on the other hand, will tend to lead to commensurate behavior toward them.

Any viable personalism at the close of the twentieth century and the dawn of the twenty-first century must necessarily give prominence to an integrated mind and body. And unlike much of traditional personalism, it will be necessary to emphasize the dignity and sanctity of the body, and thus the need to love, care for, and preserve it. This means, minimally, that personalism must become the philosophy par excellence that stresses the sacredness of the human body. In this regard personalism can learn much from the best Afrikan American experiences have to offer on the subject.

We-Centeredness Plus I-Centeredness

In addition, Afrikan and Afrikan American ancestors emphatically rejected the idea of a privatized self or the view that the individual is capable of being all that she or he can be apart from the group or community. The emphasis is on *we* rather than I, although we will see momentarily that efforts must also be made to ensure that the I is not lost in or swallowed up by the we or community.

The we-centered outlook is prevalent in the writings of many thinkers of Afrikan descent. Gabriel M. Setiloane writes:

Community is not by human choice for the sake of self-preservation. It is given in an unaccountable way like humanness itself and Divinity or religion. African Christians' first dis-enchantment with Christianity in its Western version is at the point of its denial of community or dealing with it as something dispensable at the human's will and whim… Christianity could be enriched immensely if it were to learn from African tradition about community: that it is of the very essence of being.[14]

Archbishop Desmond Tutu looks both to the Bible and to Afrikan tradition to make the same point and to argue against racism.

According to the Bible, a human being can be a human being only because he belongs to a community. A person is a person through other persons, as we say in our African idiom. And so separation of persons because of biological accidents is reprehensible and blasphemous.[15]

John S. Mbiti also stresses the Afrikan view that a person can only be a person-in-community.

Whatever happens to the individual happens to the whole group, and whatever happens to the whole group happens to the individual. The individual can only say: "I am, because we are; and since we are, therefore I am." This is a cardinal point in the understanding of the African view of man.[16]

We see the same emphasis in the work of Afrikan American scholars like Archie Smith, Jr., who stresses the idea that "people are eminently relational beings," and that "reality is fundamentally interrelated and social and perspectival or plural in character."[17] This idea is also present in the earliest stage of Bowne's movement toward personalism. We saw in chapter 1 that in the objective idealism stage he focused on the fact that the person always finds in her or his experience something that she or he did not create, but finds. There is an objective presence that is given. This implies that the individual is never alone, from birth to death. For at birth the child is greeted at least by its mother and God, while at death one is still not alone, since we are greeted by the Creator as we make our way from this world to the next.

The caution that must be continuously raised, however, is that we not place so much emphasis on relationality that the worth and integrity of the person as such is undermined or lost. For example, it could be disastrous from the standpoint of ethics if the individual person were somehow lost or swallowed up in the we-ness of community,[18] for it is the individual who is the basic moral unit. Carolyn Hardville concretizes this point and makes the following observation:

This is what often times happens to women. We become so wrapped up in family (husbands and children) that we lose sight of who we are as individuals…A lot of the submissiveness and the taking care of the family actually results in the bondage of lost identity. How can one love what one doesn't see and know?[19]

This is why it is crucial that militant personalism retain we-centeredness *plus* I-centeredness in both the metaphysical and ethical outlook. In this way we avoid the danger of the we swallowing up the I.

As noted in the previous chapter, Harold Oliver looked to the East for contributions to the relational character of the person. As for me, I need only look to Afrikan and Afrikan American religio-cultural heritage. Efforts to develop more meaningful and relevant discussions on the nature of the person must be done in light of contributions of groups like Afrikan Americans who contribute so much to what greatness remains in this country. Personalistic method requires that we be inclusive, synoptic, and critical in approach.

Preference for the Poor and Oppressed

No ethic for which the person is not the central and highest value may be deemed adequate and intelligible for Afrikan Americans and others in whom the image of God is desecrated on a massive scale by socioeconomic and political forces. In addition, for a viable personalism there needs to be an emphasis not simply on the centrality of the person, but on the centrality of the systematically oppressed, brutalized person. For when we get right down to the actual concrete state of affairs of persons in the world, it is these whose dignity is trampled upon. It is these who are treated like nonpersons. Therefore, it is not enough to merely stress the dignity of the abstract person or of persons in general. Since particular persons and groups are the victims of systematic dehumanization, it is necessary to be concrete and particular when talking about the centrality of persons and their inviolable sacredness.[20] The type of oppression and dehumanization persons experience is concrete and specific, not general and abstract. Therefore, militant personalism requires the naming of both the persons and groups, in addition to the types of oppression suffered. This is what the late Archbishop Oscar Romero had in mind when he said that the glory of God is not merely the human person, but the poor, oppressed person.[21]

Beyond Melioristic Ethics

Militant personalism's emphasis on preference for the systematically poor and oppressed necessarily means that we will have to move beyond melioristic ethics. A preference for the poor and the oppressed means that there must be a focus on immediate, radical change in their societal condition. As seen in chapter 8, meliorism is the view that the world can be made better through human endeavor. This in itself is not problematic. But what is troublesome is the tendency of early personalists to imply that because of the developmental nature of the world it is permissible that change should come slowly. We see this, for example, in Bowne's decided or adamant meliorism.[22] In *Principles of Ethics* he writes:

> Without doubt the possession of power, talents, riches imposes obligation; but there is no jural way of reaching those who do not feel it. The slow formation of conscience, of humanity, and of public opinion must be our chief reliance.[23]

It may well be true that conscience, humanity, and public opinion generally develop slowly in society, but this is the case only if it is allowed to be so. There is no question that Bowne was optimistic about the goodness of the world in the most fundamental sense. "For man as moral and active...the goodness of the world consists in the possibility of making it indefinitely better, and in its furnishing the conditions of a truly human development."[24] Those who, like Bowne, have an essentially developmental view of the world and societal change will tend to focus on steady, but slow change. But this is a serious moral problem in a society where massive numbers of persons are forced to endure dehumanizing socioeconomic and political practices, and thus are in need of immediate relief from the day-to-day hardships that result from these practices. Yet at some point it will also be necessary to work toward long-term, deep-rooted structural changes.

Bowne was convinced that the world was created in such a way that it would respond positively to the active and aggressive good will of persons. This is an important point, but the systematically oppressed are not likely to be comforted by the idea that the goodness of the world consists in the fact that it has built into it the conditions that make human development and the goodness of the world possible. This in itself is too abstract, and must be made to relate to what is actually happening to poor, oppressed persons in this world. What would be more meaningful, humane, and considerate of the dignity of such persons is the recognition that it may be necessary to take steps to force radical transformative change in their condition. This means that personalism will have to move beyond meliorism or developmentalism and take on a much more militant and radical tone. This means focusing on more than simply altering the attitudes and practices of large numbers of individuals. It requires much more emphasis on the need for radically altering or even dismantling the structures of dehumanization and oppression and replacing them with structures that are more consistent with the idea of the enhancement and uplift of all persons. In the new system no person or group will be the superior of any other, and none will be allowed to possess surplus goods until the basic human needs of all have been met.

Respect for Nonhuman Life Forms

The dignity of nature and other areas of creation is not necessarily diminished because of the insistence that the person is the highest value in the created order.[25] It is the Western tendency to think in either-or or dualistic terms that often leads to the view that affirming this or that necessarily means that one must reject something else. But this need not be the case. For example, that I love myself and my people does not necessarily mean that I either hate or have strong disregard for some other group. That I am a race person (i.e., that I believe in racial and cultural pride) does not mean that I hate Anglos. That I like the color blue does not necessarily mean that I dislike the color red. It simply means that I like the color blue! Or, I may prefer the color blue, but still like the color red. Furthermore, I may insist that I like both blue and red, even though I am told that I have to decide in favor of one or the other. The contention that persons are the highest intrinsic values of which we humans know does not preclude either the value and worth of other areas of creation or our recognition of, or respect for, their worth. Indeed, because personalism is deeply relational, it is more reasonable to acknowledge the value and interrelatedness of all that God has created.

The fact that all that exists depends on God for its being and that all is related to everything else in creation are good grounds for respecting the value of all things, although all things, do not possess the same level of value. In respecting the value of all things, one respects self and the Creator. Furthermore, the debate on whether personalism emphasizes the dignity of nature is not the chief problematic for the Afrikan American community, nor, I suspect, for the Native American community (from which all of the Americas and other parts of the West can take a lesson in environmental ethics). If, as these groups contend, the entire cosmos is sacred; if all being is interrelated and depends for its existence on God and is related to all others, then this includes relationship between persons and nature. This implies that nature is good in itself, and therefore has its own dignity. In this regard Setiloane writes: "*Motho* [the quality of being human] is part of Nature and Nature is *Motho's* companion from the beginning. Nature is not therefore an object for human exploitation, for like the human it came out of the same Source." [26] If all derives from a common Source that is good and loving, this in itself implies the duty to respect all human and nonhuman life forms.

In addition, Native American cultural beliefs highlight the centrality and sacredness of the land (which implies respect for the earth). Vine Deloria, Jr., writes of the Indian's complete "reverence for land." "Earth, they believed, was mother of all."[27] In 1854 Chief Seattle told the Governor of Washington Territory: "Every part of this soil is sacred in the estimation of my people."[28] The land provided food (life), a place to live, and a place to return to in death. The land, for Indians, holds "the bodies of the tribe in a basic sense." According to Deloria, this idea "testified in a stronger sense to the underlying unity of the Indian conception of the universe as a life system in which everything had its part."[29] In 1938 John Collier, then Commissioner of Indian Affairs, wrote: "So intimately is all of Indian life tied up with the land and its utilization that to think of Indians is to think of land. The two are inseparable."[30] Unlike those who ultimately stole the entire country from them, Indians felt less of a sense of ownership of the land than "devotion and veneration befitting what is not only a home but a refuge."[31]

Militant personalism will be intentional about uplifting the need for respect for all life forms—human and nonhuman. It will be just as adamant that these be treated accordingly. This personalism accepts and appropriates Paul W. Taylor's distinction between moral subjects and moral agents. Any conscious being is a moral subject, even if it is not able to make responsible moral choices. All moral subjects are beings to whom moral agents owe responsibilities. Moral agents, on the other hand, are moral subjects whose mental and other faculties are such that they are capable of making responsible moral choices and anticipating the consequences of those choices, willing to take responsibility for choices made, able to evaluate the outcome and apply what is learned to new situations calling for moral choice.[32] Yet militant personalism insists on the need to acknowledge that although all life forms have a value of their own, not all are of the same value. There are, in this regard, gradations of intrinsic value, a point that even Bowne— unknown to critics—acknowledged in *The Immanence of God* (1905).

> Some weak heads have been so heated by the new wine of immanence as to put all things on the same level, and make men and mice of equal value. But there is nothing in the dependence of all things on God to remove their distinctions of value.[33]

Militant personalism retains the view of early personalists that persons are the highest intrinsic values. It does not deny the intrinsic value of non-human life forms, but is adamant in its insistence that persons are the supreme values in the world.

Conclusion

It is not clear whether the recent emphasis on environmental ethics is just another fad introduced by progressive white scholars, professionals, and students as a way of redirecting attention, energy, and resources away from socioeconomic and political policies and practices that continue to destroy massive numbers of persons of color. Any adequate metaphysics today must necessarily ground the dignity of all areas of creation. But as an Afrikan American male—whose life-chances and very life are threatened everyday precisely because I am an Afrikan American male—I must acknowledge my suspicion of many ecological and environmental ethicists, recognizing as I do the tendency of many Anglos today to exhibit such strong concern about the well-being of nonhuman life forms while barely raising their voices against the massive and systematic oppression of black, brown, and red peoples in this country. In this regard Garth Baker-Fletcher is not wrong when he challenges ecological ethicists to learn from King's (and personalism's) focus on the dignity of persons.

> Much of contemporary ecological discussion could gain moral depth from King's view of the dignity and value of persons, and of oppressed persons in particular. It is disturbing that so much academic attention is given to the nonhuman world when human beings are still allowed to exist in undignified living conditions. Strong theological censure of human injustice as well as concern for the nonhuman world is needed. Without such censure one suspects that ecological concern could become an abstract exercise of those detached from and unconcerned about genuine human oppression. Expressing moral concern for the nonhuman world without an explicit call for human dignity leads to an inadequate view of dignity.[34]

To critics who say that personalism has so elevated the value of persons that the door has been opened for the exploitation and destruction of the environment, it must be pointed out that both historically and contemporaneously this idea of the elevation of the worth of persons has generally not been applied to persons of Afrikan descent to the same degree as to those of European descent. And while there has been much destruction of the environment, most of this is the result of the malicious greed, selfishness, and racism of powerful white male capitalists. Therefore, when well-meaning Anglo environmental thinkers write so cogently and passionately about what "we" have done and are doing to the environment (as if to suggest that *all* persons participate in this equally) it is important to be specific and to name the "we." To be sure, any meaningful personalistic ethic requires this today, especially since there is no evidence that the traditionally exploited and the poor have contributed in significant ways to the destruction of the environment. They might well be willing participants in such destruction of life had they the power and the resources, but the fact is that they do not.

Although in the final analysis all who are moral agents owe responsibilities to the environment, as an Afrikan American I urge that the highest ethical principle must point in the direction of the absolute dignity of persons as such, and most especially the systematically poor, oppressed person. Indeed, it is this principle that must condition all others. After all, was it not Bowne who urged the need to develop the highest possible conception of the sanctity and worth of both persons and nature? Both experience and history teach that a low conception of either is generally followed by corresponding treatment and behavior.[35]

The type of personalism discussed in this book is an axiological metaphysics. As such it provides more than adequate grounding for the aforementioned emphases in this and the previous chapter. Although when analyzed and unpacked, personalism is an elaborate philosophy that provides what proponents believe to be most reasonable answers to the chief problems of philosophy and life, the entire philosophy of personalism is built on two chief ideas: (1) the idea that reality itself is personal; and (2) the idea of both the dignity and worth of persons as such, and of the rest of creation.

According to this personalism, metaphysics, epistemology, and ethics all eventuate in theism. This means that there can be little hope of providing adequate answers to the questions raised by these short of belief in the existence of a personal God who is the creator and sustainer of all that is good and perfectible in the world. All life forms depend on God for their existence. God chooses to create these life forms and therefore loves and values them all. It is therefore reasonable to conclude that much more emphasis than has heretofore been the case should be placed on the value of all creation in general, and on the worth of the bodies and entire lives of persons. This should particularly be the case for persons who have historically been systematically deprived of their God-given right to be fully human and to be recipients of all the benefits their God-given humanity warrants. That God willingly creates and sustains persons, the environment, and the animal kingdom is evidence enough that God values these highly. An obvious conclusion—often conveniently disregarded—is that created persons are to value these highly as well, and that our treatment of all life forms should be consistent with an ethic of dignity that values all forms of life.

Consistent with its synoptic-analytic method and its criterion of truth (viz., coherence) personalism combines created persons, the plant and animal kingdoms, ethics, and so on, in a coherent whole. This type of personalism does not allow one to merely address the separate parts of reality. Rather, one is forced by personalistic methodology to see the parts in relation to each other and to the whole. Therefore, though one may choose to abstract a given aspect or element for isolated discussion, for example, nature, one must finally consider it in relation to the other aspects, and finally in relation to the whole of reality. As a worldview, personalism presents its own case for the interrelatedness of all things. Although personalism sees persons as the highest intrinsic values in the world, it has from the time of Bowne sought to see them in relation both with each other and with the other areas of creation. This relational aspect of personalism means that all that is created by God warrants respect and corresponding treatment precisely because it was called into existence by a personal and loving God.

Notes

Preface

[1]See my articles, "Moral Laws in Borden P. Bowne's *Principles of Ethics*," *The Personalist Forum* 6/2 (Fall 1990), pp. 161–81; "Borden Parker Bowne's Doctrine of God," *Encounter* 53/4 (Autumn 1992), pp. 381–400.

Introduction

[1]Rachel Metheny, "Personalism's Message to the Church and to the World," (unpublished Master of Divinity paper, class on Introduction to Personalism, Christian Theological Seminary, May 6, 1993), p. 6.

[2]And yet we find an interesting statement on the back cover of Eileen Cantin's book, *Mounier: A Personalist View of History*. Here a reviewer of Cantin's book writes that Emmanuel Mounier (1905–1950) "was the founder of the 20th century school of thought known as 'personalism'" (New York: Paulist Press, 1973). The reviewer's name is not included. The statement is an interesting one because Mounier was born five years before Bowne died, and by this time Bowne had already developed personalism systematically and had a large following. In addition, the French philosopher Charles B. Renouvier (1815–1903) and the American George Holmes Howison wrote major texts on personalism or personal idealism before Mounier began his work. Indeed, Renouvier entitled his book *Le Personnalisme* (1903).

[3]Johannes Hirschberger, *The History of Philosophy*, trans. Rt. Rev. Anthony N. Fuerst (Milwaukee, Wis.: The Bruce Publishing Company, 1959), 2:681.

[4]The French political personalist, Emmanuel Mounier thought similarly about personalism. He said that it "offers no 'solutions.' It presents a method of thinking and of living." Mounier, *A Personalist Manifesto* (New York: Longmans, Green and Company, 1938), p. 271.

[5]Robert Neville, Review of Paul Deats, Jr., and Carol Robb, eds., *The Boston Personalist Tradition* (1986), *The Personalist Forum* 5/1 (Spring 1989), p. 63.

[6]John H. Lavely, "Reflections on a Philosophical Heritage," Deats and Robb, eds., *The Boston Personalist Tradition* (Macon, Ga.: Mercer Univ. Press, 1986), p. 258.

[7]Deats, "Conflict and Reconciliation in Communitarian Social Ethics," Deats and Robb, eds., *The Boston Personalist Tradition*, p. 273.

[8]Edgar S. Brightman, "Why Is Personalism Unpopular?" *Methodist Review* (July 1921), p. 534.

[9]Brightman, *An Introduction to Philosophy* (New York: Henry Holt and Company, 1925), p. vi.

[10]"Why Is Personalism Unpopular?"pp. 534–35.

[11]J. Deotis Roberts, *A Philosophical Introduction to Theology* (London: SCM Press, 1991), p. 162.

[12]See Andrew J. Reck's essay on the development of philosophy in the United States from 1945–1980 in John R. Burr, ed., *Handbook of World Philosophy: Contemporary Developments Since 1945* (Westport, Conn.: Greenwood Press, 1980), p. 379.

[13]J. Philip Wogaman, *Faith and Fragmentation* (Philadelphia: Fortress Press, 1985), pp. x–xi.

[14]Lavely, p. 257.

[15]Albert C. Knudson, *The Philosophy of Personalism* (New York: Abingdon Press, 1927).

[16]L. Harold DeWolf, "Albert Cornelius Knudson as Philosopher," *The Personalist* 35/4 (1954), p. 366.

[17]William H. Werkmeister, *A History of Philosophical Ideas in America* (New York: Ronald Press, 1949), chaps. 7, 8, 15.

[18]Werkmeister, ed., *The Forest of Yggdrasill: The Autobiography of Ralph Tyler Flewelling* (Los Angeles: Univ. of Southern California Press, 1962).

[19]Lucyle Werkmeister and E. F. Kaelin, "In Memoriam: William H. Werkmeister," *The Personalist Forum* 10/1 (Spring 1994), p. 65.

[20]Werkmeister, "Some Aspects of Contemporary Personalism," *The Personalist* 32 (October 1951), p. 350.

[21]Elizabeth Flower and Murray G. Murphy, *A History of Philosophy in America* (New York: G. P. Putnam's Sons, 1977), 2:490.

[22]It is important to note, however, that Knudson himself attends to these in his book, *The Principles of Christian Ethics* (New York: Abingdon Press, 1943). However, in my judgment, his discussion leaves much to be desired.

[23]See Borden P. Bowne, *Metaphysics* (New York: Harper, 1882), p. 460.

[24]Bowne, *The Principles of Ethics* (New York: American Book Company, 1892), chaps. 9, 10.

[25]The discussion on Afrikan American personalism is brief, inasmuch as I have dealt with this subject extensively in a presently unpublished book-length manuscript on the Afrikan American as person. I include a discussion on Afrikan American personalism in the present volume because any text on American personalism must.

Chapter 1. What is Personalism?

[1]Ernest N. Merrington, *The Problem of Personality* (New York: Macmillan, 1916), p. 143.

[2]Borden P. Bowne, *Theory of Thought and Knowledge* (New York: American Book Company, 1897), pp. 234, 236.

[3]See Bowne, *Studies in Theism* (New York: Phillips & Hunt, 1879), p. 284.

[4]Edgar S. Brightman, *An Introduction to Philosophy*, rev. ed., ed. Robert N. Beck (New York: Holt, Rinehart and Winston, 1963), p. 330.

[5]See my article "Francis John McConnell and Personalistic Social Ethics," *Methodist History* 31/2 (January 1993), p. 91. In an unpublished paper on McConnell I note the following types of personalism: atheistic, absolutistic, pantheistic, relativistic, teleological or ethical, theistic or "normative," realistic, political, panpsychistic, anthropomorphic, and Afrikan American. There is also the hierarchical personalism of "the most important" of the Russian philosophers, Nicholas Losskij (1870–). [See Johannes Hirschberger, *The History of Philosophy*, trans. Rt. Rev. Anthony N. Fuerst (Milwaukee, Wis.: Bruce Publishing, 1959), 2:613.] There is also the ethical personalism of Max Scheler (1874–1928). Scheler argued that "the most primitive and most powerful element in man is the vital power and drive with which he is endowed…" (See Hirschberger, *The History of Philosophy*, 2:583). Scheler's personalism is similar to that of Howison in that he believed that "God stands only at the conclusion of the world process…" But it is different in that his is a form of pantheism (ibid.), which Howison consistently argued against. I have also been trying to determine whether womanist (Afrikan American women's feminism) and mujerista (Hispanic women's feminism) might be hybrids of personalism. My present sense is that they are. If so, this will mean the existence of even richer forms of personalism.

[6]Albert C. Knudson, *The Philosophy of Personalism* (Nashville: Abingdon Press, 1927), p. 87. According to Brightman, Knudson's working title for this book was *Bowne and Personalism*. [See Brightman, *An Introduction to Philosophy* (New York: Holt Rinehart and Company, 1925), p. 374.]

[7]Knudson, *The Philosophy of Personalism*, pp. 85, 87, 433.

[8]Ralph T. Flewelling, *Personalism and the Problems of Philosophy: An Appreciation of the Work of Borden Parker Bowne* (New York: The Methodist Book Concern, 1915), p. 12.

[9]Flewelling, *Personalism and the Problems of Philosophy*, p. 13.

[10]See Brightman, *An Introduction to Philosophy* (New York: Henry Holt & Company, 1925), p. 374. Brightman lists this title as a book that Knudson was working on.

[11]Knudson, *The Philosophy of Personalism*, p. 78.

[12]Ibid., p. 87. Although Richard Morgan Cameron claims that this was a definition that Knudson quoted "presumably from Bowne," my research does not bear this out. As far as I can tell this was Knudson's definition, although it is quite consistent with what Bowne thought personalism to be.

[13]James McLachlan, "George Holmes Howison: The Conception of God Debate and the Beginnings of Personal Idealism," *The Personalist Forum* 11/1 (Spring 1995), p. 1.

[14]Ralph B. Perry, *The Present Conflict of Ideals* (New York: Longmans, Green & Company, 1922), p. 203. It is of interest to note here that, having devoted several pages to discussing Howison, Perry does not even include Bowne's name in the index.

[15]Howison, *Preface to the Second Edition*, in *The Limits of Evolution* (New York: Macmillan, 1904), pp. xxx–xxxi.

[16]Perry, *The Present Conflict of Ideals*, p. 203n.

[17]Howison, "Introduction by the Editor," in *The Conception of God*, by Josiah Royce et al. (New York: Macmillan, 1897), p. xv.

[18]Ibid., pp. xv, xxxiii, xxxv.

[19]Ibid., p. xxxiv.

[20]Howison, "The City of God, and the True God as its Head," in *The Conception of God*, p. 114.

[21]Ibid., pp. 85, 89, 97, 114, 119.

[22]Indeed, William L. Reese tells us that the term was first introduced by Schleiermacher in 1799 and then by Ludwig Feuerbach in 1841 "to characterize the position that God is personal, a person rather than an abstract principle." [Reese, *Dictionary of Philosophy and Religion* (New Jersey: Humanities Press, 1980), p. 425].

[23]And yet I concede the possibility that Howison is the author of the term *personal idealism*. Although this may be the case, it is most assuredly the case that it was not he who first introduced the term *personalism*, even though the two terms would eventually be considered to be synonymous by some thinkers. Furthermore, I know of no place in Howison's writings where he actually uses the term personalism.

[24]Wilbur Long, "Flewelling and American Personalism," in *The Forest of Yggdrasill: The Autobiography of Ralph Tyler Flewelling*, ed. William H. Werkmeister (Los Angeles: Univ. of Southern California Press, 1962), p. xxxiv.

[25]See Frank W. Collier's foreword to the 25th Anniversary Edition of *Personalism*, privately printed (Norwood, Mass.: Plimpton Press, 1936), p. vii.

[26]Richard Morgan Cameron, *Boston University School of Theology 1839–1968*, Nexus 11/2 and 3 (May, 1968), p. 44.

[27]See William James, *Some Problems of Philosophy* (New York: Longmans, Green and Company, 1911), p. 165n.

[28]Cameron, *Boston University School of Theology 1839–1968*, p. 44.

[29]George C. Cell, "Bowne and Humanism," *Zion's Herald* (March 27, 1935), pp. 297–99.

[30]See William James, *The Varieties of Religious Experience* (New York: Longmans, Green and Company, 1928) [1902], p. 501n.

[31]Cell, "Bowne and Humanism," p. 298.

[32]James, *The Varieties of Religious Experience*, p. 502n.

[33]Cell, "Bowne and Humanism," p. 298.

[34]See Bowne, *The Immanence of God* (Boston: Houghton Mifflin, 1905), p. 32.

[35]William H. Werkmeister, *A History of Philosophical Ideas in America* (New York: Ronald Press, 1949), p. 103.

[36]Flewelling, "This Thing Called Personalism," *The Personalist* 28/3 (Summer 1947), p. 233.

[37]Flewelling, "Personalism," in *A Survey of American Philosophy*, ed. Ralph B. Winn (Paterson, N. J.: Littlefield, Adams, and Company, 1965), p. 156. This is somewhat confusing since Flewelling contends in another essay with the title "Personalism" that Walt Whitman was the first American to coin the term, and Bronson Alcott subsequently named his own type of theism personalism. See Flewelling, "Personalism," in *Twentieth Century Philosophy*, Dagobert D. Runes, ed. (New York: Philosophical Library, 1947), p. 323.

[38]Brightman, *An Introduction to Philosophy*, rev. ed., p. 313n.

[39]Francis J. McConnell, "Bowne and Personalism," Brightman, *Personalism in Theology* (Boston: Boston Univ. Press, 1943), p. 21.

[40]Bowne, "The Philosophical Outlook," in *Congress of Arts and Sciences*, ed. Howard J. Rogers (Boston: Houghton Mifflin, 1905), p. 172.

[41]Quoted in McConnell, *Borden Parker Bowne* (New York: Abingdon Press, 1929), p. 280.

[42]Bowne, *Metaphysics* (1882), pp. 450–87.

[43]Ibid., p. 452.

[44]Ibid.

[45]Ibid., p. 466. Bowne actually preferred the term *phenomenalism* rather than idealism, since the latter implies that the world is only an idea. However, he was aware that phenomenalism had gotten a bad reputation by being associated with positivism. Commenting on the worldview connoted by objective idealism he said: "This view is not well described as idealism, because it makes the world more than an idea. If the word had not been appropriated to denote positivistic doctrines, phenomenalism would be a much better title. This word sufficiently implies the objective nature of the world-process, while at the same time it implies that, apart from mind, the phenomena would not exist. Perhaps, with all its disadvantages, there is less risk of misunderstanding in using phenomenalism than in using idealism."

[46]Ibid., p. 460.

[47]McConnell, *Evangelicals, Revolutionists and Idealists* (New York: Abingdon-Cokesbury, 1942), p. 139.

[48]Bowne, *Metaphysics*, rev. ed. (New York: American Book Company, 1898), p. 423. Hereafter, any reference will be to this edition unless otherwise noted.

[49]McConnell, *Evangelicals, Revolutionists and Idealists*, pp. 134–35.

[50]George Berkeley, *Alciphron*, in *George Berkeley: Alciphron in Focus,* ed. David Berman, (New York: Routledge, 1993). See Fourth Dialogue, especially sections 7, 12, 14.

[51]Joseph A. Leighton, *The Field of Philosophy* (New York: D. Appleton & Company, 1923), p. 244.

[52]Bowne, *Metaphysics* (1898), p. 295.

[53]Ibid., p. 265.

[54]John Wright Buckham, *Christianity and Personality* (New York: Round Table, 1936), p. 44.

[55]Bowne, *Metaphysics* (1882), p. 451.

[56]George Berkeley, *A Treatise Concerning the Principles of Human Knowledge,* in *British Empirical Philosophers,* ed. A. J. Ayer and Raymond Winch, (New York: Simon and Schuster, 1968), pp. 190, 191.

[57]Ibid., p. 180.

[58]Bowne, *Metaphysics* (1882), p. 452.

[59]Ibid., p. 477.

[60]Knudson, *The Philosophy of Personalism,* pp. 226, 230.

[61]Bowne, *Metaphysics* (1882), p. 455.

[62]McConnell, *Evangelicals, Revolutionists and Idealists,* pp. 136–37, 146.

[63]Ibid., p. 143.

[64]Ibid., p. 149.

[65]Ibid., p. 134.

[66]Bowne, *Metaphysics* (1882), p. 461.

[67]McConnell, *Evangelicals, Revolutionists, and Idealists,* p. 137.

[68]Bowne, *Metaphysics* (1882), p. 483.

[69]Bowne, *Kant and Spencer* (Port Washington, N.Y.: Kennikat Press, Inc., 1967) [1912], p. 136.

[70]Ibid., p. 148.

[71]Ibid., p. 133.

[72]Bowne, *Studies in Theism,* p. 37.

[73]Bowne, *Kant and Spencer,* p. 133.

[74]Ibid., p. 135.

[75]Knudson, *The Philosophy of Personalism,* p. 137.

[76]Bowne, *Metaphysics* (1898), pp. 66, 91, 119, 186, 340, 341.

[77]Knudson, *The Philosophy of Personalism,* p. 139.

[78]Bowne, *Theism* (New York: American Book Company, 1902), p. 43.

[79]Knudson, *The Philosophy of Personalism,* p. 162.

[80]Bowne, *Metaphysics* (1898), p. 424.

[81]Ibid., (1898), p. 425.

[82]Charles B. Pyle, *The Philosophy of Borden Parker Bowne and Its Application to the Religious Problem* (Columbus, Ohio: S. F. Harriman Company, 1910), p. 51.

[83]Bowne, *Personalism* (Boston: Houghton Mifflin, 1908), p. 20.

[84]McConnell, *Borden Parker Bowne,* p. 37.

[85]George Santayana, *Lotze's System of Philosophy,* Paul Grimley Kuntz, ed. (Bloomington, Indiana: Ind. Univ. Press, 1971), p. 52.

[86]McConnell, *Borden Parker Bowne,* p. 37.

[87]Bowne, *Studies in Theism,* p. vi.

[88]Ibid., p. 275.

[89]Bowne, *Metaphysics* (1882), p. vii.

[90]Flewelling, *Personalism and the Problems of Philosophy,* p. 108.

[91]See McConnell, "Borden Parker Bowne," *Methodist Review* (May 1922), p. 342.

[92]Bowne, *Personalism,* p. 218.

[93]Knudson, *The Philosophy of Personalism,* pp. 429–30.

[94]Bowne, *Personalism,* p. 88.

[95]Bowne, *Metaphysics* (1898), p. 27.

[96]Ibid., pp. 24, 25.

[97]Ibid., p. 119.

[98]This was a favorite term of Berkeley's, which Bowne himself frequently used. See Berkeley, *A Treatise Concerning the Principles of Human Knowledge,* p. 216.

[99]Bowne, *Theory of Thought and Knowledge* (New York: Harper & Brothers, 1897), p. 57.

[100]This was essentially the view of Leibniz, who held that the world is both the thought and the will of God. Bowne was much influenced by this view. See *Metaphysics* (1882), pp. 470, 472, 474.

[101]See Berman, ed., *George Berkeley: Alciphron in Focus*, p. 95.
[102]Bowne, *Metaphysics* (1898), p. 28.
[103]Bowne, *Theory of Thought and Knowledge*, p. 7.
[104]Ibid., p. 119.
[105]Ibid., p. 155.
[106]L. Harold DeWolf, "Personalism in the History of Western Philosophy," *Philosophical Forum* 12 (1954), pp. 29–51.
[107]See chapter 3 of this text.
[108]Knudson, *The Philosophy of Personalism*, p. 420.
[109]See Andrew J. Reck's essay on the development of philosophy in the United States in John R. Burr, ed., *Handbook of World Philosophy: Contemporary Developments Since 1945* (Westport, Conn.: Greenwood Press, 1980), p. 379.

Chapter 2. Some Less Typical Types of Personalism

[1]Edgar S. Brightman, *A Philosophy of Religion* (Englewood Cliffs, N. J.: Prentice Hall, 1940), p. 296.
[2]J. M. E. McTaggart, *Some Dogmas of Religion* (London: Edward Arnold, 1906), p. 219. See chapters 6 and 7.
[3]McTaggart, *The Nature of Existence* (Cambridge: Cambridge Univ. Press, 1927), 2:176.
[4]Ibid.
[5]Arthur K. Rogers, *English and American Philosophy Since 1800: A Critical Survey* (New York: Macmillan Company, 1923), p. 300.
[6]L. Harold DeWolf, "Personalism in the History of Western Philosophy," *Philosophical Forum* 12 (1954), p. 41.
[7]William Sahakian, *History of Philosophy* (New York: Barnes & Noble Books, 1968), p. 278.
[8]Albert C. Knudson, *The Philosophy of Personalism* (Nashville: Abingdon Press, 1927), p. 23.
[9]Martin Luther King, Jr., "Doctrine of Freedom," in *The Papers of Martin Luther King, Jr.*, ed. Clayborn Carson (Berkeley, Calif.: Univ. of California Press, 1994), 2:73.
[10]Floyd W. Matson, *Being, Becoming and Behavior* (New York: George Braziller, 1967), p. 143.
[11]Ibid.
[12]Ibid., p. 147.
[13]George F. Thomas, *Philosophy and Religious Belief* (New York: Scribners, 1970), p. 87.
[14]Borden Bowne, *Metaphysics* (New York: Harper, 1882), p. 483.
[15]Knudson, *The Philosophy of Personalism*, p. 31.
[16]P. Magg, "The Personalism of Mary Calkins," *The Personalist* 28/3 (Summer 1947), p. 45.
[17]Mary Calkins, "The Philosophical Credo of an Absolutistic Personalist," in *Contemporary American Philosophy*, ed. George P. Adams and William P. Montague, (New York: Russell & Russell, Inc., 1962), 1:212n.
[18]Ibid.
[19]Ibid., 1:212.
[20]See the quote from that letter in Knudson, *The Philosophy of Personalism*, p. 32n.
[21]Knudson, *The Philosophy of Personalism*, p. 33.
[22]Calkins, *The Persistent Problems of Philosophy* (New York: Macmillan Company, 1907), pp. 406–17.
[23]Calkins, "The Philosophical Credo of an Absolutistic Personalist," 1:203n.
[24]Flewelling, "Studies in American Personalism," *The Personalist* 31/4 (Autumn 1950), p. 345.
[25]Brightman writes that "Bowne is being more explicitly recognized than heretofore." However, he is misleading when he lists the fifth edition of Calkins' text as an example of a historical work that takes Bowne's personalism seriously. [See Brightman, "Personalism and the Influence of Bowne," in *Proceedings of the Sixth International Congress of Philosophy ed. Brightman* (New York: Longmans, Green & Company, 1927), p. 166.] Calkins does not list Bowne's name in the index. The most she does is include his name and the titles and dates of three of his books in a list of twentieth-century philosophers. She also includes Brightman's name there along with the title of one of his articles (see the 1925 edition of *The Persistent Problems of Philosophy*, p. 587).

[26]Quoted in Bruce Kuklick, *The Rise of American Philosophy* (New Haven, Conn.: Yale Univ. Press, 1977), p. 590.

[27]Ibid., p. 46.

[28]Quoted in Ibid., p. 46.

[29]Calkins, *The Good Man and the Good* (New York: Macmillan, 1918).

[30]P. Magg, "The Personalism of Mary Calkins," p. 48.

[31]Calkins, "The Personalistic Conception of Nature," *The Philosophical Review* 28/2 (March 1919), p. 122.

[32]Ibid.

[33]Calkins and Brightman, "The Personalistic Platform," *Journal of Philosophy* 30/16 (August 3, 1933), pp. 434–35.

[34]Brightman, *An Introduction to Philosophy* (New York: Henry Holt and Company, 1925), p. vi.

[35]Calkins, "The Philosophical Credo of an Absolutistic Personalist," ed. George P. Adams and William Montague, *Contemporary American Philosophy* (New York: Russell and Russell, 1962), pp. 200–209.

[36]Ibid., p. 212.

[37]Ibid., p. 212n.

[38]Calkins, *The Persistent Problems of Philosophy* (1908), p. 562.

[39]Knudson, *The Philosophy of Personalism*, p. 34.

[40]Calkins, *The Persistent Problems of Philosophy*, fifth rev. ed. (New York: Macmillan Company, 1925), p. 449n.

[41]Bowne, *Metaphysics* (1882), p. 486.

[42]George H. Howison, "The City of God, and the True God as its Head" in *The Conception of God*, by Josiah Royce et al. (New York: Macmillan Company, 1897), pp. 98–99.

[43]Bowne, *Theism*, p. 216.

[44]Ralph T. Flewelling, *Personalism and the Problems of Philosophy* (New York: The Methodist Book Concern, 1915), p. 186.

[45]See Walter G. Muelder, Laurence Sears, and Anne Schlabach, eds., *The Development of American Philosophy*, second ed. (Boston: Houghton Mifflin Company, 1960) [1940], p. 214.

[46]Quoted in Ibid., pp. 212–13.

[47]See John J. Ansbro, *Martin Luther King, Jr.: The Making of a Mind* (Maryknoll, N. Y.: 1982), p. 299n.

[48]Brightman, *An Introduction to Philosophy*, rev. ed., p. 332.

[49]Knudson, *The Philosophy of Personalism*, p. 33.

[50]Knudson, *The Doctrine of God* (New York: Abingdon, 1930), p. 307.

[51]Brightman, *Person and Reality*, Peter A. Bertocci, ed. (New York: Ronald Press, 1958), p. 248.

[52]Brightman, "The Finite Self," in *Contemporary Idealism in America*, Clifford Barrett, ed. (New York: Russell & Russell, 1964), p. 179.

[53]Bowne, *Metaphysics* (1882), pp. 5–8.

[54]Radoslav A. Tsanoff, *The Great Philosophers* (New York: Harper, 1953), p. 597.

[55]William James, *Some Problems of Philosophy* (New York: Longmans, Green and Company, 1911), p. 165n.

[56]Knudson, *The Philosophy of Personalism*, p. 43.

[57]Ibid., p. 42.

[58]Ibid., p. 50.

Chapter 3. Some More Typical Types of Personalism

[1]I examine Afrikan American contributions to personalism extensively in a separate book.

[2]See Ralph Tyler Flewelling, *The Person or the Significance of Man* (Los Angeles: The Ward Ritchie Press, 1952), p. 334.

[3]George H. Howison, "Personal Idealism," in *George Holmes Howison, Philosopher and Teacher: A Selection from His Writings with a Biographical Sketch*, ed. John W. Buckham and George M. Stratton (Berkeley, Calif.: University of California Press, 1934), p. 125.

[4]Ibid., p. 127.

[5]Ibid., p. 92.

[6]See William H. Werkmeister, *A History of Philosophical Ideas in America* (New York: Ronald Press, 1949), chapters 7–8, where he treats the personalism of Bowne and Howison, respectively.

[7]John Wright Buckham, *Christianity and Personality* (New York: Round Table Press, 1936), p. 38n.

[8]See Howard J. Rogers, ed., *Congress of Arts and Sciences* (Boston: Houghton Mifflin, 1905), p. 1.

[9]Werkmeister, *A History of Philosophical Ideas in America*, p. 123.

[10]Howison, *The Limits of Evolution* (New York: Macmillan, 1901), p. 11, chap. 1; Bowne, *The Philosophy of Herbert Spencer* (New York: Hunt & Eaton, 1874).

[11]Ibid., p. 7; Bowne, *Theism* (New York: American Book Co. 1902), pp. 51–63; idem, *Personalism*, p. 278; idem, *The Philosophy of Theism* (New York: Harper & Brothers, 1887), pp. 50–51, 52.

[12]Howison, *The Limits of Evolution* pp. 58–69, 75, 76; Bowne, *Theism*, pp. 216, 217–218, 246; *Idem., The Philosophy of Theism*, idem, p. 183.

[13]Howison, *The Limits of Evolution*, pp. 7, 43; Bowne, *Metaphysics*, pp. 406, 416.

[14]Buckham and Stratton, *George Holmes Howison*, pp. 131, 139; Bowne, *Theism*, pp. 182–83, 186, 224.

[15]See my article "Borden Parker Bowne's Doctrine of God," *Encounter* 53/4 (Autumn 1992), pp. 390–92.

[16]See José Franquiz Ventura, *Borden Parker Bowne's Treatment of the Problem of Change and Identity* (Rio Piedras, Puerto Rico: Univ. of Puerto Rico, 1942), p. 204. See also Bowne, *Kant and Spencer* (Port Washington, N. Y.: Kennikat Press, 1967) [1912]. Here Bowne implied the reality of time for God (p. 49).

[17]See Howison, *The Limits of Evolution*, p. xviii.

[18]Werkmeister, *A History of Philosophical Ideas in America*, p. 319.

[19]Buckham and Stratton, *George Holmes Howison*, p. 137; Bowne, *Metaphysics*, p. 8.

[20]Bowne, *Metaphysics*, pp. 265, 295.

[21]See George Berkeley, *Alciphron or the Minute Philosopher*, in *The Works of George Berkeley*, ed. Alexander Campbell Fraser, (New York: Oxford Univ. Press, 1901), 2:163–77.

[22]Buckham and Stratton, *George Holmes Howison*, p. 132; see Bowne's letter to Mrs. Bowne in *The Personalist*, 1921, p. 10. In a letter to Thomas Davidson (September 26, 1898), Howison responded to some comments Davidson made about something he had written about Kant. "...I do *not* think I am 'too pious toward Kant.' I love him, and think his central thought (of the free self-activity of the human reason a priori) to be of ultimate value, and unperishable, but I feel that he needs to be judged, corrected, amended, extended. And I strongly hope I have learned the true way of doing all this" (Buckham and Stratton, *George Holmes Howison*, p. 95).

[23]Buckham and Stratton, *George Holmes Howison*, pp. 133, 134; Bowne, *Theory of Thought and Knowledge* (New York: Harper and Brothers, 1897), pp. 48, 50, 55, 56, 113–16, chap. 3.

[24]Buckham and Stratton, *George Holmes Howison*, p. 133; Bowne, *Kant and Spencer*, pp. 142–51, chap. 5.

[25]Buckham and Stratton, *George Holmes Howison*, p. 132; see Bowne's letter to Mrs. Bowne.

[26]Ibid.

[27]Ibid., pp. 140, 150; Bowne, *Theism*, pp. 277, 280.

[28]Ibid., p. 128; Bowne, *Theism*, p. 190.

[29]Knudson, *The Philosophy of Personalism*, pp. 78, 80, 250.

[30]Buckham, *Christianity and Personality*, p. 33.

[31]Buckham and Stratton, *George Holmes Howison*, p. 232; Howison, "The City of God, and the True God as its Head," in *The Conception of God*, Howison, Josiah Royce, Sidney Edward Mezes, and Joseph LeConte (New York: Macmillan, 1897), p. 84; Bowne, *Metaphysics*, p. 423.

[32]Buckham and Stratton, *George Holmes Howison*, pp. 132, 139.

[33]Ibid., p. 131.

[34]Ibid., pp. 96, 129, 131, 139, 141.

[35]Ibid., p. 132.

[36]Ibid., p. 139.

[37]Ibid., p. 147.

[38]Ibid., p. 140.

[39]Ibid., p. 84.

[40]James Iverach, "A British Estimate of Dr. Bowne," reproduced in Buckham, "A Group of American Idealists," *The Personalist* 1/1, April 1920, pp. 32, 33.

[41]Rudolph Eucken, "The Work of Borden Parker Bowne," in *Personalism and the Problems of Philosophy*, Ralph T. Flewelling (New York: The Methodist Book Concern, 1915), p. 17.

[42]Ibid., p. 31.

[43]Buckham, "The Contribution of Professor Howison to Christian Thought," pp. 297–98.

[44]This is the case in the following: Mary W. Calkins, *The Persistent Problems of Philosophy* (New York: Macmillan, 1907), pp. 413–16; Bruce Kuklick, *The Rise of American Philosophy:*

Cambridge, Massachussetts, 1860–1930 (New Haven: Yale Univ. Press, 1979), pp. 135–36, 260, 50; John Passmore, *A Hundred Years of Philosphy* (New York: Penguin Books, 1978) [1957], pp. 74–75, 540, n. 5. In each of these books the authors discuss Howison's personalism but do not mention Bowne. Only in the fifth edition of her book did Calkins at least list Bowne, although she did not discuss his personalism.

[45]Brightman, "Personalism and the Influence of Bowne," in *Proceedings of the Sixth International Congress of Philosophy*, ed. Brightman, (New York: Longmans, Green and Company, 1927), p. 166.

[46]See Elizabeth Flower and Murray G. Murphey, *A History of Philosophy in America* (New York: Capricorn Books, 1977), 2:486–90.

[47]Ibid., 1:xx, 2:490.

[48]Ibid., 1:xx.

[49]See Buckham and Stratton, *George Holmes Howison,* p. 112.

[50]William James, *Varieties of Religious Experience* (New York: Longmans, Green and Company, 1902), p. 502n.

[51]James, *The Principles of Psychology* (New York: Dover, 1950) [1890], 1:219–20.

[52]James, *Pragmatism* (New York: Longmans, Green, and Company, 1907), pp. 17, 18.

[53]Quoted in McConnell, *Borden Parker Bowne* (New York: Abingdon Press, 1929), pp. 276, 277.

[54]Buckham and Stratton, *George Holmes Howison,* pp. 19–20.

[55]McConnell, *Borden Parker Bowne*, p. 259.

[56]Buckham and Stratton, *George Holmes Howison*, p. 13.

[57]Quoted in Gustavus W. Cunningham, *The Idealistic Argument in Recent British and American Philosophy* (Manchester, N. H.: Ayer Company, 1977), p. 303.

[58]Howison, *The Limits of Evolution*, p. xii.

[59]Ibid., p. xiii.

[60]Ibid., p. 65.

[61]Ibid., pp. xiii–xiv.

[62]Ibid., pp. xvii–xviii.

[63]Ibid., p. 329.

[64]Ibid., p. xiv.

[65]Knudson, *The Philosophy of Personalism*, p. 54.

[66]Buckham and Stratton, *George Holmes Howison*, p. 131.

[67]Howison, "The City of God, and the True God as its Head," in *The Conception of God*, p. 98.

[68]Howison, *The Limits of Evolution*, p. 81.

[69]Werkmeister, *A History of Philosophical Ideas in America*, p. 123.

[70]Howison, *The Limits of Evolution*, pp. x–xi.

[71]Ibid. p. xiv.

[72]Buckham and Stratton, *George Holmes Howison*, p. 145.

[73]Ibid., p. 147.

[74]Ibid.

[75]Bowne, *The Philosophy of Theism* (New York: Harper and Brothers, 1887), pp. 173–74.

[76]Ibid., p. 178.

[77]Ibid., p. 179.

[78]Ibid., p. 180.

[79]Quoted in James Ward, *The Realm of Ends* (Cambridge: Cambridge Univ. Press, 1920), p. 455.

[80]Buckham, *Personality and the Christian Ideal* (Boston: The Pilgrim Press,1909), p. 182.

[81]Ibid., p. 183.

[82]Augustine, *The Confessions of St. Augustine,* J. G. Pilkington, trans. and annotated (New York: Liveright Publishing Corp., 1942), p. 1. See Buckham, *Personality and the Christian Ideal*, p. 184.

[83]Quoted in Buckham, *Personality and the Christian Ideal*, p. 184.

[84]Bowne, *Studies in Christianity* (Boston: Houghton Mifflin, 1909), pp. 95, 98, 144.

[85]Buckham and Stratton, *George Holmes Howison*, p. 151.

[86]Brightman, *Nature and Values* (New York: Abingdon Press, 1945), p. 25.

[87]See Rosemary Skinner Keller, *Georgia Harkness: For Such a Time as This* (Nashville: Abingdon Press, 1992), chap. 6.

[88]Ibid., pp. 113, 119.

[89]Ibid., p. 162.

[90]Ibid., p. 169.

[91]Ibid., pp. 215, 236–38.
[92]Ibid., p. 167.
[93]Ibid., pp. 114, 167.
[94]Ibid., p. 98.
[95]Ibid., p. 58.
[96]Ibid., p. 111.
[97]Ibid., p. 173.
[98]Pastor Mulligan wrote this to me in a letter dated September 2, 1997.
[99]Keller, *Georgia Harkness,* pp. 240–41.
[100]Ibid., pp. 242–43.
[101]Ibid., p. 243.
[102]Ibid., p. 143.
[103]Wilbur Long, "Idealism," in *Dictionary of Philosophy,* rev. ed., ed. Dagobert Runes, (New York: Harper), p. 153.
[104]Bowne, *Metaphysics,* p. 423.
[105]Brightman, *An Introduction to Philosophy* (New York: Henry Holt and Company, 1925), p. 389.
[106]Brightman, "Personalism," in *An Encyclopedia of Religion,* ed.Vergilius Ferm (New York: The Philosophical Library, 1943), p. 576. It is important to point out, however, that Brightman was not consistent in this regard. For in the last revised edition of *An Introduction to Philosophy* (1963) we still find the view that personalism "makes the further assertion that persons and selves are the only reality…" (p. 330).
[107]Brightman, "Personalism as a Philosophy of Religion," *The Crozer Quarterly* 5/4 (October 1928), pp. 394–95.
[108]Harkness, *The Recovery of Ideals* (New York: Scribners, 1937), p. 165.
[109]Ibid., p. 167.
[110]Harkness, "The Abyss and the Given," *Christendom* 3 (1938), pp. 519–20.
[111]Harkness,*The Recovery of Ideals,* pp. 161, 169.
[112]Dianne E. S. Carpenter, "Georgia Harkness's Distinctive Personalistic Synthesis," (Ph.D. diss., Boston University, 1988).
[113]Brightman, *Is God A Person?* (New York: Association Press, 1932), p. 22.
[114]Knudson, *The Philosophy of Personalism,* p. 87. See also pp. 85, 433.
[115]In *The Philosophy of Personalism* Knudson writes that his aim is to determine whether there is a "true or normal type" of personalism (p. 21).
[116]In *The Philosophy of Personalism* Knudson discusses atheistic, pantheistic, absolutistic, relativistic, and teleological forms of personalism before introducing the Bowne type as the most typical or "normative."
[117]See Jewelle Taylor Gibbs, ed., *Young, Black, and Male in America: An Endangered Species* (New York: Auburn House, 1988).
[118]Bowne, *The Immanence of God* (Boston: Houghton Mifflin, 1905).
[119]See McConnell, "Bowne and the Social Questions," in *Studies in Philosophy and Theology* (by Former Students of Borden Parker Bowne) ed. E. C. Wilm, (New York: Abingdon Press, 1922), p. 136.
[120]Bowne, *The Philosophy of Herbert Spencer* (New York: Hunt & Eaton, 1874), p. 282.
[121]Ibid., p. 32.
[122]Ibid., p. 49.
[123]Ibid., p. 148.
[124]Ibid. Bowne makes scathing criticisms of British philosophers. See pp. 28, 60, 67, 96–97, 112.
[125]Knudson, *The Philosophy of Personalism,* p. 62.
[126]John Macquarrie is quite right to point to the centrality of the idea of dignity in James Cone's work. [See Macquarrie, *Twentieth Century Religious Thought: The Frontiers of Philosophy and Theology, 1900–1980* (New York: Charles Scribner's Sons, 1981), p. 407.]
[127]Martin Luther King, Jr., *Stride Toward Freedom* (New York: Harper, 1958), p. 100.
[128]L. Harold DeWolf, "Martin Luther King, Jr., As Theologian," *The Journal of the Interdenominational Theological Center* 4/2 (Spring 1977), p. 10.
[129]See Clayborne Carson, ed., *The Papers of Martin Luther King, Jr.* (Berkeley, Calif.: Univ. of Calif. Press, 1992), 1:390.
[130]John J. Ansbro, *Martin Luther King, Jr.: The Making of a Mind* (Maryknoll, N. Y.: Orbis, 1982), p. 120. Bertocci and Brightman co-taught the seminar on Hegel. King also took a seminar with Bertocci on the history of philosophy, in which he sometimes earned only average grades (see Carson, ed., *The Papers of Martin Luther King, Jr.,* 2:196n.–197n., 15–16).

[131]King, *Stride Toward Freedom*, p. 100.

[132]King, "Pilgrimage to Nonviolence," in *Stride Toward Freedom*, p. 100.

[133]See Stephen B. Oates, *Let the Trumpet Sound: The Life of Martin Luther King, Jr.* (New York: Harper & Row, 1982), p. 35.

[134]James H. Cone, *Martin & Malcolm & America* (Maryknoll, N. Y.: Orbis, 1991), pp. 29, 132.

[135]Garth Baker-Fletcher, *Somebodyness: Martin Luther King, Jr., and the Theory of Dignity* (Minneapolis: Fortress Press, 1993), chaps. 1–3. Baker-Fletcher, more than most King scholars, pays considerable attention to the preseminary and graduate school influences on King's thought development. Baker-Fletcher helps us see that King learned much about a personal and loving God and the absolute dignity of persons (especially that of his own people) from his parents and maternal grandparents.

[136]See Lewis V. Baldwin, "Martin Luther King, Jr., The Black Church, and the Black Messianic Vision," in *Martin Luther King, Jr., and the Civil Rights Movement*, ed. David Garrow (New York: Carlson Publishing, 1989), 1:93–108.

[137]See David Garrow, "The Intellectual Development of Martin Luther King, Jr.: Influences and Commentaries," in *Martin Luther King, Jr., and the Civil Rights Movement*, ed. Garrow, pp. 438, 444, 451, n. 20.

[138]Kenneth L. Smith and Ira G. Zepp, Jr., *Search for the Beloved Community: The Thinking of Martin Luther King, Jr.* (Valley Forge, Pa.: Judson Press, 1974), chap. 5.

[139]Ansbro, *Martin Luther King, Jr.: The Making of a Mind*.

[140]Baker-Fletcher, *Somebodyness*, chap. 3.

[141]Bowen was not, in the strictest sense, the first Afrikan American personalist. The long tradition among Afrikan Americans of belief in a personal God and the sanctity of all persons long antedates Bowen. But from the standpoint of formal academic training relative to personalism, it must be said that Bowen was the first personalist among Afrikan Americans. Indeed, he studied under Bowne long before the well-known Anglo personalists discussed in this book.

[142]Richard Morgan Cameron, *Boston University School of Theology 1839–1968, Nexus* XI, nos. 2 and 3 (May 1968), p. 43.

[143]This material is located in the John Wesley Edward Bowen collection at the Gammon Theological Seminary Archives housed in The Atlanta University Center Woodruff Library, Archives and Special Collections Department, (185) reel 23.

[144]Bowne, *Metaphysics* (1882), p. 126.

[145]John Wesley Edward Bowen, "A Psychological Principle in Revelation," *Methodist Review* (September 1891), p. 737.

[146]Bowen, "Apology for Higher Education of the Negro," *Methodist Review* (1897), p. 724.

[147]Ibid., p. 725.

[148]See Bowne, *Metaphysics* (1882), p. 87, and idem, *Theory of Thought and Knowledge*, p. 57.

[149]Bowen, "Apology for Higher Education of the Negro," p. 724.

[150]Ibid., p. 731.

[151]Ibid., p. 742.

[152]Ibid., p. 728.

[153]Ibid., p. 730.

[154]Bowen, *What Shall the Harvest Be?* (Washington, D.C.: Asbury Methodist Episcopal Church, 1892), pp. 5, 6.

[155]Ibid., p. 9.

[156]Ibid., pp. 10–11.

[157]See Bowne, *Theism*, p. 278.

[158]Bowen, *What Shall the Harvest Be?* pp. 13, 14.

[159]Ibid., p. 25.

[160]Ibid., p. 34.

[161]Bowen, *An Appeal for Negro Bishops, But No Separation* (New York: Eaton & Mains, 1912), p. 86.

[162]Ibid., p. 66.

[163]Ibid., pp. 67–68.

[164]Ibid., pp. 75–76.

[165]Ibid., p. 83.

[166]Ibid., p. 85.

[167]See J. Deotis Roberts, *A Philosophical Introduction to Theology* (Philadelphia: Trinity Press International, 1991), pp. 162–64.

[168]See Roberts, "Black Consciousness in Theological Perspective," in *Quest for a Black Theology*, ed. James J. Gardiner and J. Deotis Roberts, Sr. (Philadelphia: Pilgrim Press, 1971), pp. 72–74.

[169]Roberts, *A Philosophical Introduction to Theology*, p. 164.
[170]Roberts, *A Black Political Theology* (Philadelphia: Westminster Press, 1974), p. 75.
[171]Ibid., p. 51.
[172]Ibid., p. 87.
[173]Ibid., p. 92.
[174]See *The Personalist Forum* 5/1 (Spring 1989).
[175]Roberts, *The Prophethood of Black Believers* (Louisville, Ky.: Westminster/John Knox Press, 1994), p. 28.
[176]Roberts, *A Black Political Theology*, p. 97.
[177]Ibid., p. 109.
[178]Ibid., p. 105.
[179]Ibid., p. 104.
[180]Ibid., p. 102.
[181]Ibid., p. 69.
[182]Knudson, *The Philosophy of Personalism*, p. 79.
[183]Bowne, *Theism*, p. 167.
[184]Roberts, *A Black Political Theology*, p. 75.
[185]However, Roberts does not tell us that he is here appropriating the language and ideas of Brightman.
[186]See Roberts' further discussion on existentialism's emphasis on human freedom in *Liberation and Reconciliation: A Black Theology* (Maryknoll, N. Y.: Orbis, 1994), p. 55.
[187]Brightman, "Personality as a Metaphysical Principle,"in *Personalism in Theology* (Boston: Boston Univ. Press, 1943), pp. 44, 58.
[188]Brightman, *Nature and Values*, p. 53.
[189]McConnell, *Personal Christianity* (New York: Fleming H. Revell Company, 1914), p. 48. See also p. 185.
[190]Nels F. S. Ferré, *Christianity and Society* (New York: Harper & Brothers Publishers, 1950), p. 118.
[191]Roberts, *A Black Political Theology*, p. 166.
[192]Ibid., pp. 91, 99.
[193]See Walter G. Muelder, *Moral Law in Christian Social Ethics* (Richmond, Va.: John Knox Press, 1966), pp. 29, 113, chap. 2.
[194]Roberts, *A Black Political Theology*, p. 99.
[195]Ibid., pp. 165–66.
[196]See my as yet unpublished book on the Afrikan American person.
[197]Buckham, *Christianity and Personality*, pp. 165–66.
[198]Harkness, *The Recovery of Ideals*, p. 139.
[199]Brightman, *Nature and Values*, p. 117.
[200]Other types of personalism include, but are not limited to: political personalism (Emmanuel Mounier, 1905–1950), panpsychistic personalism (James Ward, 1843–1925), anthropomorphic personalism (Henri Bois, 1862–?), and existential personalism (Nicolas Berdyaev, 1874–1948).

Chapter 4. Person: The Key to Reality

[1]See Peter A. Bertocci, "The Personalism of Edgar S. Brightman and Ultimate Reality," *Ultimate Reality* 6/1 (March 1983), p. 35.
[2]Edgar S. Brightman, *Nature and Values* (New York: Abingdon Press, 1945), p. 53.
[3]Brightman, *A Philosophy of Religion* (Englewood Cliffs, N. J.: Prentice Hall, 1940), p. 534.
[4]Bertocci, *The Person God Is* (London: Allen and Unwin, 1970), p. 95.
[5]Bertocci, "Brightman's View of the Self, the Person and the Body," *The Philosophical Forum* 8 (1950), p. 22n.
[6]Brightman, *Nature and Values*, p. 53.
[7]Bertocci, *Introduction to the Philosophy of Religion* (Englewood Cliffs, N.J.: Prentice Hall, 1951), p. 204.
[8]Ibid., p. 224.
[9]Bowne, *Studies in Theism* (New York: Phillips & Hunt, 1879), pp. 230, 231.
[10]Bowne, *Metaphysics*(New York: Harper, 1882), pp. 16, 17, 24, 26.
[11]Ibid., p. 142.
[12]Ibid., p. 41.
[13]Ibid., p. 40.
[14]Albert C. Knudson, *The Philosophy of Personalism* (Nashville: Abingdon Press, 1927), p. 204.

[15]Ibid., p. 43.

[16]Bowne, *Personalism* (Boston: Houghton Mifflin, 1908), p. 76.

[17]Bowne, *Theism,* (New York: American Book Co., 1902) p. 30.

[18]Ibid., p. 130.

[19]Bowne, *Metaphysics* (1882), pp. 470, 472, 474.

[20]Bowne, *Theory of Thought and Knowledge* (New York: American Book Company, 1897), pp. 342–43.

[21]Knudson, *The Philosophy of Personalism*, p. 87.

[22]Brightman cites as one of the key victories of idealistic thought that it historically "insisted that the social problem is an integral part of philosophy. It was Plato [the idealist], not Democritus [the materialist], who wrote the *Republic*; it was Berkeley, and not Hume, who was concerned about the economic sufferings of the proletariat; it was Fichte and not Bolzano who unified his nation; it was Hegel and not Herbart who wrote a *Philosophie des Rechts*; it was the idealistic method that led Marx to write *Das Kapital*" (see Brightman, "From the Standpoint of an Idealist," in Wieman and Meland, eds., *American Philosophies of Religion*, pp. 320–21).

[23]Knudson, *The Philosophy of Personalism*, pp. 76, 83, 237, 244. See also Brightman, *Person and Reality: An Introduction to Metaphysics*, ed. Bertocci, Newhall, and Brightman, (New York: Ronald Press, 1958), pp. 353–66.

[24]Brightman, "Personality As A Metaphysical Principle," in *Personalism in Theology* (Boston: Boston Univ. Press, 1943), p. 42.

[25]Ibid., p. 54.

[26]Knudson, *The Philosophy of Personalism*, p. 246.

[27]Bowne, *Metaphysics*, pp. 63, 64.

[28]Knudson, *The Philosophy of Personalism*, pp. 209, 210; see also p. 106.

[29]Bowne, *Metaphysics*, p. 138.

[30]Brightman, "Personality As A Metaphysical Principle," pp. 55–56.

[31]Ibid., p. 54.

[32]Harkness, *The Recovery of Ideals* (New York: Scribner's, 1937), p. 139.

[33]Brightman, *A Philosophy of Religion*, p. 350.

[34]Ibid. Although aware of Brightman's view and Wolfgang Kohler's report that apes have a high degree of conceptual thinking, Harkness did not consider them to be persons. Only persons have the capacity to worship God; to reflect on the meaning of selfhood, as well as past, present, and future; have power of conscious development and reflective thought; and the capacity to plan and work toward achievement of goals and spiritual aspirations (see Harkness, *Conflicts in Religious Thought* [New York: Henry Holt, 1949], pp. 153, 155).

[35]Brightman, *A Philosophy of Religion*, pp. 351–52.

[36]Knudson, *The Philosophy of Personalism*, pp. 33–34.

[37]Brightman, *A Philosophy of Religion*, pp. 352–53. But the trait of privacy cannot mean that human persons and God do not commune, or that God does not know directly their thoughts and feelings. By definition God should be able to know these immediately, although it is not empirically sound to say that we humans should know directly the thoughts and feelings either of each other or of God. And, the element of privacy holds up when individual persons commune with God. What happens is only between God and the individual, and in this sense remains a very private experience. God can know and appreciate our feelings and thoughts without these being God's own, as would be the case in classical pantheism (see Bowne, *Personalism*, p. 282).

[38]Ibid., p. 359.

[39]Ibid., p. 361.

[40]Ibid., pp. 363–64.

[41]Ibid., p. 364.

[42]Ibid., pp. 364–68.

[43]Bowne, *Personalism*, p. 267.

[44]Bowne, *Theism*, p. 168. Here Bowne follows the view of his teacher, Lotze, idem, *Studies in Theism*, p. 275.

[45]See Bowne, *Theism*, p. 162; and idem, *Metaphysics*, p. 116.

[46]Ibid.

[47]Bowne, *The Principles of Ethics* (New York: American Book Company, 1892), p. 97.

[48]Bowne, *Theism*, p. 170.

[49]Bowne, *Metaphysics*, p. 116.

[50]Bertocci, "The Essence of a Person," *The Monist* 61/1 (January 1978), p. 29.

[51]Bowne, *The Principles of Ethics*, p. 124.

[52]See McConnell, "Bowne and Personalism," Brightman, ed., *Personalism in Theology*, p. 39.

[53]Bowne, *Personalism*, p. 277.

[54]Francis J. McConnell, *Personal Christianity* (New York: Fleming H. Revell Company, 1914), p. 185.

[55]See Muelder, *Moral Law in Christian Social Ethics* (Richmond, Va.: John Knox Press, 1966), pp. 29, 113, chap. 2.

[56]Bowne, *Philosophy of Theism* (New York: Harper & Brothers, 1887), pp. 50–51.

[57]Ibid., p. 53.

[58]Brightman, *Nature and Values*, p. 117.

[59]Howison, *The Limits of Evolution*, (New York: Macmiilan, 1901) p. 7.

[60]Buckham, *Personality and the Christian Ideal* (Boston: The Pilgrim Press, 1909), chap. 4.

[61]See Harold H. Oliver, *Relatedness: Essays in Metaphysics and Theology* (Macon, Ga.: Mercer University Press, 1984), p. 160 and chap. 10. Oliver maintains that much of Western thought has been more concerned about either the subject (idealism) or the object (realism) than about relation. "Relational metaphysics, to the contrary, affirms the fundamentality of *relatio*, the relation, the relating. Thus it maintains the coherence, or better, the coin*herence*, of the act. By definition, there can be no actor (agent) or thing-acted-upon prior to the acting (*actio*). Every attempt to posit them outside the act fails, because we can do so only by appeal to other acts where the same restrictions obtain" (p. 160). For Oliver subject and object derive from the relation, and therefore are abstractions. But clearly what is fundamental for him is the relation, not the subject or the object.

[62]Knudson, *The Philosophy of Personalism*, p. 83.

[63]Knudson, *The Doctrine of Redemption* (New York: Abingdon Press, 1933), pp. 85–86.

[64]In addition, my reading of Knudson leads me to conclude that he was at best racially insensitive. Paul Deats, Jr., a fourth-generation personalist, contends that Knudson "was concerned with racism as it found expression in the union of Methodist Churches" [see *The Boston Personalist Tradition* (Macon, Ga.: Mercer Univ Press, 1986), p. 11]. With this point one cannot take issue. But if Deats means to convey the idea that Knudson sought to eradicate racism I must beg to differ, for such a view is not consistent with the conclusion of others who knew Knudson and his work well. S. Paul Schilling maintains, for example, that one of the "regrettable gaps in Knudson's treatment of Christian social ethics" is his failure to mention "racial segregation and other forms of injustice to minorities within nations like the United States." This conclusion is consistent with my own findings. In addition, Knudson condemned Hitler and the Nazis, but was silent on the issue of anti-Semitism among Nazis and their brutal murder of more than six million Jews (see Schilling in ibid., pp. 102–3).

[65]Brightman, "Authority and Personality," *The Journal of Bible and Religion* 12 (February 1944), p. 6.

[66]In *The Spiritual Life* Brightman says that no self that is not able to reason and strive toward ideal value is a person. At best such a self may be subpersonal. Brightman writes: "…there are human selves…so abnormal that, as far as we know, they can never develop any ideal values at all, certainly not in this life, perhaps not in the world to come. Such beings would be subpersonal selves, without eventual potentialities of any real development or redemption. Selves incapable of reflective and critical self-consciousness, unable to devote themselves to any ideal enterprise, are not persons." [Brightman, *The Spiritual Life* (New York: Abingdon Press, 1942), p. 61.]. But one must wonder about the parents who gave birth to such a self. They and God were cocreators who intended the birth of a "healthy" baby. The intention was that the baby be "a candidate for humanity." That an imbecile was born, for example, would seem to say more about God than the child and its parents. It was, after all, God who called the child into existence. Since God is love, God's intention was that the child be mentally and physically healthy. What enters here is the problem of evil. Experience shows that human persons give birth to human persons. That some are "abnormal" at birth should not minimize the fact that in a much deeper sense the intention was that they be healthy in every respect. In either case they should be treated with love and respect, preferably because it was intended that they be persons. But if for no other reason they should be treated with love and respect because of the humanity of the persons responding and reacting to them.

[67]Paul Tillich, *Love, Power, and Justice* (New York: Oxford Univ. Press, 1960), p. 59.

[68]Knudson, *The Philosophy of Personalism*, p. 168.

[69]Brightman, *Person and Reality*, ed. Peter A. Bertocci (New York: Ronald Press, 1958), p. 358.

[70]Bowne, *Theism* (New York: American Book Company 1902), p. 134.

[71]Bowne, *Studies in Theism*, p. 57.
[72]Ibid.
[73]Knudson, *The Philosophy of Personalism*, pp. 237–38.
[74]Brightman, "From Rationalism to Empiricism," *The Christian Century* (March 1, 1939), p. 277.
[75]See Muelder, "Edgar Sheffield Brightman: Person and Moral Philosopher," *The Boston Personalist Tradition* (Macon Ga.: Mercer Univ. Press, 1986), pp. 110–11.

Chapter 5. Personalistic Method and Criterion of Truth

[1]Bowne, *Metaphysics* (New York: Harper, 1882), p. 23.
[2]Ibid., p. 5.
[3]Bowne, *Theory of Thought and Knowledge* (New York: Harper & Brothers, 1897), p. 293.
[4]Bowne, *Theism* (New York: American Book Co., 1902), pp. 15–43.
[5]Bertocci, Course Syllabus on Philosophy of Religion, p. 2.
[6]David Elton Trueblood, *Philosophy of Religion* (New York: Harper, 1957), p. 48.
[7]Bowne, *Theism*, pp. 15, 24, 27, 35, 272.
[8]Bertocci, *Introduction to the Philosophy of Religion* (Englewood Cliffs, N.J.: Prentice Hall, 1951), p. 61.
[9]Bertocci, *The Goodness of God* (Washington, D.C.: Univ. Press of America, 1981), p. 7.
[10]A. C. Ewing, "Criteria of Truth" in *The Range of Philosophy*, ed. Harold Titus and Maylon Hepp (New York: Van Nostrand Reinhold Company, 1970), pp. 43, 45.
[11]Bowne, *Theory of Thought and Knowledge*, pp. 293, 271.
[12]Trueblood, *Philosophy of Religion*, p. 53.
[13]Bowne, *Theism*, p. iv.
[14]See Frederick Copleston, *A History of Philosophy* (New York: Image Books, 1967), 8:48.
[15]Brightman, *Person and Reality*, ed. Peter A. Bertocci, (New York: Ronald Press, 1958), pp. 22–23.
[16]Brightman, *An Introduction to Philosophy* (New York: Henry Holt and Co. 1925), p. 29.
[17]See Bowne, *Studies in Theism* (New York: Phillips & Hunt, 1879), pp. 4, 5.
[18]Brightman, *An Introduction to Philosophy*, third rev. ed., p. 42.
[19]Harkness, *The Recovery of Ideals* (New York: Scribners, 1937), p. 93.
[20]Bowne, *Metaphysics* (1882), p. 5.
[21]Ibid., p. 6.
[22]Bertocci, *Introduction to the Philosophy of Religion*, p. 62.
[23]Bowne, *Studies in Theism*, p. 57.
[24]Bowne, *Theism*, p. 130.
[25]Harold H. Titus and Marilyn S. Smith, *Living Issues in Philosophy* (New York: D. Van Nostrand, 1974), pp. 267–68.
[26]Bowne, *Metaphysics* (1882), p. 7.
[27]Ibid., pp. 7–8.
[28]Ibid., p. 8.
[29]Bertocci, *Introduction to the Philosophy of Religion*, p. 78.
[30]V. J. McGill, "Pragmatism," in *Dictionary of Philosophy*, ed. Dagobert D. Runes, (New York: Philosophical Library, 1942), p. 245.
[31]William James, *Essays in Pragmatism* (New York: Hafner Publishing Company, 1961), p. 144.
[32]Knudson and others described personalism in this way as well [see *The Philosophy of Personalism* (Nashville: Abingdon Press, 1927), p. 17]. In addition, Ralph T. Flewelling implies this in his article, "Personalism," when he writes that "the personalistic system has at various times been designated as Voluntarism, the Philosophy of Freedom, of Effort, of Probability, of Contingency, of Continuity, of *Idées Forces*, of Change, Spiritual Realism, Transcendental Empiricism, Personal Idealism, Humanism, Vitalism, Activism, Personal Realism, and Personalism," with the latter becoming the most popular of the designations [See Flewelling, "Personalism," in *Twentieth Century Philosophy*, ed. Dagobert D. Runes, ed. (New York: Philosophical Library, 1947), pp. 323–24].
[33]James, *Essays in Pragmatism*, p. 144.
[34]Quoted in McGill, "Pragmatism," in *Dictionary of Philosophy*, ed. Runes, p. 245.
[35]Quoted in Joseph Leighton, *The Field of Philosophy* (New York: D. Appleton and Company, 1923), p. 535.
[36]Quoted in Titus and Hepp, eds., *The Range of Philosophy*, p. 49.
[37]Bowne, *Metaphysics* (1898), pp. 16, 17, 26, 25.
[38]Norman Pittenger, *Loving Says It All* (New York: Pilgrim Press, 1978), p. 73.

[39]Bowne, *Kant and Spencer* (Port Washington, N. Y.: Kennikat Press, 1967) [1912], p. 146.

[40]Bertocci, *Introduction to the Philosophy of Religion*, p. 78.

[41]Titus and Smith, *Living Issues in Philosophy*, p. 273.

[42]Brightman, "Personality as a Metaphysical Principle," in *Personalism in Theology* (Boston: Boston Univ. Press, 1943), p. 57.

[43]James, *Essays in Radical Empiricism*, and *A Pluralistic Universe* (one volume) (New York: Longmans, Green and Company, 1943), p. 42.

[44]Brightman, "Personalistic Metaphysics of the Self: Its Distinctive Features," in *Radhakrishnan*, W. R. Inge et al., eds. (New York: Harper, 1950), pp. 290–91.

[45]Brightman, *The Spiritual Life* (New York: Abingdon Press, 1942), p. 211.

[46]See Bowne, *The Principles of Ethics* (New York: American Book Company, 1892), chap. 5.

[47]David Ray Griffin, "Charles Hartshorne's Postmodern Philosophy," *Hartshorne: Process Philosophy and Theology*, ed. Robert Kane and Stephen Phillips (Albany, New York: SUNY Press, 1989), p. 22.

[48]Bowne, *Theory of Thought and Knowledge*, p. 293.

[49]Ibid., pp. 293–94.

[50]Brightman, *An Introduction to Philosophy* (1925), p. 60.

[51]Harkness, *Conflicts in Religious Thought*, rev. ed. (New York: Henry Holt, 1949), p. 65.

[52]Brightman, "Religion as Truth," in *Contemporary American Theology*, ed. Vergilius Ferm (New York: Round Table Press, 1932), 1:59.

[53]Bertocci, *Introduction to the Philosophy of Religion*, p. 54.

[54]Bowne, *Theism*, p. 18.

[55]Brightman, "Authority and Personality," *The Journal of Bible and Religion* 12 (February 1944), p. 7.

[56]Ibid., p. 5.

[57]Brightman, *A Philosophy of Religion*, pp. 128–29.

[58]Brightman, *Religious Values* (New York: Abingdon Press, 1925), p. 30.

[59]Brightman, *A Philosophy of Religion*, p. 129.

[60]Bertocci, *Introduction to the Philosophy of Religion*, p. 78.

[61]Brightman, *An Introduction to Philosophy* (1925), p. 64.

[62]Bowne, *The Philosophy of Herbert Spencer* (New York: Phillips & Hunt, 1874), p. 270.

[63]McConnell, *Religious Certainty* (New York: Eaton J. Mains, 1910), p. 6.

[64]Bowne, *Theism*, p. 35.

[65]Bertocci, *Introduction to the Philosophy of Religion*, p. 78.

[66]Brightman, *Religious Values*, p. 261.

[67]Ibid., p. 234.

[68]Bowne, *The Immanence of God* (Boston: Houghton, Mifflin and Company, 1905), p. 103.

Chapter 6. Borden P. Bowne's Theism

[1]See Knudson, *The Philosophy of Personalism* (Nashville: Abingdon Press, 1927), pp. 21, 50, 51, 61, 261.

[2]Bowne, *Theism* (New York: American Book Co., 1902), p. 61.

[3]Calkins, *The Persistent Problems of Philosophy*, fifth rev. ed. (New York: Macmillan Company, 1936) [1907], p. 436.

[4]Bowne, *Personalism* (Boston: Houghton Mifflin, 1908), p. 297.

[5]Bowne, "The Logic of Religious Belief," in Steinkraus, ed., *Representative Essays of Borden Parker Bowne* (Utica, N.Y.: Meridian Publishing, 1980), p. 154.

[6]Bowne, *Personalism*, p. 297.

[7]McConnell implies this in *Borden Parker Bowne* (New York: Abingdon Press, 1929). "Bowne was profoundly religious by nature, and approached philosophy from the religious point of view" (p. 91). Elsewhere McConnell writes: "Bowne was a product of Methodism, and his evangelical training did much to influence his philosophy" [McConnell, *Evangelicals, Revolutionists and Idealists* (New York: Abingdon-Cokesbury, 1942), p. 134.].

[8]Bowne, *Studies in Theism*, p. 360.

[9]Muelder and Sears, eds., *The Development of American Philosophy* (Boston: Houghton Mifflin, 1940), p. 489.

[10]It should be noted, however, that Harkness' brand of theistic finitism differed from Brightman's since she believed that God is limited by extramental realities, for example, events, things, and eternal forms.

[11]Bowne, *Studies in Theism* (New York: Phillips & Hunt, 1879), p. 360.

[12]Ibid., p. 4.

[13]Ibid., p. 411.

[14]Bowne, *Metaphysics* (New York: Harper, 1882) p. 296.
[15]Bowne, *Theism*, p. 33.
[16]Bowne, *Metaphysics*, p. 379.
[17]Ibid.
[18]Bowne, *Theism*, p. 34.
[19]Bowne, *The Philosophy of Herbert Spencer* (New York: Phillips & Hunt, 1874), p. 76.
[20]Ibid., pp. 77–78.
[21]Bowne, "The Logic of Religious Belief," p. 153.
[22]Bowne, *Theism*, pp. 18, 43, 259, 291.
[23]Ibid., p. 42.
[24]Ibid., pp. 129–30.
[25]Ibid., p. 130.
[26]Ibid., p. 134.
[27]Bowne, *Metaphysics*, pp. 66, 91, 101, 119, 186, 340–41.
[28]Ibid., p. 134.
[29]McConnell, *Borden Parker Bowne*, p. 123.
[30]Bowne, *Theism*, p. 154.
[31]Ibid.
[32]Ibid., p. 161.
[33]Ibid., p. 155.
[34]Ibid., pp. 50, 62.
[35]Ibid., p. 49.
[36]Ibid., pp. 48, 77.
[37]See Bertocci, *Introduction to the Philosophy of Religion* (Englewood Cliffs, N. I.: Prentice Hall, 1951), chaps. 13–15, and Frederick R. Tennant, *Philosophical Theology* (Cambridge: University Press, 1930), 2: chap. 4.
[38]Bowne, *Theism*, p. 86.
[39]Ibid., p. 53.
[40]Bertocci, "Borden Parker Bowne and His Personalistic Theistic Idealism," *Ultimate Reality* 2/3 (1979), p. 219.
[41]Bowne, *Theism*, p. 57.
[42]Ibid.
[43]Ibid., p. 172.
[44]Ibid., p. 315.
[45]Ibid., p. 173.
[46]Ibid., pp. 173, 177.
[47]Bertocci, "Borden Parker Bowne," p. 221.
[48]Bowne, *Theism*, p. 178.
[49]Ibid., pp. 182–83.
[50]Bowne, *Metaphysics*, p. 178.
[51]Bowne, *Kant and Spencer*, (Port Washington, N.Y.: Kennikat Press, 1967) [1912] p. 49.
[52]José Franquiz Ventura, *Borden Parker Bowne's Treatment of the Problem of Change and Identity* (Rio Piedras, Puerto Rico: Univ. of Puerto Rico, 1942), p. 204.
[53]Bowne, *Theism*, pp. 184–85.
[54]Ibid., p. 185.
[55]Ibid., pp. 212, 183, 184.
[56]Bowne, *Metaphysics*, p. 190.
[57]Bowne, *Theism*, p. 179.
[58]Bertocci, "Borden Parker Bowne," p. 222.
[59]Bowne, *Theism*, p. 185.
[60]Ibid., p. 186.
[61]Bowne, *Metaphysics*, p. 133.
[62]Ibid., pp. 133–34.
[63]Ibid., p. 137.
[64]Ibid., p. 139.
[65]Bowne, *Theism*, pp. 64, 200.
[66]Ibid., pp. 179–80.
[67]Ibid., p. 180.
[68]Ibid., pp. 180–81.
[69]Bowne, *Metaphysics*, pp. 154–55.
[70]Bowne, *Theism*, pp. 186–87.
[71]James, "The Dilemma of Determinism," in *The Will to Believe and Other Essays in Popular*

Philosophy (New York: Dover Publications, 1956) [1897], pp. 181–83.

[72]Bowne, *Theism*, p. 188.

[73]Ibid., p. 190.

[74]What is interesting in this is that Bowne was criticizing a similar view of God that Brightman would later develop in a unique and radically different way, viz., theistic finitism.

[75]Bowne, *Theism*, p. 245.

[76]Bowne, *Studies in Theism*, p. 352.

[77]Ibid., p. 275.

[78]Bowne, *Theism*, p. 249, chap. 5.

[79]Bowne, *Studies in Christianity* (Boston: Houghlin Mifflin, 1909), p. 97.

[80]Bowne, *Theism*, p. 251.

[81]Ibid., pp. 251–52.

[82]Ibid., p. 254.

[83]Ibid., p. 255.

[84]Ibid., pp. 257–58.

[85]Ibid., p. 258.

[86]Ibid.

[87]Bowne, *The Philosophy of Herbert Spencer*, p. 264.

[88]Ibid.

[89]Bowne, *Studies in Christianity*, p. 94.

[90]Ibid., p. 217.

[91]Ibid., p. 218.

[92]Ibid., p. 94. Interestingly, many present-day theologians seem to prefer the God of the philosophers—a God who seems abstract, emotionless, detached, and unconcerned about what happens in the world. One scholar expresses this concern well: "Even today much theological opinion prefers the God of philosophy to the God of history. Emotions, feelings and activities are considered accidental to what God is in himself and extrinsic to his divine nature. When applied to God in human discourse, they are simply anthropomorphic representations of him, necessary in order that man have a way of thinking and speaking about deity. However, these modes of speaking do not tell us anything about the deity itself." [Robert B. Mellert, *What is Process Theology?* (New York: Paulist Press, 1975), pp. 41–42]. Neither Bowne nor those who adhere to the basic outline of his personalism have much interest in the God of the philosophers. This explains personalism's chief emphasis on the ethical attributes of God.

[93]Ibid., p. 144.

[94]Ibid., p. 98.

[95]Bowne, *The Philosophy of Herbert Spencer*, p. 263.

[96]Ibid., p. 266.

[97]Bowne, *Theism*, p. 280.

[98]Bowne, *Studies in Theism*, p. 360.

[99]Ibid., pp. 355, 159.

[100]Ibid., p. 360.

[101]Knudson, *The Doctrine of Redemption* (New York: Abingdon Press, 1933), p. 220. This appears to be an interpretation of a portion of Bowne's discussion in *Studies in Theism*. Here he writes: "Finally, we do not recognize the need of limiting either the divine power or benevolence to account for unmoral evil. We believe it much more rational to confess that we have no sufficient data for the speculative solution of this problem. When, then, belief in the divine benevolence seems to conflict with belief in the divine omnipotence, except always in the case of contradiction, we limit neither, but decide that the solution of the problem lies at present beyond the horizon of the human mind" (p. 360). See also Hermann Lotze, *Microcosmus* (Edinburgh: T. & T. Clark, 1885), 2:717.

[102]Bowne, *Studies in Christianity*, p. 151.

[103]Bowne, *Theism*, p. 281.

[104]Bowne, *Studies in Theism*, p. 367.

[105]Bowne, *Theism*, pp. 269, 282.

[106]Ibid., p. 283.

[107]Ibid., p. 280.

[108]Ibid., pp. 256, 233.

[109]Ibid., p. 284.

[110]Bowne, *Studies in Theism*, pp. 4, 6.

[111]Ibid., pp. 370–71.

[112]Bowne, *The Philosophy of Herbert Spencer*, p. 263.

[113]Ibid.

[114]Bowne, *Theism,* pp. 224, 219.

[115]Bowne, *Studies in Christianity,* p. 92.

[116]In my mind this at least approximates Whitehead's notion of the primordial and consequent natures of God, and Hartshorne's abstract essence of God and concrete actuality.

[117]I address the idea of dipolarity in Bowne's theism more fully in "Borden Parker Bowne's Contribution to Theistic Finitism," *The Personalist Forum* (forthcoming).

[118]Bowne, *Studies in Christianity,* p. 91.

Chapter 7. Edgar S. Brightman's Theism

[1]Brightman, "Religion As Truth," in Ferm, ed., *Contemporary American Theology* (New York: Round Table Press, 1932), 1:57.

[2]Joseph A. Leighton, "Temporalism and the Christian Idea," *The Chronicle* 18 (1918), pp. 283–88, 339–44.

[3]Ibid.

[4]Brightman, *A Philosophy of Religion* (Englewood Cliffs, N.J.: Prentice Hall, 1940) p. 274.

[5]Brightman, *An Introduction to Philosophy* (New York: Henry Holt and Company, 1925), pp. 332–33.

[6]Jannette Newhall, "Edgar Sheffield Brightman: A Biographical Sketch," *Philosophical Forum* 12 (1954), p. 14.

[7]Brightman, "Religion As Truth," 1:75.

[8]Brightman, *The Problem of God* (New York: Abingdon Press, 1930), pp. 10, 176.

[9]Brightman, "An Empirical Approach to God," in Walter G. Muelder and Laurence Sears, eds., *The Development of American Philosophy* (Boston: Houghton Mifflin Company, 1940), p. 514.

[10]Brightman, *A Philosophy of Religion,* p. 321.

[11]Ibid., p. 246.

[12]Quoted in Brightman, *Person and Reality,* p. 333n. In the 1940 edition of *A Philosophy of Religion* we find: "If there be any truly surd evil, then it is not in any sense an instrumental good; good comes in spite of it, not because of it" (p. 246). In later editions he writes: "If there be any truly surd evil, then it is not in any sense an intrinsic good; good comes in opposing it, not in enjoying it" (p. 246).

[13]L. Harold DeWolf, *The Religious Revolt Against Reason* (New York: Harper and Row, 1949), pp. 47–54.

[14]Ibid., p. 170.

[15]Brightman, *A Philosophy of Religion,* p. 284. See Aristotle, *Metaphysics,* trans. Richard Hope (Ann Arbor, Mich.: Univ. of Michigan Press, 1983 [1960]), book lambda, chap. 7, pp. 259–60.

[16]Brightman, *The Problem of God,* pp. 172–73.

[17]Henry Nelson Wieman and Bernard Meland, eds., *American Philosophies of Religion* (Chicago: Willett, Clark, & Company, 1936), p. 139.

[18]It is interesting to note that for a number of years Whitehead taught at Harvard, just across the Charles River from Brightman at Boston University. Brightman cites Whitehead's ideas in many of his writings, and yet there is no indication that Whitehead made use of Brightman's work in his published writings. Nor is it clear that the two men corresponded or otherwise dialogued. We do know, however, that there was extensive correspondence between Brightman and Charles Hartshorne, the neoclassical philosopher who served as Whitehead's teaching assistant and became a giant in his own right.

[19]Brightman, *A Philosophy of Religion,* p. 309.

[20]Ibid., p. 312.

[21]Ibid., p. 313.

[22]Ibid.

[23]Ibid., p. 302.

[24]Ibid., p. 303.

[25]Bertocci, *Introduction to the Philosophy of Religion* (Englewood Cliffs, N. J.: Prentice Hall, 1951) p. 426.

[26]Brightman, *A Philosophy of Religion,* p. 314.

[27]Ibid., p. 319.

[28]Brightman, *The Problem of God,* p. 189.

[29]Brightman, *Personality and Religion* (New York: Abingdon Press, 1934), p. 82.

[30]Ibid.

[31]Ibid., p. 83.

[32]Ibid.

[33]This may be likened to Bowne's reference to, but rejection of, the idea of an "intractable element" in the nature of things that works against God's achievement of the divine purpose in the world. See Bowne, *Theism*, p. 280.

[34]Brightman, *Personality and Religion*, p. 84.

[35]Brightman, *The Problem of God*, p. 192.

[36]Ibid., p. 193.

[37]Ibid., p. 174.

[38]Ibid., p. 187.

[39]Ibid., p. 176.

[40]Ibid., p. 177.

[41]Ibid.

[42]Brightman, *A Philosophy of Religion*, p. 338.

[43]Ibid.

[44]Brightman, "The Given and Its Critics," *Religion in Life* 1 (1932), p. 138. See also idem, *A Philosophy of Religion*. Here Brightman acknowledges Knudson's as "the best statement of objections" to his doctrine of the Given (p. 324n.).

[45]Knudson, *The Doctrine of Redemption* (New York: Abingdon Press, 1933), p. 203.

[46]Ibid., p. 204.

[47]Ibid.

[48]This is also the criticism of Andrew Banning. See his article "Professor Brightman's Theory of a Limited God: A Criticism," *Harvard Theological Review* 27/3 (July 1934), p. 152.

[49]Knudson, *The Doctrine of God* (New York: Abingdon Press, 1930), p. 212. For a full discussion of Knudson's seven points against Brightman's theory of the finite-infinite God see pp. 204–12.

[50]Brightman, "The Given and its Critics," *Religion in Life* 1 (1932), pp. 134–45. It should be noted that Brightman's response is to the criticisms Knudson makes in *The Doctrine of God* (1930). Here Knudson makes four criticisms: (1) The nonrational Given thwarts permanently God's ability to achieve God's purpose in the world; (2) The denial of divine omnipotence is also a denial of God's goodness and moral perfection; (3) There is too sharp a distinction between God's nature and God's will; (4) There is no scientific or religious ground for the claim that some evils are absolutely irrational and irreducible to good. In my discussion I basically followed Knudson's more extended criticisms in his later book, *The Doctrine of Redemption* (1933). However, in a brief selection, "The Given and Its Critics," (*Religion in Life* 11/1 [1941–42], pp. 19–20), Brightman does refer to Knudson's critique in the latter book. He said he would try to show more clearly that "the finiteness of God's power is compatible with the infinity of His eternal duration and of his goodness," and "that God's will to create man under the conditions of The Given does not involve him in the same responsibility as if he had created the Given" (pp. 19–20).

[51]Ibid., p. 141.

[52]Flewelling, "Brightman: Ex Umbras in Lucem," *The Personalist* 34/4 (October 1953), p. 345.

[53]Ibid., p. 346.

[54]Brightman, "The Given and its Critics," p. 137.

[55]S. Paul Schilling, *God and Human Anguish* (Nashville: Abingdon Press, 1977), pp. 242–43.

[56]Ibid., p. 242.

[57]Ibid., p. 243.

[58]Ibid.

[59]Ibid.

[60]Brightman, *The Finding of God*, p. 186.

[61]Brightman, "The Given and Its Critics," (1932), p. 136.

[62]William James, *The Varieties of Religious Experience* (New York: Modern Library, 1902), pp. 507, 514.

[63]Brightman, "The Given and Its Critics," (1932), p. 142.

[64]Ibid.

[65]Brightman, *The Finding of God*, p. 186.

[66]Ibid.

[67]Bertocci, *Introduction to the Philosophy of Religion*, pp. 436–37. See also Brightman, *The Problem of God*, p. 185.

[68]Bertocci, *Introduction to the Philosophy of Religion*, p. 436.

[69]Ibid.
[70]Brightman, *A Philosophy of Religion*, p. 340.
[71]Brightman, *The Finding of God*, p. 183.
[72]Ibid.

Chapter 8. Chief Elements in Personalistic Ethics

[1]See Francis J. McConnell, "Bowne and Personalism," Brightman, ed., *Personalism in Theology* (Boston: Boston Univ. Press, 1943), p. 33.
[2]Brightman, "Personalism and the Influence of Bowne," Brightman, ed., *Proceedings of the Sixth International Congress of Philosophy* (New York: Longmans, Green and Company, 1927), p. 164.
[3]Bowne, *The Principles of Ethics* (New York: American Book Company, 1892), p. 293.
[4]Ibid., p. viii.
[5]Bowne, *Studies in Christianity* (Boston: Houghton Mifflin Company, 1909), p. 334.
[6]Ibid., p. 344.
[7]See Brightman, *Moral Laws* (New York: Abingdon Press, 1933), chap. 6.
[8]Bowne, *The Principles of Ethics*, pp. 97, 189, 193, 203, 216–17.
[9]Ibid., p. 190.
[10]Ibid., p. 97.
[11]Ibid., p. 190.
[12]Ibid., pp. 150–51.
[13]Ibid., p. 200.
[14]Ibid., p. 202.
[15]Ibid., pp. 194–95.
[16]Brightman, "Tasks of Personalistic Philosophy," *The Personalist* 7 (1921), p. 263.
[17]Bowne, *The Principles of Ethics*, p. 203.
[18]Ibid., p. 161.
[19]Frederick Douglass, *The Life and Times of Frederick Douglass* (New York: Collier Books, 1962) [1892], p. 474. It is also important to note that this third version of Douglass' autobiography appeared the same year as Bowne's book *The Principles of Ethics*. One wonders why there is no mention of Douglass and his people, the race problem, and black women's suffrage. Indeed, it is noteworthy that the first National Conference of Colored Women convened under the leadership of Josephine St. Pierre Ruffin in Boston, July 29–31, 1895, during a time Bowne was teaching at Boston University. Although Douglass died that year, he gave numerous speeches and lectures on race in Boston and the New England area. Yet to date no evidence has surfaced indicating that Bowne, the father of American Personalism, was in dialogue with any of this. Indeed, from all apparent indications, the same criticism that S. Paul Schilling makes of Albert C. Knudson's social ethics may be made of Bowne: "There are some regrettable gaps in Knudson's treatment of Christian social ethics. He is quite realistic in listing attitudes of racial superiority among the major causes of war, but he makes no mention of racial segregation and other forms of injustice to minorities within nations like the United States" (Schilling, "Albert Cornelius Knudson: Person and Theologian," Deats and Robb, eds., *The Boston Personalist Tradition* (Macon, Ga.: Mercer Univ. Press, 1986), pp. 102–3).
[20]Bowne, *The Principles of Ethics*, p. 161.
[21]Plato, *The Republic of Plato*, trans. Francis M. Cornford (New York: Oxford Univ. Press, 1976), pp. 144–55.
[22]See Richard McKeon, ed., *The Basic Works of Aristotle* (New York: Random House, 1941), pp. 1143–45.
[23]Rosemary Agonito, ed., *History of Ideas of Women: A Source Book* (New York: Perigee Books, 1977), pp. 41, 43–54.
[24]Bowne, *The Principles of Ethics*, pp. 161, 193. See also McKeon, ed., *The Basic Works of Aristotle*, pp. 1130–32. Aristotle made clear that both reason and fact reveal that by nature some are destined to be slaves and others masters. "For that some should rule and others be ruled is a thing not only necessary, but expedient; from the hour of their birth, some are marked out for subjection, others for rule" (p. 1132).
[25]Bowne, *The Principles of Ethics*, p. 193.
[26]Etienne Gilson, *The Spirit of Medieval Philosophy* (New York: Scribners, 1936), p. 190.
[27]Quoted in Walter G. Muelder and Laurence Sears, eds., *The Development of American Philosophy* (Boston: Houghton Mifflin Company, 1940), p. 221.
[28]Bowne, "Concerning Miracle," *The Harvard Theological Review* (1910), p. 162. This article was published posthumously.
[29]Bowne, *Metaphysics* (New York: Harper, 1882), p. 293.

³⁰Bowne, "Concerning Miracle," p. 146.
³¹Bowne, *Metaphysics*, pp. 285, 292.
³²Ibid., p. 289.
³³Bowne, "Concerning Miracle," p. 148.
³⁴Bowne *Metaphysics*, pp. 291–92.
³⁵Bowne, "Concerning Miracle" p. 159.
³⁶Bowne, *The Principles of Ethics*, p. 161.
³⁷McConnell, "Bowne and the Social Questions," Wilm, ed., *Studies in Philosophy and Theology* (New York: Abingdon Press, 1922), p. 131.
³⁸Bowne, *The Principles of Ethics*, p. 150.
³⁹Ibid., p. 152.
⁴⁰Ibid., p. 150.
⁴¹Ibid., pp. vii, 106, 132, 133.
⁴²McConnell, "Bowne and the Social Questions," p. 131.
⁴³Bowne, *The Principles of Ethics*, p. 72.
⁴⁴Ibid., 133.
⁴⁵Bishop Joseph Butler (1692–1752) characterized conscience or the "ought imperative" in this way. "Had it strength, as it has right; had it power, as it has manifest authority, it would absolutely govern the world." [*Five Sermons* (New York: Liberal Arts Press, 1950), p. 41].
⁴⁶Bowne, *The Principles of Ethics*, p. 134.
⁴⁷Ibid., p. viii.
⁴⁸Ibid., p. 139.
⁴⁹Ibid., p. 140.
⁵⁰Ibid., p. 133.
⁵¹Ibid., p. 307.
⁵²I first heard Muelder characterize Bowne's ethics this way during the summer of 1989 when he and I did a critical study of Bowne's text *The Principles of Ethics*. Inasmuch as Bowne placed so much emphasis on development and pursuit of moral ends, I think this an accurate description.
⁵³Bowne, *The Principles of Ethics*, p. 139.
⁵⁴Ibid., p. 132.
⁵⁵Ibid., p. 150.
⁵⁶Ibid., p. 133.

Chapter 9. Personalism and Moral Laws

¹See Walter G. Muelder, "Martin Luther King, Jr., and the Moral Laws," Paper read at Morehouse College, 24 March 1983.
²Bowne, *The Principles of Ethics* (New York: American Book Co., 1892) p. 165.
³Bowne, *Metaphysics* (New York: Harper, 1882) part 3, chap. 4; also pp. 92, 406, 407.
⁴Bowne, *Theory of Thought and Knowledge* (New York: Harper&Brothers, 1897), pp. 239–44.
⁵Bowne, *Metaphysics*, p. 407.
⁶Bowne, *The Principles of Ethics*, p. 166. Bowne discusses much of his view on ethical freedom in chapter 4.
⁷For example, see pp. 77, 105, 164, 196, 197, 201, 255.
⁸For a discussion of moral laws in Bowne's work see my article "Moral Laws in Borden P. Bowne's *Principles of Ethics*," *The Personalist Forum*, (Fall 1990), pp. 161–81.
⁹Ibid.
¹⁰Muelder and Sears, eds., *The Development of American Philosophy* (Boston: Houghton Mifflin Company, 1940), p. 489.
¹¹See Knudson, *The Philosophy of Personalism* (New York: Abingdon Press, 1927) Flewelling, *Personalism and the Problems of Philosophy* (New York: Methodist Book Concern, 1915); idem, *Creative Personality* (New York: Macmillan Company, 1926); idem, *The Person* (Los Angeles: Ward Ritchie Press, 1952).
¹²Paul Deats, Jr., a fourth-generation personalist, suggests that there is a connection between Francis J. McConnell and Brightman's formulation of the moral law system. Deats contends that five of the laws are implicit in various of McConnell's books written between 1923 and 1932. "There is the obligation to pursue self-imposed ideals or goals; the requirement that one consider consequences of an action; the necessary attention to be given to the most inclusive end; the need to specify the good particular to a situation; and the injunction to cooperation (the last foreshadowing the communitarian laws)." Deats then draws the conclusion that Brightman's systematic formulation of the moral laws grew out of his discussions with

McConnell and others. [See Deats, "Bishop Francis J. McConnell and Social Justice," Deats and Robb, eds., *The Boston Personalist Tradition* (Macon, Ga.: Mercer Univ. Press, 1986), pp. 151–52.] There is no doubt that several of the moral laws that later appear in Brightman's system are implicit in McConnell's writings. But we need to go further and say that Deats's discovery merely lends more credence to my thesis that all of the moral laws appear in some form in Bowne's text on ethics. We must not forget that McConnell was a disciple of Bowne. In addition, he wrote the only book-length biography of Bowne.

[13]Brightman, "The Tasks Confronting a Personalistic Philosophy," *The Personalist* 2 (1921) p. 163.

[14]Quoted in ibid.

[15]Alfred N. Whitehead, *Process and Reality* (New York: Free Press, 1978) [1929], p. 39.

[16]Brightman, "The Tasks Confronting a Personalistic Philosophy,"pp. 164–65.

[17]Brightman, *Moral Laws* (New York: Abingdon Press, 1933), pp. 9, 13, 29, 30, 94.

[18]Bertocci, "The Personalism of Edgar S. Brightman and Ultimate Reality," p. 44.

[19]L. Harold DeWolf, *Responsible Freedom* (New York: Harper, 1971), p. 144.

[20]Ibid., chap. 7.

[21]Brightman, *Moral Laws*, p. 94.

[22]Ibid.

[23]Ibid., p. 95.

[24]Ibid., p. 107.

[25]Ibid., p. 87.

[26]Ibid., p. 135.

[27]DeWolf, *Responsible Freedom*, p. 145.

[28]Brightman, *Moral Laws*, p. 30.

[29]Ibid., p. 31.

[30]Ibid., p. 164.

[31]Ibid., p. 156.

[32]Knudson, *The Philosophy of Personalism*, chap. 1.

[33]Brightman, *An Introduction to Philosophy*, rev. ed., ed. Robert N. Beck (New York: Holt, Rinehart and Winston,1963), chap. 3.

[34]Brightman, *Moral Laws*, pp. 129–32.

[35]Muelder, "Personalism's Debt to Hegel," *The Boston Personalist Tradition*, p. 47.

[36]Brightman, *Moral Laws*, p. 204.

[37]Ibid., p. 242.

[38]Ibid., p. 94.

[39]Bowne, *The Principles of Ethics*, p. 69.

[40]Ibid., p. 210.

[41]Brightman, *Moral Laws*, p. 235.

[42]See DeWolf, "Ethical Implications for Criminal Justice," *The Boston Personalist Tradition*, p. 222; idem, *Responsible Freedom*, chap. 7.

[43]See Muelder, *Moral Law in Christian Social Ethics* (Richmond, Va.: John Knox Press, 1966).

[44]DeWolf, *Responsible Freedom*, chap. 7.

[45]DeWolf, "Ethical Implications for Criminal Justice," p. 223.

[46]See McConnell, *Personal Christianity* (New York: Fleming H. Revell Company, 1914), pp. 48, 185.

[47]DeWolf, "Ethical Implications for Criminal Justice," p. 224.

[48]Muelder, "Communitarian Dimensions of the Moral Laws," *The Boston Personalist Tradition*, p. 241.

[49]Brightman, "Personality as a Metaphysical Principle," Brightman, ed., *Personalism in Theology* (Boston: Boston Univ. Press, 1943), pp. 59–60.

[50]Muelder, "Communitarian Dimensions of the Moral Laws," *The Boston Personalist Tradition*, p. 244.

[51]John W. Buckham, *Personality and the Christian Ideal* (Boston: The Pilgrim Press, 1909), p. 21. Although more influenced by Howison, Buckham acknowledged his appreciation for Bowne (p. vi).

[52]Muelder, "Communitarian Dimensions of the Moral Laws," *The Boston Personalist Tradition*, p. 240.

[53]Muelder, "Edgar S. Brightman: Person and Moral Philosopher," *The Boston Personalist Tradition*, p. 110.

[54]See McConnell, *By the Way: An Autobiography* (New York: Abingdon-Cokesbury Press, 1942). McConnell characterizes Niebuhr as one of the "notables" who impacted his life in significant ways. "Any account of what I have seen during the past years would be incomplete

without some reference to Reinhold Niebuhr. I have known 'Reinie' since the days of his pastorate in Detroit. From those days on I have thought of him as introducing a note of seriousness and solidity into American theological thinking otherwise infrequent, not to say lacking…Even those who find Niebuhr hard to understand see that his thought is God-centered and that out from that transcendent source stream the influences which can be made immanent in a transformed society" (p. 254). Indeed, McConnell even anticipated Niebuhr's provocative thesis in *Moral Man and Immoral Society* (which lambasted the naive sentimentality of liberal theology regarding individual and group relations) by ten years. Niebuhr essentially argued that individuals tend to be more moral than groups. He failed, however, to point out that the individual in the group may also be more inclined to do the right thing as opposed to the isolated individual outside the group. Anticipating the Niebuhrian thesis, McConnell's view of the relation between the individual and the group was more far-reaching. "A group of men, all of them individually sane, can as a group act insanely. [Here we see the influence of both Niebuhr and McConnell's experience working with groups.] Or, to take the other side, a group of persons individually rather selfish can as a group act unselfishly. Men find loosed within them in groups forces different from those they know when they are alone. The purpose of any gospel that understands itself is to get hold of these group powers and use them for righteousness" [McConnell, *Christian Citizenship* (New York: Methodist Book Concern, 1922), p. 11]

Niebuhr was also influenced by McConnell and did not hesitate to praise him. In one place he wrote that McConnell is "our most outstanding social prophet" [Niebuhr, "Religion: True or Useful?" *Christian Century* (September 23, 1926), p. 1161]. In the journal he kept during his pastorate in Detroit, Niebuhr wrote: "I am glad to hear of the new honors which have come to Bishop M[cConnell]. He seems to me to be the most glorious figure in American church life. To have a philosopher, prophet and statesman all rolled into one, and to have that one achieve a peculiar eminence in our religious life is a clear illustration of how the richest character is achieved when various, seemingly incompatible, tendencies and functions are fused in one personality…For years he has carried heavy responsibilities as a church leader; and it is always more difficult for a responsible leader, tied to an organization, to speak bravely than an irresponsible prophet. Yet he has accomplished it. Here is a vindication of the power of the Christian life. Here is a Thomas Aquinas and an Innocent III and something of a Francis all under one hat. He is not as much of an absolutist as Francis, of course; and his power is not as great as that of Innocent. But his learning would compare favorably with that of Aquinas, and like the great medieval philosopher, he has combined the study of metaphysics with that of social economy" [Niebuhr, *Leaves from the Notebook of a Tamed Cynic* (New York: Harper, 1980) [1929], pp. 193–94].

[55]McConnell, "Bowne and the Social Questions," Wilm, ed., *Studies in Philosophy and Theology* (New York: Abingdon Press, 1922), p. 135.

[56]Ibid.

[57]Oldham defined middle axioms as "attempts to define the directions in which, in a particular state of society, Christian faith must express itself. They are not binding for all time, but are provisional definitions of the type of behavior required of Christians at a given period and in given circumstances" [W. A. Visser't Hooft and J. H. Oldham, *The Church and Its Function in Society* (Chicago and New York: Willett, Clark and Company, 1937), p. 194.

[58]Muelder, "Christian Social Ethics Looks Forward," *Nexus* (May 1964), pp. 4, 5.

[59]Deats, "Conflict and Reconciliation in Communitarian Social Ethics," *The Boston Personalist Tradition*, p. 276.

[60]Ibid., p. 274.

[61]Ibid., p. 273.

[62]Ibid., pp. 280–81.

[63]Ibid., p. 285.

[64]See the following books by J. Philip Wogaman: *Guaranteed Annual Income* (Nashville: Abingdon Press, 1968); *A Christian Method of Moral Judgment* (Philadelphia: Westminster Press, 1976); *The Great Economic Debate* (Philadelphia: Westminster Press, 1977); *Faith and Fragmentation* (Philadelphia: Westminster, 1985); *Economics and Ethics* (Philadelphia: Fortress Press, 1986); *Christian Moral Judgment* (Louisville, Ky.: Westminster/John Knox Press, 1989). The latter text is a revision of *A Christian Method of Moral Judgment* (Philadelphia: Westminster Press, 1976).

[65]Wogaman, *Faith and Fragmentation*, pp. x–xi.

[66]See Wogaman, *Christian Moral Judgment*.

[67]Wogaman, *A Christian Method of Moral Judgment*, p. 40.

[68]Ibid., pp. 36–37.

[69]Brightman, *Moral Laws*, p. 171. We also see this tension between perfectionist principles and situation in Bowne. For example, there was for Bowne what amounted to a dialecti-

cal tension between the formal principle of good will and the actual situation in which one tries to actualize or apply it. Therefore the form that good will takes will be shaped to a large extent by the specific situation.

[70]Wogaman, *A Christian Method of Moral Judgment*, pp. 52–59.

[71]Ibid., pp. 70–104.

[72]Ibid., p. 106–10.

[73]Ibid., pp. 136–51.

[74]Ibid., p. 132.

[75]Ibid., p. 133.

[76]Brightman, *Moral Laws*, p. 135.

[77]Wogaman, *A Christian Method of Moral Judgment*, p. 97.

[78]Bowne, *The Principles of Ethics*, p. 199.

[79]Ibid., pp. 106, 108, 190–91, 216.

[80]Wogaman, *A Christian Method of Moral Judgment*, pp. 94–95.

[81]Muelder, "Pilgrimage to Communitarian Personalism," Leroy S. Rouner, ed., *Foundations of Ethics* (South Bend, Ind.: Univ. of Notre Dame Press, 1983), pp. 89–90.

[82]Bertocci and Millard, *Personality and the Good: Psychological and Ethical Perspectives* (New York: David McKay, 1966), pp. 411–618.

[83]Ibid., p. 413.

[84]Ibid., p. 428.

[85]Wogaman, *A Christian Method of Moral Judgment*, p. 29.

[86]See Stephen B. Oates, *Let the Trumpet Sound: The Life of Martin Luther King, Jr.* (New York: Harper & Row, 1982), p. 6.

[87]Kenneth L. Smith and Ira G. Zepp, Jr., *Search for the Beloved Community: The Thinking of Martin Luther King, Jr.* (Valley Forge, Pa.: Judson Press, 1974), p. 22.

[88]Cited in Leo Sandon, Jr., "Boston University Personalism and Southern Baptist Theology," *Foundations* 20 (April–June 1977), p. 105. King wrote about Brightman's influence in a 1957 publication in *Bostonia* (Spring 1957), p. 7. He also mentioned in his application to Boston University Graduate School the influence of Brightman's ideas on his thinking as a seminarian at Crozer Theological Seminary [See Clayborne Carson, ed., *The Papers of Martin Luther King, Jr.* (Berkeley, Calif.: Univ. of California Press, 1992), 1:390]. King noted Brightman's presence at Boston University as one of two reasons that the institution appealed to him.

[89]Carson, ed., *The Papers of Martin Luther King, Jr.*, 1:390.

[90]John J. Ansbro, *Martin Luther King, Jr.: The Making of a Mind* (Maryknoll, N.Y.: Orbis, 1983), p. 77. The research paper was written for DeWolf and entitled "The Personalism of J. M. E. McTaggart Under Criticism" (p. 287 n. 32). King found McTaggart's rejection of freedom to be repulsive, since he accepted the Bowne-Brightman view that freedom is essential to what it means to be a person.

[91]See King's doctoral dissertation, "A Comparison of the Conceptions of God in the Thinking of Henry Nelson Wieman and Paul Tillich," (Ph.D. diss., Boston University, 1955). Here King opts for a doctrine of God similar to that of Bowne and DeWolf.

[92]Coretta Scott King, *My Life With Martin Luther King, Jr.* (New York: Holt, Rinehart and Winston, 1969), p. 92.

[93]See David Garrow, ed., *Martin Luther King, Jr., and the Civil Rights Movement* (New York: Carlson Publishing Inc., 1989), 1:xiv. Garrow also argues that King often used the phrase "the dignity and worth of all human personality" in sermons and speeches because "it was the consonance between King's already-developed views and the principal theme of personalism that led King to adopt and give voice to that tenet so firmly and consistently" (Garrow, "The Intellectual Development of Martin Luther King, Jr.: Influences and Commentaries," Garrow, ed., *Martin Luther King, Jr. and the Civil Rights Movement*, 2:445.) In addition, Garrow complains in an endnote that King's teachers and mentors at Boston University "have badly overstated the formative influence their instruction and personalism had on King" (ibid., p. 451, n. 23). He then invites the reader to examine writings by DeWolf ["Martin Luther King, Jr., as Theologian," *Journal of the Interdenominational Theological Center* 4 (Spring 1977), pp. 1–11]; and Muelder ["Communitarian Christian Ethics: A Personal Statement and a Response," Deats, ed., *Toward a Discipline of Social Ethics* (Boston: Boston Univ. Press, 1972), pp. 295–320, at 299 and 314; and "Martin Luther King, Jr.'s, Ethics of Nonviolent Action," unpublished paper, 1985, King Center].

[94]See Keith D. Miller, *Voice of Deliverance: The Language of Martin Luther King, Jr., and Its Sources* (New York: The Free Press, 1992), pp. 7, 17.

[95]James H. Cone stresses this point in *Martin & Malcolm & America* (Maryknoll, N.Y.: Orbis, 1991), as does Garth Baker-Fletcher in *Somebodyness: Martin Luther King, Jr., and the Theory of Dignity* (Minneapolis: Fortress Press, 1993).

[96]King, *Stride Toward Freedom* (New York: Harper & Row, 1958), p. 100.

[97]King, *My Life With Martin Luther King, Jr.*, p. 92.

[98]Baker-Fletcher, *Somebodyness*, p. 61.

[99]In his senior sermon, King "declared that 'there are moral laws of the universe that man can no more violate with impunity than he can violate its physical laws'" [Branch, *Parting the Waters:America in the King Years, 1954–1963* (New York: Simon and Schuster, 1989), p. 68].

[100]See Smith and Zepp, Jr., *Search for the Beloved Community: The Thinking of Martin Luther King, Jr.*, pp. 110–13.

[101]Muelder, "Martin Luther King, Jr. and the Moral Laws," (Unpublished paper read at Morehouse College, March 24, 1983), p. 2.

[102]Ibid., p. 12. See Thomas Hill Green, *Prolegomena to Ethics* (Oxford: Clarendon Press, 1884), p. 193.

[103]Muelder, "Martin Luther King, Jr. and the Moral Laws," p. 2.

[104]Ansbro, *Martin Luther King, Jr.: The Making of a Mind*, p. 79.

[105]See King, "A Time to Break Silence," Washington, ed., *A Testament of Hope*, pp. 231–44.

[106]See Brightman, *Moral Laws*, p. 181.

[107]Ibid.

[108]Ansbro, *Martin Luther King, Jr.: The Making of a Mind*, p. 82.

[109]Ibid., p. 85.

[110]Ibid., p. 86.

[111]Ibid., pp. 76, 86.

[112]Muelder, *The Ethical Edge of Christian Theology: Forty Years of Communitarian Personalism* (New York: The Edwin Mellen Press, 1983), pp. 6–7.

[113]Bertocci, "The Personalism of Edgar S. Brightman and Ultimate Reality," p. 47.

[114]DeWolf, *Responsible Freedom*, p. 174; also pp. 174–76.

[115]William James, *Psychology* (The Briefer Course) (New York: Henry Holt and Company, 1910), p. 139.

[116]Ibid., p. 143.

Chapter 10. The "Unpopularity" of Personalism

[1]Deats was comforted by the discovery that Bowne, the father of American personalism, came to call himself a personalist rather late in his career, between 1905 and 1907. Deats studied with several of the chief third-generation personalists, including Walter G. Muelder, S. Paul Schilling, L. Harold DeWolf, Paul E. Johnson, John Lavely, and had close contact with Peter A. Bertocci. In this sense he could not avoid being influenced by personalism. He remained "a closet personalist" until he "initiated the seminar on 'Ethics and Theology in Personalism' in 1980 and persuaded John Lavely to be coteacher and personal tutor." Deats gradually came to recognize himself as a personalist. [See Deats, "Conflict and Reconciliation in Communitarian Social Ethics," Deats and Robb, eds., *The Boston Personalist Tradition* (Macon, Ga.: Mercer Univ. Press, 1986), pp. 274, 276].

[2]Brightman, "The Unpopularity of Personalism," *Methodist Review*, January 1921, p. 16.

[3]Knudson, *The Philosophy of Personalism* (Nashville: Abingdon Press, 1927), p. 20.

[4]Ibid. W. D. Weatherford wrote that "the most interesting and far-reaching tendency of modern philosophy is that toward personalism." This was in 1916, just five years before Brightman wrote two articles addressing the "unpopularity of personalism." See Weatherford, *Personal Elements in Religious Life* (Nashville: Publishing House Methodist Episcopal Church, South, 1916), p. 33.

[5]Flewelling, *The Person* (Los Angeles, Calif.: The Ward Ritchie Press, 1952), p. xi.

[6]Johannes Hirschberger, *The History of Philosophy*, trans. Rt. Rev. Anthony N. Fuerst (Milwaukee, Wis.: The Bruce Publishing Company, 1959), 2:681.

[7]Brightman, "Why is Personalism Unpopular?" *Methodist Review* (July 1921), pp. 534–35.

[8]Bertocci, et al., "The Renaissance of Bowne," *Bostonia* 34 (Fall 1960), p. 23.

[9]Bowne, *The Philosophy of Herbert Spencer* (New York: Hunt & Eaton, 1874), p. 283.

[10]Ibid.

[11]Bowne, *Metaphysics* (New York: Harper, 1882), p. v.

[12]Bowne, *Metaphysics* (1898), pp. v–vi.

[13]Wolfhart Pannenberg, *Metaphysics and the Idea of God* (Edinburgh: T. & T. Clark, 1988), chap. 1.

[14]King, "The Ethical Demands for Integration," Washington, ed., *A Testament of Hope*, p. 122.

[15]See Walter G. Muelder, "Edgar S. Brightman: Person and Moral Philosopher," Deats and Robb, eds., *The Boston Personalist Tradition*, p. 110.

[16]Bowne, *Personalism* (New York: American Book Co., 1902), p. 277.

[17]Bowne, *Theism* (Boston: Houghton Mifflin, 1908), p. 57.

[18]Muelder, *Moral Law in Christian Social Ethics* (Richmond, Va.: John Knox Press, 1966), p. 113, and chap. 2.

[19]McConnell, *Personal Christianity* (New York: Fleming H. Revell Company, 1914), p. 48. See also p. 185.

[20]Nels F. S. Ferré, *The Christian Understanding of God* (New York: Harper, 1951), p. 39.

[21]Ferré, *Christianity and Society* (New York: Harper & Brothers, 1950), p. 118.

[22]John W. Buckham, *Personality and the Christian Ideal* (New York: Pilgrim Press, 1909), p. 21. See also pp. 42, 44, 53, 54. In the preface, Buckham writes of "the exceeding value" of Bowne's book *Personalism*, though his own book was nearly completed before its appearance in 1908. He thought highly of Bowne's philosophy and used the aforementioned book in his courses. The single most important book that expresses Buckham's personalism is *Christianity and Personality* (New York: Roundtable Press, 1936).

[23]Harold H. Oliver, "Relational Personalism," *The Personalist Forum* 5/1 (Spring 1989), p. 39.

[24]See Erazim Kohak, *The Embers and the Stars* (Chicago: Univ. of Chicago Press, 1984). See especially pp. 124–30, 205–18.

[25]Oliver, "Relational Personalism," *The Personalist Forum* 5/1 (Spring 1989), p. 36.

[26]Ibid., p. 38.

[27]"The narrow isolation of personality in modern individualism," writes the Russian personalist Nicolas Berdyaev (1874–1948), "is the destruction and not the triumph of personality." Bowneans concur with this point. See Berdyaev, *The Destiny of Man* (New York: Harper, 1960), p. 58. Berdyaev, exiled from his Russian homeland, was clearly himself a personalist, and was encouraged by the work of French personalists with whom he was acquainted. In his posthumously published autobiography, *Dream and Reality: An Essay in Autobiography* (1951), he writes that he was present at the founding meeting of the personalist journal *Esprit*. "I was greatly moved when at the foundation meeting it was unanimously adopted that the fundamental purpose and concern of *Esprit* should be the vindication of man. I felt that here was a place where a new spirit was blowing" (New York: Macmillan, 1951), p. 274.

[28]Knudson, *The Philosophy of Personalism*, pp. 76, 230–31. Knudson called this "panpsychistic personalism." Indeed, a student of Bertocci's and Millard's concluded: "Although Whitehead cannot, without some modification, be classified as a personalist, his similarity to Brightman in fixing the locus of values in the concrescent experience of actual entities, and his stress on the realization and stabilization of the higher types of values in personal order suggest a stronger personalistic emphasis than is usually attributed to him" [Wilbur Handley Mullen, "A Comparison of the Value Theories of E. S. Brightman and A. N. Whitehead" (Ph.D. diss., Boston Univ. Graduate School, 1955), p. 359]. Brightman himself had written: "The greatest Anglo-American philosopher of recent times, A. N. Whitehead (1861–1947), came from a realistic tradition, but his doctrines of creativity, actual occasions, prehensions, subjective aim, and God all point to panpsychistic personalism" [Brightman, "Personalism (Including Personal Idealism)," Vergilius Ferm, ed., *A History of Philosophical Systems* (New York: The Philosophical Library, 1950), p. 344]. Elsewhere Brightman wrote that "even Whitehead is essentially personalistic" [Brightman, "Personalistic Metaphysics of the Self," Warren E. Steinkraus and Robert N. Beck, eds., *Studies in Personalism: Selected Writings of Edgar Sheffield Brightman* (Utica, N. Y.: Meridian Publishing Company, 1984), p. 16].

[29]Gottfried Wilhelm von Leibniz, *Monadology and Other Philosophical Essays*, Paul Schrecker and Anne Martin Schrecker, trans. (Indianapolis: Bobbs-Merrill Company, 1965), p. 159.

[30]Brightman, "Personalism (Including Personal Idealism)," p. 341.

[31]Whitehead, *Process and Reality*, corrected edition by David Ray Griffin and Donald W. Sherburne (New York: The Free Press, 1978) [1929], Part 3.

[32]John Lavely, "Personalism Supports the Dignity of Nature," *The Personalist Forum* 2:1 (Spring 1986), p. 37.

[33]Mullen, "A Comparison of the Value Theories of E. S. Brightman and A. N. Whitehead," p. 334.

[34]Ibid., p. 336.

[35]William James, *Pragmatism* (New York: Longmans, Green and Company, 1907), p. 18. Yet it is clear that Bowne and James had the highest admiration for each other. We see evidence of this in a letter James wrote to Bowne in 1908 commenting on Bowne's recently published

book, *Personalism*. In part James wrote: "It seems to me a very weighty pronouncement, and form and matter taken together a splendid addition to American philosophy…It seems to me that you and I are now aiming at exactly the same end, though, owing to our different past, from which each retains special verbal habits, we often express ourselves so differently. It seemed to me over and over again that you were planting your feet identically in footprints which my feet were accustomed to—quite independently, of course, of my example, which was what made the coincidences so gratifying. The common foe of both of us is the dogmatist-rationalist-abstractionist. Our common desire is to redeem the concrete personal life which wells up in us from moment to moment." Cited in McConnell, *Borden Parker Bowne* (New York: Abingdon, 1929), pp. 276, 277.

[36]Robert Neville, Review of Deats and Robb, eds., *The Boston Personalist Tradition*, *The Personalist Forum* 5/1 (Spring 1989), p. 62.

[37]Knudson, *The Philosophy of Personalism*, p. 165.

[38]John Howie, "Can Personalism Provide a Theoretical Basis for an Environmental Ethics?" *The Personalist Forum* 7/2 (Fall 1991), pp. 35–36.

[39]McConnell, "Bowne and Personalism," Brightman, ed., *Personalism in Theology* (Boston: Boston Univ. Press, 1943), p. 36.

[40]Brightman, "Personalism as a Philosophy of Religion," *The Crozer Quarterly* 5/4 (October 1928), p. 394. It is interesting to note that one of the critics to whom Brightman is responding is his former student, Georgia Harkness, who came to reject idealistic for realistic personalism.

[41]Brightman, *Is God A Person?* (New York: Association Press, 1932), p. 14.

[42]Ibid., pp. 4–5.

[43]See Brightman, *Nature and Values* (New York: Abingdon Press, 1945).

[44]McConnell, *Humanism and Christianity* (New York: Macmillan, 1928), pp. 140–41.

[45]Paul W. Taylor, *Respect for Nature: A Theory of Environmental Ethics* (Princeton, N. J.: Princeton Univ. Press, 1986), pp. 14–16.

[46]Howie, "Human-Centered or Ecocentric Environmental Ethics?" (Unpublished paper read at the meeting of the Personalistic Discussion Group in Boston, 1993), p. 2.

[47]Ibid., p. 3.

[48]Bowne, *Theism*, p. 279.

[49]Bowne, *The Principles of Ethics* (New York: American Book Company, 1892), p. 150.

[50]See Bowne, *Theism*, pp. 275, 279.

[51]Harkness, *The Gospel and Our World* (New York: Abingdon-Cokesbury Press, 1959), p. 108.

[52]Ibid.

[53]Ibid., p. 109.

[54]Ibid., p. 108.

[55]DeWolf, *Responsible Freedom* (New York: Harper and Row, 1971), p. 246. See chap. 11.

[56]Quoted in ibid., p. 247.

[57]Brightman himself writes that "the personal mind is not any part of the body or of any other mind" [Brightman, *Person and Reality* (New York: Ronald Press, 1958), p. 272]. In addition, Brightman believed the unconscious to be a Situation Believed-in, and therefore "entirely inferential" (ibid., p. 273).

[58]See Brightman, *A Philosophy of Religion* (Englewood Cliffs, N.J.: Prentice Hall, 1940), p. 347. The point Lavely makes about Brightman's heavy emphasis on mind at the expense of the body is quite evident in this text. At one point Brightman writes that "no portion of an experient's nervous system nor any part of his body has ever been or can be a Situation Experienced by that experient" (ibid., p. 348). Later he says that "personal consciousness alone is experience, and all bodies, brains, and gods are objects of belief." And then: "But I—the experient, the person, the Situation Experienced—am not to be identified with what sustains any being. I am not my nervous system, the sun, or God" (ibid.). And yet it seems to me that it may be argued that as long as I am in this world I am these things, although I am most assuredly more than these. The truth is that in this world I never experience myself as disembodied. At least disembodiment is not a "normal" occurrence.

[59]Buckham, *Personality and the Christian Ideal*, p. 57.

[60]Brightman, *Person and Reality*, p. 271.

[61]Lavely, "Personalism Then and Now and Perhaps Hereafter," *The Personalist Forum* 4/2 (Fall 1988), p. 38.

[62]Jack F. Padgett, "Key to Personalism: A Moral Relation," *The Personalist Forum* 4/2 (Fall 1988), p. 45.

[63]Oliver prefers the term "self" since for him it is more universal than "person." See Oliver, "Relational Personalism," p. 27.

[64]See Tom Buford, "Person, Identity, and Imagination," *The Personalist Forum* 5/1 (Spring 1989), pp. 7–25.

[65]See Peter A. Bertocci, *The Person and Primary Emotions* (New York: Springer-Verlag, 1988). See especially chap. 3 regarding the mind-body relation.

[66]Bertocci, *The Person God Is* (London: Allen & Unwin, 1970) p. 42.

[67]King, *The Measure of a Man* (Philadelphia: Fortress Press, 1988) [1959], pp. 13–14.

[68]Ferré, *The Christian Understanding of God* (New York: Harper and Brothers, 1951), p. 34.

[69]DeWolf, *A Theology of the Living Church* (New York: Harper & Brothers, 1960) [1953], p. 153.

[70]Ibid., p. 155.

[71]Emmanuel Mounier, *Personalism* (Notre Dame, Ind.: Univ. of Notre Dame Press, 1952), p. 10.

[72]Ibid., p. 3.

[73]Ibid., p. 11.

[74]James Baldwin, *The Price of the Ticket* (New York: St. Martin's/Marek, 1985), p. 440.

Chapter 11. Toward a New Personalism

[1]Carolyn Hardville is a student of both womanist thought and personalism. She was one of the chief readers and respondents to this manuscript as it has unfolded over the past several years. The quote is from her critique.

[2]Imam Benjamin Karim, ed., *The End of White World Supremacy: Four Speeches by Malcolm X* (New York: Arcade Publishing, 1971), pp. 119–20.

[3]Steve Clark, ed., *Malcolm X Talks to Young People* (New York: Pathfinder, 1991) [1965], pp. 36–37.

[4]Alice Walker, *In Search of Our Mothers' Gardens: Womanist Prose* (New York: Harcourt Brace Jovanovich, 1983) [1967], pp. 244–49, 271, 376.

[5]Ibid., p. 250.

[6]Maya Angelou, *Poems* (New York: Bantam Books, 1986), p. 121.

[7]Audre Lorde, *Sister Outsider: Essays and Speeches* (Freedom, Calif.: The Crossing Press, 1984), pp. 174–75.

[8]Ibid., p. 173.

[9]Ibid., p. 114.

[10]Margaret Homans, "Audre Lorde," Valerie Smith, et al., eds., *African American Writers: Profiles of Their Lives and Works—From the 1700s to the Present* (New York: Macmillan, 1993) [1991], p. 211.

[11]Lorde, *Sister Outsider*, p. 175.

[12]Ibid., p. 62.

[13]Toni Morrison, *Beloved* (New York: Alfred Knopf, 1987), p. 88.

[14]Gabriel M. Setiloane, *African Theology: An Introduction* (Johannesburg: Skotaville Publishers, 1986), p. 41.

[15]Desmond Tutu, *Crying in the Wilderness* (Grand Rapids, Mich.: Eerdmans, 1982), p. 99.

[16]John S. Mbiti, *African Religions and Philosophy* (New York: Anchor Books, 1970), p. 141.

[17]Archie Smith, Jr., *The Relational Self* (Nashville: Abingdon Press, 1982), pp. 55, 58. See chaps. 2, 3.

[18]Here I take a clue from Berdyaev. Ethics must oppose "the final socialization of man which destroys the freedom of spirit and conscience." [*The Destiny of Man* (New York: Harper, 1960), p. 58.]

[19]Taken from Hardville's critique of this work during the developing manuscript stage.

[20]Few have written more eloquently and cogently about this need to be concrete and specific about both the image of God in persons in both genders and all races than the nineteenth-century black feminist Anna Julia Cooper (1858–1964). [See Cooper, *A Voice From the South* (New York: Oxford Univ. Press, 1988) {1892}, pp. 124–25)]. By all accounts Cooper was a forerunner to the present-day womanist movement. [See Karen Baker-Fletcher, "A 'Singing Something': The Literature of Anna Julia Cooper as a Resource For a Theological Anthropology of Voice" (Ph.D. diss., Harvard Univ., 1990), chaps. 7, 8.]

[21]Romero cited Saint Irenaeus' celebrated maxim: "'The glory of God is the living person.' And he translated this for El Salvador as: 'The glory of God is the living poor person.' God sincerely wills life, not death. And so God takes sides. God takes sides for life, and actively struggles against the idols of death…" [Jon Sobrino, *Archbishop Romero: Memories and Reflections* (Maryknoll, N. Y.: Orbis, 1990), p. 197].

[22]Bowne, *Theism* (New York: American Book Co., 1902), p. 269.

[23]Bowne, *Principles of Ethics* (New York; Harper & Brothers, 1892), p. 267.

[24]Bowne, *Theism*, p. 281.

[25]Berdyaev, *The Destiny of Man*, p. 55.

[26]Setiloane, *African Theology*, p. 40.

[27]Vine Deloria, Jr., *Custer Died for Your Sins* (Oklahoma: Univ. of Oklahoma Press, 1988) [1969], p. 103.

[28]See Frederick W. Turner III, ed., *The Portable North American Indian Reader* (New York: The Viking Press, 1974), p. 253.

[29]Deloria, *God Is Red* (New York: Grosset & Dunlap, 1973), p. 175. See also pp. 162–64, 266–67.

[30]John Collier, "A New Deal for the Red Man," Wilcomb D. Washburn, ed., *The Indian and the White Man* (New York: Anchor Books, 1964), p. 394.

[31]Ibid.

[32]See Paul W. Taylor, *Respect for Nature: A Theory of Environmental Ethics* (Princeton, N. J.: Princeton Univ. Press, 1986), pp. 14–16.

[33]Bowne, *The Immanence of God* (Boston: Houghton Mifflin, 1905), p. 130.

[34]Baker-Fletcher, *Somebodyness: Martin Luther King, Jr., and the Theory of Dignity* (Minneapolis: Fortress Press, 1993), pp. 171–72.

[35]Bowne, *The Principles of Ethics*, pp. 150, 161–62.

A Selected Bibliography of Works on Personalism

First Generation

Borden Parker Bowne (1847–1910)

BOOKS

The Philosophy of Herbert Spencer. New York: Nelson & Phillips, 1874, 1881; Hunt and Eaton, 1902.
Studies in Theism. New York: Phillips & Hunt, 1879; Cincinnati: Cranston & Stowe, 1907.
Metaphysics: A Study in First Principles. New York: Harper & Brothers, 1882.
Philosophy of Theism. New York: Harper & Brothers, 1887.
Principles of Ethics. New York: Harper & Brothers, 1892, 1898.
Theory of Thought and Knowledge. New York: Harper & Brothers, 1897; American Book Company, 1925; Kraus Reprint Corp., 1968.
Metaphysics, Revised Edition. New York: Harper & Brothers, 1898, 1910, 1926; Boston Univ. Press, 1943.
Theism. New York: American Book Company, 1902 (revision of *Philosophy of Theism* includes the Deems Lectures at New York University).
The Immanence of God. Boston: Houghton Mifflin, 1905.
Personalism. Boston: Houghton Mifflin, 1908; Norwood, Mass.: The Plimpton Press, 1936 (revised edition includes the N. W. Harris Lectures at Northwestern University in 1907).
Studies in Christianity. Boston: Houghton Mifflin, 1909.
Kant and Spencer: A Critical Exposition. Boston: Houghton Mifflin, 1912. (Posthumous.)

ARTICLES

"The Philosophical Outlook." In *Congress of Arts and Science,* edited by Howard J. Roger. Boston: Houghton Mifflin & Company, 1905.
"The Logic of Religious Belief." In *Representative Essays of Borden Parker Bowne,* edited by Warren Steinkraus. Utica, N. Y.: Meridian Publishing Co., 1980.
"Concerning Miracles." *The Harvard Theological Review* (1910). (Posthumous.)

George Holmes Howison (1836–1916)

BOOKS

The Limits of Evolution, and Other Essays Illustrating the Metaphysical Theory of Personal Idealism. New York: The Macmillan Company, 1901, 1904 (second edition, revised and enlarged).

ARTICLES

"The City of God, and the True God as Its Head." In *The Conception of God,* by Howison, Josiah Royce, Sidney Edward Mezes, and Joseph Le Conte. New York: Macmillian, 1897.
"Personal Idealism on the Solution of the Enigma of Evil." *Hibbert Journal* 1 (October, 1902) London.
"Personal Idealism and Its Ethical Bearings." *International Journal of Ethics* 13 (July, 1903).
"In the Matter of Personal Idealism." *Mind: A Quarterly Review of Psychology and Philosophy* 12 (April, 1903) London.

Second Generation

John Wesley Edward Bowen (1855–1933)

"A Psychological Principle in Revelation." *Methodist Review* (September, 1891).
"What Shall the Harvest Be?" Washington, D.C.: Asbury Methodist Episcopal Church, 1892.
"Apology for Higher Education of the Negro." *Methodist Review* (1897).

Edgar Sheffield Brightman (1884–1953)

BOOKS

An Introduction to Philosophy. New York: Henry Holt, 1925 (revised editions 1951, 1963).
Religious Values. New York: Abingdon Press, 1925.
A Philosophy of Ideals. New York: Henry Holt, 1928.
Is God a Person? New York: Association Press, 1932.
Moral Laws. New York: Abingdon Press, 1933.
Personality and Religion. New York: Abingdon Press, 1934.
A Philosophy of Religion. Englewood Cliffs, N.J.: Prentice Hall, 1940.
Personalism in Theology (ed.). Boston: Boston Univ. Press, 1943.
Nature and Values. New York: Abingdon-Cokesbury Press, 1945.
Persons and Values. Boston: Boston Univ. Press, 1952.
Person and Reality: An Introduction to Metaphysics, edited by Peter A. Bertocci, Janette G. Newhall, and Robert S. Brightman. New York: Ronald Press, 1958. (Posthumous.)

ARTICLES

"Why is Personalism Unpopular?" *Methodist Review* (July 1921).
"The Finite Self." In *Contemporary Idealism in America*, Clifford Barrett ed. New York: Russell & Russell, 1964.
"Personalism and the Influence of Bowne." In *Proceedings of the Sixth International Congress of Philosophy*, Brightman, ed. New York: Longmans, Green and Company, 1927.

John Wright Buckham (1864–1945)

Personality and the Christian Ideal. Boston: The Pilgrim Press, 1909.
The Humanity of God. New York: Harper and Brothers, 1928.
George Holmes Howison, Philosopher and Teacher: A Selection from His Writings with a Biographical Sketch, co-edited Buckham with George Malcolm Stratton. Berkeley, Calif.: Univ. of California Press, 1934.
Christianity and Personality. New York: Round Table, 1936.

Mary Whiton Calkins (1863–1930)

BOOKS

The Good Man and the Good. New York: Macmillan, 1918.
The Persistent Problems of Philosophy, fifth rev. ed. New York: Macmillan Company, 1925.

ARTICLES

"The Personalistic Platform." *Journal of Philosophy* 30/16 (August 3, 1933).
"The Philosophical Credo of an Absolutistic Personalist." In *Contemporary American Philosophy*, George P. Adams and William P. Montague, eds. New York: Russell & Russell, 1962.
"The Personalist Conception of Nature." *The Philosophical Review* 28/2 (March 1919).

George Albert Coe (1861–1951)

BOOKS

Education in Religion and Morals. New York: Revell, 1904.
A Social Theory of Religious Education. New York: Scribners, 1917.

ARTICLES

"My Search for What is Most Worthwhile." *Religious Education,* vol. 47 (1952).

Ralph Tyler Flewelling (1871–1960)

BOOKS

Personalism and the Problems of Philosophy: An Appreciation of the Work of Borden Parker Bowne. New York: Methodist Book Concern, 1915.
Bergson and Personal Realism. New York: Abingdon Press, 1920.
Creative Personality: A Study in Philosophical Reconciliation. New York: The Macmillan Co., 1926.
The Person, or the Significance of Man. Los Angeles: The Ward Ritchie Press, 1952.

ARTICLES

"Bergson, Ward, and Euken, in their Relation to Bowne." *The Methodist Review* 46/3 (May–June 1914).
"To the Gentle Personalist." *The Personalist* 1 (April 1920).
"Bergson and Personalism." *The Personalist* 14 (1933).
"James, Schiller and Personalism." *The Personalist* 23 (1942).
"Studies in American Personalism." *The Personalist* 31/4 (Autumn 1950).
"George Holmes Howison: Prophet of Freedom." *The Personalist* 38 (1957).

Albert Cornelius Knudson (1873–1953)

BOOKS

The Religious Teaching of the Old Testament. New York: Abingdon Press, 1918.
The Philosophy of Personalism. New York: Abingdon Press, 1927.
The Doctrine of God. New York: Abingdon Press, 1930.
The Doctrine of Redemption. New York: Abingdon Press, 1933.
The Principles of Christian Ethics. New York: Abingdon-Cokesbury Press, 1943.
Basic Issues in Christian Thought. New York: Abingdon-Cokesbury Press, 1950.

ARTICLES

"Borden Parker Bowne." *Bostonia* (1917).
"A Personalistic Approach to Theology." In *Contemporary American Theology, Volume 1,* Vergilius Ferm, ed. New York: Round Table, 1932.
"Personalism and Theology." *The Personalist* (1939).

Francis J. McConnell (1871–1953)

BOOKS

Personal Christianity. New York: Fleming H. Revell Company, 1914.
Democratic Christianity. New York: Macmillan, 1919.
Borden Parker Bowne: His Life and Philosophy. New York: Abingdon Press, 1929.
Is God Limited? New York: Abingdon Press, 1924.
Evangelicals, Revolutionists and Idealists. New York: Abingdon-Cokesbury Press, 1942.
By the Way: An Autobiography. New York: Abingdon-Cokesbury Press, 1952.

ARTICLES

"Bowne and the Social Questions." In *Studies in Philosophy and Theology,* E. C. Wilm, ed. New York: Abingdon Press, 1922.

William H. Werkmeister (1901–1993)

BOOKS

A History of Philosophical Ideas in America. New York: Ronald Press, 1949.
The Autobiography of Ralph Tyler Flewelling: The Forest of Yggdrasill. Los Angeles: Univ. of Southern California Press, 1962.

ARTICLES

"Some Aspects of Contemporary Personalism." *The Personalist* 32 (October, 1951).

Third Generation

Peter Anthony Bertocci (1910–1989)

BOOKS

The Empirical Argument for God in Late British Thought. Cambridge, Mass.: Harvard Univ. Press, 1938. New York: Kraus Reprints, 1970.
Introduction to the Philosophy of Religion. Englewood Cliffs, N. J.: Prentice Hall, 1951.
Free Will, Responsibility and Grace. New York: Abingdon Press, 1957.

Person and Reality. (Written by Edgar S. Brightman. Edited by Peter A. Bertocci, with Jannette E. Newhall and Robert S. Brightman.) New York: Ronald Press, 1958.
Personality and The Good: Psychological and Ethical Perspectives. With Richard M. Millard. New York: David McKay, 1963.
The Person God Is. London: Allen & Unwin, 1970.
Is God For Real? New York: Sheed and Ward, 1971.
The Goodness of God. Washington, D.C.: University Press of America, 1981.
The Person and Primary Emotions. New York: Springer-Verlag, 1988.

ARTICLES

"The Person, Obligation, and Value." *The Personalist* 40 (1959).
"Foundations of Personalistic Psychology." In *Scientific Psychology*, Benjamin B. Wolman and Ernest Nagel, eds. New York: Basic Books, 1964.
"The Perspective of a Teleological Personalist." In *Contemporary American Philosophy*, John E. Smith, ed. New York: Humanities Press, 1970.

L. Harold DeWolf (1905–1986)

BOOKS

A Theology of the Living Church. New York: Harper & Brothers, 1953.
Responsible Freedom: Guidelines to Christian Action. New York: Harper and Row, 1971.

ARTICLES

"A Personalistic Re-examination of the Mind-Body Problem." *The Personalist* 34 (Winter 1953).
"Personalism in the History of Western Philosophy." *Philosophical Forum* 12 (1954).
"Martin Luther King, Jr., as Theologian." *The Journal of the Interdenominational Theological Center* 4/2 (Spring 1977).

Nels F. S. Ferré (1908–1971)

Christianity and Society. New York: Harper and Brothers, 1950.
The Christian Understanding of God. New York: Harper and Brothers, 1951.
Searchlights on Contemporary Theology. New York: Harper and Brothers, 1961.

Georgia Harkness (1891–1974)

The Recovery of Ideals. New York: Charles Scribner & Sons, 1937.
Conflicts in Religious Thought. New York: Henry Holt, 1949 (revised edition).
Foundations of Christian Knowledge. New York: Abingdon Press, 1955.
Christian Ethics. Nashville: Abingdon Press, 1957.
The Providence of God. Nashville: Abingdon Press, 1960.
Women in Church and Society: A Historical and Theological Inquiry. Nashville: Abingdon Press, 1972.

Paul E. Johnson (1898–1974)

BOOKS

Christian Love. Nashville: Abingdon-Cokesbury Press, 1951.
Personality and Religion. Nashville: Abingdon-Cokesbury Press, 1957.

ARTICLES

"The Trend Toward Dynamic Interpretation." *Religion in Life* 35 (1966).

Willis Jefferson King (1886–1976)

"Personalism and Race." In *Personalism in Theology*, Edgar S. Brightman, ed. Boston: Boston Univ. Press, 1943.

Walter George Muelder (1907–)

BOOKS

"Individual Totalities in Ernst Troeltsch's Philosophy of History." Boston University, Graduate School. Ph.D. Dissertation, 1933.

The Idea of the Responsible Society. Boston: Boston Univ. Press, 1955.
In Everyplace a Voice. Cincinnati, Ohio: Woman's Division of Christian Service, Board of Missions, The Methodist Church, 1957.
Foundations of the Responsible Society. New York: Abingdon Press, 1960.
Moral Law in Christian Social Ethics. Richmond, Va.: John Knox Press, 1966.
The Ethical Edge of Christian Theology: Forty Years of Communitarian Personalism. New York: Mellen Press, 1984.

ARTICLES

"Personality and Christian Ethics." In *Personalism in Theology: A Symposium in Honor of Albert Cornelius Knudson*, Edgar S. Brightman, ed. Boston: Boston Univ. Press, 1943.
"Personalism, Theology, and the Natural Law." *Philosophical Forum* 14 (1956).
"What Has Theology to Do with Social Action?" *Nexus* 30 (1967).
"Martin Luther King, Jr., at Boston University." *Currents* (April, 1970). Boston University.
"Personal and Cultural Autonomy in 'Third World' Ideologies of Development." In *Contemporary Studies in Philosophical Idealism: Essays in Honor of Peter Bertocci*, John Howie and Thomas O. Buford, eds. Cape Cod, Mass.: C. Stark, 1975.
"Philosophical and Theological Influences in the Thought of Martin Luther King, Jr." *Debate and Understanding*. Boston University, 1977.

Jannette Newhall (1898–1979)

"Edgar Sheffield Brightman: A Biographical Sketch." *Philosophical Forum* 12 (1954).

S. Paul Schilling (1904–1994)

God in an Age of Atheism. New York: Abingdon Press, 1969.
God in Cognito. New York: Abingdon Press, 1974.
God and Human Anguish. New York: Abingdon Press, 1977.

Warren E. Steinkraus (1922–1990)

BOOKS

Representative Essays of Borden Parker Bowne, Steinkraus, ed. Utica, N. Y.: Meridian Publishing Company, 1980.
Studies in Personalism: Selected Writings on Edgar Sheffield Brightman, Steinkraus, ed. Utica, N. Y.: Meridian Publishing Company, 1984.

ARTICLES

"Martin Luther King's Personalism and Nonviolence." *Journal of the History of Ideas* 34/1 (January–March, 1973).
"Martin Luther King's Contributions to Personalism." In *Martin Luther King, Jr., and the Civil Rights Movement*, David J. Garrow, ed., vol. 3. New York: Carlson Publishing, 1989.
"The Dangerous Ideas of Martin Luther King." In *Martin Luther King, Jr., and the Civil Rights Movement*, David J. Garrow, ed., vol. 3. New York: Carlson Publishing, 1989.

Fourth Generation

Paul K. Deats, Jr. (1918–)

BOOKS

Toward a Discipline of Social Ethics: Essays in Honor of Walter George Muelder, Deats, ed. Boston: Boston Univ. Press, 1972.
The Boston Personalist Tradition in Philosophy, Social Ethics, and Theology, coeditors Deats and Carol S. Robb. Macon, Ga.: Mercer Univ. Press, 1986.

ARTICLES

"Conviction, Conflict, and Consensus in Ethics." *Nexus* 23/2 (Summer 1980). Boston University School of Theology, 1980.

Martin Luther King, Jr. (1929–1968)

BOOKS

Stride Toward Freedom. New York: Harper, 1958.
The Measure of a Man. Philadelphia: Fortress Press, 1988 (1959).
Where Do We Go From Here: Chaos or Community? Boston: Beacon Press, 1967.

ARTICLES

"Doctrine of Freedom." In *The Papers of Martin Luther King, Jr.* Clayborn Carson, ed. Berkeley, Calif.: Univ. of California Press, 1994.

Fifth Generation

Randall E. Auxier (1961–)

"Guest Editor's Introduction: The Relevance of Bowne." *The Personalist Forum* 13/1 (Spring 1997).
"Time and Personality: Bowne on Time, Evolution, and History." *Journal of Speculative Philosophy* 12/4 (1998).

Rufus Burrow, Jr. (1951–)

BOOKS

"A Critique of E. S. Brightman's Conception of God, With Special Reference to Excess Evil." Ph.D. Dissertation, Boston University, 1982. Unpublished.

ARTICLES

"Moral Laws in Borden P. Bowne's *Principles of Ethics.*" *The Personalist Forum* 6/2 (Fall 1990).
"The Personalistic Theism of Edgar S. Brightman." *Encounter* 53/2 (Spring 1992).
"Borden Parker Bowne's Doctrine of God." *Encounter* 53/4 (Autumn 1992).
"Two Elements in Francis J. McConnell's Social Ethics." *The Personalist Forum* 8/2 (Fall–Winter 1992).
"Francis John McConnell and Personalistic Social Ethics." *Methodist History* 31/2 (January 1993).
"Personalism and Ecological Ethics." *The A. M. E. Church Review* 110/357 (January–March 1995).
"Martin Luther King, Jr., and the Ethics of Dignity." *Lexington Theological Quarterly* 30/1 (Spring 1995).
"John Wesley Edward Bowen: The First Afrikan American Personalist." *Encounter* 56/2 (Summer 1995).
"Borden Parker Bowne and the Dignity of Being." *The Personalist Forum* 13/1 (Spring 1997).
"The Personalism of John Wesley Edward Bowen." *The Journal of Negro History* 82/2 (Spring 1997).
"Martin Luther King, Jr., Personalism and Moral Laws." *The Asbury Theological Journal* 52/2 (Fall 1997).
"Borden Parker Bowne: The First Thoroughgoing Personalist." *Methodist History* 36/1 (October 1997).
"Martin Luther King, Jr., Personalism, and Intracommunity Violence." *Encounter* 58/1 (Winter 1997).
"Afrikan American Contributions to Personalism." *Encounter* 60/2 (Spring 1999).

Carol Sue Robb (1945–)

BOOKS

Making the Connections: Essays in Feminist Social Ethics, Beverly Wildung Harrison, ed., and with introduction by C. S. Robb. Boston: Beacon Press, 1985.
Sexuality and Economic Justice: Where Economic and Sexual Ethics Converge. Boston: Beacon Press, 1990.
Equal Value: An Ethical Approach to Economics and Sex. Boston: Beacon Press, 1995.

ARTICLES

"Race and Sex, Challenges to the Center," with Preston Williams (Society of Christian Ethics, Annual Meeting, 1984).
"Sexual Ethics." *Dialog* (1994).

Index